ATHLETIC ADMINISTRATION
for College, High School, Youth, and Club Sport

Dina Gentile, EdD

Professor
Sport Management Program
School of Sport Science and Fitness Studies
Endicott College
Beverly, MA

JONES & BARTLETT
LEARNING

World Headquarters
Jones & Bartlett Learning
5 Wall Street
Burlington, MA 01803
978-443-5000
info@jblearning.com
www.jblearning.com

Jones & Bartlett Learning books and products are available through most bookstores and online booksellers. To contact Jones & Bartlett Learning directly, call 800-832-0034, fax 978-443-8000, or visit our website, www.jblearning.com.

Substantial discounts on bulk quantities of Jones & Bartlett Learning publications are available to corporations, professional associations, and other qualified organizations. For details and specific discount information, contact the special sales department at Jones & Bartlett Learning via the above contact information or send an email to specialsales@jblearning.com.

15807-6

Production Credits
Director of Product Management: Cathy L. Esperti
Product Manager: Sean Fabery
Product Assistant: Andrew LaBelle
Director, Project Management: Jenny L. Corriveau
Project Manager: Jessica deMartin
Director of Marketing: Andrea DeFronzo
VP, Manufacturing and Inventory Control: Therese Connell
Composition and Project Management: Exela Technologies
Cover Design: Kristin E. Parker
Text Design: Kristin E. Parker
Rights & Media Specialist: Maria Leon Maimone
Media Development Editor: Shannon Sheehan
Cover Image: © miodrag ignjatovic/Getty Images
Chapter Opener Image: © Audrey Kwok/EyeEm/Getty Images
Printing and Binding: LSC Communications
Cover Printing: LSC Communications

Library of Congress Cataloging-in-Publication Data
Names: Gentile, Dina, author.
Title: Athletic administration for college, high school, youth and club sport
    /Dina Gentile.
Description: Burlington, MA : Jones & Bartlett Learning, [2020] | Includes
    bibliographical references and index.
Identifiers: LCCN 2018053647 | ISBN 9781284107302 (pbk. : alk. paper)
Subjects: LCSH: Sports administration–United States. | School sports–United
    States–Management. | Sports for children–United States–Management.
    | Sports–Vocational guidance–United States.
Classification: LCC GV713. G458 2020 | DDC 796.06/9–dc23 LC record available at https://lccn.loc.gov/2018053647

6048

Printed in the United States of America
23 22 21 20 19   10 9 8 7 6 5 4 3 2 1

Dedication

To Quinn and Laine

You are both so kind and loving.
Always be proud of who you are.
Set your goals high and you will surpass them!
I will always be by your side.

Forever,
Your Madi

Brief Contents

© Audrey Kwok/EyeEm/Getty Images

Contents

Preface

Given the transformation of sport from a purely recreational endeavor to a multibillion-dollar entity, attention is warranted to how administrators manage and deliver sport as a product. The movement toward a business-focused approach to operating sport across all forms and settings has forced administrators to take a closer look at how their daily management of teams and programs fit into the changing landscape of sport. Future sport administrators will be faced with evolving issues in the realm of organizing and implementing athletic programs. In order to create, maintain, and sustain athletic programs, sport administrators must have the ability to analyze problems, develop solutions, craft plans of action, and determine the effectiveness of their decisions. With that in mind, *Athletic Administration for College, High School, Youth, and Club Sport* explores the skill sets needed to be a successful and effective sport administrator across collegiate athletics, interscholastic sport programming, youth and community sport, and club sport settings in order to prepare the next generation of athletic administrators.

The contents within each chapter of this text speak to the timely issues impacting collegiate sport and student-athletes, the changing landscape of high school sport, the challenges of organizing developmental programs in community sport, and the rise in select clubs and leagues in the United States. The exercises and information included in each chapter place the reader in the role of administrator, leader, and decision-maker for sport programs.

▶ Why a New Text?

There are a variety of academic programs, including Sport Management, Sport Administration, Recreation Management, and Athletic Administration, which feature both undergraduate and graduate courses addressing current topics in the management of athletics. However, until now, there has been no all-in-one text that thoroughly addresses organizing and administering sport in collegiate athletics, interscholastic sport programming, youth and community sport, and club sport settings for the aspiring athletic administrator. Indeed, the texts that do address athletic administration and organization tend to take a physical education approach, even though both athletic administration and sport management programs have shifted away from the physical education domain into specific sport domains. Because of this, for more than 25 years, I have been teaching this subject matter both in traditional classrooms and online, I have always used current-event articles versus a full text to discuss this dynamic subject. With that in mind, *Athletic Administration for College, High School, Youth, and Club Sport* highlights the managerial applications across growing and dynamic sport settings from the collegiate to club domains.

This text can serve as an ideal resource for courses including—but not limited to—Organization and Administration of Sport, Athletic Management, and Athletic Administration. Additionally, this text can also be used as a learning tool for coaching courses, particularly those that introduce students to the practical aspects of athletic administration.

From a curriculum development perspective, this text, coupled with instructor resources, addresses Commission on Sport Management Accreditation (COSMA) key content areas. Part of the accreditation process requires programs to demonstrate teaching in specific curriculum content areas, also referred to as the Common Professional Component. In keeping with this, *Athletic Administration for College, High School, Youth, and Club Sport* highlights student learning outcomes at the start of each chapter to guide instructors seeking to tie in accreditation standards within course syllabi and course materials.

Each setting addressed in *Athletic Administration for College, High School, Youth, and Club Sport* plays a significant role in providing education opportunities, outlets for achievement, social skills, and enhancement of personal development. Athletic administrators are spearheading the values and ideals that sport contains for masses of people across a variety of populations. Athletic administrators are ultimately accountable for making sure athletes within our care not only get the very best preparation for athletic success but also receive educational opportunities and decision-making skills, which will formulate their character.

▶ Features and Benefits

To better distinguish subject matter relevant to each of the four sport domains, this text is organized so that content within chapters is color coded by domain: Collegiate sport (blue), high school sport (yellow), youth sport (green), and club sport (red). This feature gives readers the opportunity to quickly locate the setting-specific content in each chapter.

In each chapter, various features prompt readers to respond to the practical scenarios athletic administrators manage and resolve within their specific sport setting. Readers can experience the role of athletic administrator, weighing possible outcomes based on cases or scenarios within specific sport settings through the *Decision Making Challenge* feature. In addition, each chapter includes *Managerial Applications* in the form of scenarios and case studies for students to complete in order to demonstrate their knowledge and ability to apply the information to specific tasks. To bridge theoretical concepts with practical administrative responsibilities, readers receive professional tips, advice on handling problems, guidance to assist with planning, and suggestions to manage programs within *Feedback from the Field* sections.

Each chapter closes with a *Wrap-Up* section, including end-of-chapter *Activities* and *Questions*. The activities prompt students to develop plans of action to resolve the scenarios, problems, and tasks. The *questions* direct students to reflect on the materials conveyed within the specific chapter, allowing readers to test their knowledge of the core topics of the text along with the development of individual management style across collegiate, high school, youth, and club sports.

The exercises and information included in this text place the student in the role of the decision-maker for sport programs. There are a number of challenges, risks, and opportunities in athletic administration across these diverse sport settings that are dissected within this text. For the first time in the marketplace, all four athletic settings (collegiate athletics, high school sport programming, youth sport, and club sport) are examined in one comprehensive text addressing the current and timely issues impacting sport in society. Students will gain valuable tools from the information and exercises in the text that they will carry with them as they move from setting to setting in their athletic administration careers. Instructors can easily facilitate course discussions based on the chapter components and variety of best practices within the athletic administration domain. Within each chapter, students study each of the four domains of athletics, allowing them to investigate specific scenarios, highlighted issues, or practical situations that fully examine the challenges and opportunities within a dynamic professional setting that is athletic administration.

▶ Student and Instructor Resources

Each new copy of this text is accompanied by an access code for the **Navigate 2 Companion Website**, which includes the following study materials:

- Practice Quizzes
- Glossary
- Flashcards

Additionally, qualified instructors can request access to the following materials:

- Test Bank
- Slides in PowerPoint Format
- Instructor's Manual
- Sample Syllabus

Athletic Administration for College, High School, Youth, and Club Sport incorporates the analysis of prominent issues that administrators are challenged to resolve in their specific sport setting. Students looking for careers outside of professional sports will learn from both the content provided in *Athletic Administration for College, High School, Youth, and Club Sport* and the highlighted practical activities, empowering them to face decision-making opportunities in these growing sport settings.

Acknowledgments

This book was written with my deep passion for the field of athletic administration. I am continually motivated to share my experiences in the field of athletics to empower current and future athletic administrations to enhance the opportunities for young people through and with sport participation. Thank you to my partner and children for the unwavering support through the writing and research process. A special thank you to my undergraduate and graduate Sport Management and Athletic Administration students who continually demonstrate their core desire to learn and develop sport programming that is both positive and enriching.

I want to acknowledge the professionals in the field of athletic administration who are featured in this text. Their words of wisdom and contributions make this text truly unique in an ever-changing and dynamic field—that is, athletic administration.

Thank you to Sean Fabery for guidance throughout the entire process of writing and organizing the text. To Nancy Hoffmann, thank you for the editing skills and probing to enhance the content areas throughout the writing process. Finally, thanks to the entire Jones and Bartlett family for the support of this project.

About the Author

Dina Gentile, EdD is a professor of Sport Management at Endicott College, teaching at both the undergraduate and graduate levels. Prior to joining the faculty, Dr. Gentile served in a variety of roles at the college in athletic administration and coaching the women's soccer team. Dr. Gentile has organized soccer camps for more than 25 years and currently serves as an administrator and coach for a nationally recognized club. Dr. Gentile presents nationally and internationally, with her research spanning numerous topics including sport management accreditation, technology in sport management, athletic administration, volunteerism, and coaching. She previously published *Teaching Sport Management: A Practical Guide* in 2010.

Reviewers

W. Scott Bradshaw, EdM
Professor
Kinesiology and Sport Studies
Bucks County Community College
Newtown, PA
and
Professor
Sport Management and Leadership
   Studies
College of Business
Kutztown University
Kutztown, PA

Scott Branvold, EdD
Professor
School of Business
Robert Morris University
Moon, PA

Chris Brown, PhD
Assistant Professor
Department of Exercise Science and
   Sport Management
WellStar College of Health and Human
   Services
Kennesaw State University
Kennesaw, GA

Tammy Crawford, PhD
Clinical Assistant Professor
Department of Educational Leadership
   and Counseling Psychology
College of Education
Washington State University
Pulman, WA

Sean Daly, EdM
Program Director and Associate Professor
Sports, Entertainment, Event Management
College of Hospitality Management
Johnson and Wales University
Denver, CO

Lisa Olenik Dorman, PhD
Dean
School of Teacher Education and Sport
   Science
Professor
Physical Education and Sport Studies
Huntingdon College
Montgomery, AL

Brooke Forester, PhD
Assistant Professor
Department of Health, Kinesiology, and Sport
College of Education
University of South Alabama
Mobile, AL

Paul Hogan, MEd
Director and Professor
Sports Management Program
Sport, Recreation, and Tourism Studies
New Hampshire Technical Institute
Concord, NH

Christopher M. Keschock, MBA, PhD
Program Director and Associate Professor
Department of Health, Kinesiology, and Sport
College of Education
University of South Alabama
Mobile, AL

CHAPTER 1

Role of Athletic Administrators

After reading this chapter, students will be able to:

1. Identify the role of the athletic administrator across a variety of sport settings.
2. Define athletic administration, including the challenges and benefits of managing sport.
3. Categorize and describe the roles of athletic administration in college, high school, youth, and club sport settings.
4. Outline the differences and similarities between the governing bodies in athletics.
5. Compare the scope of administration in college, high school, youth, and club sport settings.

▶ Sport Landscape

A new landscape of athletics from youth to collegiate levels is currently developing. What used to be a purely recreational endeavor has evolved into a multibillion-dollar sport industry. Current-day athletic administrators must adapt to the dynamic shift in management, which warrants enhanced attention on how to manage all facets of sport programming and deliver sport to a highly engaged and educated consumer group of athletes, participants, parents, spectators, and fans. Consequently, because of the mass participation in sport from the youth to collegiate levels coupled with the revenue generated by these programs, the organization and

administration of sport has inevitably shifted to a professional business orientation. Today, the skills needed to be a successful and effective sport administrator mirror the requisite skills and competencies desired in a traditional business environment. Brower (1979) defined the professionalization of sport as "the degree of seriousness and importance given to it by athletes, management, and spectators" (p. 445). It is not surprising that tens of millions of children playing organized sport and parents overspending to create sport opportunities for their children (Hyman, 2012) mean that athletic administrators are now held to a higher standard of athletic management. As Horch and Schutte (2003) summarized in their study of youth club sports managers, there is a need for "specially trained sport managers; that is, experts who do not only understand something about general business administration but also about the particulars of sport products and organization" (p. 82). Clearly, athletic administrators today are charged with understanding not only the rules of competition but also the trends associated with the changing landscape of sport.

▶ Role of Athletic Administrator

To elevate offerings and fully support the growing and changing needs of sport organizations in collegiate athletics, interscholastic sport programming, youth sport, and club sport settings, the preparation of the next generation of athletic administrators must evolve. Athletic administration preparation must be geared toward the management of resources and meeting the desires of a knowledgeable and demanding consumer group. As the ultimate decision maker within the sport entity, athletic administrators monitor the pulse of their specific settings. Along with creating, maintaining, and sustaining athletic programs, the sport administrator must have the ability to analyze problems, develop solutions, craft plans of action, and determine the effectiveness of their decisions. Administrative leadership drives the organization to create positive and influential experiences for both athletes and their families.

The overarching ideals of athletic administration are to create enriching opportunities through sport offerings so participants can learn sport-specific skills, create bonds with teammates and coaches, and become physically active. For most, sport participation is a rewarding and meaningful experience that can begin in early childhood and extend to late adulthood. Athletic administrators have the task of formulating programs and securing staff not only to educate participants from a skill development and social perspective but also to challenge athletes to excel on the playing fields, work as a cohesive team, and discover their personal athletic potential. A former National Collegiate Athletic Association (NCAA) president shared his perspective regarding the role of athletics in college: "[T]he values of hard work, striving for excellence, respect for others, sportsmanship and civility, team play, persistence, and resilience that underlie the ideal of sport should be brought into the development aspects of a college education affecting all students" (Brand, 2006, p. 19). Sport participation is an integral part of the educational experience within our school system, in the community setting, and on college campuses. The ultimate goal for an athletic administrator is to deliver positive and substantial experiences to develop young people and instill a passion for engagement in a healthy lifestyle.

Today, the playbook to operate sport within the settings of collegiate sport, high school sport, youth sport, and club sport contains material that tackles challenges associated with costs, participation interest, facility availability, societal pressure to win, injuries, sport specialization, and competition within the sport marketplace. Athletic administrators are continually multitasking, planning, and managing scenarios that can and do change daily. As the pressure to add opportunities and enhance offerings becomes the norm within the sport settings, the role of the athletic administrator has been pushed not only to exceed expectations but also to absorb greater levels of responsibility and accountability for greater numbers of participants.

▶ Sport Programming

For the purposes of this text, an athletic administrator is defined as a person who plans, organizes, and operates any facet of sport-related programs in a collegiate, high school, youth sport, or club sport setting. Readers will explore administrative practices in amateur sport in a time where much attention is directed toward professional sport. Athletic administrators are more than just sport organizers; they are charged with analyzing problems, devising solutions, and preparing plans of action to enhance programmatic offerings. Athletic administrators across college, high school, youth, and club sport wear many "managerial hats" as entrepreneurs, resource allocators, schedulers, and social media promoters, among others. Modern athletic administrators are expected and required to anticipate industry trends to implement innovative programs so they can attract more participants to their organization, programs, or teams and be viable options for consumers in a cluttered sport landscape.

© Debby Wong/Shutterstock.

▶ Athletic Settings

As leaders, athletic administrators continually evaluate issues that affect their specific sport entities from a managerial, strategic, and social perspective. Athletic administrators work in youth sport settings in which sport offerings are delivered by towns or cities, volunteer programs, YMCAs, or church programs; these are often referred to as *community sport*. Club sports are now a prominent option for sport participants. Club sports are programs offered to players across several towns or regions that attract competitive players and professional coaches. Club sports are typically focused on one specific sport to deliver high-level training and competitive league games to players across an entire year. Sports such as soccer, softball, baseball, lacrosse, and basketball are typically team-based sports contained under the club sport umbrella. Community sport focuses on participants' comprehension of skills, techniques, and tactics connected to the specific sport (Anderson-Butcher, Riley, Amorose, Iachini, & Wade-Mdivanian, 2014). Youth sport associations are generally volunteer and nonprofit agencies "supported primarily by

 FEEDBACK FROM THE FIELD

Best Practices: Youth Sport

Robert Elliot has been instrumental in youth sport in the town of Wilmington, Massachusetts. Elliot lives and raises his children in town and has been an active volunteer, serving as a coach and board member for Wilmington Youth Soccer Association (WYSA). Elliot has several different hats to support WYSA in its offerings, including vice president of player and coach development, referee coordinator, chair of all in-town programs, and member of the fundraising committee. Defining his role within WYSA is not easy, but Elliot summarizes his efforts by stating he does "whatever [I] can to make the program better." Most recently, he was the vice president of development, overseeing player and coach development, including the hiring of a director of coaching; creating new programs to improve developmental opportunities for the players; and improving the existing training structure. In the community youth sport setting, Elliot has found that the use of web-based sport management sites for rosters and registration has made the administration of the programs easier, adding communication with players, families, and coaches can always be streamlined. A successful youth sport athletic administrator,

(continues)

FEEDBACK FROM THE FIELD   *(continued)*

according to Elliot, pays attention to detail, is an effective time manager, demonstrates a love for the program, possesses excellent communication skills, and wants to constantly improve.

From Elliot's perspective, parents can be challenging for those managing community youth sport. Elliot explained that although most parents are well intentioned, some are a hindrance because they forget that youth soccer athletes are not professional players and learn at different levels. He added that if youth sport administrators are able to work with the parents in a positive way, then parents can be an organization's greatest asset. In terms of communicating organizational goals and expectations to athletes, parents, and spectators, Elliot says this could be achieved in several ways, including through rules and regulations from the overall program and then reinforced through program directors, coaches, and administrators. The importance here, in his opinion, is the creation of open communication channels with the parents and players.

In terms of cost to operate the program, Elliot indicated there are fiscal concerns because of decreasing interest in soccer: Other sports are pulling players or not allowing them to play multiple sports, club sports are pulling players out, and the costs of league and state fees for insurance and registration are increasing. Elliot was named Massachusetts Youth Soccer Administrator of the Year in 2015. When asked how he decides what gets top priority when managing within a program, he added, "It is simple: what is best for the kids." For college students hoping to land a career in athletic administration, Elliot advised that they learn as much as possible about communication and the psychology of people, stressing the importance of being able to interact with players and families.

membership fees and/or community funds that develop, implement, or manage recreation/sport programs and/or facilities" (Desensi, Kelley, Blanton & Beitel, 1990, p. 33). Youth and community sport constitute a variety of options for participants, including YMCAs, town- and city-based programs, travel-based programs through towns and cities, and recreational offerings. Traditional athletic programs at the collegiate and high school levels consist of broad-based programs, including team and individual sports offered to student-athletes across the academic year.

▶ Stakeholders in Athletic Administration

Managing sport programming equates to balancing a variety of needs from stakeholders, including athletes, parents, coaches, officials, fans, and community members. Each stakeholder is invested in the outcomes of the sport programming on several levels. To deliver valuable experiences to each stakeholder, athletic administrators must understand each group's needs to continually satisfy interest and meet demand. From an administrative perspective, there must be an appreciation of each group's unique needs to sustain business operations and retain the base of members or participants.

Participants are defined as athletes and coaches who desire to compete and achieve within their specific sport. The spectator category encompasses parents and fans of the teams or sport. Both groups strongly crave connections with the team and players. Most will show their affiliation by their sideline support and donning fan gear at each game. In some cases, athletic programs will also cater to consumers or patrons who are fans of the sport even if they do not have a family connection or tie to the program. Within college and university programs, athletic administrators may tap the interest of these groups by selling tickets to events and games along with merchandise. Consumer fans constitute alumni of the institution or people who have a strong bond with supporting the team or program because of the team's talent level, location, or reputation. The ways in which athletic administrators manage each stakeholder will be deliberately different in order to tap into the emotional and psychological elements of each group. Athletic administrators constantly examine and monitor the motivation of the stakeholder groups as each cluster of the sport environment spends time, money, and energy to connect with athletic programs and sport organizations.

As participation rates rise in youth sport and community-based sport memberships and new player opportunities increase each year at the high school and college levels, one can only conclude that sport plays a prominent role in our lives on several levels. The skills needed to keep up with the changes within these sport settings have dramatically transformed the position of athletic administrator, requiring business savvy that can help the administrator tackle the financial and administrative sides of managing and delivering sport-specific experiences head-on while implementing sport programming to targeted groups. The athletic administrator position has transformed along with the core competencies to direct sport programming.

▶ Growth Across All Settings

Across various athletic settings, sport continues to evolve. Decades ago, when children wanted to play recreational basketball for their local town program, they just signed up, paid a fee, and played. Today, we require online sign-ups, tryouts, team-selection days, and higher fees to participate. When you add the hundreds of dollars in required gear and equipment associated with the team membership, it makes opportunities for all children who desire to play a sport financially out of reach for many families. Within the community sport setting, the YMCA (or just Y) boasts 22 million people, including 13 million adults and 9 million youth of diverse ages, economic status, and backgrounds, taking advantage of a wide range of sport-related offerings each year (YMCA, n.d.). In the high school setting, a report by the National Federation of State High School Associations depicts an increase in participants for the academic year of 2014–2015 with the total number of athletes at more than 7.8 million. The NCAA provided 460,0000 opportunities to student-athletes enrolled in Division I, Division II, and Division III colleges and universities from 2014 to 2015 (NCAA, "2013–14 Guide," n.d.). In 2015, NCAA membership included 346 active Division I members, 291 active Division II members, and 439 active Division III members (NCAA, "Student-Athlete Participation," n.d.). To give insight into the growth of youth sport, the U.S. Youth Soccer organization reported more than 3 million children registered to play soccer in 2014 compared to slightly more than the reported 100,000 participants in 1974 (U.S. Youth Soccer, 2014).

▶ Family Costs for Sport Participation

For athletic administrators, understanding how much parents are paying for their children to engage in sport allows them to see the challenges families experience when weighing the benefits of sport participation. The pull for athletes to participate in multiple sports for a variety of programs within just one town is

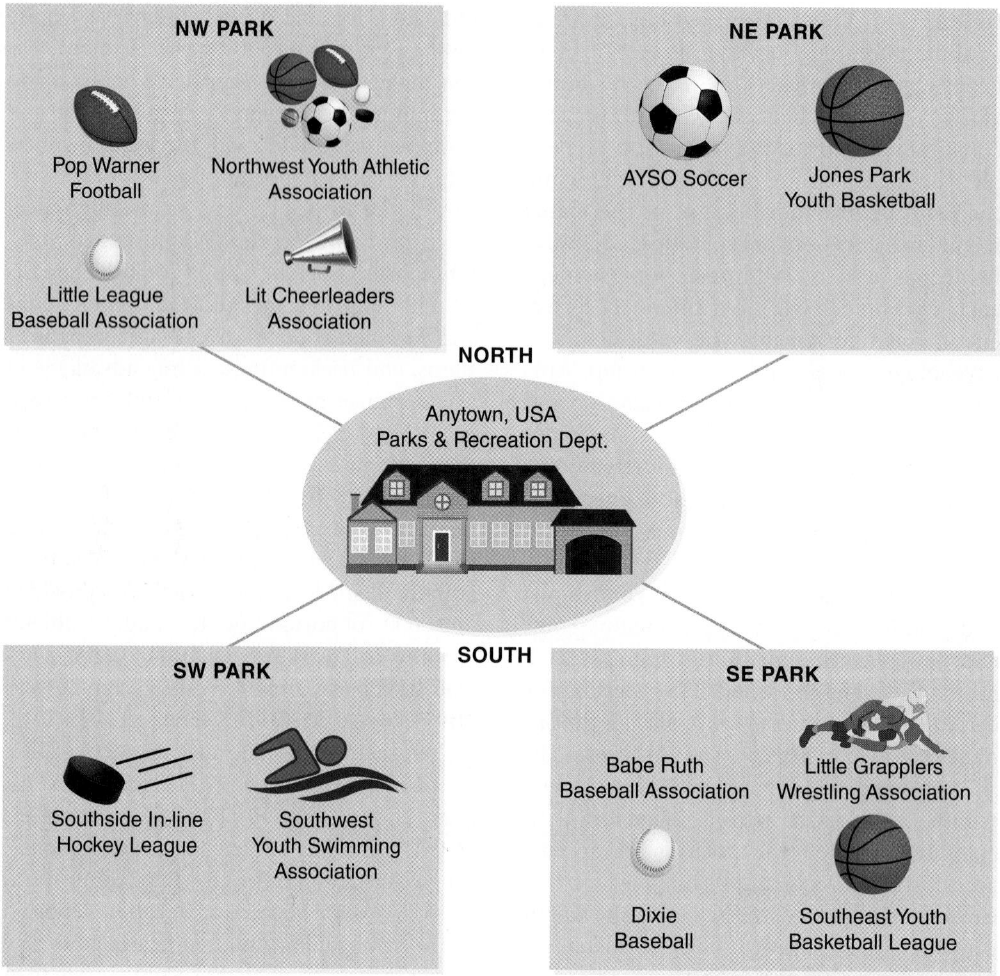

FIGURE 1.1 Typical Sport Landscape

National Alliance for Youth Sports (2012). Background screening in youth sports 2012. Retrieved March 22, 2016 from http://www.nays.org/CMSContent/File/nays_community_recommendations.pdf.

depicted in **FIGURE 1.1**. Managing athletic programs from a family perspective has evolved into organizing and juggling multiple sport schedules for children along with securing carpools to transport athletes from one site to another across the week.

The National Collegiate Athletic Association reported growth in student-athlete participation (see **FIGURE 1.2**) from 1984 to 2015. The growth in sport participation in higher education, coupled with the high levels of interest in high school sports (see **FIGURE 1.3**), shows how families support the progress of young athletes from town sport to higher levels. Along the sport journey, the costs for athletic participation affect family economics with participation fees ranging from $100 to $1,000 per child each season (Dougherty, 2016). The cost for athletics across the youth, club, high school, and collegiate settings shows how athletic administrators must be able to decipher the motives of parents and athletes as families invest in their children's sport careers.

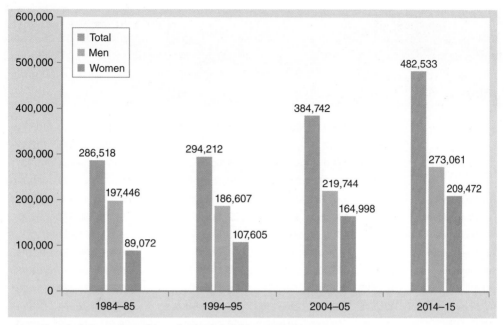

Note: Data include student-athletes in championship sports only.

FIGURE 1.2 Number of NCAA Student-Athletes from 1984–85 to 2014–15

Modified from National Collegiate Athletic Association (n.d.). Retrieved March 22, 2016 from http://www.ncaa.org/sites/default/files/Participation Rates Final.pdf.

▶ From Recreation to Business Model to Administer Sport

The sports that children and adults play, watch, compete in, and organize have transitioned from simple recreational endeavors to formalized businesses. Today, athletic administrators manage with state-of-the-art technology and tools to track participants, market events, and constantly and instantaneously inform parents and athletes about programming news and opportunities through social media platforms.

Another core task for athletic administrators is understanding how the overall experience affects the sport participants. Garcia (2015) found the two principal aspects of a high school student-athlete's experience are the influence of family and friends and the opportunity to participate in a competitive activity. Conversely, the most negative aspects

of high school sport participation were problems with coaches (Garcia, 2015). Notably, sport provides an avenue for young people to develop a sense of community, and it has proven to have numerous benefits for both individuals and groups (Garcia, 2015; Warner, Kerwin, & Walker, 2013). In the youth athletic setting, youth sport coaches have the greatest positive influence on young athletes' behaviors (Martin, Ewing, & Gould, 2014). Youth sport provides socializing benefits not only to young athletes but also to parents as they become increasingly engaged in their child's athletic experiences (Dorsch, Smith, Wilson, & McDonough, 2015).

The movement toward a business model to operate sport in all forms and settings has prompted administrators to adopt methods to analyze how the daily management of teams and programs fits into the dynamics of sport today. Decades ago, our youngest participants gathered at local town playing fields for instructional clinics to get their feet wet and become

2014-15 SUMMARY OF ATHLETICS PARTICIPATION TOTALS BY STATE

State	Boys	Girls	Total[1]	State	Boys	Girls	Total[1]
1. Texas	488,224	316,374	804,598	27. Tennessee	69,839	39,510	109,349
2. California	462,401	334,700	797,101	28. Kansas	61,722	40,871	102,593
3. New York	215,447	174,028	389,475	29. Louisiana	61,677	39,634	101,311
4. Illinois	199,595	141,377	340,972	30. Oregon	56,577	43,599	100,176
5. Ohio	189,955	129,974	319,929	31. Kentucky	52,529	43,996	95,525
6. Pennsylvania	169,312	150,250	319,562	32. South Carolina	59,719	35,671	95,390
7. Michigan	171,027	124,633	295,660	33. Nebraska	45,716	31,421	77,137
8. New Jersey	162,919	116,458	279,377	34. Arkansas	36,876	24,387	61,263
9. Florida	154,650	113,304	267,954	35. Utah	35,265	24,723	59,988
10. Minnesota	121,027	114,216	235,243	36. Maine	27,592	24,032	51,624
11. Massachusetts	126,748	100,177	226,925	37. New Mexico	27,349	22,364	49,713
12. Georgia	118,704	78,833	197,537	38. Nevada	26,511	18,522	45,033
13. North Carolina	111,531	82,821	194,352	39. New Hampshire	24,191	20,837	45,028
14. Wisconsin	109,827	76,768	186,595	40. Idaho	25,655	18,869	44,524
15. Virginia	99,475	73,808	173,283	41. Hawaii	20,952	15,919	36,871
16. Missouri	102,190	69,747	171,937	42. West Virginia	20,444	15,537	35,981
17. Washington	92,160	68,085	160,245	43. Montana	17,425	13,930	31,355
18. Indiana	90,890	61,662	152,552	44. Delaware	16,705	12,960	29,665
19. Iowa	80,744	55,394	136,138	45. South Dakota	16,892	12,268	29,160
20. Colorado	71,593	57,007	128,600	46. Rhode Island	16,565	11,921	28,486
21. Alabama	80,510	42,829	123,339	47. North Dakota	14,469	10,604	25,073
22. Arizona	71,259	50,926	122,185	48. Alaska	12,438	11,936	24,374
23. Maryland	67,464	50,638	118,102	49. Wyoming	10,802	8,218	19,020
24. Oklahoma	59,881	54,794	114,675	50. Vermont	8,001	6,888	14,889
25. Mississippi	67,923	45,213	113,136	51. District of Columbia	7,160	4,676	11,836
26. Connecticut	60,785	50,426	111,211				

FIGURE 1.3 2014–15 Summary of Athletics Participation Totals by State

Reproduced with permission from National Federation of State High School Associations.

more interested in a particular sport. Today, most four- to five-year-olds are placed on formalized teams that compete (i.e., keep score) rather than just play (i.e., focus on development only) against other children each weekend as parents line the sidelines in support.

The cost to register children in sport programs has escalated. Players are no longer playing on one team each season. The athletic landscape includes parents registering their athletes for multiple teams each season, athletes signing up for specialty clinics throughout the entire year, and athletes participating in multiple summer sport camps. The reliance on volunteer coaches in athletic administration has exploded, leaving many youth sport organizations scrambling to identify and train enough parents to support the growing needs of the local town programs. New to the sport arena is an injection of professional coaches who assume responsibility for the instruction of the athletes in their care and the amateur coaches (parent volunteers) who lead practice sessions and manage all facets of a game. It is common, however, for youth sport associations to pay for professional services to manage tryouts, run player clinics, organize summer camps, and develop coach education programs.

High school athletics is not immune to the changes being experienced in the youth sport setting. Athletic administrators in high schools are faced with supervising not only coaches and teams but also facilities, which mirror venues often seen at the college level. Managing state-of-the-art facilities plus the need to fund broad-based programs and the concerns of "pay for play" are paramount on the mind of the high school sport administrator. Concussion prevention has also taken center stage in youth sport and competitive athletics from high school to college. The burden to protect and maintain the health and safety of athletes must be continually tackled and addressed by athletic administrators.

 FEEDBACK FROM THE FIELD

Best Practices: High School Sport

Karen Guillemette, director of athletics at Monomoy Regional High School in Harwich, Massachusetts, was formerly the assistant athletic director and Health and Wellness Department chairperson at Bishop Fenwick High School. Guillemette has been coaching either soccer or lacrosse or both since 2001, and she had served as the health and wellness teacher for 10 years at Bishop Fenwick High along with serving as assistant athletic director for seven years. In that last role she taught a full schedule of health and wellness classes while assisting in all aspects of running a high school athletic program—from game management to scheduling, transportation, and coach contracts.

Guillemette says technology helped communication with parents and the outside world via social media, which have made communication with parents easier while also giving parents more access to coaches and administrators. Guillemette believes effective administrators should be organized, have good time-management skills, be able to multitask, be strong leaders, and be good communicators. In her role in high school athletic administration, the biggest challenge she has faced is learning that it is impossible to please everyone and administrators must do what they know is right for all student-athletes. She admits some parents can be a challenge, which is why it is so important for athletic administrators to be not only good communicators but also good listeners. In providing guidance to aspiring athletic administrators, she indicated they should get involved in coaching as soon as possible at any level because this will be important to their futures in terms of knowing what qualities to look for in good coaches. They should also take as many communication classes as possible.

Guillemette communicates organizational goals and expectations to athletes and parents in "meet the coaches" forums. In terms of defining success at the high school level, she feels it is important for student-athletes to have positive experiences no matter what their roles on a team. She stresses that one function of the athletic administrator is to hire coaches who are experts in their sport but also care about their players on and off the field. Winning games and championships is a measure of success in her department, but Guillemette believes they can measure success in many other ways and areas. Her proudest achievements as a high school athletic administrator at Bishop Fenwick were the addition of great coaches to the staff, creating a girls' hockey team, adding various freshmen and junior varsity teams to their offerings, and having 70% of the students on campus participate in sport at some level. In terms of cost to operate the athletic program at Bishop Fenwick, the department did not charge user fees for athletics, which Guillemette believes helped keep their participation numbers high.

▶ Sport Participants Across the Settings

Athletes are the primary participants of sport offerings within collegiate, high school, youth and club sport settings. Athletes of all ability levels join sport teams for a variety of reasons, including acquiring physical techniques and learning the tactics of the sport along with

enhancing social skills. Effective athletic administrators recognize the importance of both of these goals, with the value placed on athletes becoming better people through interactions with coaches and teammates. The social aspect of sport cannot be ignored because youth to collegiate athletes enjoy spending time with friends and teammates through interactions developed and fostered through the sporting experience. Athletic administrators must not dismiss the

 FEEDBACK FROM THE FIELD

Best Practices: Club Sport

Steve Moreland is the founder and chief executive officer of Advanced Placement (AP) Sports, Inc., and the New England Twisters. AP Sports comprises an indoor and an outdoor turf facility that is utilized by the New England Twisters, a youth lacrosse club serving boys and girls. In addition to his ownership in these two entities, Moreland also serves as the boy's lacrosse coach at Phillips Academy in Andover, Massachusetts. Moreland recognizes significant trends in his business, including the youth movement toward early sport specialization and early college recruiting. In his role, he has adjusted to the growing demand for year-round lacrosse instruction while also promoting the benefits of being a multisport athlete. Moreland spends time helping young high school athletes navigate the college recruiting process while also assisting them in continually developing their skills. From his perspective, video has made the most dramatic impact in his setting as both a teaching mechanism and recruiting tool.

According to Moreland, effective athletic administrators must possess a good business mind coupled with people skills. He stresses that athletic administrators need to define the vision of the sport programs, lead others to execute the vision, and relate well to the athletes they serve. The two greatest challenges Moreland deals with in his position are (1) developing character in student-athletes in an age where everything happens so fast, and (2) meeting the increasing demands and expectations of parents. To communicate organizational goals and expectations to athletes, parents, and spectators, Moreland uses both writing and oral skills to engage in open and honest communication with athletes and parents. Success for Moreland is measured by player retention; he continually works to ensure that athletes and their parents enjoy the experience enough to enroll again the following year. In terms of operating costs, fiscal realities include the costs of operating the turf facility and paying coaching and staff salaries with member and participant fees being the primary source of revenue. Moreland adds he is mindful of costs but is not obsessed with them. Instead, he focuses on providing increasing value to members and participants at fair market rates.

Lacrosse is a fast-growing sport, so the challenge of providing positive experiences to those new to the game is a tremendous opportunity for Moreland. The importance of developing strong relations with athletes is evident, as Moreland explains that his greatest accomplishment is always the next time a student-athlete thanks him for making a difference in his or her life. Staying true to his priorities of working with young people, Moreland accentuates that student-athlete development is always the priority in his decision making, adding that the decision to do or not to do something, assuming no fiscal constraints, depends on the potential value to the athletes. When asked to provide advice to college students hoping to land a career in athletics, coaching, or youth sport administration, he says young people should find something they are passionate about and figure out a way to earn a living doing it.

fact that for more seasoned athletes, the desire to compete and fine-tune advanced skills becomes the central focus, which maximizes their need to achieve and elevate their performance-oriented goals within the sport domain. Athletic administrators must keenly understand the wants and desires of the groups they serve, often striking a balance between athletic-oriented goals and the development of the entire person, from social skills to character building.

College Setting

In addition to allegiance and accountability to participants and spectators, athletic administrators are guided by governance structures within each area of management. College athletic directors fulfill roles at institutions of higher learning and manage sport teams that fall under one of the following governing bodies: the National Junior College Athletic Association (NJCAA), the National Association of Intercollegiate Athletics (NAIA), and the National Collegiate Athletic Association (NCAA). Under the scope of college athletics, several core positions help carry out the functions of the department through the organizational structure.

▶ Organizational Structure

The administrators for college and university athletics have a variety of responsibilities. Depending on the institution, position descriptions may vary, but the aims of the department tend to be consistent across campuses. *Organizational structure* refers to the positions created to effectively implement the plans and activities of the department or athletic organization (**FIGURE 1.4**).

Position Descriptions Within College and University Athletics

Athletic Director or Director of Athletics

The athletic director (AD) provides leadership, supervision, and fiscal accountability for competitive athletic programs for departments that encompass student-athletes, full-time and part-time staff, and student workers and volunteers. The AD is responsible for the planning and development of programs along with

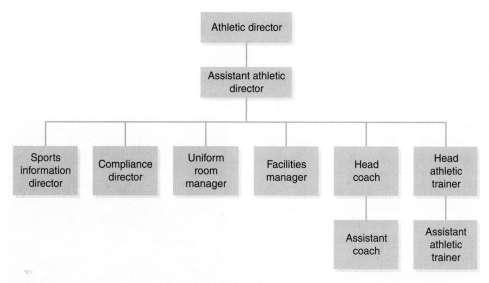

FIGURE 1.4 Organizational Structure for College Athletic Department

fundraising and budgeting for the department and individual sport teams. Division I and Division III athletic directors may have the same job title and similar roles at their respective institutions, but there are many differences in their positions relating to revenue generation at the Division I level (Wong, 2014). The AD also oversees compliance with league and conference policies and adherence to governing bodies' rules and regulations.

Associate or Assistant Athletic Director

Although the athletic director has full and complete accountability over a department's management and effectiveness, most institutions will have one to several positions at the associate or assistant levels. In these roles, the athletic administrator's expertise formulates the duties for each position. For instance, an associate director of athletics at one school may be responsible for transportation or team budgeting. At another institution the athletic administrator at this level may oversee community service or contest management for home games. The position title and description for the level directly under the athletic director depends on the skill set required to complement the department as a whole.

Sports Information Director

The sports information director (SID) is responsible for developing, administering, and distributing athletic department news and statistics through social media channels. The sports information director writes press releases for local media, websites, and social media. The SID maintains game-day statistics and provides reports to officials for the league, conference, and opposing team. In addition, the SID updates and maintains current web and social media messaging and produces season media guides and event-day publications for current sport teams.

Director of Sport Marketing

The director of sport marketing coordinates athletic department ticket sales, sponsorship opportunities, and external business relationships. The goal of the director is to maximize ticket sales, secure sponsorship deals, and ultimately increase fan attendance at events. This position title may vary from institution to institution, but marketing and promotion are functions central to the role.

Compliance Coordinator

The compliance coordinator is responsible for maintaining compliance and eligibility with designated governance entities, conference, and institutional regulations for the university. The compliance coordinator manages and monitors all aspects of athlete eligibility, oversight of regulations, and education regarding compliance regulations for student athletes and athletic department staff.

Athletic Trainer

The athletic trainer evaluates, treats, and rehabilitates intercollegiate athletes. The scope of athletic training services varies from campus to campus. Many institutions that offer athletic training as an academic major may have a greater number of certified athletic trainers on staff with dual roles in academics and athletics. Many departments may value having primary athletic trainers for each team rather than share athletic trainers across season offerings.

© Steve Skjold/Alamy Images.

For those institutions housing athletic training as a major, the athletic department becomes the beneficiary of student athletic trainers who serve a vital role in the overall operations of the athletic training department while they gain clinical experience.

Head Coach

The head coach of each college- or university-level sport team is responsible for the overall management of his or her team, including recruiting prospective student-athletes, meeting NCAA, NAIA, and NJCAA regulations, scheduling traditional and nontraditional season practices and contests, and arranging team travel schedules. Regardless of sport, each coach must support the institution's philosophy and mission.

Equipment Management

At a variety of institutions, the equipment manager may be a full-time employee who coordinates, washes, and maintains athletic team equipment and student-athlete practice and game-day apparel. In some cases, the equipment manager may have a dual appointment within the athletic department to achieve full-time employee status. The equipment manager may be assigned other duties by the athletic director based on skill set and expertise.

Game-Day Operations and Contest Management

The game-day operations coordinator or contest manager maintains all aspects of athletic game-day management, including securing work-study students, setup and breakdown of facilities, organizing concessions, and managing on-campus parking for events. In addition, the game-day operations coordinator or contest manager serves as liaison to game-day officials, communicates with away team officials regarding parking and meeting space availability, hires staff, secures game-day volunteers, and works with campus security regarding traffic and crowd control for sporting events.

Facility Manager

The facility manager works in conjunction with the physical plant on college campuses to coordinate the maintenance of field and athletic venues. With upgrades of college facilities, many outside groups such as youth and community sport enterprises vie to rent field or outdoor space when college sports are not in session. The facility manager works closely with the central planners at the institution to schedule facilities for both athletic teams and rental groups to fully use the available spaces to maximize revenue streams. As an example, at Endicott College, a Division III institution in the Northeast, all summer weeks are booked with sport camps run by college coaches associated with the institution and external sports camps operated by private entities.

Fundraising and Development

Fundraising and development personnel play significant roles in identifying and cultivating donor relationships to secure athletic department gifts and funds. The fundraising and development director manages the planning and staffing of special events such as booster club dinners or golf outings to acquire new donors while maintaining current annual giving programs for the athletic department.

▶ High School Sport Setting

Similar to the organizational structure of the college-level athletic department, high school sports mirror these positions but on a smaller scale, depending on the size and scope of program offerings. Fewer full-time and more part-time or stipend-oriented positions may exist within the high school setting. As an example, for athletic trainer services, the high school or school district may have a staffing contract with healthcare providers to secure and provide medical coverage at all home contests. Other high school athletic administrators hire

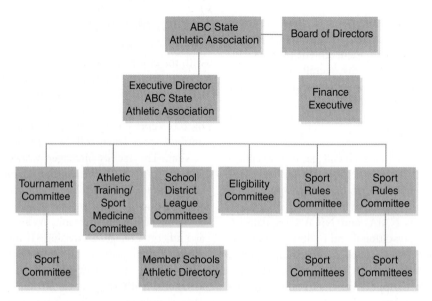

FIGURE 1.5 Constitutional Organization

Modified from Massachusetts Interscholastic Athletic Association Handbook (2016). Retrieved March 22, 2016 from http://www.miaa.net/contentm/easy_pages/view.php?sid=38&page_id=88.

full-time athletic trainers for the institution. High school athletic directors fulfill roles at educational institutions and manage sport teams that operate under state governing bodies for scholastic programs like the Massachusetts Interscholastic Athletic Association or the Connecticut Interscholastic Athletic Association (see **FIGURE 1.5**). In some instances, depending on the scope of athletics in a particular school district or region, the athletic director may oversee several programs, including recreational or middle school athletics.

▶ Position Descriptions in Youth Sport

In the youth sport setting, the majority of administrators for town or city programs are volunteers. Within community offerings from town or city programs or community recreational departments, a mix of paid staff and volunteers manage these programs. In youth sports, boards of directors are elected to assume the responsibility for organizing and operating programs similar to

the responsibilities of college or high school athletic directors. Within youth sport, athletic administrators adhere to governance structures that include sport leagues and national governing bodies. The sport leagues adopt and implement rules and regulations to assist youth sport athletic administrators in operating their specific seasons along with providing guidance on codes of conduct for coaches, players, officials, and parents (see **FIGURE 1.6**).

Board of Directors

A typical board of directors consists of a group of elected or appointed members charged with

© KidStock/Blend Images/Getty Images.

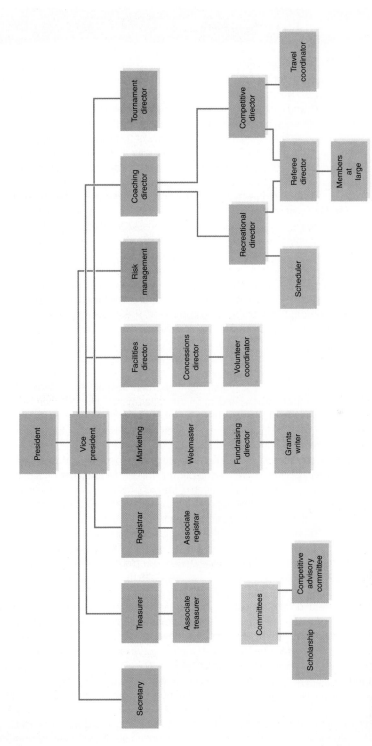

FIGURE 1.6 OSS Organizational Chart

Ocean State Soccer School (2011).

FEEDBACK FROM THE FIELD

Best Practices: Youth Sport

Mary Ellen Mayo has held several roles for the YMCA (Y) of the North Shore in Massachusetts since 1999. In her current role as youth services director for the Greater Beverly Y, Mayo is charged with overseeing youth and family, teen, adventure, and sports programs and camps, managing more than 3,000 youth in programs and camps each year. Recently, her position has evolved into specific youth and after school programs as the director of child care, managing the daily operations of two early education programs and seven after-school programs. Mayo is financially responsible for approximately $4 million in revenue for a $7 million branch, and more than 700 youth are involved in child-care and after-school programs at the Y. In addition, she manages 150 full- and part-time educational staff members.

According to Mayo, the sport program has changed dramatically over her time, especially at a nonprofit like the Y. Mayo and her staff continue to answer to the needs of the community and have changed and altered programs to ensure quality and cost-effectiveness. Of notable interest, according to Mayo, is that the Y tends to see more growth in its gymnastics and swim programs in Olympic Game years such as 2016.

In Mayo's setting of youth sport, technology is the link to parents, families, employees, and community. The Y has a strong marketing team that represents the programs so athletic administrators can continue the important work of the Y mission. Mayo uses technology in early education programs as teaching tools as well as fitness programs for the aging population. She stresses that effective administrators must be leaders, while simultaneously understanding and relating to their own staff. From Mayo's perspective, essential characteristics of an effective administrator include the ability to multitask, respecting all members of the team, communicating the goals of the department, setting expectations for staff members, and holding staff accountable through communication or continuous evaluation.

One Y challenge is recruiting and hiring quality staff members. The Y operates with a large percentage of part-time and volunteer help. Depending on the department, some staff members are 25-year employees, whereas other departments might see a high turnover on a seasonal basis. There is always a financial awareness while working in nonprofit, as well. Mayo strives for the best-quality programs while being conscious of the bottom line.

For Y offerings, safety is always the top priority. As Mayo indicates, when so many youth are involved in programs, it is important to prepare and train the team to prevent accidents and injuries. After safety, Mayo makes certain that every decision made is for the good of the organization. Some programs are strictly mission based (no revenue generated), while others are responsible for the local Y's revenue. Mayo's advice to college students looking to become athletic administrators is to grasp that it takes hard work and dedication to get to the top of any organization. The workday is never just 9 AM to 5 PM, and she urges young people to put in the work and advises that it will eventually pay off. In fact, Mayo describes herself as a product of the Y. She started at the Y as an undergraduate student completing her semester-long sport management internship in 1998. Mayo proudly shares she has been with the Y from her days as an intern, to a part-time staff member, to an associate director of youth services, to the director of operations.

When discussing communication of organization goals and expectations, Mayo makes it clear that her work is based on the Y mission statement and the organization's strong five-year strategic plan. Mayo communicates the goals of the Y on several levels. From her corporate board of directors to parents and participants, she keeps everyone informed of the Y's mission. The Y's website is a general way of explaining goals and expectations to the community.

Mayo's definition and measurement of success comes in two different ways. First, Y staff members embrace their service and understand that work is rewarded through the impacts made on particular family or community members. Measuring impact on the community is the easy part, Mayo explained. Second, as a way to define success in financial terms, she answers the question, did we balance the impact and the budget without the impact suffering? Without sacrificing quality, the Y ensures it is providing the best service with the best staff at the best price. Thankfully, Mayo expressed, the Y has departments that keep the branch financially viable even as other departments are more mission based. The Y is an ever-growing organization, Mayo says. For example, the Y is answering to a community need and plans to open a state-of-the-art child-care facility at another local site in the next year. The community support is essential because she will be embarking on the annual campaign to raise money for the building. For these reasons, the Y's leadership is always researching new and innovative programs.

overseeing the activities of the association or program. Meetings are typically held monthly to organize programs and allocate funding through a voting process. Members of the association are informed of the activities of the board and are welcome to attend monthly and annual meetings. Depending on the scope and size of the association, a small or large number of board members may be in place to carry out the needs and demands of the entity. Positions on the board may include fundraising, marketing and media relations, coach and player development, and parent education, along with the roles of president and vice president to provide oversight to the various arms of the group. Under the community sport umbrella (see **FIGURE 1.7**), many sport options exist as administered through town and travel programs, municipal recreation departments, and local Ys (formerly YMCAs).

▶ Position Descriptions in Club Sport

Club sports have increased in popularity since the mid-2000s as parents have sought more professional-level coaching and competitive training environments for their children outside of town programs. Club sports attract higher-level athletes who are instructed by coaches who have typically earned greater credentials than coaches in the youth and community settings (see **FIGURE 1.8**). The organizational operations typically consist of league officials who schedule games and regulate policies to create consistency throughout the clubs. Each club includes several

roles such as an executive director who operates much like an athletic director at a college or even a chief executive officer within a corporation.

Executive Director

The executive director is similar to the athletic director and oversees the entire management of the sponsored programs. The executive director will manage enrollment, create marketing plans to recruit players, secure facility contracts, and handle the fiscal responsibilities of the club from membership fees to coaching contracts. The executive director manages the entire operation of the club, including decisions relating to training costs, facility usage, fundraising, and marketing and development of the entity within a competitive sport environment.

Director of Coaching

The director of coaching (DOC) identifies and recruits new coaches, assigns coaches to teams, and creates and coordinates coaching development sessions. The DOC manages and supervises all player development initiatives for the program, including team selections and tryouts, team placement in leagues and tournaments, and developing relationships with local youth sport groups to promote the program initiatives. The player development arm of clubs rests with the DOC. The DOC oversees the training elements or curriculum of the program, including development of practice plans, season-long outcome assessments for players and teams, and curriculum development. Under the DOC administrative

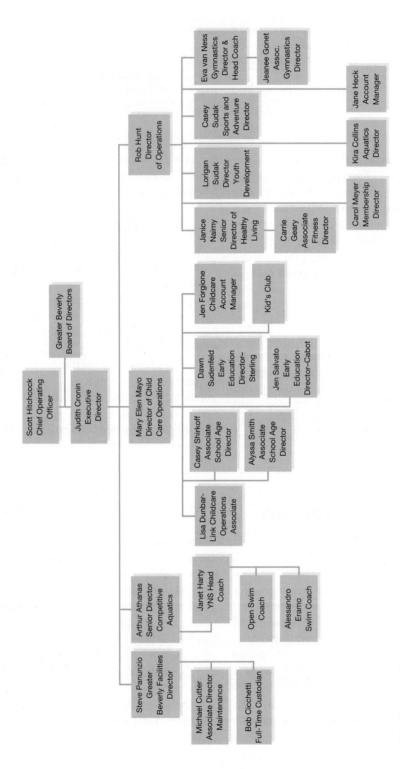

FIGURE 1.7 YMCA Organizational Chart

Courtesy of the Greater Beverly YMCA, Beverly MA.

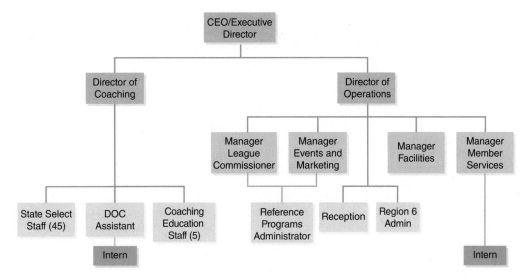

FIGURE 1.8 UYSA Staff Organizational Chart

With permission UYSA Staff Organizational Chart, Utah Youth Soccer Organization.

 FEEDBACK FROM THE FIELD

Best Practices: Club Sports

Arthur Dimitrakopoulos is the founder, president, executive director, and director of coaching for Benfica USA, a Massachusetts-based soccer club. Along with his duties managing day-to-day operations for a growing and innovative club, Dimitrakopoulos also coaches academy-level teams and is a holder of advanced licenses that afford him the ability to instruct United States Soccer Federation coaching courses. Dimitrakopoulos is responsible for all aspects of the soccer club, including planning, implementing, and supervising all programs; developing and implementing the club philosophy and policies; hiring coaches and staff; setting the yearly budget; and securing contracts with personnel, players and parents, and training facilities. As Dimitrakopoulos explained, the soccer landscape in Massachusetts is unique in that 11 town leagues or recreational leagues represent 291 towns. In addition, three club leagues serve more than 135 clubs. This environment has created an enormous political struggle between towns and clubs. The results include duplicating resources, creating fatigue and burnout for the players, and providing conflicting information to the players, which results in declined performance, diluting the talent pool for players and coaches, and competition to secure field space. From Dimitrakopoulos's perspective, the governing bodies in soccer—including the US Soccer Federation, US Youth Soccer, and US Club Soccer—are slowly reacting to the growing need for changes in the soccer landscape. Within the club soccer setting, it is extremely difficult to set budgets and long-term goals because parents and players can essentially just leave their current clubs without notice because no sanctions exist to force families or players to fulfill their contractual responsibilities.

In Dimitrakopoulos's opinion, technology has revolutionized club soccer from both a management and communication perspective. Today, families can register and pay online, which speeds up the process and allows administrators to work on other areas of need within the organization. Social media in the club setting offers a faster communication vehicle and—more importantly—provides free

(continues)

FEEDBACK FROM THE FIELD   *(continued)*

and effective advertising and promotion of all club events. The creation and availability of free club applications for smartphones has also aided the organization.

When asked what types of characteristics or qualifications effective administrators should possess, Dimitrakopoulos stressed knowledge first, emphasizing that administrators must be well versed in all aspects of the business while surrounding themselves with a support team with expertise in different areas of the operation. Second, athletic administrators must be energetic and willing to devote time to not only "doing" but also delegating and supervising. As far as leadership, Dimitrakopoulos believes athletic administrators must put the operation's performance ahead of their ego, which is more difficult for some people than others.

When dealing with staff, Dimitrakopoulos highlights that leaders must free their coaches to fulfill their talents to the utmost. The challenge of getting the most out of coaches depends on three variables: the leader's needs, the organization's atmosphere, and the coaches' potential competence. Dimitrakopoulos must keep in mind that the coaches are part-time employees and therefore have full-time jobs, which understandably take precedence. This sometimes causes a breakdown in communication, preparation, and attention to their coaching duties.

The coaching soccer pool also has become diluted because of the sheer number of clubs and teams in this setting. It is extremely difficult to find coaches with experience, Dimitrakopoulos laments, and it is also difficult to find committed coaches who can clear their schedules for a year-long program. A consistent challenge for Dimitrakopoulos is finding the balance between granting coaches the independence to learn and be in charge of their team while simultaneously steering them in the right direction without seeming overbearing.

When prompted to provide advice to college students studying for a future in athletic administration, Dimitrakopoulos stressed they must love what they are doing. According to him, when working with young players as either administrator or coach, personal characteristics are far more important than knowledge. "If you do not enjoy working with kids no matter your knowledge, you will fail." Dimitrakopoulos's greatest accomplishment within sport administration starts with staying true to the organizational mission statement of "player development over team development" in all of his decisions.

level, many clubs have program directors to manage all of the girls' teams and boys' teams. These program directors will manage and hire coaches and determine the needs of each age level consistent with the curriculum planning from the DOC to measure the programs' effectiveness. Under each program director are the coaches who must implement the plans to fully develop and prepare their athletes for club-level training and competition.

Screening Requirements for Volunteers

Across all sectors of the sport landscape, volunteers are secured to operate programming that happens behind the scenes and alongside youth participants. The establishment of a comprehensive screening process is more than a background check [National Alliance for Youth Sports (NAYS), 2012]. Sport organizations must take preventive steps to ensure the safety of their participants by adhering to legal requirements for background checks, including criminal offender records and sexual offender records. Even if these reports come back without any violations, sport entities are wise to conduct further investigation into the character and conduct of volunteers via personal and professional references, along with phone conversations with previous employers or other sport associations. In addition to the screening process, athletic administrators cannot dismiss and must recognize

FEEDBACK FROM THE FIELD

Best Practices: Youth Sport

Nick Campion has worked in various roles in sport administration as a volunteer, a coach, an administrator, and currently as a community sport professional. Campion started his professional career at a tennis club in member services, later advancing to club supervisor and managing daily operations, member services, and facility maintenance. The clientele at this specific club was an older population, typically retired or established wealthy business professionals from the Boston suburbs. Seeking interaction with a broader, more diverse population, Campion moved on from the tennis club after three years and began working for a seasonal special needs program (Camp Starfish) as the athletics coordinator, developing activities that ranged from swim instruction to organized field games such as soccer and flag football. This experience opened the door to an opportunity at Phillips Exeter Academy, where Campion worked in the athletics office holding a variety of roles ranging from contest management to pool supervisor. Although brief, these two opportunities—Camp Starfish and Phillips Exeter Academy—helped diversify Campion's résumé and were critical components in helping him secure the recreation supervisor position for the City of Somersworth in New Hampshire. As recreation supervisor, Campion was involved with coaching basketball, running summer camps, offering educational classes, and maintaining and improving city parks. After three years in Somersworth, Campion changed positions to join a much larger program with the Town of Danvers in Massachusetts.

As assistant recreation director in Danvers, Campion is responsible for the planning, development, implementation, and management of a wide variety of recreation programs year round. Campion emphasizes that key characteristics of athletic administrators include listening to the community to gauge its interests and dislikes and to adjust programs accordingly. The areas of growth and opportunity in a community recreation department are constantly evolving—much like peoples' interests and hobbies. Campion uses social media to monitor what his community is currently engaged in and what residents would like to see more of. In his role, conducting surveys and reaching out for feedback have been excellent tools in managing programs while looking for more growth and opportunity across all facets of community recreation.

In terms of the cost to operate programs, Campion is always mindful that his programs and event pricing must be oriented to what families can afford. The department does offer financial aid and scholarships to community members. Campion highlights that, ultimately, his organization is looking to build a stronger, happier, and more unified community at the end of the day, and if they have to operate in the red to do so, it is understood by community leaders that their efforts are made with the community's best interest in mind.

the staggering statistic that less than 20% of volunteer coaches are appropriately trained (NAYS, 2012).

▶ Community Outreach

Although the primary focus is on participants, athletic administrators at all settings and levels devote a great deal of effort and time to fostering relationships with parents and community members. These external relationships materialize in many forms, including volunteers for programs, donors, coaches, and support groups that communicate to other groups the value and benefits of the specific sport entity. Time and effort are invested in cultivating relationships to create links and external bonds with business and banking professionals, as well as parents within the community to better position the program financially.

Administrative Applications

Because of the variety of tasks athletic administrators must execute on a daily basis, the operational aspects within these sport organizations are both dynamic and exhilarating. Athletic administrators' tasks vary, depending on the seasonal nature of the industry and the demands for project completion based on the priorities of the entity. Decisions of athletic administrators significantly affect the experiences and opportunities of their target audiences. Critical to the effectiveness of athletic administrators is the foresight to determine how each decision or opportunity contributes to the creation of enhanced programs, improved services, and elevated opportunities to advance the athletes' personal interests and desire for sport achievement.

Many people believe working in athletic administration is an enchanting career that involves working with athletes and coaches and dealing with the fun and entertainment aspects of sport. However, the "behind-the-scenes" operation of athletic administration is often time consuming. What is central to the focus for athletic administrators is the reach and impact of their decisions on the athletes and families they serve. Deliberate management of actions within each program and activity has immeasurable but important impacts on the changed and improved lives of athletes. At the heart of athletic administration is the crafting of mindful decisions even as the needs of staff and stakeholders pull administrators in multiple directions. Decisions and actions have ripple effects on the stakeholders within each setting. Athletic administrators must realize that many groups are not only interested in, but also invested in, the outcomes of the programs under their supervision.

The end result of developing and ultimately operating sport programming is the product of hours spent promoting the program in the marketplace, organizing team tryouts, hiring staff or adding volunteer coaches, securing space for the team to practice and compete in games, ordering uniforms and practice equipment, hiring officials, maintaining budgets, and constantly dealing with issues that may arise after each game or practice. The position of athletic administrator means fielding many questions and working to educate many groups of people about the underlying purpose of athletics in our culture and the specific sport setting. In the end, the fulfillment comes from the successes on the playing fields, as well as perhaps years later when athletes return to express satisfaction with the impact these athletic activities had on their lives.

Values and Mission

Athletic administrators are stewards of a sport entity. At the core, athletic administrators embrace and execute the values of the organization's mission statement through their decision-making process and through the creation of programming options for its stakeholders. On its own merit, a mission statement serves to guide, inform, and inspire stakeholders. From an athletic administrator's perspective, the words and values embedded within the mission statement influence decision making. Decisions stem from the guiding principles expressed in the mission statement and executed by the athletic administrators. When new programs are considered, athletic administrators must be sure to question how the components or ideas mesh with current offerings and recognize how the program will advance the core values of the entity as detailed in the mission statement. For many administrators, the mission statement is a living, breathing document that serves to guide decision and policy making, as well as provide directional posts for confronting challenges.

When making decisions during the sport entity's seasons or programs, athletic administrators must be grounded by the values and ideals of the organization. Continually questioning the purpose of the sport entity is essential to ensure that the actions taken and decisions made by the athletic administrator are all geared toward realizing the organization's mission and ultimate goals. Athletic administrators must constantly question whether or not the decision makers are fulfilling the mission and accomplishing the organization's original goals. To simplify, athletic administrators constantly measure their effectiveness by determining whether they are meeting the expectations of their primary participant group—the athletes.

Functional Roles

Many functional managerial roles are assumed by athletic administrators to help a high-performing sport entity meet its organizational goals and desired daily outcomes. Athletic administrators are obligated not only to play a leadership role but also to use their capabilities to accomplish core tasks within the department.

In addition to carrying out the day-to-day operations of their organizations, athletic administrators advocate for increases in funding for new programs or the enhancement of existing programs. Athletic administrators negotiate for field and gymnasium space within the towns and regions they operate to provide more training experiences for their teams. In addition, many athletic administrators have the task of raising funds from outside sources to operate programs of the highest possible quality.

As a figurehead for the entity, athletic administrators provide guidance at meetings and develop relationships with key town officials to create opportunities relating to

© Mike Powell/Photodisc/Getty Images.

community affairs or even field and gymnasium use. Athletic administrators who work with boards of directors, community members, and volunteers must recognize that the motives of these participants to be involved in sport are quite different than those of paid staff members. Some volunteer parents may lack or have limited knowledge in sport, but tapping their professional expertise in marketing, business, technology, or fundraising is paramount. To foster strong ties in the community, athletic organizers reach out to parents and families to help strengthen programs for the youth of the area. The combination of sport management professionals and volunteers provides professional skills and personal experiences to generate new programs and complete needed tasks to effectively manage and operate sport programs across all settings.

▶ Organizational Culture

In addition to written mission statements, athletic administrators work to create and implement local corporate cultures to highlight shared beliefs and value systems to be accepted and adopted by staff members. Just like coaches, athletic administrators look for tools and methods to create a seamless unit within their departments. Athletic administrators must recognize that staff members sometimes advocate so much for their own program needs that they simply lose sight of the bigger picture. It is the duty of the athletic administrator to refocus the coaches and staff to help them embrace a corporate identity that aspires to provide equitable experiences to all athletes. Creating and fostering a strong organizational culture assists athletic administrators in promoting acceptable standards within the department.

An organizational culture comprises shared beliefs and values by a group and patterns of behaviors that reflect those beliefs and norms (Trice & Beyer, 1993). Through shared attitudes, staff members develop trust and bonds that lead to a collegial, supportive, and ultimately more productive environment. Within a high-paced and high-intensity sport-oriented department, staff members use the guiding foundation of the organizational culture to work cooperatively on projects, resolve issues, and communicate ideas. The end result is to have a cohesive team working to achieve departmental tasks and goals. The culture identity begins with the development, cultivation, and implementation of the mission statement. The mission statement is a clear and cohesive snapshot of the department's purpose embedded with values and aims. In some cases, the mission statement can be a single sentence; in other organizations, it can range from 6 to 12 sentences. It takes time to construct a mission statement that systematically communicates the essence of the organization or department.

Some institutions have taken organizational culture development to a new level. Athletics at Butler University in Indiana focus on five pillars that embody the university's strong sense of culture. A close look at both the institution's mission statement and the athletic department's specific mission statement show why Butler has been a focus for the study of culture building in athletics. Butler University's mission statement is "to provide the highest quality of liberal and professional education and to integrate the liberal arts into professional education, by creating and fostering a stimulating intellectual community built upon interactive dialogue and inquiry among faculty, staff and students." Butler University's athletic department mission statement reads, "The intercollegiate athletic department's mission is to support the university's purpose by providing exceptional educational and athletic experiences for all student-athletes. . . *The Butler Way*." Furthermore, "*The Butler Way* demands commitment, denies selfishness, accepts reality, yet seeks improvement everyday while putting the team above self." The goals for Butler athletics include: "Exceptional

[student-athlete] experiences, successful teams, source of unity and pride for students, faculty, staff, alumni and friends of Butler, and fiscal sustainability" (Butler, n.d.). The importance of these statements is greater than the words on paper. From the institutional mission to the goals of the department, every staff member, every student athlete, and every parent understands the values and is strongly encouraged to live by the Butler Way to reinforce the ultimate direction of the institution—creating exceptional experiences for its stakeholders in both academics and athletics.

Another organization, the Positive Coaching Alliance (PCA), offers culture-shaping ideas to assist sport organizers from collegiate to youth sport define how to create an enriching sport experience through an organizational lens. PCA is a national nonprofit that works with a variety of programs within youth sport, community sport, club sport, and high school and college athletics (www .positivecoach.org). In *Developing Better Athletes, Better People: A Leader's Guide to Transforming High School and Youth Sports into a Development Zone* (Thompson, 2013), the PCA considers three stages of culture. First, "setting the table" means that athletic administrators must outline clear expectations of behavior from coaches, parents, and athletes. Second, "fixing broken windows" symbolically represents an organization protecting the culture's identity from people who disregard its values. This idea is based on the work of social scientist James Q. Wilson, who pointed out that neighborhoods with unkempt and disheveled homes would be subject to higher crime rates. If windows were not mended, more broken windows and decay would follow and the quality of living in those areas would decline. The PCA stresses that negative sport behavior will affect the culture of the entire organization if not corrected or stopped. Third, integrating structural pillars that shield the culture of the organization from wearing away over time can protect the organization into the future. How athletic administrators nurture the aims of the department depends not only on what staff members value but also on what the organization or institution embraces as goals in athletics and academics.

Ultimately, athletic administrators represent their particular organization in all aspects of the operation. Athletic administrators manage with the understanding that their actions reflect on themselves as well as the entity they epitomize and ultimately embody. The commitment to nurturing and fully developing athletes should never waiver because the aim of administration is to create programs and hire staff members who can direct the goals and objectives of the sport organization with the highest standard of care. Although the field of athletic administration is desirable and the daily work rewarding, it is important to note the amount of time required to successfully manage sport.

 MANAGERIAL APPLICATIONS

Collegiate Athletics: Mission of Athletics

The term *student-athlete* has long been used to stress that academics takes priority over athletics within the walls of academia. Athletic administrators are charged with ensuring that student-athletes understand their commitment to earning their degree and fulfilling coursework obligations as the first priority over athletics. Many seminars and meetings have occurred on campus to present strategies for student-athletes to manage their time. The lacrosse coach has decided to have 5 AM practices because of facility availability Monday through Friday during the academic semester. Student-athletes have been arriving late or missing morning classes entirely because they are falling asleep after lacrosse practices. The instructors are sending out academic warnings to alert students that they are missing core work or have failed in-class assignments.

Questions to Consider

1. As the athletic administrator accountable for monitoring student-athlete success in the classroom, how will you handle this situation with the coach and with the student-athletes?
2. Review athletic department policies on academic regulations for two college athletic departments. What actions would you consider to strengthen the priority of academics within an athletic department?
3. In what ways can you communicate the importance of a "student first and athlete second" philosophy to your coaching staff?

 DECISION-MAKING CHALLENGE: HIGH SCHOOL SPORT

Hazing has become a destructive ritual within many sport teams across many levels. As a high school athletic administrator, you are trying to build a strong organizational identity that does not tolerate negative behavior from coaches or athletes. What types of programs will you create to combat hazing? To tackle this task, locate an operational definition of hazing and then craft two programs to deliver to your student-athletes and another to deliver to your coaching staff to address hazing as a significant problem in athletics. What external resources can you use to create a powerful and meaningful educational program to stress the importance of eliminating any and all forms of hazing from your programs?

DECISION-MAKING CHALLENGE: CLUB SPORT

Club sports play a large role in our culture. High school coaches are dealing with athletes and parents who are paying a great deal of money to play club sports, attend tournaments, and receive professional coaching. These athletes are often not signing up to play for high school teams or they place a priority on club activities over athletic practices and contests at the scholastic level. As a high school athletic administrator, how would you explain the benefits of high school athletics over club sports? As a club sport organizer, how would you communicate expectations to parents and players who wish to continue to participate in their school programming while also being involved in your club at an elite level? Is there a balance that can be struck so athletes can participate in both high school and club sports, or are there rules from governing associations that prevent this scenario?

FEATURED INTERVIEW: BEST PRACTICES IN ATHLETIC ADMINISTRATION

Diana Cutaia is the owner and founder of Coaching Peace. Her experience in athletic administration spans 20 years in a variety of capacities, including director of athletics at Wheelock College, acting executive director of the Massachusetts Governor's Committee on Physical Fitness and Sport, and emcee for the NCAA National Student-Athlete Leadership Forum, in addition to presenting to colleges on topics ranging from diversity and gender equity to sportsmanship. Cutaia served as the Boston Public Policy consultant for the Women's Sports Foundation, cofounded the Boston Women's Athletic Administrators Network, and coached basketball at Curry College, Mount Holyoke College, and Norwalk Community College, as well as for three years at the high school level. Cutaia's latest endeavor is with her new company, Coaching Peace. Its mission is to coach organizations, schools, departments, and teams to create cultures and be leaders who will employ empathy, seek balance, and ensure equality and acceptance.

Changes Across Settings

Cutaia has been instrumental as a change agent across multiple sport settings, including youth, high school, and college athletics. When prompted to reflect on the changing sport landscape, Cutaia pointed to a shift that has occurred across all sectors of sport from youth to collegiate levels, where the focus is no longer on the process of learning or development but on outcomes. Adults between the ages of 40 and 60 have memories of playing neighborhood sport in their backyards or playgrounds. The desire to win was important but the difference, according to Cutaia, is that the act of playing was more enjoyable than the result, even if the kids kept score. Those children enjoyed playing, learning, and working toward improving their skills. The difference, summarized by Cutaia, is that today's parents and athletes are more focused on winning "the golden ticket" because of media exposure on college athletics and the escalation of professional athlete salaries which has sapped the enjoyment of sport away from the athletes because of the focus on money and athletic scholarships. Even at the college level, Cutaia admits that players will leave teams after one year simply because they are burned out because sport is all they have known and identified with from such an early age.

Who Is Coaching the Athletes?

One area of deep concern for Cutaia is the shift in who teaches sport to young people. In the 1980s and 1990s, coaches were educators teaching sport—that is, they were teachers who understood the basic tenants of teaching and made teaching a focus. From Cutaia's perspective, there is no longer any widespread involvement of educators in sport. Coaches in the past were trained in the basic skills of teaching and made that the focus of practices and games. Today, many career coaches working with athletes are making a living and basing their entire careers on coaching club soccer or club basketball or the Amateur Athletic Union. This trend has been growing over time, but it is now a major force in coaching.

What does this mean for today's athletes? Coaches are not trained in the basic principles of education, sport psychology, outcome assessment, practice plan development, or teaching in a progressive model. Most important of all, they are not ensuring that athletes have a positive experience. Simply put, many coaches are career coaches who are in it to just pad a résumé, increase their status in the community, or get more perks. As Cutaia explains, when programs lose educators in sport, the athletes ultimately are the ones who lose out. Within sports today there are more injuries, coaches talk to athletes in ways that are too often debasing, athletes are experiencing overuse injuries at extremely young ages, there are high rates of concussion, and violence has generally proliferated for its own sake in sport. Add to that mix parents and coaches on the sidelines because there is a lack of educators teaching sport. Cutaia warns that if educators or individuals who are focused on teaching are not involved in sport, then society as a whole will see many more issues with bullying, hazing, interpersonal problems between coach and athlete, and performance challenges. Many of today's coaches, stresses Cutaia, just do not know how to manage these player and team issues, which contributes to young athletes not being able to reach their full potential and falling short of enjoying the process of learning through a positive sport experience.

Values and Organizational Culture

When asked to address how to empower athletic administrators to think outside the box, Cutaia says it comes down to courage, adding the first thing any athletic administrator needs to do is follow his or her values. According to Cutaia, the first step to developing a value system is to identify what is important to you. She further elaborates that she paid attention to what was happening around her and recognized a lack of positive attributes associated with the way administrators were positioning kids in sport and what the administrators were focused on. In her experience, she never saw kids come away and say "I love it when my coach is screaming at me all the time." Athletes may say such behavior is motivating, but it only motivates them temporarily.

Cutaia's values became critically important, and it was a journey that included opening one's eyes to focus on what is important and what athletic administrators are trying to achieve. As much as Cutaia thought outside the box to some extent, especially at an institution like Wheelock College, she thought inside the box as well. Cutaia took an introspective look at Wheelock College's institutional mission statement which simply states, *to improve the lives of children and families*. The mission is just one line, and all students enrolled at the institution majored in education or were service-oriented majors all focused on improving the experiences of members of society. As athletic director, Cutaia decided to embed those values within the athletic department, committing the department to living the values of the institution. It became clear that the direction of the department should be focused on what Cutaia wanted; it was what the institution valued that was most important. What she saw when the athletic department meshed its values with the institution was that the student-athletes had better experiences that translated to measurable outcomes recorded through senior surveys. Surveys of student-athletes revealed that 90% reported they had a successful sport experience regardless of the win–loss record, and their satisfaction had no connection to wins. Cutaia felt it would be hypocritical and contradictory of her to measure coach success by wins and losses if students and the entire institution did not use that same criteria.

Learning About the Athlete Experience

One way to learn more about the student-athlete experience was to live it. Cutaia spent a full week of each sport season participating as an athlete. After meeting with student-athletes in her office and

(continues)

hearing the normal complaints and challenges that come from college-age students, she decided to find a better way to understand the student experience by immersing herself into their athletic lives. She did everything the athletes did and acted like an athlete to get the full experience. She stressed to the coaches that this was not an evaluation but rather a chance for Cutaia to examine and learn from the athlete experience. Through this process, she experienced several different things from how far the athletes traveled to the field, to meal times, to what was being served in the dining hall—all aspects that affect the overall student experience. Without spending time at practices and talking with athletes, she believes she would have never really understood the root of what her student-athletes were communicating to her during their meetings.

Culture Building

Cutaia cultivates bonds with her coaches, describing the process as a blind trust when she asks staff members to try new ideas. She consistently challenges coaches to focus on what is ultimately important and to measure effective coaches in several different ways, not just through wins and losses. Cutaia describes shaping an organizational culture among her staff to pinpoint values and make sure they match the culture of the department and the institution. Sometimes, she acknowledges, individual values are not consistent with the department culture and both coaches and administrators must figure out how to make small changes under their control to integrate within the established culture.

Mentoring Role of Athletic Administrator

Instead of judging coaches, Cutaia spends time asking questions to understand the value system of staff members. Ultimately, she mentors coaches as a way to provide feedback and be a resource in their professional development. She underscores the importance of athletic administrators being aware of what is happening with all teams and intervening in a timely fashion to offset negative consequences. Blame is not part of the process of mentoring; instead, modeling positive behavior—guiding that behavior and celebrating that behavior—are the ingredients that Cutaia incorporates to mentor effectively.

One aspect of Cutaia's department focus was to complement rather than compete with the student-athletes' overall experience at the institution. In a vibrant athletic department, coaches want to spend as much time as possible working with athletes, but Cutaia would not approve any extra activities. Instead, she placed the accountability on the coaches. She prompted coaches to review the mission statement; if a request was in line with the values of the department and institution, then the answer was easy. If the activities did not align with the values, then the coaches had the answer as well. Through that process, Cutaia mentored coaches to examine the core aspects of the department to guide decision making and ultimately to live the mission of the institution.

Development of a Philosophy

As Cutaia explains, spending time communicating to athletes and coaches is essential to ensuring that all stakeholders understand the fundamentals of the philosophy of the coach or administrator or both. In a time when parents are investing in sport programs, the demand to see improvement in the skill sets of their children is real. To make sure parents and athletes have a clear understanding of the values of the coach, administrator, or program, open meetings must be required for all families before practices start. Expectations about standards of behavior can be communicated not only to the athletes but also to their parents. Coaches and athletic administrators must clearly indicate how they want the program to be operated by being firm and honest with the policies and boundaries. Cutaia points out that athletic administrators and coaches must first provide athletes with a positive experience and then should set learning outcomes to map skill acquisition and character development.

Questions for Discussion

1. Review the website and mission statement of Coaching Peace. What are the offered programs you would select within an athletic department? What other types of organizations provide athletic administrators and coaches with the resources to make powerful changes in their operations?
2. List the values an athletic administrator should hold. Please prepare your script or slideshow to present your philosophy to your staff and a second one to present to parents. Point out any differences that may exist from one presentation to the other.
3. What impresses you the most about Cutaia's story and experience? What ideas will you implement as an athletic administrator and why?
4. Select two other seasoned administrators to write about. Describe their experiences and journey to create a positive experience for athletes across youth, high school, club, and collegiate sport settings.
5. Examining the work of Cutaia with Butler University athletics, what are the similarities of the message conveyed? What aspects would you incorporate into your culture-building toolbox?
6. Take some time to think about the positive impact you will make in athletic administration. What would you want your staff and your athletes to say about you when describing your efforts to enrich the sporting experience for young people? Create a list of words and phrases they would use to highlight your values, your personality, and your legacy as an athletic administrator.

Good Ware from flaticon.com

Wrap-Up

End-of-Chapter Activities
College Athletics

1. You have been hired as the first athletic director at a newly established college. You have the chance to name the institution and set the location of the institution (city and state), size of the institution, academic offerings, and athletic sport teams. Let's get started:
   a. Name of institution
   b. Location of institution
   c. Type of athletic institution (NCAA or NAIA) and level (Division I, II, III)
   d. List of academic majors
   e. Size of institution (enrollment)
   f. List of sponsored sport teams
2. To fully operate a new sport program, create a hiring plan for the athletic department, including job titles and descriptions. Research similar institutions to assist with creating the hiring plan.
3. List and describe all of the athletic facilities you will construct for the sponsored teams (you can set the budget for the construction).
4. Craft a mission statement for the athletic department.

Youth Club Sport

1. You are now the executive director for Club Elite. In this position, you must establish the entire club from players to staff.
   Let's get started:
   a. Indicate what sport Club Elite encompasses (example: Club Elite Soccer or Club Elite Softball).
   b. Pinpoint club location (please be sure to indicate a region or

several towns to recruit elite-level athletes).

c. Determine the league for Club Elite's affiliation for games.

d. List the teams, including gender, age, and level specific to the league and sport regulations.

e. In the area you selected for Elite Sport, research playing facilities you can acquire for rent or purchase for practices and games.

f. According to the league you selected, indicate length of the season and number of games played for each team.

g. How many staff and coaches will be hired to operate an effective club program? For Elite Club, craft position titles and descriptions for all staff members. Please indicate part-time or full-time for each staff member.

h. Determine the cost for players to join the club (annual or seasonal membership costs).

i. After reviewing similar sport clubs online, use a free web-design platform and create the Elite Club website, logo, and club colors to help market the new club to prospective players. Include as much detail as possible on the website.

End-of-Chapter Questions

1. Locate mission statements for a local youth sport organization, amateur sport club, and high school athletic department. List and describe the core values expressed in each mission. Based on your research, are there any values these organizations may have overlooked?

2. Locate college athletic department missions for Division I, II, and III schools and compare and contrast differences. What words can you highlight that embody the values and aims found in the mission statements of the NCAA for each divisional classification?

3. The NCAA's core ideal is to subscribe to the principles of amateurism. Describe how an athletic director can enforce the mantra of student first, athlete second on your college campus.

4. Visit the website of two colleges of varying sizes to identify the staff differences at each institution. Pay attention to the number of staff at each institution, staff titles, and whether people have more than one role at the institution.

5. Develop your personal philosophy for athletic administration. What are the guiding principles you used when developing your philosophy? Share one experience when you needed to rely on your fundamental ethics to provide direction in making an important decision.

6. List words you would use to describe a cohesive department. What are some ideas you can implement to ensure a strong organizational culture among your staff members and coaches within community sport, high school sport, and collegiate athletics?

7. What are the trends associated with the community, high school, club, and college athletic competition? What resources will you use to stay current with the changing aspects of the settings discussed in this chapter?

8. Mentors are a critical part of developing a personal and professional philosophy. List the people you would turn to for guidance in dealing with difficult issues relating to the topics covered in this chapter.

9. *Change* is the buzzword across sport organizations. Explain the attributes and experiences you have to embrace to change and lead your organization into new endeavors.

10. Look at participation data for a specific sport in your town. What other options do families have within a 30-mile radius from their homes to join? How do

these competitive factors influence the participation rates and marketing reach of community sport relations?

11. What role does college or university athletics play in developing youth sport in their specific area in terms of community outreach? As a college athletic director, what do you regard as the importance of community outreach and marketing to youth sport teams? Is this an added value or should this be part of college sports?

12. Create a list of questions you think you would be asked during interviews for the following positions:
    - Club Sport: director of coaching
    - College associate athletic director: finance
    - Fundraising coordinator: high school athletics
    - Board of directors position: community sport
    - High school: director of athletics
    What follow-up questions will you ask at the end of your interview?

13. Look up two professionals in each setting and review their expertise and academic preparation. Why did you select these people and how has this assignment helped you understand the industry settings?

14. To stay current and abreast of trends within athletic administration, many participants embark on professional development opportunities. Research professional organizations to which athletic administrators would secure memberships. What are the names of these organizations, what is the annual fee to join, and what are the benefits of membership?

15. Research online a professional organization that is hosting a seminar, workshop, training, or conference on a topic of interest to you in athletic administration. Indicate the professional organization or institution hosting the event, the name of event, the cost to attend (as a student and as a professional), featured or highlighted speakers, and the location of the event. In three to five sentences, describe why you selected this event and how the information will help you in the field of athletic administration.

16. Research online the types of assessment tools that institutions, schools, community programs, and clubs use to measure effectiveness and whether they are fulfilling their mission statements.

17. Track the history and evolution of the athletic administration profession since the mid-1990s. What has surprised you the most about the profession?

18. Illustrate the core differences between the goals of the NCAA for Division I, Division II, and Division III schools.

19. Being an athlete is a source of identity for sport participants. As an athletic administrator in the youth sport and college settings, how can you promote or encourage athletes to engage in other activities outside of sport through your mission or policies?

20. The staff members you hire or secure as volunteers will most likely have diverse backgrounds. How will you as the athletic administrator create a cohesive unit within the department or organization to deliver high-quality sport programming to your participants? How would you find out what each staff person brings (e.g., expertise, creativity, unique skills) to the department or organization?

21. Craft a professional philosophy with regards to athletics. If you were to be interviewed for a position, what would the script look like for sharing your philosophy of athletics (include your goals, core values relating to sport participation and management of staff and student athletes)?

22. What recent stories or research point to the fact that sport is adopting a more business-like orientation? Reflect on how you as an athletic administrator would manage the business side of sport.

References

Anderson-Butcher, D., Riley, A., Amorose, A., Iachini, A., & Wade-Mdivanian, R. (2014). Maximizing youth experiences in community sport settings: The design and impact of the LiFE Sports Camp. *Journal of Sport Management*, 28(2), 236–249.

Brand, M. (2006). The role and value of intercollegiate athletics in universities. *Journal of the Philosophy of Sport*, 33(1), 9–20.

Brower, J. J. (1979). The professionalization of organized youth sport: Social psychological impacts and outcomes. *Annals of the American Academy of Political and Social Science*, 445(1), 39–46.

Butler University Athletic Department. (n.d.). Retrieved March 22, 2016, from http://butlersports.com /information/school_bio/mission_statement.

DeSensi, J. T., Kelley, D. R., Blanton, M. D., & Beitel, P. A. (1990). Sport management curricular evaluation and needs assessment: A multifaceted approach. *Journal of Sport Management*, 4, 31–58.

Dougherty, M. (2016, September 21). How much does it cost to play youth sports? Retrieved October 10, 2018, from https://www.lohud.com/story/sports/2016/09/21 /youth-sports-cost/90313836/.

Dorsch, T. E., Smith, A. L., Wilson, S. R., & McDonough M. H. (2015). Parent goals and verbal sideline behavior in youth sport. *Sport, Exercise, and Performance Psychology*, 4(1), 19–35.

Garcia, A. C. (2015). Understanding high school students' sports participation. *Sport Science Review*, 24 (3/4), 121–145.

Horch, H., & Schütte, N. (2003). Competencies of sport managers in German sport clubs and sport federations. *Managing Leisure*, 8(2), 70–84.

Hyman, M. (2012). *The most expensive game in town: The rising cost of youth sports and the toll on today's families*. Boston: Beacon Press.

Martin, E. M., Ewing, M. E., & Gould, D. (2014). Social agents' influence on self-perceived good and bad behavior of American youth involved in sport: Developmental level, gender, and competitive level effects. *Sport Psychologist*, 28(2), 111–123.

Massachusetts Interscholastic Athletic Association (2016). MIAA handbook [online]. Retrieved March 22, 2016, from http://www.miaa.net/contentm/easy_pages/view .php?sid=38&page_id=88.

National Alliance for Youth Sports (2012). Background screening in youth sports 2012. Retrieved March 22, 2016, from https://www.nays.org/default/assets/File /Background%20Screening%20Guidelines%202012 .pdf.

National Collegiate Athletic Association (NCAA). (n.d.). 2013–14 guide for the college-bound student-athlete [online]. Retrieved March 22, 2016, from http://www .ncaapublications.com/productdownloads/CBSA .pdf

National Collegiate Athletic Association (NCAA) (n.d.). Student-athlete participation, 1981–92 to 2014–15. Retrieved March 22, 2016, from http://www.ncaa.org /sites/default/files/Participation Rates Final.pdf.

Ocean State Soccer School (2011, October 17). OSS organizational chart. Retrieved from http://oceanstatesoccer.org /Page.asp?n=43790&org=OCEANSTATESOCCER .ORG.

Thompson, J. (2013). *Developing better athletes, better people: A leader's guide to transforming high school and youth sports into a development zone*. Mountain View, CA: Positive Coaching Alliance.

Trice, H. M., & Beyer J. M. (1993). *Cultures of work organizations*. Englewood Cliffs, NJ: Prentice Hall.

U.S. Youth Soccer (2014, January 21). U.S. Youth Soccer celebrates 40th anniversary in 2014. Retrieved October 10, 2018, from https://www.usyouthsoccer .org/us_youth_soccer_celebrates_40th_anniversary _in_2014/.

Warner, S., Kerwin, S. & Walker, M. (2013). Examining sense of community in sport: Developing the multidimensional SCS' Scale. *Journal of Sport Management*, 27(5), 349–362.

Wong, G. (2014, June). The path to the athletic director's office. *Sport Business Journal*, p. 32.

YMCA. (n.d.). Retrieved March 22, 2016, from http://www .ymca.net/sites/default/files/news-media/About-the -Y-Fact-Sheet.pdf

CHAPTER 2

Managerial Aspects of Athletic Administration

LEARNING OBJECTIVES

After reading this chapter, students will be able to:

1. Outline and analyze the management tools used by athletic administrators across a variety of sport settings.
2. Define leadership within athletic administration.
3. Describe and compare the managerial functions of athletic administration in college, high school, youth, and club sport settings.
4. Illustrate the importance of policy making and construction of athletic-specific regulations.
5. Evaluate the role of the athletic administrator in a high-demand workplace.

Effective and sustained athletic administration is a powerful force that elevates the performance levels of staff through deliberate use of managerial applications and tools. Successful athletic administrators personify leadership while initiating positive change within sport entities. The growth and increased demands within the sport setting have stimulated change in how athletic administrators operate, analyze, and approach the total management of their department. Today's athletic administrators embrace innovative managerial tools to help staff achieve organizational objectives and goals, adequately meet consumer demand, and offset competition in the sporting domain. An administrator's *management style* refers to

the methodology he or she uses to direct and motivate staff to achieve organizational tasks.

Athletic administrators use a combination of managerial tools, expertise, and theory to cultivate high-performing staff who will efficiently and effectively move the sport organization forward to provide programming to its core market. The effectiveness of athletic administrators rests with their ability to understand and nurture their leadership role within the sport entity. "Leadership involves day-to-day interactions between manager and their subordinates" (Gibson, Ivanenvich, Donnelly, & Konopaske, 2006, p. 19). The athletic administrator in command embraces a variety of tasks that need to be accomplished, not only by him or her but also by staff members and volunteers. *Leadership* is a buzzword used in the explanation and research of management theory. Kruse (2013) describes leadership as "a process of social influence, which maximizes the efforts of others, towards the achievement of a goal" (p. 2).

From an athletic administrator's perspective, leadership reinforces many values embodied in sports such as teamwork, respect, collaboration, selflessness, and decision making. Leadership characteristics are typically learned from and nourished by parents, teachers, and coaches. The expectation to lead by example is paramount, especially for the highly visible athletic administrator. Because of that visibility, the athletic administrator must not only communicate the ideals of the department and organizational mission but also live them. Athletic administrators continually promote the ideals expressed in the mission statement of the sport entity and systematically evaluate two specific questions: What is our purpose? Are we doing what we say we are doing?

The nature of any athletic administrative position requires a level of accountability unlike other roles in the professional sector simply because the delivery of programming deeply influences the target groups, whether they are athletes or family members. All roles assumed by athletic administrators should uphold the organization's values to satisfactorily meet stakeholders' core needs. In summary, the athletic administrator reinforces the goals of the sport entity by deliberately using such managerial tools as planning, organizing, scheduling, budgeting, and marketing. Applying these tools within and outside the sport entity results in two important achievements: elevated programming for athletes and a strengthened workplace environment for staff.

Undoubtedly, effective leadership injects motivation and passion into the work environment, resulting in increased performance levels by staff. Performance and productivity are measures that dictate the functional effectiveness of athletic administration. Nonetheless, many

interchangeable parts exist within athletic management, and this requires administrators to focus on the task at hand to create a seamless entity. Furthermore, because of the pressures to succeed and obligations to serve multiple target groups, many professionals and researchers classify management as both art and science. From a creative standpoint, athletic administrators deal with many fiscal constraints, forcing them to do more programming with less funding. Leaders rise to the challenge, evoking creativity and innovation to calculate methods to elevate programs even when budgets remain the same or decrease. On the other hand, the athletic administrator's dashboard includes the ability to forecast change and anticipate challenges to quantitatively solve problems by using formulas and equations to determine needs, expenses, or revenue-related opportunities. "The myth that coaching and directing athletic programs are simple and without undue pressures is misleading" (Green & Reese, 2006, p. 318.). The dynamic nature of athletic administration makes the daily work environment invigorating and challenging at the same time. Undeniably, athletic administrators play a prominent role in all aspects of the sport entity but, in reality, they go unnoticed because "the athletic director's job is often viewed like that of a referee—if no one notices you are there, you're doing it well" (Kalahar, 2011, p. 1).

▶ Managerial Theories

Over the decades, research in managerial theory has evolved as changes emerged within business management. Theoretical aspects of management are critical to learn and comprehend because athletic administrators continually analyze and decipher the best ways to increase motivation and productivity within their designated sport entities. Commonly studied management theories are the classical approach, the behavioral approach, the scientific management approach, and the systems approach. Under the classical approach, business managers in the 1900s developed an organized approach to increasing productivity with the core responsibilities focusing on planning, organizing, implementing, and controlling. The end result or the final product was the desired focus of managers operating within the classical approach.

The behavioral approach developed because of managers' core need to better understand what motivates and drives employees to become more productive. The scientific management approach evolved from these two concepts and focused on administrative tasks and operating the business entity efficiently. Efficiency adheres to the tenant of producing high-quality work with little waste (both physical and human resources). This helps organize the functions of the workplace into more streamlined units. The systems approach recognizes that all people within the organization are valued and significant to the end result. By using the systems approach, athletic departments ultimately become more effective when staff members work together to complete projects and tasks.

Managerial Functions of the Athletic Administrator

Athletic administrators execute the following functions: planning, budgeting, organizing, staging, coordinating, reporting, innovating, and representing (Judge & Judge, 2009). In addition, they must perform tasks, including hiring staff, scheduling games, communicating with parents, facility management, marketing, budgeting, and fundraising (Sullivan, Lonsdale, & Taylor, 2014). Because of the far-reaching scope and intensity of the athletic administrator's responsibilities, there are many challenges and demands associated with the management of sport programs (Judge & Judge, 2009). These demands further accentuate the need for athletic administrators to prepare and use staff to perform tasks and complete

projects to share the burden of the daily stressors associated with sport programming and to become more effective.

Planning

Planning allows athletic administrators to conceptualize ideas for the sport entity for the immediate future and for long-range endeavors. From the athletic administrative perspective, creating multiple blueprints to visualize the requisite components for moving ideas from the conceptual stage to finished stage is a continual function. On a daily basis, athletic administrators are tasked with calculating the needs of the sport entity while determining the best course of action for the program. Planning envelops not only understanding the needs of the sport organization but also outlining a process to satisfy those needs. Plans are categorized as *short term* (months to three years) or *long term* (three to four years or more). In some cases, plans will be revised and adapted to mesh with changes in the sport setting or to effectively address the desires of the target groups. Flexibility and the ability to adapt to changes are tools athletic administrators assume because plans are not always concrete but may in fact be subject to minor alterations to best serve the sport entity. "The planning function includes defining the ends to be achieved and determining appropriate means to achieve the defined ends" (Gibson et al., p. 17).

© fizkes/Shutterstock.

Organizing

Once a plan is crafted, athletic administrators will next begin organizing. The organizational hierarchy or flowchart depicts each staff position, unit, and department. Based on the job descriptions, the athletic administrator assigns tasks and projects to be completed to meet the department's goals. The function of organizing has two features: (1) ensuring enough personnel are assigned to carry out the designated tasks and (2) providing enough support (physical, fiscal, and human resources) to accomplish those tasks. Many aspects associated with understanding the core needs of the staff emerge during the organizing process. A successful athletic administrator serves to make everyone else's job operationally easier through the design of their positions within the organization. "In a theoretical sense, the organizing function involves (1) designing the responsibility and authority of each individual job and (2) determining which of these jobs will be grouped in specific departments" (Gibson et al., pp. 17–18).

Job Design

Job design allows athletic administrators to establish positions that include specific role descriptions while also balancing responsibilities throughout the workday. The core outcome for each staff person employed within the sport entity is to satisfactorily complete all tasks efficiently and effectively. Many contributing factors can be considered when designing jobs to get the most productivity from staff while promoting a sense of accomplishment in each person. When employees travel to work, they are thinking about the meetings, emails, assignments, and reports they need to complete to meet the requirements of their specific position.

Athletic administrators also can assign specialty projects to staff members to allow them to explore tasks that are outside their normal job descriptions. For example, the athletic training staff can be tasked with a schoolwide challenge to develop healthy eating habits among students, or coaches can organize a charity basketball game with proceeds donated to a local cause. New and exciting projects build morale, but a simple addition or change in the workday can also provide a different outlook on daily operations. Certainly, there are times when projects and tasks are lackluster, but for the majority of time at work professionals desire to feel challenged with task variety throughout the day and a sense of fulfillment or accomplishment. How athletic supervisors create those opportunities will depend on the tools used to manage the staff.

Another way to ensure the staff feels challenged and productive is to create a balance in the workday by combining small tasks and larger projects with individual and group-related tasks. Certainly, there will be times when the focus needs to be on major projects for the sport entity. In daily operations, athletic administrators deliberately construct roles and responsibilities to ensure that high-performing staff are productive. In turn, staff members satisfy their core need to contribute to the goals of the organization.

Delegating

Delegating is assigning responsibility or a task to a staff member (subordinate). When athletic administrators entrust staff members to complete projects autonomously, delegation serves as a motivation tool. Through delegation, staff members are empowered to complete a project from start to finish, which in turn generates staff creativity and confidence. Within athletic administration, it is common for staff to work independently to accomplish small and large tasks; this allows for better allocation of task completion. Delegating, however, requires a great deal of time on the part of the supervisor, who must determine which tasks need to be delegated, select the appropriate person to handle the task, and explain the specific details of the task. However, the results of allowing staff to assume full responsibility and accountability to execute the project have long-lasting effects, including building self-confidence and loyalty within the sport entity. Gallo (2012) stresses that managers should use delegation because it is a critical skill and is underutilized in practice.

© SmartPhotoLab/Shutterstock.

Implementing

Implementing is simply the action that drives the plan forward by the designated staff member or departmental unit. The strength of planning is that it moves the ideas, staff, or resources in a positive direction to meet the program's aims. Under the umbrella of implementing, athletic administrators formulate activities within the workplace that helps create and sustain cohesion and strengthen the organizational culture.

Cohesion is "the degree to which individual members stick together" and is "required for a group to exist" (Spink, Ulvick, McLaren, Crozier, & Fesser, 2015, p. 294). Athletic administrators use the values of the organization (culture) to motivate the staff to add effort and be professional when completing all roles and responsibilities. Athletic teams often operate under these conditions as they perform like a well-oiled machine, just as staff members work in tandem to use the quality skills of each member of the unit. When all members of the group work simultaneously

toward the same goal, high-level results typically follow.

Implementation serves the purpose of making sure the plans are communicated, accepted, and followed. Under this managerial function, athletic administrators demonstrate motivational skills to create a seamless environment in which all members of the organization, department, and unit are valued, feel significant, and contribute to the end result. Motivation and leadership can be defined in the same manner as athletic administrators aim to change and sustain valued staff behaviors through the process of implementation. Clearly, motivation and leadership are tools that allow athletic administrators to influence others to accomplish both small tasks and larger projects.

Controlling

Once plans are crafted, the staff secured, and the drive to complete each task is in motion, the athletic administrator must supervise all aspects of the operations to maintain high quality and be certain staff remains on task to meet expectations. The function of *controlling* creates a system of checks and balances that ensures tasks are understood and accomplished. *Monitoring* consists of providing oversight for the projects but also allows athletic administrators the ability to counsel, fix, or revise any element of the work to see the project to fruition and completed with the highest quality and care. Under this managerial function, athletic administrators determine whether the tasks are being met throughout the control process and determine the next course of action if they are not (Gibson et al., 2006). The managerial functions of an athletic administrator are not stand-alone concepts. Athletic administrators must continually seek out emerging resources and support from colleagues and staff members to operate efficiently and effectively, especially when modern-day athletic administrators are "performing increasing managerial functions such as planning, budgeting, organizing, staging, coordinating, reporting, innovating, and representing" (Judge & Judge, 2009, p. 38).

Management Styles

Another aspect of being an effective leader is using a range of styles to elevate the performance levels of staff and ultimately the sport organization's overall effectiveness. The organizational effectiveness of athletic administrators is contingent on using leadership skills comprising a variety of roles (Baghurst, Murray, Jayne, & Carter, 2014). According to Kirkpatrick and Locke (1991), effective leaders possess six traits: (1) drive, (2) the desire to lead, (3) honesty and integrity, (4) self-confidence, (5) cognitive ability (analysis and decision making), and (6) knowledge of the business. Athletic administrators who embody these traits are not automatically thrusted into leadership roles or experience success, but those who possess these attributes are likely to have an advantage over others who do not.

The priority athletic administrators place on values and goals within their sport entity affect the programs' overall management. Within athletic administration research, many operative goals exist, such as entertainment, national sport development, financial, transmission of culture, career opportunities, public relations, the athlete's personal growth, prestige, and achieved excellence, all of which have been studied within the college athletics setting (Chelladurai & Danylchuk, 1984; Chelladurai, Inglis, & Danylchuk, 1984). The athletic administrator's ranking of high-priority goals may not align with the perceptions of those groups served by the department, which constitutes a clear dilemma. Research indicates that these stated values and goals may not mesh with what stakeholders (participants and spectators) expect from athletic programs

(Trail & Chelladurai, 2002), which prompts administrators to determine how to manage with these existing differences. Notwithstanding, athletic administrators must recognize the polarizing viewpoints of university faculty and staff with regard to their perception of athletics on college campuses, specifically relating to academic performance, standards, integrity, governance, and the financing of intercollegiate athletics (Lewinter, Weight, Osborne, Brunner, 2013). The culture of athletics evokes strong emotion from athletes and fans and is embedded into "student cultures of U.S. universities" (Beyer & Hannah, 2000, p. 126). Undeniably, sports on many campuses are defined as the college ideal, serving as a powerful connector for stakeholders to identify with and ultimately support (Toma, 2010). Clearly, there are many competing thoughts and perspectives regarding the value of sport in our culture, but athletic administrators inevitably have a distinct task to take value from stakeholder perspectives. Striking the balance between academics and athletics is not a new challenge for athletic administrators, but they are constantly under the microscope to showcase how sport and academics can coexist.

The importance of analyzing the priorities of the department and its stakeholders serves to reinforce the values of the department. Athletic administrators use goals as pathways to craft responsibilities for task completion within the department. The movement of the staff toward the achievement of those tasks and to ultimately reaching the stated goals constitutes effective leadership. The leadership style adopted by athletic administrators directly affects relationships between manager and subordinate and is transferred into the formulation of a satisfied and cohesive work unit. Gratton and Erickson (2007) utilize the term *gift culture* when describing the collaborative workplace because the interactions are considered "valuable and generously offered" (p. 5).

The following are nine principal objectives and their general descriptions.

1. Entertainment: to provide a source of entertainment for the student body, faculty and staff, alumni, and the community.
2. National sport development: to contribute to the national sport development.
3. Financial: to generate revenue for the university.
4. Transmission of culture: to transmit the culture and tradition of the university and society.
5. Career opportunities: to provide those athletic experiences that will increase career opportunities for the athletes.
6. Public relations: to enhance the university community relations.
7. Athlete's personal growth: to promote the athlete's personal growth and health (physical, mental, and emotional).
8. Prestige: to enhance the prestige of the university, students, faculty and staff, alumni, and community.
9. Achieved excellence: to support those athletes performing at a high level of excellence (relative to athletes in other universities).

Adapted from Chellandurai & Danylchuk (1984).

Athletic administrators across all settings share core responsibilities. With the movement toward a business orientation in the administration of sport, required competency areas include communication, public relations, business and athletic management (Williams & Miller, 1983). As with any business-related organization, sport entities with a culture of collaboration can experience benefits such as increased staff engagement, motivated staff, and staff who are more

invested in the goals of the entity (Wallace & Mello, 2015). Leadership can be considered the primary ingredient to ensure streamlined success and effectiveness within sport entities across the youth sport, high school, collegiate, club, and community sport settings.

Leadership Styles

Athletic administrators' leadership styles vary in terms of how they manage, communicate, and ultimately lead their sport department. Perhaps athletic administrators will adopt one core methodology and style to lead. On the other hand, some athletic administrators may extract methods from various styles, depending on the situation. To elevate performance levels of staff and get the most productivity from each member of the department, athletic administrators need to challenge employees to excel. Effective athletic administration lends to the discovery of individual talents and special characteristics of workers.

Burns (1978) describes leadership in two forms: transactional leaders and transformational leaders. *Transactional leaders* are those who "take the initiative in making contact with others for the purpose of an exchange of valued things" (p. 19). A *transformational leader*, however, "looks for potential motives in followers, seeks to satisfy higher-level needs, and engages the full person of the follower" (Burns, 1978, p. 4). Furthermore, the four essential behaviors to classify a transformational leader are (1) vision builder, (2) standard-bearer, (3) integrator, and (4) developer (Bottomley, Burgess, & Fox, 2014). The vision builder encourages full staff participation and creates specific goals for the department. The standard-bearer understands the significance of ethics and accountability and establishes a culture of high moral conduct. Integrators engage staff to foster and initiate change and create an inclusive work environment to reach common goals. The developer cultivates an environment that promotes professional development and continuous professional improvement (Bottomley et al., 2014).

Transformational leadership evolves into morality because "it raises the level of human conduct and ethical aspiration of both leader and led" creating a "transforming effect on both" (Burns, 1978, p. 20). Burton and Peachey (2009) concluded "the key managerial implications is that both male and female athletic directors, as well as others in leadership in intercollegiate athletics, should strive to display transformational leadership behaviors to better achieve organizational outcomes" (p. 255). Davis (2002) found that "in athletics in general, and in junior college athletics specifically, transformational leadership is essential for success," adding, "as budgets and human resources diminish and the need to do more with less increases, leadership ability to transform and inspire individuals to act in organizations' best interests will be vital." The ultimate outcome of leadership for the athletic administrator is to get the most productivity from employees. The power to make impactful changes and create a cohesive unit rests with the athletic administrator who, as the leader, has "influence over the attitudes and behavior of subordinates and groups of individuals" (Soucie, 1994, p. 6).

BOX 2.2 Transformational Versus Transactional Leadership

Transformational Leadership

Charisma: provides vision and sense of mission, instills pride, and gains respect and trust.

Inspiration: communicates high expectations, uses symbols to focus efforts, and expresses important purposes in simple ways.

Intellectual stimulation: promotes intelligence, rationality, and careful problem solving.

Individualized consideration: gives personal attention, treats each employee individually, coaches, and advises.

Transactional Leadership

Contingent reward: contracts exchange of rewards for effort, promises rewards for good performance, and recognizes accomplishments.

Management by exception (active): watches and searches for deviations from rules and standards and takes corrective action.

Management by exception (passive): intervenes only if standards are not met.

Laissez-faire: abdicates responsibilities and avoids making decisions.

Reproduced from Bass, B. M., & Avolio B. J. (1990). The implications of transactional and transformational leadership for individual, team, and organizational development. Research in Organizational Change and Development, 4, 231–272.

 FEEDBACK FROM THE FIELD

Best Practices: High School Athletics

Thomas Bendt is athletic director at Aloha High School in Aloha, Oregon, a Portland suburb, which boasts a school enrollment of 1,900 students with 650 to 700 student-athletes participating in the program each year. Bendt has also taught social studies, comparative advanced placement politics, and U.S. government classes. In addition, he has held a variety of coaching positions at the high school level for boys' basketball (21 years), boys' and girls' golf (12 years), and baseball (three years). He assumed the athletic director position at Aloha High School in 2014 and recognizes the variety of challenges that come with working with new groups of coaches, athletes, and parents. Bendt currently oversees the construction of a new turf field for the stadium along with additions to the gymnasium and lobby area of the athletic building.

Bendt supervises several staff members in the athletic department. To stay connected with each coach, Bendt schedules monthly meetings with them to keep in touch with the pulse of the teams. In 2017, he initiated an assistant coach seminar on weekends to highlight communication tools when dealing with young athletes and their parents. In addition to meeting with the coaches, Bendt holds a monthly "Captain's Club" to give and receive feedback with athletes. The meetings with the high school captains educate him about team issues and assist athletes dealing with any issues or concerns on and off the playing field.

Bendt encourages his staff to work independently. It is an ongoing process for him to figure out the personality of coaches and determine which coaches need help while allowing those who have experience to continue to find success. Bendt admits it is a balancing act to determine how to best serve each program's needs in a large athletic department. Through the evaluation process, he discovers areas that need improvement; through open dialogue, he prompts coaches to reflect on their purpose and role in the athletic department.

One challenge Bendt encountered was the number of coaches employed who are "off-campus coaches," meaning they are not teachers within the building and thus do not have the advantage of seeing students in class or school hallways every day. Teacher coaches who work in the building have a better idea of the school culture and typically attend games out of season. Bendt feels fortunate to have veteran coaches on staff who support other programs, which sends positive messages throughout the program.

Bendt emphasizes that athletic administrators must spend time out of the office nurturing relationships with coaches. He strongly believes building those relationships is vital to the success of the athletic department. As athletic director, Bendt makes it a priority to be at all events because he feels the student-athletes and their parents need to see the athletic director as a supporter of all sports and student-athletes. When prompted to provide advice to aspiring athletic administrators, Bendt expresses the importance of leading in a manner that fits one's personality. He urges future administrators to avoid being something they are not. Athletic administrators should get to know the strengths and weaknesses of each coach to help them improve. He stresses "we are in the people business," whereby administrators should be positive and ask "what you can do" to help the coaches and their programs. Bendt leads by example, aiming to get the best out of people. He constantly reminds people that they need to always do "what is best for kids."

Part of Bendt's role as athletic director is to have a sound relationship with the academic staff. He works diligently with student-athletes who may be failing classes, and during progress report time he advocates for open communication to monitor athletes to help them become successful. Part of being an athletic director is multitasking, says Bendt. Every day is different, and sometimes items come across his desk that he would never have thought of. He urges athletic administrators to be adaptable as crises happen, which can take up a portion of the day. In closing, he expressed that future administrators "must not think the calendar will remain constant, as it will change all of the time."

Decision Making

In daily operations and within long-range planning, athletic administrators are continually prompted to make choices through a thoughtful and systematic process. The decision-making process requires timely choices to achieve organizational objectives. Four steps to improve the decision-making process include identification of high-level or priority decisions needed to meet established goals, an inventory of the

© Lucky Business/Shutterstock.

roles and factors that go into each decision, intervention throughout the process to deliver the outcome of the decision, and institutionalization, which constitutes giving staff the tools to deliver decisions (Davenport, 2009). Athletic administrators share the responsibility of selecting viable options for programming and "when employees feel that they are heard in the decision-making process, they are more likely to support—rather than merely comply with—those decisions, their bosses, and the organization as a whole" (Brockner, 2006, p. 128). Drucker (1963) simplifies the athletic administrator's decision-making role by focusing on three core questions (p. 2):

1. What is the manager's job?
2. What is the major problem in it?
3. What is the principle for defining and analyzing this problem?

Drucker further explains the need for managers to "attack" a problem using a "plan of action" (1963, p. 16).

Rubin (2013) also provides helpful leadership and management information regarding processes and theories. He poses the following questions that athletic administrators can consider when managing staff:

- Is my current leadership style working in my current situation?
- What kind of evidence do I have that my style is or is not effective?
- What aspects of my working environment might affect my leadership style?
- How might I consider leading differently?
- Am I willing to do what it takes to change my current leadership style?
- Will the potential results be worth the effort I expend? (p. 64).

Another perspective in the study of leadership was created in the 1980s by John D. Mayer and Peter Salovey, who identified a concept called *emotional intelligence*. Daniel Goleman has since popularized emotional intelligence, connecting the theory to the management setting and its role in performance. The five

Commanding: someone who demands immediate compliance

Visionary: someone who mobilizes people toward their vision

Affiliative: someone who creates harmony and builds emotional bonds

Democratic: someone who forges consensus through collective and fair participation

Pace-setting: someone who sets his or her own high standards for performance and expects the team to match them

Coaching: someone who develops people for the future through nurturing and training

FIGURE 2.1 Leadership Styles in the Workplace

Modified from Goleman, D. (1995). Emotional intelligence. New York: Bantam Books. Goleman, D. (2000). Leadership that gets results. *Harvard Business Review*, 78(2), 78–90. Goleman, D. (2004). What makes a leader? *Harvard Business Review*, January, 1–10.

components of emotional intelligence are self-awareness, self-regulation, internal motivation, empathy, and social skills (Goleman, 1997).

Athletic administrators use various methods to manage, depending on the scenario. The leadership style they adopt directly affects the performance levels of their staff. Six leadership styles used in the workplace stem from emotional intelligence (**FIGURE 2.1**).

The manner in which athletic administrators implement their leadership styles translates into performance success and ultimately the achievement of goals. In the dynamic and fast-paced environment that is athletics, managers need to determine which style best suits the department and how to systematically use administrative tools to generate an energetic and productive workplace environment that will ultimately serve its stakeholders.

Policy Making

One essential responsibility of the athletic administrator is to establish policies and procedures to manage day-to-day operations. Policies are clear statements that provide guidance to employees in specific areas of the operations of the sport entity. Procedures give employees direction in the form of steps or instructions. Policies and procedures not only serve to regulate the operations of the program but also enable administrators to make decisions based on written rules, which provides consistency in decision making. Meaningful decisions, therefore, are grounded in the philosophy of the department, entity, or program. Before formulating any policy, administrators must reacquaint themselves with the ultimate direction (goals) of the entity as written in its mission statement.

The publication of a policies and procedures manual is important to achieve an efficient department aiming for high standards of excellence. Each area of responsibility, plus the actions needed to carry out the functions of the department, is communicated clearly through policies and procedures. Uniformity is achieved when all staff members understand

the desired mechanisms required to fully operate each area of the sport entity.

Policies and procedures serve to guide the staff in the daily management of the sport entity. A policies and procedures manual encompasses a wide range of areas to illustrate the pertinent recurring themes, questions, concerns, and steps in the operation of the programs. The guide or manual will change and evolve as emergent challenges or areas present themselves to the athletic administration field. As an example, in the mid-2000s, social media usage policies were not incorporated into policies and procedure manuals; today, these guidelines are commonly included in athletics. The policies and procedures should be specific and comprehensive, and they should assist in clarifying the standards of the athletic entity.

 FEEDBACK FROM THE FIELD

Best Practices: Youth Sport

Christine Habermann
Executive Director of Mass Bay Girls Lacrosse

Christine Habermann has a wealth of experience in athletics as a youth lacrosse coach and youth lacrosse official, while she has also worked full-time in event management and marketing. She has been executive director with Mass Bay Girls Lacrosse since 2007. The Mass Bay Girls Lacrosse League (MBGLL) has 400 teams. When asked about the challenges associated with the MBGLL, Habermann explained the difficulty in securing volunteers because, as in society in general, so many people are overbooked. People who she normally relied on in the past for assistance are booked in other areas.

The MBGLL is primarily a volunteer association comprising divisional directors and board members. Managing the operations of the largest girls' youth league in the nation requires a great deal of effort and planning. As Habermann indicates, before the current season has even started, she is already planning for the following year. There are many changes Habermann and the league look to implement based on feedback received from its membership (town programs, divisional directors, coaches). Habermann attributes her ability to effectively manage the MBGLL to her education, experience in the event-management setting, and her passion for the game she developed as a former player, youth coach, and official. Habermann offers that a leader needs to communicate effectively but nicely when working with others. As Habermann clarified, part of being a leader means finding a way to communicate in a positive fashion to get people to work together. She feels that the more people get involved, the more invested and supportive they are toward the league. Three designated board meetings take place to deal with league tasks. Habermann encourages professional and coach

(continues)

education of members and board members, especially to learn from presenters not only at the national level but also from peers who share a diverse viewpoint on youth lacrosse administration.

Habermann's leadership style has evolved since she started with the MBGLL. From an involvement standpoint, she has encouraged more conversations with constituents to learn about needs. In addition, she created feedback surveys to gather input that could be included in new action plans. As Habermann articulated, sometimes swift decisions are needed to emphasize the league's mission. During her tenure a few years ago, when representatives from town programs did not attend required meetings, coaches and players missed important information. Now, to be in compliance for league play, one representative from the town program must be in attendance.

Unfortunately, sportsmanship issues arise throughout the season and Habermann communicates often to coaches, reminding them that they are dealing with youth players who may or may not have played lacrosse. She continually supports the ideals of the MBGLL mission, focusing on teaching the game and creating a love for the game. Because of the priority placed on education and training, Habermann has instituted a policy that every league must have a representative at the New England regional convention. She strongly believes training leads to better retention of players.

Habermann serves on the chapter board for US Lacrosse. Although the rules of checking or modified checking are within the scope of US Lacrosse, the MBGLL may not adopt all rules so that it can ensure that safety is the priority and the game environment promotes enjoyment for all. For players and coaches who want a different experience, they can opt to play at the club level, which endorses all of the US Lacrosse rules. As Habermann explains, the MBGLL is a recreational league in which the focus is on participation and fun. When asked about her legacy, she conveyed that she is passionate about providing opportunities for young players to get introduced to the sport and become part of the sport. Her background of business skills has allowed her to effectively administer the league, but she notes her involvement stemmed from being a volunteer coach and her desire to teach children to lead healthy lifestyles.

The mission statement is a powerful grouping of ideals that is read by participants, spectators, sponsors, and any interested party related to the sport entity. Details within the mission statement include past accolades of the entity along with a vision of where the entity is heading. A direct relationship between the mission statement and policies exists when athletic administrators set out to consistently regulate and monitor the sport programs. Seasoned athletic administrators retain a strong understanding of the areas that tend to repeatedly need attention in terms of policy guidance. Athletic administrators must familiarize themselves with the governing body within their sport offerings. Governing bodies such as leagues and conferences set standards on issues ranging from participant eligibility to participation outcomes, game-scheduling procedures,

season start and end dates, and sportsmanship policy. They also provide codes of conduct for athletes, parents, spectators, and coaches. Policies within collegiate, high school, youth and community, and club sports develop from the guidelines and regulations provided by governing associations. Athletic administrators tailor policies to address recurring issues, questions, or challenges that continually affect decisions.

The policies and procedures manual can be formatted to encompass content areas that are relevant to the department while also providing a general overview of the role of the department within the larger organizational or school system. Examples of content areas to be included in a departmental policy manual for college athletics are shown in **FIGURE 2.2** and examples of manuals for program participants are shown in **FIGURE 2.3** and **FIGURE 2.4**.

Table of Contents for College/University Athletic Department Policies and Procedures Manual	High School Athletic Department Manual for Parents, Players, and Coaches
■ Philosophy ■ Message from athletic director ■ Admission policy for student-athletes ■ Chain of command/flow chart ■ Camps and clinics ■ NCAA compliance ■ Professional development ■ Student-athlete advisory committee ■ Equipment distribution/maintenance ■ Purchasing/budgeting ■ Facilities ■ Financial aid ■ Contest management/home game administration ■ Human resources ■ Scheduling of games/practices ■ Athletic department communications ■ Athletic training ■ Student-athlete policies and procedures ■ Ticketing ■ Travel (per diem/charter bus) ■ Weight room ■ Non-traditional season regulations ■ Social media conduct	■ Table of contents ■ Message from the athletic administration ■ Athletic philosophy ■ Athletic goals and objectives ■ Student-athlete responsibilities ■ Sportsmanship philosophy and guidelines ■ Coach responsibilities (practice/game days) ■ Ejection of coaches from athletic contests ■ Ejection of student/athletes from athletic contests ■ Spectators code of conduct ■ Student-athlete eligibility requirements for participation ■ Code of conduct of student-athlete ■ Practice rules ■ Travel rules ■ Team behavior rules ■ Student transportation in private vehicles ■ Interscholastic extracurricular eligibility ■ Weekly progress checks for students on academic probation ■ Student drug, tobacco & alcohol policy ■ Offenses and disciplinary action ■ Hazing and bullying ■ Sexting, texting and emailing ■ Financial obligations and equipment

FIGURE 2.2 Table of Contents for College or University Athletic Department Policies and Procedures Manual

FIGURE 2.3 High School Athletic Department Manual for Parents, Players, and Coaches

Athletic Administration Preparation

The next generation of athletic administrators will confront new challenges and obstacles that affect the delivery of specific sport programming. The best preparation for the athletic administration industry is a combination of essential coursework and experiences, including volunteering and internships. Career paths of collegiate-level athletic administrators should focus on earning advanced degrees in sport management or athletic administration coupled with experience in the field for elevated positioning within the industry (Lumpkin, Achen, & Hyland, 2015). At the level of the National Collegiate Athletic Association (NCAA), athletic directors, along with professional sport managers, believe courses such as athletic administration, speech communication, public relations, marketing, and business management are the most important for career preparation

Town Recreation Policy Manual	**Sample Table of Contents for Club Program:**
■ Table of contents	■ Organization policies
■ Mission statement	■ Organizational leadership
■ Recreation objectives	■ Mission
■ Philosophy of youth sports	■ Vision and core values
■ Fair play	■ Administration (organizational chart and
■ Participation	position descriptions)
■ Registration/sign-ups	■ Club registration policies
■ Creating balanced teams	■ Financial policies
■ Team formation process	■ Program fees
■ Practice and game schedules	■ Refund policy
■ Game cancellation procedures	■ Camp or additional program refunds
■ Practice/game sites and contact information	■ Tournaments expenses
■ League rules	■ Financial assistance procedures
■ Medical emergencies	■ Insurance protocol
■ End of season awards	■ Player development
■ Fundraising	■ Coach development
■ Selection of volunteer coaches	■ Parent and fan code of conduct
■ Zero tolerance policy	■ Social media and communications
■ Weather	■ Chain of communication practices
■ Players code of ethics	■ Game cancellation and postponement
■ Guidelines for supportive parents	■ Field assignments (game and practices)
■ Parents code of ethics	■ Travel and tournament policies

FIGURE 2.4 Town Recreation Policy Manual

FIGURE 2.5 Sample Table of Contents for Club Program

(Hatfield, Wrenn, & Bretting, 1987). Bravo, Won, and Shunck (2012) and further support the need for experience within the athletic administration domain. They state that when hiring athletic administrators, the most important attributes to consider are career-related experiences, positive recommendations, and leadership experience. Athletic administrators must have the personality to manage people effectively as they come to appreciate the variety of roles they will play within the organization while satisfying the needs of a variety of stakeholder groups.

When dealing with a population consisting of youth to college-age participants, athletic administrators can never accurately pinpoint when and where issues will arise. However, athletic administrators troubleshoot on a daily basis. As figureheads, athletic administrators provide guidance to many groups from the athletes to their families, to staff and the external community. Because of the immense pressures associated with sport, many athletic administrators must manage demands from superiors (executive directors, principals, or presidents) and requests from coaches wanting more resources, or from entitled players acting like professional athletes.

Athletic administrators may wear several hats, but the impact they have on the lives of athletes is immeasurable. Whatever decisions they make behind closed doors affect and have ripple effects on stakeholders across all settings. An effective leader in the realm of athletics must balance a variety of tasks and challenges. Oftentimes the athletic administrator plays more of a decisional role over all others when it comes to resource allocation and disturbance mediation. As athletes become more sophisticated in their training and the pressure to win at all levels continues to be the measure of success, the position of athletic administrator holds not only a decisional piece

but also an ethical one. Many decisions made by athletic directors have a moral element to them. The decision to act is an administrative duty. Athletic administrators may handle scenarios of misconduct by staff (e.g., a coach knowingly allows athletes to play in games when they are ineligible, a club coach allows a player who is not age appropriate to play in a game) but it is the beliefs and philosophy of athletic administrators that guide them as they make difficult decisions to enhance the sporting experience for all.

💬 FEATURED INTERVIEW: BEST PRACTICES IN ATHLETIC ADMINISTRATION

Jodi Kenyon has been associate athletic director at Endicott College (Division III) since 2005 while also coaching the women's soccer team. She is the highest-ranking female in the department, serving as the senior woman administrator. Kenyon's coaching career at the collegiate level spans 24 years: She held coaching positions at two levels—Division I (University of Vermont, head soccer coach; Harvard University, assistant soccer coach) and Division II (Adelphi University, Assistant Soccer Coach). At Endicott College, Kenyon oversees all of the women's athletic programs. She also assists with the men's programs, primarily in mentoring coaches, providing staff evaluations, and offering program development. Kenyon coordinates all of the schedules for the teams for the 20 varsity sports in the department. The schedule coordination includes monitoring season game limitations, contracting games, official assigning and payroll, event and practice scheduling, overseeing any cancellation or rescheduling of events, preparing and submitting postseason declarations for opportunities to host championship events, serving as tournament director, and overseeing budgets for these events. In addition, Kenyon serves on various college committees, acting as a liaison and the voice of the athletic department. From a coaching perspective, her managerial functions revolve around recruiting, budget management, fundraising, team activities beyond practice and game planning, team building, community service, player development, advising and counseling, video, and scouting.

The landscape of college athletics, according to Kenyon, has affected the internal operations, especially since 2010. For one, the Internet has changed how the athletic department does everything from social media, recruiting, communication, event reporting, and even daily communication within a department. In one respect, the Internet has taken the human element out of athletic administration.

The evolution of athletes who are specialists and no longer multisport athletes has also greatly affected the Division III model of participation and involvement. Kenyon believes society has placed a much bigger emphasis on the athletic arena of bowl games, March Madness, the Super Bowl, and the World Series, which she strongly feels has affected sport at all levels from collegiate athletics and, perhaps even more so, to high school, town, and recreational leagues across the country. In her words, "Everyone gets a trophy now for participation and there is such a huge emphasis placed on winning and organizing that young athletes don't play for the love, they play for the reward."

At the college level, the Internet has dramatically changed how sport is organized, reported, and communicated. The Endicott College athletic department tracks every statistic. It also films every game, including practice sessions, to review later or even instantaneously to show athletes what the coaches are looking for. From an outreach perspective, families from all over the world can watch an event live on the web from the comfort of their own home. In turn, coaches post to Instagram and send

(continues)

Snapchats to potential recruits with footage of their team working out or scoring a goal. Coaches will use the latest and hottest trends in their communications to get recruits interested in their programs.

As an administrator and coach, Kenyon spends more time on her computer with Google docs and sheets, online programs, email, and Internet searches than she does on the phone, out on the field, or in the office of a colleague. Although the Internet has dramatically improved her workload and increased her efficiency, she laments that in some ways it has also taken out the personal aspect of sport. Kenyon indicates that she always has to be cognizant of time and how best to use it so that she saves time for mentoring and advising student-athletes.

Leaders of athletic departments or teams need to possess qualities, including having a vision, character, and confidence, says Kenyon, and they need to be effective communicators. A vision is critical so that leaders know what direction to guide their programs or teams. Kenyon adds that if they don't have a vision of what they want things to look like, they cannot set clear goals or standards for team members to strive for. Kenyon articulates that once the athletic administrator has a vision, sharing those ideals and getting "buy in" is critical to the success of the program. Leaders must also possess good sound judgment and have quality character. A leader with good character, as defined by Kenyon, "is totally invested in the direction of the program, does the little things well, makes good decisions, and owns their decisions even when they don't work." From Kenyon's managerial perspective, leaders must be able to communicate their vision, goals, and standards but must also listen and be open to opinions and differences of opinion. Lastly, she subscribes to the fact that leaders must be confident in themselves and be able to make tough decisions even when faced with adversity or challenges.

Many challenges exist when managing sport at the intercollegiate level. Kenyon explains that more than 40 years after Title IX was first adopted, athletics and sport are still male dominated and women still face challenges unknown to their male counterparts. Unequal pay, longer paths to career advancement, back room conversations, and under-the-table deals are still prevalent and continue to be a big challenge for women in coaching and athletic administration. Unfortunately, from Kenyon's experience, there also tends to be a high rate of women leaving the athletics profession, whether as coaches or administrators, to have families. Many departments make it challenging to be flexible with women or even provide salaries that allow for child care. Kenyon points out that some women leave the profession because they put so much in and get so little back and end up "burned out" or feeling frustrated with the lack of support or opportunity. In athletics, losing key personnel is a managerial concern because of the cost to secure and then train new people. Plus, when a person leaves, part of the institutional history is lost with that departure.

From a coaching perspective, recruiting and the method in which the college fills its freshmen classes have changed a great deal. There is growing pressure to win and to get the best players into programs. In addition, high school players are committing and starting their search at a much younger level, so the department is forced to cast its net wider and see more players. This has changed how Kenyon recruits, she says. She has needed to become more efficient and creative with her time and energies, especially with limited resources for staffing.

New challenges arise every day, explains Kenyon, and some may push higher priority items down the list. Athletic administrators must be able to multitask and prioritize not based on what is easy to get done, but what needs to get done. Tools that work for Kenyon include making lists, setting a schedule, and establishing a routine. To prioritize tasks, it is important to set goals and figure out a way to best accomplish those to meet the needs of the program. She is constantly reevaluating how she does things and is not afraid to make changes when necessary. Being flexible, adapting to change, making sacrifices, and being decisive are key to accomplishing tasks on a daily and weekly basis.

In terms of communicating department goals and expectations, Kenyon reinforces the importance of putting those components in writing and being clear in the oral communication of goals, objectives, and expectations. A thorough understanding will lead to fewer issues within a program if an administrator has communicated effectively, she says. Kenyon finds it useful to involve her athletes in reevaluating, discussing, and getting feedback every six to eight months on team and individual goals and objectives. The creation of a team mission statement with input from the athletes, according to Kenyon, is a useful tool to get buy-in and execution. She indicates that making athletes part of the process has ensured their clear understanding of the expectations and holds them to the standards they create. When it comes to parents and spectators, though, it is often a different challenge because everyone these days is a critic and has an opinion about what should be done with a program, she says. Being steadfast, decisive, and confident are critical when handling situations with parents and spectators. When Kenyon meets with a family, whether the athlete is a recruit for her team or for any other team, she always reinforces the notion that student-athletes at the college level are adults and must be able to address problems or concerns head-on; it is no longer the parent's "job." Helping collegiate student-athletes develop skills such as handling adverse situations, clearly communicating issues, and problem solving are valuable life tools that will help them in the real world.

Although many people would define success by wins and losses in the athletic world, Kenyon finds that to be just a small piece of the measuring stick. Success for Kenyon as a coach is answering questions such as, Did we get better on the field from day one to the last day? Did we achieve our goals? Have I provided them the opportunity to succeed on the field, in the classroom, in their internships, and in life? Do I challenge them enough? Have I developed these young women into better wives, partners, and mothers? Are they still involved as alumni? Are they successful in their lives?

For administrators, the reflective questions are not much different: Did I accomplish my goals and objectives to the best of my ability? What did I learn? Am I able to adapt to change and make change? Did I give my best? Have I been effective in communicating the department goals and objectives and held those in my charge to a high standard? Success in the world of collegiate athletics is too often defined in those measurable tools of wins and losses when in reality, it is a profession that relies heavily on the decisions of 18- to 25-year-old student athletes. How we affect their decisions as coaches and administrators, says Kenyon, is paramount to our success.

Collegiate-level athletics have evolved much over the last 20 years, and Kenyon fully believes they will continue to grow and provide more opportunities for future generations. The Division III level is starting to see the influence of Division I athletics and even professional sport, she observes. Emergent areas of Division III athletics revolve around technology, coverage of events, sport reporting, recruiting, the pressure to commit to a college, youth sport, and the importance of being seen by a college coach. In addition, many Division III athletic departments are creating leadership programs for student-athletes, turning to resources with the department or on campus to develop, creating academic monitoring and support services for student-athletes, hiring recruiting services, and getting creative with the Internet and social media tools to better communicate with families, athletes, and students. Kenyon asserts that athletics is constantly evolving and will continue to provide great areas of opportunity as long as technology and funding continue to grow.

At the Division III level, fundraising for teams and departments is a top priority for Kenyon and staff. Tuition costs, limited budgets, and increasing demand for the latest technology, finest gear, and equipment stretch the wallets for some of her student-athletes and families. To provide opportunity, equipment, and gear, she needs to be as creative as possible when offsetting costs. Operating budgets for equipment upgrades, facility improvements, and general maintenance expend much of the budget because of the high costs of technology upgrades. A growing trend in Division III athletics is to provide live video of games for audiences who are unable to attend. This is done at significant cost with camera equipment, Internet access, and in-game analysis. Kenyon explains "as sport in society evolves, so do the ways in which we view it and reproduce it."

Kenyon is a professional who likes to see things through to a finished product. She considers herself to be a hands-on administrator. She delegates tasks effectively but keeps a close eye to ensure

(continues)

productivity and success. Although she does not think micromanaging is effective, staff sometimes need direction and guidance as well as constructive criticism and approval when completing tasks.

When asked about transformational leadership, Kenyon describes that it is how coaches act everyday with student-athletes. She believes her staff guides student-athletes and supports them in a positive fashion through all of their interactions to motivate them to achieve at high levels. Kenyon explains that in the recruitment process of student-athletes, coaches share their style of leadership so high school prospects and families can see their passion and commitment. Kenyon is steadfast in her efforts to get players to understand the goals and motivation behind her strategies so they will be more inclined to perform at their best. She adds that coaches motivate with quotes, positive encouragement, success stories, and locker room pump-up speeches.

As an administrator, Kenyon encourages colleagues to perform at their best and to think "outside the box" to try new approaches. She is the answer person for many staff members, helping them with a problem, looking for resolutions or suggestions. The staff knows she will do her best to help them with any issues they may have or help them find solutions. Kenyon stresses the "importance of staff to feel respected, necessary, and valued in order for them to completely buy in to you as a leader." She feels when athletic administrators include staff in key decision-making situations and strategic-planning processes, it keeps them on task and engaged in what they are doing. Kenyon also notes it is incredibly important to provide positive encouragement, especially when morale is low or folks are having an off day. Sometimes little things like just spending time, asking questions, and showing concern can greatly affect how staff members perform. Kenyon compares her administrative role to coaching, explaining that the staff is a team with a role and a purpose; making members feel they are a valued and worthy department can only enhance performance and productivity. Getting to know staff members, how they operate, evaluating their strengths and areas of needed improvement in relation to an administrator's own are important for him or her to be effective in motivation and encouragement, says Kenyon. She believes athletic administrators must know what drives staff in order to push them, help them reach their goals, and challenge them to make improvements when necessary. Being an effective communicator with the staff will only help your relationship and their success within the department.

Kenyon explains that it is important for the staff to know that as their superior you care about them, are willing to listen to them, and are available to help them become better at their job while it is equally important to hold them accountable for their actions. When meeting with staff, she believes administrators need to be active listeners, even when there are many distractions and priorities. She emphasizes that if a superior seems unavailable, distant, or nonresponsive, staff members will probably avoid reaching out when dealing with future issues. In addition, Kenyon indicates "when communicating with staff it is imperative to offer solutions in a way that seems like a collaborative solution, not simply just your way of handling an issue." Kenyon adds that trust is a critical ingredient in relationship building with staff. Professional development in any position in athletic administration is a key element to success and growth as a professional. As athletics evolve, so do modern trends and technology. Kenyon believes coaches and administrators should never stop seeking to get better at their careers, adding that the quest for knowledge, learning new ways to do things, and networking are critical to continuing to stay fresh in the field. Professional development enables staff members to use available resources in the athletic department, to become better informed while making core decisions, and to be more prepared to handle problems and issues within the college sport setting.

Questions for Discussion

1. How would you define Kenyon's management style? What attributes could you pull from Kenyon's experiences to craft your own management style? Reflect on your own personality; are you similar or different to the ways Kenyon works with her staff?

2. Professional development allows staff to become exposed to a variety of viewpoints and ideas established by others outside the athletic department. Research two professional-development opportunities in intercollegiate athletics offered by the NCAA or member institutions you found interesting enough to attend.

3. Staff turnover is a real concern for many in the sport industry. There are many competitive positions in all settings from youth to collegiate sport in which staff may be recruited to work, leaving your entity with an open position. Describe how you would create a culture of sharing in order to understand and address the needs of your staff members so they feel valued and not motivated to look for another position elsewhere.

4. Your athletic staff wants to be respected and valued. What are some of the activities you plan to incorporate into your sport entity to create a collaborative spirit along with celebrating the accolades of your staff members?

5. Kenyon mentions the importance of relationship building within a department. Describe some team-building experiences in which you have been involved. Could those programs be adapted to fit the work environment? Locate a team- or staff-building idea online; describe the activity and benefits for the department.

6. Kenyon has worked in athletic departments at the Division I, II, and III levels. Find an article relating to job satisfaction of athletic administrators. What, if anything, surprises you about the findings? Please indicate which aspects of athletic administration are important to you when considering job satisfaction.

Good Ware from flaticon.com

 MANAGERIAL APPLICATIONS

Youth Sport: Functions of Management

On a town sport board are several members of the board of directors, along with several standing committees, that carry out a variety of duties, including special events as fundraisers for the entity. Many eager and experienced committee members are ready to work on a new event called "Field Day" to kick off the spring lacrosse season. The purpose of Field Day is to celebrate the start of the season on the turf field. At the event will be vendors with giveaways, music, food, and many lacrosse-oriented events to test the skill level of the players. With 1,200 registered players, this event can also serve as a major fundraiser for the sport organization. There is one problem: The athletic administrator in charge of event management (board member) is not using the functions of management and the committee has not been productive in moving any ideas forward.

Questions to Consider

1. What can the committee members do to get more effort and execution of ideas from the athletic administrator in charge?

2. Have you ever worked for a manager or administrator who did not establish priorities for your ideas or support staff members in their activities? Explain how you handled this situation.

3. What checks-and-balances system could the board of directors adopt to avoid the pitfall of having an administrator who is not putting forth genuine effort to move the ideas of the committee forward?

4. If you were the president of this sport organization, what would you do if this issue was brought to your attention? How would you make sure committee members are retained and that their efforts do not go unnoticed and underappreciated?

MANAGERIAL APPLICATIONS

Collegiate Athletics: Leadership

At Gentile State University are two associate athletic directors who carry out the functions for the entire department. The athletic director handles the overall management of the department but has entrusted Joe Winn and Amy Fletcher to administer the program, which consists of 18 sports (nine women's and nine men's) along with the supervision of 40 staff members and 20 work-study students. Winn and Fletcher have the same educational background and identical years of experience in athletic administration. However, they lead in two quite different ways. Winn is more of a transformational leader, whereas Fletcher tends to favor the transactional approach. The issue is that staff members are confused on the appropriate way to act and relate to each athletic administrator.

Questions to Consider

1. If you were the athletic director at Gentile State University, how would you handle these diverse styles?
2. What are the positive aspects of each leadership style? Can you describe a scenario in athletics in which one leadership style is more appropriate than the other?
3. If you were a staff member, would you feel comfortable discussing this issue with Winn and Fletcher? What methods could both athletic administrators use to create an environment in which feedback is accepted and appreciated?
4. Which type of leadership style would you adopt in college athletics? Would this style change if you were in a different setting (youth or club sports)?

 DECISION-MAKING CHALLENGE – CASE STUDY: MANAGING IN CLUB SPORTS

In Anywhere Town, USA, competing recreational opportunities exist for children ages 4 to 16. Today, parents are becoming smart and savvy consumers and want to make sure the cost associated with any program correlates with skill development and positive experience for their children. As an athletic administrator for a club basketball program, you are dealing with an issue of coaches who are not fully trained in the aspects of management. The majority of coaches you have hired are excellent clinicians and run efficient practices. However, these coaches are also required to fulfill managerial roles for the club such as coming up with fundraising ideas, maintaining inventories of equipment, ordering supplies, and managing the facilities where practices are being held. As the athletic administrator, you need to find a way to make sure the operational tasks are completed so you can run a profitable club program and satisfy the needs of the participants. First, prepare an email to send to all staff members outlining the job requirements of coaches in a club sport setting. Second, describe two topics you will cover at the next staff meeting to empower the coaches to take more leadership in the administration of the program. Third, find an article online to share with the staff that depicts the importance of multitasking and understanding the total management of operating a sport team.

DECISION-MAKING CHALLENGE – CASE STUDY: LEADERSHIP STYLE

Youth Sport Club

You are the owner of an Amateur Athletic Union basketball program with 30 teams offered to both girls and boys from third grade to high school. The coaches you have secured range in experience from first-time coaching to those who have been instructing youth players for more than five years. You attended a tournament to observe the styles of the coaches because you were alerted by a few parents that one coach (Coach Freemont) is using punishment by quick substitutions when a player misses a shot, travels with the ball, or makes a bad pass. You have always stressed to coaches that your program is in the reward business when dealing with players, whereby when effort is high, players will play more and mistakes will only be used as a teaching tool. What kind of leader is Coach Freemont—transactional or transformational? What tools can you give the coach to help make the experience beneficial for the players so mistakes are not punishable by quick removal from the court? How will you address these situations with Coach Freemont, the other coaches, and parents?

 MANAGERIAL APPLICATIONS

Youth Sport: Policy Development

The town you reside in has a travel basketball opportunity for both girls and boys starting in fourth grade and lasting until ninth grade. The boys' travel basketball program has created a nonprofit association with residents acting as board members and coaches. One resident, Gary Smith, has organized the girls' travel basketball program for more than 20 years with little to no involvement from parents of the athletes participating in the program. Gary Smith does not have any children in the program and has not incorporated the program as a nonprofit even though he is advertising it as such in multiple townwide publications. There is no oversight of the management of the girls' program from the town or parents. In fact, the coaches who are working with the girls' teams do not have experience in coaching or teaching and do not have children on the team. Many residents have suggested the coaches are being paid, which goes against the spirit of a volunteer-based community program.

Because of many complaints and concerns from the girls' parents, the boys' travel basketball entity has reached out to Gary Smith to merge so the girls can have similar training opportunities, gymnasium space, coaching education, and game scheduling. Gary Smith is also the league president handling the scheduling for teams for both the girls' and boys' sides. Gary Smith has refused to merge with the boys' program even though there has been an outcry from residents supporting the merge. Within this town, all sport programs (lacrosse, soccer, ice hockey) combine both the girls' and boys' programs as one entity. One mother, Kathy Stockton, has more than 20 years' coaching experience at the collegiate level and has played on a Division I basketball team; she has requested to coach her daughter's fifth-grade team.

Kathy Stockton sent an email in the spring to Gary Smith giving him plenty of time to strike a dialogue with the girl's organizer so she could be involved in fall tryouts. In October, when tryouts were announced, Kathy Stockton inquired again to see if she could become a coach for the girls' team.

(continues)

MANAGERIAL APPLICATIONS   *(continued)*

The teams were announced in late October, and Kathy Stockton was never considered for the position of volunteer coach. Instead, the organizer hired his close friend Tom Dalton to coach the team. Tom Dalton has never been a head coach of any youth team and does not have the same qualifications as the interested mother. A formal complaint was filed by the mother and supported by many parents who wanted a female coach with a résumé filled with both athletic coaching and teaching experiences to develop their daughters in a mapped-out progression that includes skill building and character development throughout the season.

Questions to Consider

1. Identify the current issues within the town when it comes to comparing the boys' and girls' programs.
2. What policies should be implemented for the girls' travel basketball program? Do the parents of the fifth-grade girls' team have a legitimate complaint? From your perspective, what should happen to the girls' program?
3. What are the benefits of using parent coaches for youth sport teams?
4. What kinds of background checks need to be used for adults working with children? Review two sport teams in your hometown and identify the background and coaching certification requirements for volunteers. Did any of the findings surprise you? Why or why not? What changes would you make? What role should the town play in monitoring the programs that are using town facilities?

 DECISION-MAKING CHALLENGE

You are currently serving as a member of the board of directors for your town's field hockey youth association. The board has approved $3,000 college scholarships to 10 worthy applicants from a pool of more than 40 high school students who have participated in the town program as youth members. After a closer review of the applicants, a board member revealed that one scholarship winner posted negative images and words on social media attacking the program and members of the board of directors.

Currently, a policy does not exist regarding social media misuse by applicants. The award winners have not been announced. As the president of the field hockey association, how do you handle this situation? Would your decision alter if the winners were already announced?

🔍 *CASE STUDY*

Managing in Athletic Administration

The NCAA has a policy regarding countable athletically related activities, requiring that student-athletes have one day off per seven-day cycle (http://www.ncaa.org/sites/default/files/Charts.pdf). You have an ambitious women's volleyball coach who requires players to attend "walk through" sessions with the coaching staff, demonstrating defensive positioning to prepare for upcoming games even though the team has already been practicing for six straight days. This goes against

NCAA policy and the spirit of allowing student-athletes to rest and recover from the intensity of a college athletic schedule. All of the other coaches in the department take the regulations of the NCAA seriously and literally as their athletes train for six days and are required to take the seventh day off from any athletic-related activities. The morale of the department is affected because one coach has manipulated the regulations for many years. This disregard for the rules has also affected the organizational culture within the department.

The coaching staff is looking for consistency in the message delivered by you, the new director of athletics. Prepare an email to the head women's volleyball coach. In addition, craft a script you will use when you address the entire staff at the next weekly department meeting detailing how you addressed the issue of a mandatory day off and the NCAA's policy of addressing countable athletic-related activities with the women's volleyball coach.

Good Ware from flaticon.com

🔍 CASE STUDY

Managing in Athletic Administration

During the fall season, the softball team organizes and operates the concession stand at all of the home football games. The softball team purchases all of the food and drink items to sell at each football event. The attendance at each home game is close to 5,000 spectators. The softball team has been able to raise more than $12,000 during the season through its promotional and marketing efforts. The football coach has requested that 80% of the funds raised should go to his team because the team is the entertainment that is attracting fans to the campus and leading to the concession sales. The softball program has never shared any of the profits since the inception of the idea of selling concessions at the field five years ago. As the athletic director, how will you handle this issue? Create your response to the coaches of both programs and the entire staff at the next athletic department meeting. Before crafting your response, spend time reviewing what other colleges and universities do when one team is providing concession items to sell during another program's games. Is there a universal policy that can be adopted to ensure both programs are satisfied with the end result?

Good Ware from flaticon.com

Wrap-Up

End-of-Chapter Activities
High School Athletics

1. Your institution currently lacks a policies and procedures manual for student-athletes. Review current policies regulating student-athletes in high school athletic departments. Create a table of contents that reflects all of the content area covered in the manual.

2. Your campus is facing an issue of social media misuse. What are some seminar topics and guest speakers you can invite to meet and discuss these issues with your student-athletes? Craft a clear and concise policy on social media use for the athletic department for staff and student-athletes.

3. You have been asked by the high school principal to create a seminar to address

leadership. The campus has several successful athletic programs, but those student-athletes are not living up to the ideals or expectations of leadership in the classroom or in other school activities outside of athletics. The seminar would be required for all students at the institution. What topics would you include? What themes would you choose to stress to your student-athletes?

Youth Sport Club

Parents who accept a spot on the roster for a club program commit to the rules of the organization. Players in receipt of financial aid from Super Club USA must accept additional terms before they can participate in the program. One specific term relates to paying the full tuition if the player decides to leave the club for any reason other than a documented medical condition. During the season, one scholarship player who is also instrumental on the team practices with another club team and decides to leave Super Club USA. Please find a policy online that relates to this dilemma. How would you construct a policy at your club to avoid this situation?

End-of-Chapter Questions

1. Use the *SportsBusiness Journal* "Forty Under 40" or "Thirty Under 30" lists to review leaders in the athletic administration field. Select four sport executives from these lists and describe their educational background, experiences, and current position. Indicate in your review why their story appealed to you and what you learned from their experiences.

2. Select a leader who has had an impact on your personal life. Please describe the person and how they influenced you. What characteristics resonate the most with you from this person?

3. Based on the readings in this chapter, write a document expressing your perspective on leadership, characteristics you most value in leaders, and how would you like people to describe you as a leader in athletic administration 10 years from now.

4. As a student, you have worked or volunteered in a variety of settings. Create a list of both positive and negative characteristics of a manager you are familiar with. If you do not have work or volunteer experience, think about an athletic team you were part of to complete this question. To which management approach did this person subscribe? What advice would you give to this manager to help him or her improve his or her effectiveness in dealing with the staff?

5. If you could invite any athletic administrator to be a guest in your class, who would it be and why? What message do you think this administrator would communicate to the class, and what do you think the students will learn?

6. Indicate the theory of management that best describes you as a future athletic administrator. Why did you select this theory over the others? How will you demonstrate and communicate your philosophy of management to your staff?

7. Describe your management style, leadership style, motivational style, decision-making process, and methods of policy development. Indicate in each area how you will engage your staff.

8. As the administrator, what steps will you take to make the daily tasks of your staff operationally easier?

9. After conducting online research, describe the following management styles: authoritarian, democratic, and laissez-faire. Which style best aligns with your personality and why?

10. List the essential steps in decision making. How long should the decision-making process be in a routine athletic department situation?

11. In your own words, define *management*. How can you apply your definition to the athletic administration domain?

12. Describe the following functions of an athletic administrator: planning, staffing, organizing, reporting, and budgeting.

13. Create a specific athletic situation in which the authoritarian management style is the best way to handle the situation. Why it is better than the democratic style?

References

Baghurst, T., Murray, E., Jayne, C., & Carter, D.R. (2014). Leadership and management skills of junior college athletic directors. The Sport Journal, http://thesportjournal.org/article/leadership-and-management-skills-of-junior-college-athletic-directors/.

Bass, B. M. (1990). From transactional to transformational leadership: Learning to share the vision. *Organizational Dynamics*, 18(3), 19–31. Retrieved from https://chaos.endicott.edu/cgi-bin/genauth/ecidbauth.cgi?url=http://search.ebscohost.com.proxy18.noblenet.org/login.aspx?direct=true&AuthType=ip&db=bth&AN=9607211357&site=ehost-live&scope=site.

Beyer, J. M., & Hannah, D. R. (2000). The cultural significance of athletics in U.S. higher education. *Journal of Sport Management*, 14, 105–132.

Bottomley, K., Burgess, K., & Fox, M. (2014) Are the behaviors of transformational leaders impacting organizations? A study of transformational leadership. *International Management Review*, 10(1), 5–9.

Bravo, G., Won, D., & Shonk, D. J. (2012). Entry-level employment in intercollegiate athletic departments: Non-readily observables and readily observable attributes of job candidates. *Journal of Sport Administration & Supervision*, 4(1), 63–78. Retrieved from https://www.endicott.edu/cgi-bin/genauth/ecidbauth.cgi?url=http://search.ebscohost.com.proxy18.noblenet.org/login.aspx?direct=true&AuthType=ip&db=s3h&AN=92948828&site=ehost-live&scope=site.

Brockner, J. (2006). Why it's so hard to be fair. *Harvard Business Review*, 84(3), 122–129.

Burton, L. J., & Peachey, J. W. (2009). Transactional or transformational? Leadership preferences of Division III athletic administrators. *Journal of Intercollegiate Sport*, 2, 245–259.

Burns, J. M. (1978). *Leadership*. New York. Harper & Row.

Chelladurai, P., & Danylchuk, K. E. (1984). Operative goals of intercollegiate athletics: Perceptions of athletic administrators. *Canadian Journal of Applied Sport Science*, 9, 33–41.

Chelladurai, P., Inglis, S. E., & Danylchuk, K. E. (1984). Priorities in intercollegiate athletics: Development of a scale. *Research Quarterly for Exercise and Sport*, 55, 74–79.

Davenport, T. H. (2009). Make better decisions. *Harvard Business Review*. http://hbr.org/2009/11/make-better-decisions-2.

Davis, D. J. (2002). An analysis of the perceived leadership styles and levels of satisfaction of selected junior college athletic directors and head coaches. *The Sports Journal*, 5(2), 13–17.

Drucker, P. (1963). Managing for business effectiveness. *Harvard Business Review*. https://hbr.org/1963/05/managing-for-business-effectiveness.

Gallo, Amy. (2012, July 26). Why aren't you delegating? *Harvard Business Review*. Retrieved from https://hbr.org/2012/07/why-arent-you-delegating.

Gibson, J. L., Ivanenvich, J. M., Donnelly, J. H., & Konopaske, R. (2006) *Organizations: Behavior, structure, processes* (12th ed.). Chicago: Richard. D. Irwin.

Goleman, D. (1995). Emotional intelligence. New York: Bantam Books.

Goleman, D. (2000). Leadership that gets results. *Harvard Business Review*, 78(2), 78–90.

Goleman. D. (2004). What makes a leader? *Harvard Business Review*, January, 1–10.

Gratton, L., & Erickson. T. J. (2007). Eight ways to build collaborative teams. *Harvard Business Review*, 85(11), 100–109, 153.

Green, G., & Reese, S. A. (2006). Job satisfaction among high school athletic administrators. *Education*, 127, 318–320.

Hatfield, B. D., Wrenn, J. P., & Bretting, M. M. (1987). Comparison of job responsibilities of intercollegiate athletic directors and professional sport general managers. *Journal of Sport Management*, 1(2), 129–145. Retrieved from https://chaos.endicott.edu/cgi-bin/genauth/ecidbauth.cgi?url=http://search.ebscohost.com.proxy18.noblenet.org/login.aspx?direct=true&AuthType=ip&db=s3h&AN=17567939&site=ehost-live&scope=site.

Judge, L., & Judge, I. (2009). Understanding the occupational stress of interscholastic 137 athletic directors. *Journal of Research*, 4(2), 37–44.

Kalahar, G. (2011, February 20). Job of high school athletic director evolving into multiple duties, resulting in increased burnout and turnover. *Jackson* [Michigan] *Citizen Patriot*. Retrieved from http://www.mlive.com/sports/jackson/index.ssf/2011/02/job_of_high_school_athletic_di.html.

Kirkpatrick, S. A., & Locke, E. A. (1991). Leadership: Do traits matter? *Academy of Management Executive*, 5, 48–60.

Kruse. K. (2013, April). What is leadership? *Forbes*. http://www.forbes.com/sites/kevinkruse/2013/04/09/what-is-leadership/#44b6172713e1.

Lewinter, G., Weight, E. A, Osbourne, B., & Brunner, J. (2013) A polarizing issue: Faculty and staff perceptions of intercollegiate athletic academics, governance, and finance post-NCAA investigation. *Applied Journal of Sport Management*, 5(4), 73–80.

Lumpkin, A., Achen, R. M., & Hyland, S. (2015). Education, experiences, and advancement of athletic directors in NCAA-member institutions. *Journal of Contemporary Athletics*, 9(4), 1–17.

Rubin, E. N. (2013). Assessing your leadership style to achieve organizational objectives. *Global Business & Organizational Excellence*, 32(6), 55–66. https://doi.org /10.1002/joe.21515.

Soucie, D. (1994). Effective managerial leadership in sport organizations. *Journal of Sport Management*, 8, 1–13.

Spink, K. S., Ulvick, J. D., McLaren, C. D., Crozier, A. J., & Fesser, K. (2015). Effects of groupness and cohesion on intention to return in sport. *Sport, Exercise, and Performance Psychology*, 4(4), 293–302.

Sullivan, G. S., Lonsdale, C., & Taylor, I. (2014). Burnout in high school athletic directors: A self-determination perspective. *Journal of Applied Sport Psychology*, 26: 256–270.

Trail, G., & Chelladurai, P. (2002). Perceptions of intercollegiate athletic goals and processes: The influence of personal values. *Journal of Sport Management*, 16, 289–310.

Toma, J. D. (2010). Intercollegiate athletics, institutional aspirations, and why legitimacy is more compelling than sustainability. *Journal of Intercollegiate Sport*, 3(1), 51–68.

Wallace, N., & Mello, J. (2015). Collaborative culture: The new workplace reality. *Foresight: The International Journal of Applied Forecasting*, 39, 31–35.

Williams, J., & Miller, D. (1983). Intercollegiate athletic administration: Preparation patterns. *Research Quarterly for Exercise and Sport*, 54, 398–406.

CHAPTER 3

Scheduling and Contest Management

LEARNING OBJECTIVES

After reading this chapter, students will be able to:

1. Outline the process of scheduling games and practices for college, high school, club, and youth sport programming.
2. Define the roles of athletic administrators within the scheduling and contest-management domain.
3. Identify the cost-related items associated with home and away game management.
4. Analyze the challenges associated with scheduling for broad-based programs in college, high school, club, and youth sports settings.

Athletics is about much more than just the competitions between two teams. It is true that rivalries exist among collegiate, high school, recreational, and club teams. However, before any of the games are played, the work of the athletic administrator takes center stage. Athletic administrators create seamless time lines to plan for the event and the resources (human, financial, and physical) that need to be incorporated into the administrative process. One major responsibility of an athletic administrator is scheduling for all teams and programs and dealing with such complications as inclement weather conditions, small staffs, and lack of facilities. In addition to creating

practice and game schedules, the athletic administrator collaborates with other schools and programs to match dates, times, and location of games to fulfill league obligations.

Contest management refers to the comprehensive administration of games from setup to breakdown. A *contest* is defined as a game, match, or play day between or among one or more teams. All of the intricate parts that go into scheduling and event planning fall under the umbrella of contest management. Those involved with planning sport contests are deemed *contest managers* or *event managers*; regardless of title, both roles are within the athletic administration realm.

Athletic administrators across sport settings will operate schedules differently, depending on not only the games but also on designated venues, staffing of coaches, and facility managers. From the managerial perspective, athletic administrators embark on the tasks of contest management weeks to months to years in advance to maximize scheduling opportunities. The scope and reach of contest management keeps the internal operations of the sport entity ticking and running.

 FEEDBACK FROM THE FIELD

Best Practices: Intercollegiate Athletics

Alexis Mastronardi is director of athletics and recreation at Emmanuel College. She joined the athletic department at Emmanuel College in 2001 after a five-year career in the criminal justice field. During her tenure at Emmanuel, the athletic department and institution has experienced tremendous growth and transition as it moves from an all-women's institution to a coeducational institution, to adding men's varsity sports under the National Collegiate Athletic Association (NCAA). In the 15 years Mastronardi has been employed at Emmanuel College, the athletic department has grown from five women's teams to 16 teams (eight men's and eight women's). During this time, she has been instrumental in the planning and construction of the Jean Yawkey Center (home to volleyball and basketball teams), as well as the planning and construction of Roberto Clemente Field (home to soccer, lacrosse, track and field, and softball teams). Before joining Emmanuel's athletic department, Mastronardi held various basketball coaching positions: assistant coach at Emmanuel College from 2001 to 2003, assistant coach at Reading High School, and numerous coaching positions with camps, clubs, and teams of the Amateur Athletic Union (AAU). She currently serves as the Great Northeast Athletic Conference (GNAC) sport chair for women's lacrosse.

Managing a broad-based program of athletic teams is difficult. As Mastronardi explains, finding enough gymnasium and field space for the program's needs presents many challenges. Because Mastronardi holds a dual role as the director of athletics and recreation, she is charged with finding time not only for varsity student-athletes but also for the general student body in terms of recreational programming and intramural sports. Mastronardi has come to realize that with only one gymnasium and one field, she will never be able to meet all of the time requests. She continually finds a way to do her best to adequately manage the time and put forth a tiered plan for priority programming. The college's partnership with the city of Boston to renovate Clemente Field allows the athletic department permitted time on the field from 6 PM to 10:30 PM every weeknight and from 11 AM to dusk on Saturdays. Although the 4.5-hour block on weeknights in the spring is a tremendous addition for the program, Mastronardi notes that it still is not enough time to meet the full needs of all of the teams. One method to handle the facility issue is by splitting and sharing field time. Once the athletic department gets into the overlap of nontraditional season soccer practices (in the spring), time crunches are even worse, she says.

Only three of Emmanuel College's 16 varsity coaches are full-time, and all three of them have other administrative duties (associate athletic director or assistant athletic director). Therefore, the full-time administrative team takes on a good deal of the responsibility when it comes to intercollegiate scheduling. Even though the Emmanuel College athletic department has a scheduling coordinator, all of the varsity coaches are encouraged and expected to play some role in developing their own schedules. The role of the coaches and the amount of work they put into their specific schedules varies. Some of the part-time coaches provide a wish list for teams they would like to play in nonconference competitions and teams they would like to drop for the following season. Other part-time coaches reach out to the opposing schools on their own and develop their own two-year reciprocation agreements and then work with the administrative team to find free dates to host, send contracts, and participate in the full scope of the scheduling process.

Often one sport gets more attention than others because of its popularity. However, as an athletic director, Mastronardi believes there needs to be provisions made to ensure each team has a similar fan base whenever possible. From an equality standpoint and always taking aspects of Title IX into consideration, Emmanuel College does its best to highlight men and women's sports as equally as possible. Doubleheaders at Emmanuel College are preferable because they reduce the impact on sports information and athletic training staff, which means full-time staff members can work one day with two games instead of two separate days of home games. Emmanuel College schedules doubleheaders for soccer, basketball, and lacrosse. When scheduling doubleheaders, Mastronardi selects to alternate the early and late start times to give each team a "highlight" or more prime-time contest. For example, if the women's lacrosse team plays the 12 PM game on Saturday and the men's lacrosse team plays the 3 PM game one week, then they would flip the times the following week. She also chooses the prime-time game each week based on the more competitive or rival contest. In addition, Mastronardi factors in the opponent's travel time or any preferences or wishes the part-time coaches may have about playing the early or late game.

At Emmanuel College, athletic administrators are conscientious in giving equal media coverage to all of their sports. As Mastronardi describes, when an athletic team's games are streamed on the Internet or delivered via live stats, they are certain to provide that same coverage for both teams (i.e., streaming both men's and women's volleyball matches live because a good number of the players on these teams are California natives). Emmanuel College athletics treats coverage via social media similarly (i.e., graphics, tweets, posts about all athletic teams equally with consistent messaging about all of the student-athletes and teams).

During game days, Emmanuel College athletics always have an on-site administrator at all home contests. In the past, staff administrators have been various game-day operations personnel, but athletic administrators have found it better to have an additional person available to manage situations that could potentially pull somebody away from the scorer's table, press box, or sidelines. For their athletic contests played at Roberto Clemente Field (a Boston public park), Emmanuel College athletics will staff all night games with two detailed park rangers who can help with circumstances outside the athletic department and college jurisdiction.

When working with conference officials in creating schedules, the department starts the game-scheduling process approximately 15 months in advance. The nonconference scheduling typically commences one year in advance and, according to Mastronardi, all of the holes left are filled with out-of-conference contests or tournaments. Unless otherwise specified, the athletic administrators work on a two-year reciprocation cycle in which they play one home game and one away game against each opponent. This relationship can then be renegotiated following the two-year agreement. Emmanuel College also tries to play its contests on comparable dates each year. For example, in women's basketball, Emmanuel College athletics have an annual agreement to play Eastern Connecticut State University in a nonconference game on the Tuesday before Thanksgiving every year. The home–away venue rotates and the calendar date changes, but the day remains consistent.

Mastronardi further explains that since the college has permitted time on a city of Boston field and does not own its own field on campus, it is subject to the terms of the contract with the city as to when it can host games. One stipulation in the contract is that the college is not able to use field time on holiday dates. This creates a challenge because Emmanuel College's teams can never play soccer games at home on Columbus Day or lacrosse games at home on Patriot's Day, which are typical conference playdates for their league. Mastronardi is diligent in working with the commissioner of the GNAC each year to be sure the teams are always scheduled to play away on these holidays.

When asked to provide best-practices tips to future athletic administrators, Mastronardi believes it is important to look at many different factors when it comes to filling in dates with nonconference opponents. As an athletic administrator, she not only wants to schedule such opponents who will be the right fit competitively but also consider the academic profile of the school, as well as other

(continues)

potential logistical issues (e.g., travel, facilities, and staffing). For example, she encourages her coaches to schedule Wentworth Institute of Technology as a nonconference game in every sport possible, simply because the campuses are two blocks away from each other. As a result, playing the local institution eliminates transportation costs. Both campuses have turf fields and lights, so they can play at night, avoiding missed class time and ensuring play time even in the perennial bad New England weather on either team's turf. She further clarifies that because of missed class time issues in the past and the Division III philosophy that academics come first, the department now considers whether an opposing school has a field with lights or not in determining whether they can host a night game.

© Larry St. Pierre/Shutterstock.

▶ Scheduling Across the Sport Settings

Every entity of sport from college to high school to youth sports presents different challenges for scheduling practices and games. Under the recreational and community sport setting, the responsibility of scheduling dates for practices and games and securing venues rests with one or multiple individuals serving as either paid staff or volunteers for the program. Typically, recreational departments work with municipal officials when offering seasonal programming, creating sport experiences for multiple age groups and various skill levels. Contest management in community and recreational sport comprise many tasks (see **FIGURE 3.1**).

At the club level, executive officials organize game schedules. League-level administrators dictate a season's opening and ending dates, dates for all home and away games, and dates for all postseason contests. Sport organizers work with the dates communicated to them. In most cases, club sport administrators will set the framework of dates and simply input venue locations and times for their respective club teams. Club sport administrators are, however, responsible for securing locations and facilities for practices and games. Today, many clubs may own and operate their own facilities, which improves the streamlining and control of the scheduling process, but many more clubs are purely renters, adding a layer of inconsistency to the schedule for teams and coaches. From a financial management standpoint, without owning playing spaces, club administrators will need to rent or lease space, perhaps working with several vendors. Multiple competing sport programs

- Securing venue(s)
- Establishing opening and ending dates
- Marketing programs to families and participants (discounts, early bird registration)
- Developing registration periods and method for registration (online)
- Soliciting and training volunteer coaches
- Hiring staff (officials and trainers)
- Ordering supplies (sport specific equipment, uniforms, shirts, awards).

FIGURE 3.1 Youth and Community Sport Scheduling Checklist

all vie to rent facilities, from gymnasiums or field house space to outdoor field space. Rental fees for facilities eat up much of the operating budgets for clubs; without enough space, however, the club programs would be limited in their numbers of offerings and participants. Challenges may also stem from the regional location of the club, which can affect travel for away games, as well as from managing weather-related issues. Understandably, in the New England area, wintry weather affects outdoor play from December to February, which equates to higher rental fees and fewer available facilities.

Within town programs, the process of securing municipal space follows a comprehensive process involving communication from volunteer youth sport officials with town administrators. In addition, negotiating for space is a reality for some town sports competing with other sports offered in the same season by another association. For example, youth soccer requires the same field space as youth lacrosse in the spring. Town officials may prioritize the allocation of fields to one sport over another. However, note that youth sport administrators from the same town or area need to work collaboratively to match the needs of all programs while considering the limited available space. Boards from these youth associations are charged with securing days and times to offer space for practices and games. Add to

 FEEDBACK FROM THE FIELD

Best Practices: Youth Sport

Paul Orlando works with the Reading Recreation Department and Arlington Recreation Department. Orlando has many experiences in sport management and athletic administration working in minor league baseball and corporate fitness. Since 2011, he has held positions with both Reading and Arlington. For the Reading Recreation Department, Orlando operates the youth basketball league; for the Arlington Recreation Department, he manages the futsal league. In addition, he serves as director for the Arlington Recreation Summer Camp for children ages five through 14.

Although managing youth sport is a satisfying career path, many challenges exist for an athletic administrator. From Orlando's experiences, dealing with parents is the hardest part of the job. It becomes a balancing act in dealing with parents who want their children to be placed with their friends and play on a quality team. As Orlando indicates, appeasing parents is not always possible, especially when their requests are unrealistic. Orlando articulated that in the sport and recreation field parents are extremely comfortable telling athletic administrators how they can do a better job. The difference, as Orlando explains, is that "with athletics we are dealing with peoples' children and they are so invested in their success." At times, Orlando has taken feedback to heart and made changes to programming. He made a coed program at the kindergarten level, for instance, single gender. It was a success. The recreation department in Reading, Massachusetts, takes advantage of using its new state-of-the-art high school for basketball programming. The winter basketball league, as Orlando points out, is a tradition within the town and is fortunate to have a facility with four basketball courts under one roof for its recreational offering.

One nonnegotiable aspect for Orlando is creating a safe environment for the young people he works with. He shared that he is a "safety freak" because he knows parents entrust him with their children and he takes that role seriously. When hiring staff, Orlando has strong ties with the high school program, allowing him to tap those players to work as coaches and officials for the recreation department. He makes sure that parents respect these high school workers to preserve the integrity of the program. Sometimes, however, parents become emotional and forget their role as positive sideline supporters. This season, Orlando started to use a microphone during the league play to show parents there is a supervisory presence. Using the microphone to remind parents and make updates has been a positive addition to the program.

When asked to provide advice to future athletic administrators when it comes to scheduling and managing community sport, Orlando stressed that they need to be "very flexible and you need to

(continues)

FEEDBACK FROM THE FIELD   *(continued)*

be able to talk with people. If you cannot talk with people you would have tough time. You need to kill people with kindness. You need to be able to listen." Orlando explains that athletic administrators need to be able to take criticism and work to try to please everyone, even knowing that is impossible. Athletic administrators in the recreational setting also need to be able to adapt quickly to changes, whether it be dealing with a missing official or working out a facility issue.

In the end, Orlando believes athletic administrators who have both a plan and positive social skills will be able to manage change and be effective problem solvers.

that the task of preseason training opportunities during winter months to prepare for spring practices in indoor facilities while traditional indoor sports are in full swing for the specific season. Supplemental practices cost an association in the form of rental and permit fees.

Within the high school setting, game and practice scheduling may be seem to be easier because most schools manage the facilities, but that is not always the case. Many schools share facilities with other programs or need to rent space to accommodate program needs. Similar to the collegiate level, the game dates for conference and league games are set at the executive level. Individual schools will be given a conference schedule and then secure matchups with out-of-conference teams filling in open dates. Conference games always have priority because their results determine postseason play opportunities and seedings. From an athletic administrator's perspective, it is typical to allocate time to secure opponents for out-of-conference games while also making minor alterations to accommodate teams as schedules become more current (closer to the start of the season). The intricacies of high school sports involve much more planning than youth recreational and club settings because of their larger exposure and attention of more fans and community appeal. Multiple games will often be scheduled on multiple fields and spaces on one high school campus. The administration of high school level contests requires addressing many tasks and conditions as shown in **FIGURE 3.2**.

- Field allocation and set-up
- Staff roles and responsibilities
- Confirmation of assignment of officials
- Allocation of meeting space for officials
- Payment of officials
- Monitoring fan behavior
- Management of away team (from allocation of locker room space, meeting at the facility, dining options, departure for facility)
- Ticket sales
- Concessions and fundraising activities
- Athletic training services for home and away players
- Time of games (alternating times for similar sports, males and females)
- Scoreboard/music/game day statistics/score keeper
- Parking spaces for away team (van/bus), officials, and fans
- Security (on-campus staff, teachers, or campus officers)
- Ambulance service (high impact sports like ice hockey and football)
- Entertainment and marketing (music for fans, t-shirts for events, rally towels)
- Travel (constant monitoring of poor weather conditions to avoid treacherous travel)
- Weather (conditions may quickly deteriorate, monitor changes)
- Competition

FIGURE 3.2 High School Athletics Scheduling Checklist

⚽ FEEDBACK FROM THE FIELD

Best Practices – High School Sport

Kimberly Kenny is the district director of athletics for middle and high schools for Passaic Public Schools in New Jersey. She handles the daily operations of all athletic events and practices. Under her direction, student-athletes are monitored and mentored, and athletic coaches, athletic trainers, and athletic secretaries are supervised. Kenny is responsible for all events, officials, transportation, security, and event workers for the middle school and high school. Before her current appointment, Kenny served as the district director of grades nine through 12 health, physical education, and athletics at Franklin Township High School. Kenny was also a physical educator and coach for high school basketball, tennis, and softball and college-level basketball.

The Passaic school district is an urban setting, and Kenny is responsible for students in grades seven through 12. The school district is large, and Kenny is accountable for 800 to 850 student-athletes at the high school level and 300 more student-athletes enrolled in the middle school athletic department. In addition, Kenny oversees the Saturday elementary school basketball league. Managing a broad-based program of athletic teams has its challenges, but Kenny has adopted an open-door policy to meet with coaches to ensure smooth operation of the athletic department and individual teams. She allocates time to meet once weekly with in-season coaches or, more often, to touch base if there are conflicts or to share the effectiveness of practices. During the off-season, Kenny meets once a month with coaches to review issues, learn more about student success in the classroom, or identify any students who may need additional academic support. Kenny admits that to manage the large department she needs great coaches coupled with great communication.

Kenny encourages coaches to play a role in their schedules for both practices and games. In New Jersey, the athletic leagues and conferences consist of 40 schools broken into four divisions. The league schedule rotates every two years. Athletic administrators work with a matrix of 10 to 14 games governed by the New Jersey Scholastic Coaches Association. Coaches review the established matrix and collaborate to pick independent games and scrimmages to fill out schedules. Kenny strongly believes in communication to build relationships and trust within the department. She empowers coaches to contact opponents to add contests to their schedule. To ensure games are appropriately scheduled, she has implemented a safeguard whereby she confirms game details with the opposing athletic director. In essence, the coaches will secure dates, but the athletic director will confirm the games and then post to the district's website to show the public schedule.

Because the schools are located in a city, they rely on sharing space owned by the municipality. All of the scheduling is done to cultivate good rapport with city officials and help gain access to municipal fields. Kenny meets with the city recreational director to review requests and secure field times and dates. For practices, Kenny requests that coaches collaborate to understand the needs of each program when it comes to scheduling practices and games. As an example, Kenny wants coaches to be mindful so that sports are not scheduled together in the same facility (baseball and track, for example). In her preseason coaches meeting, the staff reviews all games from grades seven through 12 for specific seasons and then determines practice schedules together to limit conflicts. All of the practices and games are shared and revised using Google Docs, a live shared document that allows all coaches to see the schedule and make any needed changes. Kenny emphasizes that being an athletic director is a large job, and will not be successful if all pieces (coaches) cannot be used.

Evident from Kenny's perspective is that coaches must be team players. In fact, she has adopted a process whereby each year a coach (regardless of years of service) is interviewed for the coaching position. The interview is a tool to learn about the professional development of coaches. Kenny also assesses whether coaches are following the department's vision. Each coach must submit a written

(continues)

FEEDBACK FROM THE FIELD   *(continued)*

self-evaluation and meet the athletic director for an interview to review the materials. In the end, Kenny decides to recommend contract renewal or not. She is serious about this process because coaches directly affect young people and developing young men and women. If the coaches are not fulfilling their coaching obligations and are not following the mission, there needs to be a change. Kenny emphasizes that this policy is clearly communicated in the department handbook provided to all coaches.

Athletic administrators are constantly challenged to provide similar fan bases to all programs. In the Passaic Schools, the football program is a storied program with several alumni playing in the National Football League and many having their jerseys retired. Football games are at 7 PM and draw a large fan base of students and community members. Because of league scheduling, the basketball teams compete at 4 PM, and coaches can select two highlighted games to be played at night. The Senior Recognition Night and Recreation Night are two "special events" coaches typically select for later start times. Recreation Night allows community children to enter the game free when wearing their jerseys. According to Kenny, there is great competition for students to attend private versus public school, so crafting events such as Recreation Night can highlight what public school athletics offer students.

Kenny also instrumented a mentoring program so younger students can meet and learn about the experiences of older student-athletes. The intent is to create a community culture in which young people want to stay in school. When it comes to spectator attendance at events, it is no surprise that teams are not supported equally by the community or student body, based on community demographics. Kenny admits that Passaic is not a wrestling community; 20 fans at contests is typical. The community is 87% to 92% Latino, which means soccer is a popular sport and girls' basketball is not. Kenny devotes a great deal of time to promoting athletics and inviting middle school and recreational members to the sporting events to introduce young people who are typically first-generation Americans to the program. Kenny provides all written communication in both Spanish and English to families and also organizes parent nights aided by an interpreter.

Kenny also uses the school's security staff for contest management. Typically, she hires people who are familiar with the school and students. In addition, the school system hires police officers who are stationed in school all day; those officers come to games as well, and there are generally no issues because of the presence of these officers. There are rare cases of problems from gang issues or rivalries, but the security staff is well informed about them and can offset major issues.

Kenny wanted to stress to aspiring athletic administrators that collaboration is essential. The coaches hired must be trusted to be leaders on and off the field, handle scheduling, and be the face of any program. In addition to her role as athletic director, she runs a summer program with 800 to 1,200 enrolled youth and 63 hired coaches. She must organize and manage all of the operations of the summer program and points out the importance of "surrounding yourself with leaders and people who are just as organized as you are."

Agreements

Athletic administrators within leagues and conferences work together to organize games for all sports across all seasons. Athletic administrators work to secure agreeable dates and times with opposing schools to compose full schedules of play. Without the support and flexibility of athletic administrators across leagues and conferences, securing a full slate of games for all teams would be difficult. Once athletic administrators find an agreeable date, time, and location to compete, a formalized process needs to take place in the form of a mutual agreement or contract. Many colleges and high schools have moved to electronic approval of games. The agreement needs to include the following content areas: contracts, budgeting for games, costs of away games, homecoming weekends and special events, off-season events, youth sport tournaments, and summer camps.

School:_____

City:_____

School Phone:_____

Sport:_____

Contests to be played as follow:

Varsity Contest(s):_____

School:_____

City:_____

School Phone:_____

Number of contests to be played:_____

Preliminary Contest:_____

    The By-laws of the Illinois High School Association are a part of this contract. The suspension or termination of its membership in the IHSA by either of the contracting parties shall render this contract null and void.

Financial Terms:_____

Signed

Principal: Coach or Athletic Director: School

From Officials Handbook - Indiana High School Athletic Association.

FIGURE 3.3 This contract is made and subscribed to by the principals and coaches or athletic directors between these two schools:

Modified from Officials Handbook Indiana High School Athletic Association (n.d.). Retrieved April 26, 2016, from http://www.ihsaa.org/Portals/0/ihsaa/documents/officials/Officials Handbook.pdf

Contract for Interscholastic Athletic Contests

The form shown in **FIGURE 3.3** is provided for use in arranging contests between member schools. Typically, any forms used for external purposes such as a game-day contracts would be reviewed and approved by the administrators of the institutions.

Budgeting for Games

Scheduling contests requires a variety of management and budgetary tools. Funding for game-management costs must be allocated for both home and away games. Once games are scheduled and confirmed, many financial components must be addressed through budgeting. Budgets are defined as estimated expenses and revenue. The act of budgeting is a universal responsibility for administrators who must consider all of the needs for their designated programs. Athletic administrators are guided by the mission of their sport entity and make budget determinations based on the cost linked to operating home and away games. The dollar amounts allocated to both contests will vary across programs and teams. In addition to

Staffing (work-study, part-time staff)

Scoreboard

Public address announcer

Security

Meet and greet for away team and officials

Sideline staff (ball retrieval)

Concession stand operators

Ambulance

Meals (college athletics: for home team if student-athletes missed dining hall hours)

Officiating fees (payment for service plus mileage, depending on league structure)

Game-day programming

Marketing and promotional events (merchandise, gifts to fans in attendance)

Rental fees for facility

Maintenance fees for facility usage

Within the youth sport setting, the largest fee would be for the rental and payment of officials.

Cost Application: Home Contests for College and High School Athletic Programs

United States Soccer Federation

funding for designated teams, the budgets also have line items associated with the expenses to support contest-management activities. Budgets are the method for allocating funds to effectively support these activities. Athletic administrators also must systematically identify costs to fully fund the games for the teams across multiple seasons.

Away Game Costs

The determination of cost for away game management requires more detail and information for the athletic administrator to analyze such as transportation, meals, and lodging. Transportation will be the core budget item for teams traveling to away games to compete, and the mode of transportation (e.g., bus or air travel) will dictate the cost. Travel

has emerged as a troubling concern that many athletic administrators have to tackle because the laws governing air travel have evolved. The NCAA has been proactive in communicating to member institutions about travel needs, informing administrators about the challenges with declining charter flights affecting championship venues, fleet reduction (partly a result of airline mergers), reduced seat availability, and the enormous task of moving so many student-athletes to various venues with little to no advanced planning as winners advance through a tournament or playoff (National Collegiate Athletic Association, 2015).

When fuel costs increase, athletic departments must find creative means to transport their teams to away games while also being fiscally responsible because travel consumes a large part of the athletic budget. Athletic administrators need to be strategic when examining travel schedules to determine the least expensive routes, transporting gear in a rental van rather than by air, and even limiting the number of student-athletes traveling with the team (Steinbach, 2008).

Coupled with transportation needs, meal times may be interrupted by travel, accounting for the added costs of eating at a restaurant or securing package meals from a dining hall. The athletic policy manual references specific guidelines to determine how much money is granted for meals on the road for teams. At many institutions, meal services on campus can pack bagged meals to offset the cost of eating at retail food establishments. A clear policy can be crafted to determine the distribution of meal funds or pre-packed meals from the dining services to accommodate traveling teams. Lodging for long-distance travel or late day or night games is another budgetary cost. Lodging includes finding and paying for enough rooms for all players, coaches, and support staff, such as athletic trainers and equipment managers. For sports that tend to have multiple-day tournaments, hotel partnerships are typically arranged

Official travel list for team (include student-athletes, coaches, athletic trainer, personnel)

Departure date and time

Return date and time

Flight details (name of airlines, flight number, time of departure) or charter bus information, including name of carrier)

Lodging details (name, phone number, address)

Contact name(s) and phone number(s) of designated staff traveling with team

Meal money for travel team during trip (designated staff will get funds approved prior to departure, per diem for travel may differ depending on school—for example, $10 for breakfast, $16 for lunch, $20 for dinner per person).

Travel Checklist for College and High School Teams

© Hero Images/Getty Images.

Homecoming Weekend and Special Events

Most colleges and universities will schedule special alumni or homecoming events throughout the year, depending on the sport season. These events are tools to connect with community members, parents, and former students. From an administrative perspective, athletic organizers must account for a range of variables, including tickets, parking, traffic and crowd control, security, giveaways, merchandising, and concessions. From a scheduling standpoint, athletic administrators must determine the full listing of teams participating in these events and times, and they must secure officials, hire game-day staff, and market the event.

to provide discounts to participating teams and programs.

High school sports are not immune to the challenges associated with travel arrangements. Some high school football programs are traveling more than 200 miles for postseason games (Young, 2015). Typically, coaches and athletic administrators collaborate to create an easy-to-follow itinerary for the student-athletes. The following itinerary template serves to ensure that student-athletes (and even their parents) know the expectations and time lines for travel associated with the team.

Youth sport programs may also have special events targeted to celebrate the unity of the teams. Even for Mother's Day or Father's Day, many programs may take time to acknowledge the parents supporting athletes in their sporting endeavors. All events require intense attention to detail, including pinpointed focus while planning and early communication to alert participants regarding special dates. Programs such as Little League organize opening day parades to celebrate the start of the season with participants, families, and community members. Sport programs are innovative on special days in an attempt to create a positive fan base and to demonstrate support to young athletes. In sum, all celebratory events present value-added opportunities for families involved with youth programs.

Departure and return dates, times, and location

Mode of transportation (air, charter bus, van)

Dress code and player equipment

Assigned rooms for trips, including lodging

Full schedule of events, including arrival times, practices, meals, team meetings, and curfew

Sample Itinerary for Student-Athletes

FEEDBACK FROM THE FIELD

Best Practices: Intercollegiate Athletics

Deana Ward is the assistant athletic director (AD), sports information director (SID), and senior woman administrator (SWA) at Farmingdale State College, a state university in New York. On completing her master's degree in athletic administration, Ward was hired as the SID and SWA at Farmingdale, which recently transitioned from a National Junior College Athletic Association institution to an NCAA Division III program. Serving as the SID, Ward covered every game and was responsible for game statistics, game recaps, photography, and website maintenance while publicizing the institution's 15 sports. By 2008, Farmingdale State College added three sports (men's and women's tennis and women's lacrosse), and Ward was promoted to assistant AD, SID, and SWA. As Ward enters her 13th year in athletic administration, she still enjoys going to work each day and continues to find excitement when watching the student-athletes succeed in competition, in the classroom, and overall to help them grow into productive members of society.

In terms of managing a broad-based program of athletic teams and challenges associated with scheduling, Ward says the college teams practice between the hours of 2 PM through 8 PM. This time frame allows the athletic trainers to stagger their start times each day to provide coverage at all practices. During the spring preseason (January through March) and winter crossover, coaches and administration may alter practice times because of winter conditions and to accommodate all teams, which may require adjusting the times to run later or start earlier. At Farmingdale State College, the athletic administrators allow coaches to construct their game schedules. One challenge is monitoring what the coaches are scheduling so that Ward can stagger their game times and allow for proper staffing at each event.

The coaches give a monthly practice schedule to the athletic administrator and athletic trainers, explains Ward. If she sees a problem with the practice times (e.g., missing dinner, midday practice, starting too early), she will not allow them to practice at those times. The coaches also handle scheduling games but are limited on night-game opportunities. The final schedule is submitted to the athletic department and ultimately approved by Ward.

Across college campuses, athletic administrators seek to create similar fan bases for all teams. At Farmingdale, the student demographics mainly consist of commuters, so game start times are at 4 PM to attract fans. Each coach is also allowed two to three night games per season when Farmingdale runs promotions at the games to get a larger fan base. Also in the fall, the college hosts an alumni day when teams are encouraged to organize an alumni game to introduce and connect alumni to current student-athletes.

In terms of contest management, Ward indicated that the facility coordinator is responsible for hiring student workers to handle game setup and breakdown, operate scoreboards, and work fields and sidelines. Ward hires public address announcers and provides statistical coverage of games with her assistant SID and student assistants. During the games, the facility staff is dispersed throughout the crowd and will mediate any fan issues. The athletic department also reads the NCAA sportsmanship statement after the game introductions, which notifies fans about promoting good sportsmanship and that any altercation will result in dismissal from the event. For some men's lacrosse and basketball games, campus police are notified, especially in anticipation of an emotional matchup or highly contested game.

When asked to describe her role working with conference and league athletic administrators in creating schedules, Ward noted that the associate athletic director serves on the conference scheduling committee. The conference commissioner creates the block schedules and sends them to the committee for review. The committee then holds a conference call to finalize any changes. The block schedules are set one year in advance.

Scheduling has its challenges, Ward explains. To create a balanced schedule, athletic administrators should secure similar numbers of home and away contests, alternating between each, and attempt to schedule them on different days of the week. Ward asks coaches to specify which teams they want to have on their wish list—or who they dislike playing in nonconference games. In addition, athletic administrators must also consider the travel time and possible missed class time. For home games, Ward stresses the many aspects to consider, including cost, number of event staffers, sports information staffing, security (if needed), the number of game administrators at each event, and whether multiple events can be run at the same time.

Ward encourages students who aim for a career in athletics to get their foot in the door by working in the athletic department at their colleges or universities. "You will learn a lot about what it takes to make an athletic department function; you will meet a lot of staff and administration from your school and opposing schools, which can only help you in the long run after graduation. Always try to make yourself available, ask questions, be on time, dress presentably." Ward also connects with athletic administrators and professors on campus who may also be aware of NCAA opportunities that are available to help build résumés while students are in school.

Off-Season Events

For many colleges and universities, athletic administrators not only concentrate on games for the traditional season but also must coordinate game times for the off-season or nontraditional season. The NCAA and other college-level governing bodies have regulations regarding the quantity and timing of any competitions outside the designated traditional season. College and university teams will organize tournaments to act not only as supplemental training experiences but also to support fundraising initiatives.

Similar to the college level, high school sport teams may also engage in activities before or after the traditional season to maintain fitness and competition. All of those activities are vetted and approved by the athletic administrator because governing bodies have many regulations regarding participation outside of designated sport seasons. Governing bodies at the high school level will define the specific parameters for any out-of-season practices or contests, including limitations on coach–athlete contact and requirements that student-athletes attend out-of-season events.

Develop promotional materials to solicit involvement from other teams or programs

Set the fees associated with program participation in the event

Create the schedule for the tournament, including play in games and tournament brackets

Provide incentives (early bird registration) to attract teams to the event

Order supplies for events such as T-shirts or awards

Work with officiating board members to determine whether referees can be assigned as training day participants to offset the costs for officials

Tournament Management

© Dreams Come True/Shutterstock.

Youth Sport Tournaments

Similar to college and high school sports, many youth and club programs are registering athletes and teams for tournaments over summer months and holidays to expose players to different levels of competition. Depending on the program structure, some of the fees for these tournaments are absorbed by a club, but others may be fully funded by parents. Under the AAU, many youth sports are organized by individual entities. AAU basketball operates across the country, fielding multiple teams for girls and boys. These programs compete in many tournaments each weekend, adding to the cost factor for parents. At each event, parents pay tournament fees to watch their children compete; some travel is within state, but out-of-state travel invokes gas or airline costs. As one AAU basketball club noted on its website to inform interested parents, "Costs to participate vary but can range from $500 to $1,000 or more per year—not counting travel, meals, and hotels" (http://www.yestoyouth.org). With all that, athletic administrators must still be sure to research each tournament request to ensure the competition level is within the abilities of the team to avoid lopsided scores. Athletic administrators ensure that distances traveled for teams is taken into account along with game start times for tournament participants.

Summer Camps

Summer camps are booming across the nation as more and more parents desire recreational and sport-specific activities when school is out of session. Many high school and college campuses operate camps and clinics for athletes who want to learn more about their sports of interest and to be engaged with trained and experienced coaches. The space allocation for camps and clinics provides athletic administrators with another challenge in ensuring all coaches have opportunities to run sport programs as fundraisers, promotional vehicles, or recruiting opportunities. A process must be implemented to determine which coaches and teams aspire to operate a sports camp along with the types of programming (e.g., day or overnight). The purpose of the camp can vary from a fundraiser, a recruiting-oriented camp, or a local camp to expose the community to the sport where all of the fees collected from participants will be deposited directly into a team-specific account. The camp director is responsible for hiring and compensating staff coaches. Typically, many coaches ask players to work these camps for little or no compensation for their time. Coaches may also operate privately owned camps as side businesses. In such cases, the institution would require certificates of insurance that would release the institution from any liability and establish that the coach will operate as a privately owned business entity. Typical budgets for the camp include staff (coaches and athletic trainers), stipends, sport-specific equipment, camper and staff shirts, and other supplies needed to fully operate the programs. Most summer sports camps run by coaches employ current players or other coaches at the high school and college level. Compensation to work the camps varies, depending on the size of the camp and registration fees.

Aside from securing dates and locations, camp operators must work closely with local boards of health to meet permit requirements. Camp operators collect paperwork from staff to conduct background checks, collect employment history, garner medical details for each staff member and camper (physical and immunization records), and gather emergency contact information. Each state

Staff Hiring Procedures

Each staff member must complete the Criminal Offender Record Information (CORI) and the Sex Offender Registry Information (SORI) forms with the Human Resources Department. The Camp Director will interview each candidate for employment. All coaches will submit their physical exam and immunization to the Camp Director prior to the start of camp for Board of Health review. The Camp Director maintains all records in the business office for all staff including [three] references and resumés. Staff documents are secured within the Precision Soccer business office for three years. Each staff person and volunteer shall have a background free of conduct that bears adversely upon his or her ability to provide for the safety and well-being of the campers. The Camp Director shall determine whether each staff person's and volunteer's conduct, criminal or otherwise, shall disqualify that person from employment or service at the camp. Staff requirements include prior work history, including name, address, and phone number of a contact person at those places of employment over the last five years, and three professional reference checks.

Staff Orientation

Prior to the start of camp, the Camp Director holds a staff meeting to discuss compliance with board of health regulations. Camp staff will read, review, and acknowledge understanding of all of the camp policies, camp procedures, emergency plans, supervision requirements of campers, staff roles and responsibilities, attendance groups for the week, lunch supervision schedule, disciplinary issues and policies, medical and emergency needs, emergency communication system athletic trainer policies, fire evacuation, disaster plan, foul weather and fire drill procedures, missing camper protocol, camper registration, camper departure policy, traffic control, care of mildly ill campers, and the campus map of facilities with automated external defibrillator locations and ambulance access.

Sample Camp Documentation

provides guidelines that must be met before permits to operate can be granted. There are many procedural elements camp operators use to safeguard the campers from a variety of potential risks associated with sport-related camps. For example, Precision Soccer, LLC, runs a youth camp in Massachusetts on a college campus. Before securing a camp permit, several documents must be received and reviewed by the local board of health. The following is a listing of some of the documentation provided to the board of health by Precision Soccer.

Identification Camps

A new trend within the scope of intercollegiate programs is the creation of camps and clinics to identify talent. Coaches hosting these programs can control the training atmosphere and work directly with athletes to determine their potential abilities to compete at a specific college level. These identification (ID) camps serve a few core purposes, such as evaluating players who may show an interest in playing for a specific team or showcasing the campus offering to prospective student-athletes (residential halls, dining halls, academic programs, athletic personnel, campus amenities, and athletic facilities). From the player perspective, high school-level athletes have an exploratory opportunity to experience firsthand playing for a college-level coach, meet current student-athletes, and spend quality time on a college campus.

The Elite 100 Lacrosse Camp provides players with advanced training and playing opportunities that can be used to take their game to new heights and is open to any and all participants. Whether you are looking to compete at the NCAA Division I, II, or III level, the Elite 100 Lacrosse Camp will help you reach your goals. The camp features a staff of coaches who have the experience and dedication necessary to help you develop on and off the field.

All coaches at Elite 100 are top Division I, II, and III coaches from the premier programs in the country. Year after year, more than 100 college coaches were in attendance. This camp is designed for players wishing to compete and play at the college level. The top college coaches as you will see on our staff list will be coaching the teams at Elite 100. Each team at Elite 100 will have a maximum of

20 college-bound players which will provide you with a ton of playing time and exposure to the college coaches. Campers will also benefit from the recruiting opportunities offered through our in-camp college recruiting seminar and our network of college coaches who work on staff at the Elite 100.

Reproduced with permission from Logo of Elite 100, Elite Lacrosse.

Identification Camps

 FEEDBACK FROM THE FIELD

Best Practices: Special Events

Sean Quirk owns and operates several specialty camps and clinics across New England. Quirk is a former collegiate lacrosse coach (18 years as head coach at Endicott College and two years as assistant coach at Springfield College) and is the current head coach of the Boston Cannons (men's professional lacrosse). Quirk serves as the associate athletic director at Endicott College and has operated his elite camps for two decades.

Quirk has seen the recruiting process for high school players start earlier and earlier. Quirk believes ID camps provide a service in educating the parents and student-athletes that not everyone is going to get recruited at an early age. The most important thing is to educate the families on the process of recruiting and finding the right fit for four years. Quirk's camps start with rising ninth graders and end with rising seniors, and his ID camps incorporate teaching, academics, and the college search process. Quirk fully appreciates that students have enough stress on them, and he tries to make the entire process fun. He plans his camps and clinics 8 to 12 months out. He and his staff are constantly revitalizing their programs to remain relevant and current with trends in athletics. The challenge with hosting events at facilities is to ensure that all aspects, from fields to dining hall services, are ready for the start of camp. The camp or clinic staff he hires put a great deal of time into organizing each event with the ultimate goal of having student-athletes and parents leave saying, "The value was unbelievable for what we paid." Quirk takes pride in having repeat customers—that is, players who return to attend camps and clinics year after year. Quirk truly wants every player to have a first-class experience and leave knowing they learned something about the game. He indicated that the entire staff "teaches a lot of lacrosse but tries our best to put it in perspective with real-life dealings. I think that is what separates our camps from others."

When asked what his greatest challenges are in hiring coaches and staff members, Quirk noted that the college coaches he hires come from the top 20 NCAA Division I, II, and III schools. He works diligently to treat the coaches well so they want to come back every year to work. In the end, Quirk stresses, "It comes down to how you treat people and the experience they have!" When prompted to give advice to administrators or coaches who want to operate ID or sport camps, he lamented that so many people are starting clinics and camps because they see dollar signs, noting that it is a growing business. He is "always focused in on the process, if you take all the right steps and do things the correct way in the process, the end results will always be positive no matter what the goal. Do things the right way for the student-athletes and families!"

Officiating

Athletic administrators work tirelessly to organize and prepare for games with the understanding that no contest can occur without the presence of an official. Although athletic administrators do not directly hire officials for games, they must understand the process to manage officials on arrival at their game sites and the requisite paperwork required for payment. Exploring the officiating domain presents many interesting details regarding the process. Athletic administrators must fully comprehend the role of the official, the codes that guide officials, and the process that certifies someone to officiate games.

As with any professional setting, there are standards and requirements to be met for employment. Officials are trained in the laws of the specific sports and must pass examinations to become certified to work games. Officiating is a flourishing career path for those interested in sports, growing five percent from 2014 to 2024, with an average wage of $24,000 in 2014, according to the U.S. Department of Labor (Bureau of Labor Statistics, 2016).

The National Association of Sports Officials (NASO) comprises 19,000 officials across a variety of sports, providing members with educational resources and research publications to improve the overall performance of its members. Undeniably, the role of the official is instrumental in athletic competition, but the position is pressure filled, taking a physical toll on officials because of negative and hostile environments created at some sporting events. Notably, sport officials leave the profession for a variety of reasons, including (1) career or other job opportunities, (2) poor sportsmanship by participants and spectators, (3) missing family, (4) low game fees, (5) relationship to assignors, and (6) difficulty to advance (Sabaini, 2001). Many youth sport assignors lament the fact there are not enough quality officials available for all of the scheduled contests. The work of Sabaini (2001) on behalf of NASO revealed troubling findings, indicating a shortage of officials coupled with the trend that many leave the profession after their first year. The majority of sport officials hold another full-time position because officiating is a second employment opportunity.

Because officiating is central to the organization of an athletic contest, it is paramount that sport organizers understand the business of officiating, along with the challenges to recruiting and retaining qualified personnel. Components to maintain a successful officiating program include (1) marketing the job, (2) setting standards for officials under consideration to be hired, (3) continually evaluating officials and the program, (4) setting up mentoring programs, (5) creating incentives for staff members, (6) creating a job structure in which students can advance within the program, (7) setting policies of how games will be assigned, and (8) holding fans, participants, and officials accountable for their behavior during an event (Titlebaum, Haberlin, & Titlebaum, p. 107).

Furst (1991) indicated that the top two responses from officials when asked how they entered the field were (1) seeking out the career on their own and (2) being recruited, usually by another official. From athletic administration research, sport entities craft outreach programming to educate people interested in becoming officials and training programs to teach peopple how to succeed in the setting. Similar to any workplace, assignors set expectations and goals to enhance performance and enjoyment in officiating games (Sabaini, 2003). Bernal, Nix, and Boatwright (2012) explored sport officials' longevity along with motives for entering the field. Their findings were similar to Sabaini (2003), who found that sport officials begin officiating because of their love for a sport and persist in the profession because of that same passion.

Scheduling officials at sport contests does not rest with the athletic administrator. Specialist sport official assignors are the professionals within athletic administration who handle the organization and management of the officials under their supervision. The official assignor role is typically held by an active referee who works with specific leagues or conferences within the college, high school, club, and youth sports setting to place officials in positions to work the games. Assignors may be required to be trained through sport association classes to handle this role; in addition, most sport associations require assignors to be certified officials or referees. For consistency, assignors will populate the games within their territory via an online service collectively used by all assignors for that conference or sport. Once all games, locations, dates, and times are entered, the sport officials or referees will log onto that same online platform to provide their specific availability for games. Then the official assignor matches the officials with the available games and dates, and the officials will accept or deny assignments and the process continues until all games are covered. Various software applications are used to populate the sport schedules, which enables officials to accept or deny games so the assignor can manage coverage throughout the given season.

Kathleen Stockman

Youth/Select Lacrosse Assignor (over 300 teams) and Active College, High School, Youth Lacrosse Official

"In my role as a referee assignor I am responsible for fully staffing all games for all teams in a particular league(s). In this role I coordinate with league officials to ensure all games have officials. There are times when I do file reports if there are issues with coach/player/fan behavior at games. I troubleshoot and re-assign games when there are schedule changes. Communication is essential to fully manage the scope of assigning coupled with meeting the needs of the designated leagues."

Assignor Position Description

Used with permission from Kathleen Stockman.

Communication of Schedules

Organizing sport schedules for participants falls under the athletic administrator's daily responsibilities. Communicating these schedules to ensure that athletes, parents, coaches, and officials have the latest updates is next in importance. Today, parents are juggling multiple schedules and rely on technology to get them to the correct places at the right time. Several applications on the market push out notifications to participants, including daily schedules, uniform colors, and directions. Sport automation companies also provide products that seek to meet the demands of busy parents and athletic administrators with user-friendly platforms. The products alert participants instantaneously of daily schedules and any field, time, or date changes. The products notify participants of any updates as soon as the athletic administrator or coach makes changes to the schedule.

 FEEDBACK FROM THE FIELD

Best Practices: Communication

Kristina O'Connell is the vice president of marketing for Korrio, the first truly integrated amateur sports solution. For clubs and organizations, it automates tasks and removes the complexity of managing registration, payments, and scheduling. For families, it simplifies payments, schedules, and sharing information while protecting their privacy. As O'Connell emphasizes, "Gone are the days of cobbling together multiple products from multiple vendors to get the job done. Korrio combines registration, team formation, scheduling, communication, [club and team] web hosting, and mobile access—all in one integrated platform."

Korrio is on the cutting edge of helping customers understand trends in the youth sporting industry and how communication tools have evolved. For O'Connell, mobility is the biggest trend the company is experiencing: "Korrio takes complex business operations and makes them simple and fast. We can help people communicate on the go. Our last-minute alerts can notify people via email, robocall or text." In her research and expertise, she and Korrio realize the importance of families who want instant notifications and alerts at their fingertips regarding the sport schedules of their children.

When prompted to give advice to aspiring athletic administrators when it comes to communication with their target groups, O'Connell indicates that "communication is everything—pregame, in game, and postgame. Good communication is the key to running a successful youth sports organization."

 FEATURED INTERVIEW: COMMUNITY YOUTH SPORT

Janet Gargan and Jeff Chambers

Janet Gargan is president of Essex County Youth Futsal League (ECYFL). She has also served as the registrar of the Essex County Youth Soccer Association (ECYSA), and treasurer of Danvers Youth Soccer (DYS), and she is a United States Soccer Federation (USSF) grade 8 referee, USSF futsal referee, USSF referee assignor, ECYSA referee advisor, and committee member of the Massachusetts Youth Soccer Association (MYSA) Leagues. Gargan has a wealth of experience in youth soccer as a coach from ages U6 to U19, president (DYS) town travel director (DYS), multiple board positions (DYS), secretary (ECYSA), and age group director (ECYSA).

Jeff Chambers is a secretary–clerk (ECYFL), education director (ECYSA), referee advisor (ECYSA), state-certified referee development advisor, USSF grade 8 referee, USSF futsal referee, USSF referee assignor, associate director (DYS), and director (MYSA). Chambers has coached teams from U6 to U19 in his hometown; he has also held several volunteer positions, including president (DYS), town travel director (DYS), multiple board positions (DYS), president (ECYSA), secretary (ECYSA), and age group director (ECYSA).

Both volunteers work closely together in the management of many levels of youth soccer and the youth futsal program. In community sport there are many competing programs, and managing

(continues)

a broad-based program composed of youth teams has its challenges. For the Danvers in-town and intramural leagues (DYS) the use of town fields requires application for a permit from the Danvers recreation department. In general, the process is completed three to four months before the season, although Gargan indicates permits may be granted much later than that. The approval process takes into consideration the sport organizations' needs for practice and training space, as well as match play and special events. Days of match play and training are set and published in advance so parents can determine what, if any, conflicts would apply to their child before registering.

Coaches and administrators must be flexible and allow children to participate in multiple activities that will vary by season (e.g., not punishing a child for missing a training session or match because of occasional conflicts). In the end, the field permits are granted to the recreational programs by the town based on participation numbers, facility requirements, and time requested. The in-town league generally has greater control of scheduling over travel programs because there is little reliance on outside programs to secure fields and set playing times. For travel leagues (ECYSA), each member town is responsible for providing fields based on the number of teams and the age groups for each registered team. The league mandates that fields are available for Saturday play for U9–U14 matches in both fall and spring and for Sunday play for U16–U19 age groups. Typically, the submitting organization will generally incorporate these requirements into a permit request as noted for the in-town programs. ECYSA does not dictate or require practice times or space; this is under the control of the town organization. For match-scheduling purposes, ECYSA requires that the member organization submit a tentative list of available facilities two to three months before the season. If submitted facilities are unavailable, then the organization must obtain and name alternate substitute facilities; ECYSA then adjusts the schedule accordingly.

Conflicts are inevitable, especially when dealing with younger ages, and they are not limited to other community youth sports organizations. Communication with the other youth sports leagues within a town can both lessen the number and frequency of conflicts, as well as any friction or hard feelings that result from them. Parents and players will at times be forced to make decisions as to what to attend and what to miss. The organization, whether a town league or travel league, needs to communicate this and make scheduling and rescheduling decisions based on the greater good, not to accommodate a minimal number of players at the expense of the majority. Other conflicts may take the form of school, religious, or scouting events. The league should have a policy in place as to how these conflicts will be managed to ensure they are handled fairly and consistently for all participants.

Aside from the traditional soccer season (fall, spring), many programs have engaged in futsal leagues. ECYFL has presented unique challenges compared to the outdoor leagues previously noted: The league must rent or otherwise secure appropriate facilities as a private organization unaffiliated with a specific community, as opposed to requesting space from a single municipality. A six- to nine-month lead time is recommended to secure space. ECYFL is a fairly new league, so it is difficult to accurately anticipate facility needs that far in advance; the growth rate of the league in numbers of teams and matches to be played is a great unknown from season to season and year to year. Ideally, a facility can be secured that will allow some flexibility in the actual number of hours required, but for the most part the league must commit in advance to a specific number of hours and times each week over some number of weeks. Failure to fill those slots quickly compromises the league's financial viability; being too conservative in booking limits the number of teams that may be accepted, whether because of the amount of space available or the ability of a team to participate on a specific day of play. Conflicts to date have been minimal and have been related to school events. Gargan and Chambers have been able to deal with them by providing alternate dates or scheduling doubleheaders when space and opponents are available.

The initial challenge for ECYFL was to form the organization, incorporate in the Commonwealth of Massachusetts, and obtain affiliation with the USSF and U.S. Youth Soccer through Massachusetts Youth Soccer. This required developing acceptable governance documents and establishing the corporation's directors and officers. After securing a facility, the greatest initial operational challenge for ECYFL was promoting the league's existence and recruiting teams. Because the league started later than anticipated, many local teams had already committed financially to other forms of "indoor soccer." Subsequent challenges have been varied, the first of which was educating coaches and parents about the registration process and requirements, which by necessity vary somewhat from individual town or travel league requirements.

An additional and ongoing challenge is educating parents, coaches, players, and officials about the rules and their application. Spectator management in terms of what court a specific match is on, acceptable viewing areas, and off-court management is another ongoing issue but has been minimized by posting signage throughout the facility. The final challenge Gargan and Chambers have managed successfully is the recruitment, selection, and development of qualified match officials, a challenge for all sports, not just futsal. ECYFL had the additional challenge of not only being a startup league but also of being a new sport to the area with few existing certified officials. Chambers and Gargan were able to leverage their contacts as referees and assignors to identify and recruit officials to obtain appropriate certifications and work matches.

When dealing with management of the support for the futsal league (setup and breakdown, spectator direction, and management), on-site administration is currently provided by ECYFL directors but these functions will probably be handled by paid staff in the future. Match officials are registered and assigned in advance and are responsible for in-game management and postgame reporting. Volunteer coaches are less of an issue because most teams are entered into the league and registered by existing coaches. ECYFL has three so-called house teams made of players who registered independently of a team. ECYFL staff coaches two of these teams, and one is coached by a parent volunteer who is a certified futsal official and active coach in the town and travel leagues.

For the travel league (ECYSA), there is no on-site staff provision; the home team and organization are responsible for field setup and breakdown and spectator management. A central league assignor secures match officials for games, with officials being responsible for all aspects of in-game management and postgame reporting. Volunteer coaches are recruited and appointed by the sponsoring town or club subject to ECYSA standards, including criminal offender record information (CORI) (background) checks and concussion-awareness training.

For the in-town program, coaches are responsible for setup and breakdown. Coaches are recruited from parent ranks via on-field contact, referral or email; training and education, as well as on-field support are provided by the town or club. Referees are handled internally as part of a development program that parallels player- and coach-development programs. In all of these sport offerings, Gargan and Chambers must still deal with managing fan behavior, team behavior, and behavior toward officials from spectators and participants.

Within the futsal league, there is one league official or director present for setup and breakdown and ongoing spectator assistance and management. Referees are primarily responsible for team, coach, and spectator behavior with support from staff as necessary. To date, Gargan says, incidents have been minimal partly because of the newness of the sport and the lack of spectator and coach knowledge. For the travel programs, the league does not mandate any on-site staff. Referees are responsible for dealing with behavioral issues as instructed and provided for under league and USSF rules and laws of the game set forth by the Fédération Internationale de Football Association, better known as FIFA. There are specified degrees of management that can range from admonishments and warnings to ejection to abandonment of the match by referees. All such instances require postgame reports by the referee that are reviewed for further actions or sanctions by league officials. League action may include sanction letters to individuals, teams, or sponsoring towns or suspensions of varying lengths. Ongoing and serious team issues will often result in observation and oversight by league officials of future matches. For the in-town program, no staff oversight is mandated, but certified referee mentors are at every site to support and direct officials who are in training and to deal

(continues)

💬 **FEATURED INTERVIEW: COMMUNITY YOUTH SPORT** *(continued)*

---

with spectator and coach misconduct, which again is minimal. Any incidents are reported to league officials for review and sanction as necessary.

Gargan and Chambers created the following tips for scheduling and managing community sport.

1. Have a practical and achievable mission statement that can be adhered to.
2. Make player safety your overriding priority in any and all instances.
3. Develop appropriate governance documentation. Be transparent, especially with regard to team assignments, scheduling, and financial reporting.
4. Publish expectations of players, parents, coaches, and spectators with regard to both administrative policies (registration guidelines, fee payments, attendance expectations) and behavior.
5. Provide opportunities for parents and coaches to learn more about the game and your organization. Don't limit this training to game situations and rules; speak to training opportunities, game preparation, long-term development goals for both the individual and the organization, and support for the young athletes on and off the field.
6. Use punishment of a child for parental failings as a last resort. Children are generally not responsible for meeting registration deadlines, paying fees, buying equipment, or transporting themselves to practices and games. You are in the "kid business"; punishing parents by keeping kids out of games and practices or otherwise denying them the chance to play may be tempting but should be counter to your mission statement.
7. Organize in advance, identify all possible contacts you may need, including but not limited to town, league, or other sanctioning supporting bodies, as well as any other community-based groups you may need to work with.
8. Be prepared to deal with questions, requests, conflicts, complaints, and demands you would never have thought possible.
9. Keep perspective: Stay true to your mission statement, follow your own policies fairly and consistently, work for the greater good, and remember that in almost every case, the sun will rise tomorrow and no one will lose their livelihood regardless of what happens at a specific match.
10. Have fun. If you don't, chances are that no one else will.

Questions for discussion

1. Gargan and Chambers have a wealth of experience as volunteers in youth sports. Research two sport volunteers in your hometown. List the contributions they have made to the sports they work with. What are some of their outstanding accomplishments that positively affected the community?
2. Recruiting volunteers to assist the organization and to schedule the games is paramount. List activities you will implement to recruit and retain volunteers for game-day management for a youth program.
3. Compare the best practices comments by Mastronardi (college athletics) and Kenny (high school athletics) with the perspectives of Gargan and Chambers (youth sport). What are some of the challenges universal to all athletic settings? Which setting appeals more to you in regard to the scheduling function of an athletic administrator?
4. Review an article relating to scheduling challenges for youth sport organizers. Share findings with your classmates along with policies to manage any facility or officiating issues present with contest management.
5. Conduct an online search of league policies as they relate to rescheduling any youth or club sport games canceled because of inclement weather, lack of field space, or failure of officials to be present for a game. As a youth sport administrator, how will you communicate league mandates to your coaches (both staff and volunteer coaches)?

MANAGERIAL APPLICATIONS

Youth Sport: Field Space

The town of Springfield has operated for many decades with youth sport associations in a collaborative spirit to share its limited resources with citizens. This past year, a new lacrosse program for both boys and girls was launched in Springfield. Although town officials are excited to see a great deal of interest in the new sport, they are also concerned with the maintenance associated with so many teams using the grass fields. Because lacrosse is a spring sport only, town officials want to designate the former soccer field to the new program. Of course, the soccer association is not willing to give up the space it has been using and maintaining for more than 30 years.

Questions to Consider

1. If you are a member of the soccer board, what strategies can you use to ensure your program does not lose critical field space? Do you believe the best option would be to negotiate to share field space, surrender the space to lacrosse, or argue to maintain full use of the field space?
2. If you are a member of the lacrosse board, what can you do to work with town officials and the soccer board to ensure there would be little interruption to the soccer season (assuming you agree to share the field space versus using all of it for lacrosse programming)?
3. The town of Springfield has two fields that youth soccer has had exclusive use of for 30 years. What are some ideas you can use to work out a practice schedule for both the soccer and lacrosse programs? For example, Saturday would be a designated day for soccer games and Sunday would be the designated lacrosse game day.

 MANAGERIAL APPLICATIONS

Club Sports: Facility Rentals

The facility costs for your baseball or softball club are taking a toll on budgets and leading to raising costs on parents. As the club's executive director, you want to avoid raising fees at all costs because you are a new club in the region and competitors are not raising prices. There is also a sense of urgency about whether and how to maintain current rates, if possible.

Questions to Consider

1. In your hometown, research rates for rental fees for softball and baseball programs. Aside from privately owned facilities, can your club take advantage of using municipal space (town fields or high school facilities)? Share your findings in outline form.
2. Research a baseball or softball club in your region. Review the backgrounds of the staff members. Are there incentives you can provide if coaches can secure gym space at their workplace or through their contacts?
3. As the executive director, you may have to raise fees to accommodate the practice needs of all of your teams. How will you communicate the change in cost to parents who are looking for a high-level experience for their children?

DECISION-MAKING CHALLENGE: CONTEST MANAGEMENT COLLEGE ATHLETICS

Sharing field space is not uncommon on a Division III college campus. However, because the recreation center has been booming with new registrants for sports, the time has come to establish when field space is designated for athletics and when it is designated for recreational programs. The problem is that the football coach does not want to shift practices from 8 PM to an earlier time because many assistant coaches hold full-time positions and are not free until after 6 PM. The recreation center has requested to use the field space at 8 PM because students are more likely to be out of class and available to participate in intramurals. The other athletic coaches are open to working out a schedule because they value sport participation for all.

As the scheduling coordinator for Quinn College, how will you handle the football coach's decision to refuse to change practice times? The college president has also been notified of the pushback from athletics in regard to designated field space to the recreation center. As the athletic administrator, you now must address the staff in the next meeting. Prepare a 10-slide PowerPoint presentation to communicate the purpose of athletics and recreation on the college campus, including a plan to incorporate the recreational programming into the scheduling process.

 DECISION-MAKING CHALLENGE: SCHEDULING HIGH SCHOOL ATHLETICS

Your girls' soccer coach has been instrumental in organizing alumni events over the last 10 years. Dr. Laine, the superintendent of schools, has noticed the amount of interest from alumni coming back onto the high school campus to participate in games and cookouts. Dr. Laine now wants all programs to create similar events. The issue is that the athletic department has part-time staff members as coaches. The coaches are focused on practices and games; adding another task would not be received favorably. As the athletic administrator, how will you encourage and motivate the coaches to create one annual event for their sport-specific alumni? What are some of the positive features of incorporating alumni events into high school athletic programs? Would you consider incentives for coaches who get the most attendance at these events so you can motivate the staff to move Dr. Laine's idea forward?

CASE STUDY

College Athletic Administration

Sport University has just added men's and women's lacrosse at the Division II level. As the athletic administrator in charge, you need to manage both athletic schedules, keeping in mind there is a major alumni event on campus whereby all spring sports need to compete in home games. The conference schedules for both teams are set. Both teams have enough nonconference matchups as well. The issue is that on Saturday, May 1, you cannot find an opponent for either team.

The athletic director and university president have been asking for updates regarding the scheduling of games on May 1. All options have been exhausted except absorbing the costs for transporting and lodging an opponent (Stephen State) that is four hours away from campus. The coaches for both the women's and men's teams at Stephen State are open to an overnight trip, but their budget requests have not been approved by their athletic administrator.

Questions to Consider

1. The scheduling coordinator has placed a priority on competitions for all teams on May 1. The budget for home game management leaves little to no room for an unexpected cost for charter buses, lodging, and meals for two teams to compete on May 1. However, you have no other options. What creative solutions can you deliver to the athletic director?
2. Conference scheduling seems easier than finding out-of-conference opponents. What is the priority when scheduling for teams? Specify which games are most important to schedule first and why.
3. What kinds of relationships are important to build with other athletic department scheduling coordinators when dealing with securing contests for teams?
4. Do you think the president and athletic director should be lenient for first-year programs having difficulty scheduling games?

Wrap-Up

End-of-Chapter Activities

College Athletics

You are the athletic director for a newly established institution. Your goal is to be accepted into a conference or league within the next two years.

1. Indicate the city and state for your new institution.
2. Report the NCAA division your school aims to compete in along with a conference or league you hope to join.
3. List the schools in the specific conference or league by city and state.
4. Create a travel grid for your team and conference and league opponents; indicate distance to each institution by minutes or hours and miles. If air travel is required, be sure to indicate length of time from airport to airport.
5. Based on the travel associated with your selected conference or league, list some of the costs you will need to absorb and manage for teams competing in the fall, winter, and spring seasons.

High School Athletics

You are the athletic director for a large-sized school within a highly supportive community for sports. Your goal is to try to increase fan attendance across all of your sports to create a celebratory environment for your student-athletes. Craft a policy you will implement to (1) alternate start times for boys and girls teams of the same sport, (2) mandate coaches' attendance at games they are not coaching so they can show unilateral support for all teams, (3) require student-athletes to support other teams to increase fans at games, and (4) ensure all teams receive equitable opportunities to play in highlighted games at least one time per season.

End-of-Chapter Questions

1. Create a guideline that you would recommend for an athletic administrator to use when scheduling competitions with other institutions. List the factors you need to consider when developing an athletic team schedule.

2. Describe how your contest-management policies can affect your budget for away games, preseason events, ordering new uniforms, and meals. Please craft policies for both the high school and collegiate settings.

3. There are five teams in the XYZ High School Soccer Conference. Please create a tournament bracket for a single-elimination tournament, describe your tournament policy, and illustrate the bracket using the following final regular season records.
   a. ABC (10–2)
   b. XYZ (11–1)
   c. BOS (5–7)
   d. NJJ (8–3–1)
   e. DEN (6–6)

4. How can a well-rounded, broad-based program be adequately staffed to ensure a positive experience for participants and spectators?

5. Mascots are traditional parts of collegiate and high school games. There can be many issues associated with the conduct and safety of mascots, especially against rival teams. Through your online investigation, please research the impact of mascots on fan enjoyment and any issues relating to the misconduct of mascots during games. As an athletic administrator, how would you manage the role of a mascot at your institution?

6. As a club sport administrator, you are dealing with an official who has not arrived at the game. A parent who also coaches and is a referee steps in to officiate the game. Both coaches are in agreement the score should stand as official because the parent knew the rules of the game. Find a policy from any club or youth sport association that specifically handles any issues with an official's nonattendance at a game. What would you recommend to your coaches if an official is not present at their games?

7. Weather-related cancellations occur for outdoor sports. Athletic administrators are accountable for rescheduling any cancelled games. Describe your protocol for rescheduling games on a timely basis, identify others who need to be involved in the rescheduling process, and research one policy for a sport setting of your choice that outlines the rescheduling process for teams.

8. With field space limited for most programs, what will be your vision as an athletic administrator to accommodate the following—the space and facility needs of all teams for a youth softball program, a club lacrosse program, a spring high school program, and a winter college program? Be sure to list all teams under each setting and the realistic number of facilities for these programs.

9. Renting facilities is a major expenditure for youth and community-based programs. In your region, research the hourly cost to rent an indoor turf facility, gymnasium, and outdoor turf fields. Please indicate where these facilities are located and their amenities.

10. Transportation costs constitute a large percentage of your budget as a high school athletic administrator. Research the cost for charter bus rentals. Are there any partnerships you can negotiate to lower the overall costs for transportation needs?

11. Technology is transforming the ways in which athletic administrators communicate with coaches, athletes, parents, and officials. Conduct a quick Internet search to determine what online platforms may be appropriate for you to use as a community sport organizer. Report the highlighted features and cost of the platforms.

12. Athletic administrators aim to get coaches to work together to craft agreeable practice times. Interview one coach to ask how she or he is involved with

the scheduling process for games and practices. Craft at least five questions to ask the coach about the challenges of collaborating and sharing with other coaches.

13. Transportation costs present many challenges to athletic administrators. Locate an article dealing with creative cost-saving solutions to manage the growing expenses to travel to away games and tournaments for either the high school or collegiate setting.

14. You are the athletic administrator for a youth sport club. What are some of the limitations you would place on travel to tournaments? How would you communicate these restrictions to coaches and parents?

References

Bernal, J. C., Nix, C., & Boatwright, D. (2012). Sport officials' longevity: Motivation and passion for the sport. *International Journal of Sport Management, Recreation & Tourism*, 1028–1039.

Bureau of Labor Statistics. (2016).Umpires, referees, and other sports officials. *Occupational Outlook Handbook*, 2016–17 Washington, DC: U.S. Department of Labor. Retrieved March 2, 2016, from http://www.bls.gov /ooh/entertainment-and-sports/umpires-referees -and-other-sports-officials.htm.

Furst, D. M. (1991). Career contingencies: Patterns of initial entry and continuity in collegiate sports officiating. *Journal of Sport Behavior*, 14(2), 93–102.

Indiana High School Athletic Association. (n.d.). Officials handbook. Retrieved April 26, 2016, from https:// ihsaa.arbitersports.com/Groups/103543/Library /files/2016-17%20Officials%20Handbook.doc.

National Collegiate Athletic Association. (2015, January 14). Declining charter flights affect championships travel. Retrieved April 25, 2016, from http://www .ncaa.com/news/ncaa/article/2015-01-14/declining -availability-charter-flights-will-affect-ncaa -championships.

Sabaini, D. (2001). How to get and keep officials. Pp. 1–41 in Special Report, National Association of Sports Officials. Retrieved from https://www.naso.org/portals /0/downloads/reports/SpecReptConf.pdf.

Sabaini, D. (2003). Accountability in officiating. Pp. 1–62 in Special Report, National Association of Sports Officials. Retrieved from https://s3.amazonaws.com /my.llfiles.com/00231178/Accountability-in -Officiating.pdf.

Steinbach, P. (2008, October). Athletic departments rethinking ways to make travel dollars go farther. *Athletic Business*. Retrieved April 25, 2016, from http://www.athleticbusiness.com/Budgeting/athletic -departments-rethinking-ways-to-make-travel-dollars -go-farther.html.

Titlebaum, P. T, Haberlin, N., & Titlebaum, G. (2009). Recruitment and retention of sports officials. *Recreational Sports Journal*, 33, 102–108.

United States Soccer Federation. (2000). Entry level training manual, referee assignor. Retrieved April 26, 2016, from https://www.stsr.org/forms/Assignor-Handbook .pdf.

Young, J. H. (2015, December 13). Some football teams are traveling the distance of entire countries for Texas state championships. *Houston Chronicle* [online]. Retrieved October 23, 2018, from https://www.chron .com/sports/highschool/article/Some-football-teams -are-traveling-the-distance-of-6695766.php.

CHAPTER 4

Facility Management

LEARNING OBJECTIVES

After reading this chapter, students will be able to:

1. Explain the role athletic administrators assume within the realm of facility management in the youth, club sport, high school, and college settings.
2. Define facility management within the dynamic field of athletic administration.
3. Describe sustainability and its effect on sport entities across the youth, club sport, high school, and college settings.
4. Create a facility plan to meet the needs of youth, club sport, high school, and college settings.
5. Identify the challenges associated with facility management, including costs and spacing issues across youth, club sport, high school, and college settings.
6. Categorize the benefits of event management and recreational programming for youth, club sport, high school, and college settings.

Athletic administrators in youth, club sport, high school, and college sports don many hats and assume a variety of responsibilities to deliver positive sport programs to their target groups. The availability of facilities for use by sport programs is the glue holding together delivery of these programs. Successfully scheduling sporting activities rests with the athletic administrator's ability to manage, operate, and secure locations suitable for the athletic needs of the organization. For athletic administrators to schedule practices, clinics, special events, and games, the physical space needs to be appropriate and sport specific, and the venues need to be readily available for use.

From the management perspective, a core challenge for athletic administrators is obtaining permits or securing rentals for facilities and fields in a sport marketplace cluttered with numerous competing sport programs that all aim to use the same space. Depending on the scope of the sport entity, some facilities are privately owned by community groups, youth programs, clubs, or colleges, and others are public facilities open for use by school programs, town programs, and external programs. Athletic administrators at the collegiate and high school levels may be the sole residents and users of their athletic facilities. However, it is not uncommon for high school and college athletic programs to share or rent space in the area from city recreation departments or for recreation departments to use school space. Across the settings of youth, club sport, high school, and college athletics, athletic administrators use all the functions of management (planning, organizing, implementing, and evaluating) to fully investigate the availability of venues. This includes communicating with external agencies to secure space to effectively operate the sport programming under their charge. Without the appropriate field and gymnasium space, athletic programs simply could not operate.

There are many moving parts to be considered in facility management. Facility managers coordinate the staff and resources to obtain, maintain, and fully use space to operate broad-based athletic offerings. Facility management takes many forms, depending on the athletic setting and scheduling demands. It encompasses maintenance and operations to support the participants, spectators, and organizers in their sporting endeavors. The role of the designated facility manager varies, depending on the size and scope of the athletic program, but ultimately the role includes planning and oversight of venues, managing and allocating space to designated groups, managing budgets, adhering to governing body facility guidelines, organizing security and traffic flow, leading teams of staff, and troubleshooting in real time.

The focused attention that athletic administrators give to facility management for sport and recreational programs should come as no surprise because the number of renovated and new facilities is booming across towns and cities, schools, private sport programs, and college campuses. Facility management is a significant operational task for athletic administrators: "With more than 44 million young people already involved in organized youth sports—better than half of all people under the age of 18 in America—the concern over how we allocate use of existing resources, including playing fields and indoor facilities, across all interested parties and in a fair manner will

only increase in the future" (Tyahla, 2016). The management of athletic and recreational sites and venues has evolved into a core priority for athletic administrators looking to fully use fields and gymnasium space to effectively deliver appealing sport programs. From a recruitment perspective, athletic administrators are competing with similar entities. Athletic administrations across all settings are in a "turf war" whereby they use new facilities to attract participants. New or renovated facilities provide administrators with advantages over the competition. Spending on athletic space thus becomes more necessity than mere wish when it comes to facility management.

In the college, high school, youth, and club sport settings, athletic administrators balance the needs of multiple programs on a given day. Often, the demand for facility space exceeds the actual space available for use by each sport entity. Space and availability limitations compel athletic administrators to strategically implement schedules to fulfill season-long obligations. Facility management is a specialized role within college, high school, youth, and club sport that centralizes the task of securing, organizing, and managing sport-related programs. At the collegiate and high school settings, facility managers may comprise one person or a team of people, whereas for youth and club sport the position of facility manager may be wrapped into an existing administrative board or staff position or even be a volunteer role within the organization.

▶ Competencies of Sport Facility Managers

The domain of athletic facility management comprises many specialized duties and tasks that play significant roles in athletic programs. Sport facility managers need to master a variety of skills to operate in their position. Upper-level sport facility managers have said the skill set or competencies required in their positions include budget preparation, setting priorities, developing effective delegation skills, planning long- and short-term goals, and evaluating personnel (Case & Branch, 2003). For first-time or entry-level facility managers, highly ranked competencies encompass written and oral communication skills, recognizing facility safety hazards, using problem-solving and decision-making skills, having some knowledge of computers, and managing both time and risks (Case & Branch, 2003). Notably, evaluating facility safety requires due diligence not only by facility managers but also by athletic administrators and coaches. Facility safety spans the playing surfaces as well as the fan areas, parking, and restrooms that make up the sportscape for the athletic entity.

With new facilities being constructed, the need for prepared facility managers has never been more urgent. Even at the recreational levels where field space may be shared and allocated to youth, club, and scholastic programs, a certified park and recreation professional exam exists for facility managers (National Recreation and Park Association, n.d.). Within the youth and community sport settings, Hurd (2005) explored the competencies needed by entry-level (facility) employees. The skill set required by public parks and recreation agencies included the following tasks:

- communicate clearly with customers,
- listen to staff and customers,

- deal with public,
- communicate clearly with staff,
- act professionally, and
- manage multiple tasks (Hurd, 2005).

▶ College Athletics Facility Management

College athletic buildings are often pinnacle and highly visible venues on the campus. Athletic facilities come in many shapes and sizes, depending on the scope of the programs on a campus, the size of the institution, and the success of its athletic programs. Regardless of the size or type of athletics venue, a coordinated effort is required to assign teams to athletic facilities, schedule events, and staff and supervise activities, along with coordinating and monitoring needed maintenance and repairs. Athletic departments may have a variety of staff positions responsible for coordinating the use of venue space. Position titles including *athletic facility manager* or *athletic facility coordinator* are common within intercollegiate athletic departments and larger high school programs. In many scenarios at the college level, the athletic department may share space with the recreational department or intramurals department, or recreational programming may be housed within the athletic department for organizational purposes. Facility managers must be adept at balancing the needs of athletic programs with managing staff with the end goal of providing a safe environment for athletic participation and fan enjoyment. Facility managers not only coordinate internal programming but also oversee external programs and third-party requests for field and gymnasium rentals. During the collegiate off-season (summer), facility managers are responsible for generating rental revenue by securing outside groups to use outdoor and indoor spaces.

© Felix Mizioznikov/Shutterstock.

⚽ FEEDBACK FROM THE FIELD

Best Practices: Facility Management in Collegiate Athletics

Jason Kreamer is the rink technician at the Raymond J. Bourque Arena at Endicott College in Beverly, Massachusetts. Before entering the college facility management setting, Kreamer had managed facilities within the youth and community settings. At Endicott College, he started in his role one week before a newly constructed ice rink opened. His first order of business was to make sure all aspects of the venue—from the ice being properly groomed to safety standards being implemented, including all elements of the rink's construction—were fully completed. Because the college did not have an ice rink expert on staff while decisions about space were made, many of the ideas were generated by the architects and by visits to other comparable facilities to collect plans for the new space. On reviewing the plans, Kreamer noted that a few revisions could be made to enhance player bench areas and allocate additional storage space not only in locker rooms but also as designated throughout the building. Kreamer also noted that the size of the glass used around the boards was not a standard specification, so when glass needs to be replaced, it will be more expensive to cut and require added time for delivery. Kreamer has proactively reached out to local vendors to make sure that if the glass siding is compromised, the correct size can be ordered quickly to replace the broken spaces. In addition, Kreamer has Plexiglas in the arena in the event the glass needs to be replaced in an emergency.

In his first three months in his new role, Kreamer also needed to address some of the spacing gaps between the boards and the flooring that allowed cold air to escape and compromised the surface of the ice. Many hours were also spent replacing screws that became stripped during construction. One major oversight, which Kreamer immediately remedied, was the lack of a water drain where the Zamboni ice-resurfacing machine would be stored. The contract did have provisions in place to handle all of these issues as warranty items. Kreamer acknowledged, however, that the physical plant supervisor on campus was extremely organized during all phases of construction and was tracking paperwork from vendors and contractors.

To future athletic administrators, Kreamer shared some simple points to consider for rink facility construction.

1. Plan for proper storage for all tools and equipment used daily. Facility managers need to make provisions for workspace to fix and repair items within the arena.
2. Hire someone who is a rink expert to share his or her knowledge before construction to help avoid issues of repairs and changes after construction. A rink expert will also recognize the core products needed for the facility rather than just purchasing items that are not regularly used for an arena. For example, the college purchased half boards to divide the ice. Unfortunately, these half boards are extremely heavy. Without purchasing another piece of equipment to move them, they may never be fully used.
3. The locker room space needs careful consideration, including ample storage for team needs such as jerseys, sticks, pucks, tape, and extra gear.

In addition to his facility management role, Kreamer also works closely at securing external groups to rent the arena. The college currently has a waiting list from outside groups—including youth and community hockey programs—that desire ice time. Kreamer and the arena manager set the arena rental rates, and fees are based on time of year and duration of need by these groups. Kreamer noted that the ice rink community is tightly knit; other arena managers in the region will assist with questions and ideas. Kreamer often hosts athletic administrators and facility managers looking to build their own rinks. He welcomes the opportunity to share all the challenges associated with facility construction and management.

▶ High School Facility Management

The need for facility managers at the high school level has evolved from a staff member in the athletic department assuming an untitled role to a stand-alone position to handle oversight of multiple venues and spaces for scholastic sport. During off hours, or when school is not in session, many high school administrators rent space to external groups and charge fees for classrooms, cafeterias, media centers, auditoriums, and theater spaces along with athletic fields, athletic stadiums, and gymnasium spaces. A designated central scheduler who handles rental agreements and schedules has become the norm across high school campuses that have desirable spaces. Schools are part of a district that will employ a schoolwide facility manager to plan and implement the financial operations for all spaces. The school athletic department and the municipal physical plant staff must maintain open lines of communication to ensure the safety of the grounds, including indoor and outdoor field space. Depending on the scope of the needed work or maintenance required, the athletic administrator and schoolwide facility manager determine cost allocation and responsibility for completion of the work. In essence, facility management at the high school level is three pronged. The first prong operates the rental agreements for a revenue stream to the school while the second prong operates all aspects of the physical environment, including maintenance and upkeep. The third prong handles the internal scheduling, aiming to provide adequate facility space to the broad-based programs making up the athletic teams coupled with policies to administer all programming.

▶ Youth and Club Sport Facility Management

In the youth sport setting, many of the administrators managing the entity are volunteers serving as board or committee members, so ascertaining the needs for field and gymnasium spacing must occur months before the season starts. Town sport facilities for youth programs are typically at full capacity, with municipal officials maximizing facility usage so they can meet the needs of several sports. Although many people might argue this is a "good problem" to have, it does create a dilemma for athletic administrators trying to add new initiatives, and many fields and venues cannot be properly maintained because they are in full use at all times. School facilities may be unoccupied in the evening hours, but youth sport organizations may find some of the spaces too expensive to use because custodial staff must be paid just to be stationed at the school during sporting events. In addition, some high school athletic departments may restrict the types of external groups or sports that can be played on their property, thus limiting youth sport programs from fully using that space. Within some towns and cities, many forces push and pull to get their programs into available spaces. In the end, town and city officials weigh the priorities of each sport entity before issuing permits for facility use.

Facility managers are often challenged to manage multiple fields within a town to provide equal and ample opportunities for different community-based sport groups. Solely by their decisions, athletic administrators affect the scheduling of programs on specific fields,

© Mike Flippo/Shutterstock.

and locations dictate the environment set for the youth programs in a community. Expectations for an effective facility manager include envisioning the larger picture to fully accommodate the number of programs requesting field or venue space, forming an administrative unit to assist with decision making for field allocation, and prioritizing needs because it is impossible to fully please every program (Tarantino & Andresen, 2015). School policy makers also play a decisional role in offering field and gymnasium space to community groups. Agreements outlining facility operations, maintenance, and repair costs may ease the minds of school officials who try to limit liability concerns and expenditures associated with sport programming (Kanters et al., 2014).

The extent of investment in facilities by youth sport clubs cannot be underestimated. Notable high-level investments include River City FC's plans to construct an $8 million, 80-acre soccer complex in western Michigan near Grand Rapids (Evans, 2016) and the Lonestar Soccer Club's purchase of a 22-acre parcel for construction of a new soccer facility as a nonprofit entity (Mather, 2016). Many private indoor and outdoor sport facilities are also filling the space gap for recreational teams and club sports when town venues are unavailable (Steinbach, 2008).

 FEEDBACK FROM THE FIELD

Best Practices: Club Sport Facility Management

Ian Burgess is the chief operations officer for Seacoast United Soccer Club based in Hampton, New Hampshire. Seacoast United was formed in 1992 and is devoted to promoting the game of soccer and serves more than 5,000 players in New Hampshire, northern Massachusetts, and Maine. The club is proud to be a Nike Premier Club since 1998. In the 2015–16 season, Seacoast United consisted of 55 teams (more than 850 players) and ages U-9 through minor league teams. The club is a member of the U.S. Soccer Development Academy, U.S. Club Soccer, National Premier Leagues, United Soccer League's Premier Development League, Northeast Pre-Academy League, New England Premiership, National Premier Soccer League, and Women's Premier Soccer League (http://www .seacoastunited.com/).

Seacoast United manages and operates several facilities. A systematic communication process has been incorporated into the planning to ensure that all locations operated by Seacoast United are managed effectively. Staff members participate in an annual retreat and dedicate a full day to discussing the indoor facilities, including schedules, marketing, field space, and maximizing capacity. Seacoast United staff hold weekly conference calls and sometimes in-person meetings to discuss updates at the various sites.

All Seacoast United facilities have one "manager," but several full-time staffers are responsible for each one. Each staff member reports to Burgess or to another designated facility manager in the company's management ranks. The ultimate goal for all facility spaces is to maximize opportunities for Seacoast United. The club employs two full-time maintenance people who update and ensure functionality at each site, and club cleanup days are held for painting and outside maintenance in which all staff members partake in facility upkeep.

Securing new facilities certainly has advantages, but there are also challenges associated with managing sites in so many locations. Burgess points out that each acquired venue has a different story and unveils different opportunities and challenges. The first facility for Seacoast United was Hampton Indoor, and the club dedicated the first two years of its existence to getting everyone in local communities playing indoor sports. Two years later, Seacoast United doubled the size of Hampton Indoor. According to Burgess, the core challenge when the club opens or takes over a

(continues)

FEEDBACK FROM THE FIELD   (continued)

new venue is finding people capable of dedicating the time to manage it. Seacoast United has improved on this front, but if giving a staff member sole responsibility for facility management is not addressed at the outset, it becomes more of an afterthought. Now, Seacoast United is building incentives for staff management to assist with facility management at the sites.

When the club is not using the sites, it successfully secures external groups to use the space six months out of the year, although there are downtimes in the summer months when the space is not as desirable. Burgess encourages staff to think out of the box for programming initiatives. The facilities have organized play times with bouncy houses and classes for children under age five. In addition, facilities have seven-versus-seven adult soccer leagues in the summer and lunch-hour pickup soccer games. Burgess adds that there are many opportunities for rentals when the club programs are not in operation but Seacoast United running its own programs is a bigger key to success than renting to outside groups.

Burgess explains that the process for buying land for facilities or acquiring existing facilities is the case of being at the right place at the right time. If the decision is to buy land for facility construction, then financing is initiated and coupled with planning for all aspects of the venue, including number of fields, office, parking, and lights.

Seacoast United's model and philosophy is to "own our own destiny" rather than rent from others. In terms of advice to future athletic administrators, facility managers should find partners who are business oriented and not just soccer or sport oriented, explains Burgess.

© Pataradon Luangtongkum/Shutterstock.

▶ Field and Indoor Space Permits

Towns, cities, and recreation departments frame policies around facility requests, approvals, and regulations. Scheduling procedures include the application process; costs per hour per venue per day; requests for multiple days, weeks, and months; and deadlines for facility requests. Within the policies for permit requests, officials include space regulations for players and fans, maintenance responsibilities and costs, fees associated with facility use, and billing procedures. In many cases, municipalities dealing with school and community sport programs may create a priority hierarchy for field usage. The priority of use may start with high school athletic programs, then middle school events and larger youth sports, and finally external groups with few or no ties to the community. Typically, usage requests are submitted by a deadline and permits are granted on a first-come, first-served basis following the priority of usage. Each municipality communicates facility use rules and regulation policies to preserve the integrity of the program and keep maintenance of facilities at the highest standard. Once permits are issued, the athletic entities are expected to follow and adhere to the facility rules set within the application process. When sport programs violate regulations, municipalities can withdraw permits and shut down venue space at will and without ample notice. Furthermore, athletic administrators are required to provide the municipality with a certificate of liability insurance from an insurance company licensed to conduct business within the specific state. The policy requirements may differ from municipality to municipality, but typically there is a general liability policy with a minimal coverage along with naming the city or town as an additional insured entity for comprehensive liability protection. One core aspect of facility management is setting policies for usage along with a fee schedule to cover costs associated with facility operation and overall maintenance.

Community and school partnerships are formed to ease the burden associated with the lack of facilities and the high demand for athletic space. Effective athletic administrators simply build creative options for sport programming needs in a time of limited resources for space. The challenges of scheduling and offering indoor space to competing sport programs must also be considered along with outdoor field space. In a time when children need to increase their activity, sport organizers must work together to find solutions to adequately accommodate and promote sport within the community through joint agreements between schools and community resources (Howard, Bocarro, & Kanters, 2013).

▶ Multipurpose Venues

Many college campuses have multipurpose athletic facilities to accommodate larger numbers of sport teams by design, space, sport-specific lined boundaries, and equipment. College administrators use new athletic buildings for office space, meeting rooms, and academic classrooms. Given the multipurpose nature of some athletic venues, facility managers must appease a variety of occupants within the buildings and fields. Some campuses open athletic venues to the community. It is not uncommon for community members to access indoor tracks and weight-room facilities.

College administrators recognize the instrumental role that new buildings play in retention and recruitment of students. Many athletic buildings include academic classrooms for a variety of reasons, including connection to the mission of education at the institution

and space availability when athletic programs are not in session. Adding classroom and meeting spaces to an athletic venue can serve many diverse student and faculty groups on campus, creating positive outreach by athletic administrators.

▶ Intramural and Recreational Sport Programming

High school students visiting college campuses are often wooed by the appeal of the facility for use by the general student population (weight room, fitness areas) along with the opportunities to participate on sport teams in a club versus varsity-level setting. The effect of recreation centers on enrollment is tangible as athletic facilities and recreational centers are "built due to three major reasons—the need for students to be involved in wellness activities, recruitment, and retention" (Kampf, 2010). When athletics and recreation have an impact on retention (Kampf & Teske, 2013), athletic administrators may have an easier time gaining institutional support, leading to increased funding for future projects. Notably, club sport versus varsity sport participation coupled with students being employed by recreational centers adds to increased retention rates on campus (Henchy, 2011; Kampf & Teske, 2013). Nonstudent-athletes compete in leagues or club-level teams instead of competing at the National Collegiate Athletic Association (NCAA) and National Association of Intercollegiate Athletics (NAIA) levels of competition. Some college students may have played high school athletics and decided not to compete for a variety of reasons or just did not have the appropriate skill set to compete at the collegiate level. Competition thrives in these programs but just not at the same level as NCAA and NAIA programs. Recreational opportunities foster the desire for the student population to stay active while also reaping the social benefits of team affiliation. The influence of recreational activities gives students a greater sense of community (Elkins, Forrester, & Noël-Elkins, 2011), and those students benefit intellectually, socially, and physically compared to students who do not participate (Lower, Turner, & Petersen, 2013). These data points are important for athletic administrators to consider when they leverage campus administrators while seeking funding and ultimately approval for newly constructed venues or renovations.

In addition to the formalized athletic practice, game day, and special events organized through the athletic departments at the collegiate and high school levels, intramural and recreational offerings require not only specialized attention but also highly coveted facility space. Facility managers at the collegiate and high school levels work in collaboration with intramural staff to create opportunities for recreational activities offered across the campus. To demonstrate the power of intramural and recreational sports, Boston College announced in early 2016 the plan to construct a $200-million, 240,000-square-foot facility to house and "enhance" intercollegiate, intramural, and club sports (Boston College, 2016). Students participate in intramural activities for a wide range of social and health reasons. Campus recreation opportunities help retain and recruit college students (Blumenthal, 2009).

Aside from the traditional menu of intercollegiate athletic sport participation, many institutions have a history of sport club programs available to students. Sport clubs traditionally are organized and led by students with supervision and oversight provided by college administrations. These clubs are important in fostering opportunities for student leadership (Blumenthal, 2009), but because of the pressure to schedule numerous sport programs within the athletic department, recreational and club offerings may not be considered priorities during scheduling. "Ultimately, however, how extensive future facilities will be depends on

a number of factors, including student enrollment, how closely recreational sport programs are aligned with student life, and whether facilities are dedicated solely to student recreation or shared with other university departments, including athletics" (Blumenthal, 2009). Implementing intramural or recreational programs on college campuses serves to satisfy both the athletic and social needs of participants (Webb & Forrester, 2015), as well as employ students on campus to manage and promote these events, which creates experiential learning for many studying in the fields of athletic administration and sport management (Toperzer, Anderson, & Barcelona, 2011). Tangible outcomes such as leadership opportunities, performance assessment, training and orientation, personal relationships, and professional development emerge through employment and volunteering in recreational departments (Toperzer et al., 2011). "The importance of having a bona fide campus recreational sports program in place is understood at all levels of higher education administration, whether its focus is to recruit or retain students, to complement academic missions while enhancing student life, or simply to foster and improve the health and wellness of the larger campus community" (Blumenthal, 2009). Evidence points to the benefits recreational programs can provide to diverse campus groups such as physical activity, promotion of education, and the overall development of a healthy lifestyle (Lower et al., 2013).

Intramural Sport: High School Setting

Similar to the college level, high school programs recognize the opportunities and benefits associated with intramural sports. Byl (2004) provides a framework to assist school administrators in developing intramural programs at the elementary and high school levels, including establishing a welcoming environment for students, being creative with use of equipment and facility space, varying scheduling opportunities and team formation, promoting events across the school, and celebrating the success across the campus. Brookline High School in Massachusetts upholds that "intramurals are an informal way to have fun, get exercise, relieve stress, and meet new people" (BHS Intramurals, n.d.). Athletic administrators, physical educators, and student development staff at the scholastic level can come together to formulate intramurals by determining student interest in planned sport-related activities, crafting a budget for promotions and participation awards, linking the activities to the mission of the school, creating schedules for the programs, and designating schedules for supervisors. At Mount Lebanon High School in Pennsylvania, the "focus is to provide as many athletic [and] competitive opportunities as possible, while simultaneously increasing school spirit" (Mt. Lebanon School District, n.d.). At Dana Hall High School in California, intramurals are promoted through the school's website as a "stress-free activity with no tryouts required, and absolutely anyone can participate (even the staff)" (Dana Hills High School, n.d.).

▶ Sustainability

Sustainability is a new thrust in the operation of facility management. Many athletic administrators are adopting an environmentally focused mindset by integrating sustainable practices into their departments. According to the report of the World Commission on Environment and Development (commonly known as the Brundtland Commission Report, 1987), sustainability is "development that meets the needs of the present without compromising the ability of future generations to meet their own needs." Across the nation in all athletic settings from college to youth sports, administrators are moving toward initiatives to promote environmental sustainability. Ideas for waste reduction and limiting energy use are interwoven into strategic planning discussions and implementation.

Trailblazers in the area of sustainability provide benchmarking for other athletic administrators to follow in the quest to create greener environments. Many models exemplify sustainability on college campuses, including at Amherst College, where students have initiated projects to meet the sustainability challenge—from tennis ball recycling, to lighting reduction in the athletic facility, to reduction of plastic and food waste in the dining halls; their overall goal is to "achieve a carbon-neutral footprint" (Zhang, 2015). Stanford University athletics also has been able to create a "greener movement" by adding compost and recycling bins throughout Stanford Stadium, using light towers with solar powering, shutting down sprinkler heads, and replacing grass with turf for campus landscaping (Sullivan, 2016). The University of Michigan is another example of an athletic department establishing sustainability efforts to reduce energy usage, chemical and water usage, and waste, and enhance sustainability education and awareness (Sustainability, n.d.). Yale University boasts the country's "first athletics and recreation greening program driven by student-athletes" (see **FIGURE 4.1**). Harnessing the influence of athletes on campus, Middlebury College athletic teams wear green shoelaces to raise awareness about sustainability efforts (NCAA, 2013).

Motivation to become a green-thinking campus may stem from the sustainability challenges promoted by college athletic conferences to student-athletes and athletic departments. A powerful entity in this quest is the Green Sports Alliance. The major charge of the Green Sports Alliance (GSA; http://greensportsalliance.org) is "inspiring sports leagues, teams, venues, their partners and millions of fans to embrace renewable energy, healthy food, recycling, water efficiency, species preservation, safer chemicals, and other environmentally preferable practices." Every PAC-12 member is part of the GSA (PAC-12 Conference, 2015). To date, 30 NCAA-affiliated universities are

- All athletics department office paper must contain recycled content. Yale Athletics currently uses office paper with 30 percent postconsumer recycled content.
- The custodial staff must use environmentally preferable cleaning products. Currently, 75 percent of department cleaning products are Green Seal certified.
- Waterless urinals must be installed in all new athletic facility construction projects.
- The athletics department is minimizing paper use by eliminating deskside printers and copiers in athletics offices, holding paperless staff meetings, and transitioning to electronic operations.
- Energy-saving power settings must be used as defaults on all athletics office computers.

Greener Sports Facilities

- Recycling infrastructure was installed at 100 percent of athletics and recreation facilities (including athletics offices), and upgrades based on student proposals are planned.
- Bike racks have been installed [in] close to 100 percent of athletics and recreation facilities (including athletics offices).
- Water fountains were installed in almost 100 percent of athletics and recreation facilities (including athletics offices).
- Energy efficiency upgrades have been made in almost 100 percent of athletics and recreation facilities, including enhancements to occupancy sensors, lighting retrofits, and variable-frequency drives for pool pumps. [Facility upgrades in 2013] are projected to save more than $100,000 in energy costs annually.
- About 80 percent of all leaf waste from athletics fields is mulched for reuse in turf maintenance.
- The Yale Boat House uses organic fertilizers, which are equivalent in cost to conventional pesticide alternatives.

FIGURE 4.1 Yale University Greener Athletics and Recreation Operations Goals

Republished with permission from the Natural Resources Defense Council National Resources Defense Council (2013, August). Collegiate game changers: How campus sport is going green. Retrieved from www.nrdc.org/resources/collegiate-game-changers-how-campus-sport-going-green.

GSA members. Sustainability is becoming an important movement within athletics as reflected in the emergence of degree-granting programs. The bachelor's and master's degrees offered by the School of Sustainability at Arizona State University are the first of their kind (NCAA, 2013). Forecasting into the next decade, many more academic programs and training programs in sustainability will likely be established.

Collegiate Game Changers is a leading sustainability resource in athletic administration. The content within the report "Collegiate Game Changers" (National Resources Defense Council, 2013), showcases the "breadth of sustainability measures underway at collegiate departments all across the country." This document details the work of athletic administrators in the areas of recycling, energy reduction, waste management, water use, and lighting efficiency (see **FIGURES 4.2** and **4.3**).

High School Sustainability

Similar to the college setting, high school athletic departments are adopting green programming within their athletic departments. Many high schools are also incorporating ideas that stimulate awareness among student bodies to help prompt even more change.

Youth and Community Sport Sustainability Efforts

The impact of sustainability and green initiatives are included in youth and community sport. Examples of Earth Day activities aimed to clean up fields and parks across the nation spark a greater awareness for protecting the environment. Online sport registration, although probably selected by athletic entities because of its convenience in registration, is

Reports have found the following green developments:

- At least 216 collegiate sports departments have installed recycling infrastructure throughout their sports facilities.
- At least 146 collegiate sports departments have invested in more energy-efficient practices by upgrading their lighting and controls.
- At least 116 collegiate sports departments have upgraded to water-efficient fixtures.
- At least 88 collegiate sports departments have pursued Leadership in Energy and Environmental Design (LEED) green building design certifications, and at least 24 have been certified sports venues.
- At least 23 collegiate sports departments have installed on-site solar energy production systems.

FIGURE 4.2 Collegiate Game Changers

Republished with permission from the Natural Resources Defense Council National Resources Defense Council (2013, August). Collegiate game changers: How campus sport is going green. Retrieved from www .nrdc.org/resources/collegiate-game-changers-how-campus-sport-going-green.

Among the benefits of college sports greening are the following:

- Cuts operational costs
- Educates and empowers students
- Enhances athletics and institutional brands
- Attracts sponsors and partners
- Strengthens community ties
- Reinforces interdepartmental ties
- Advances campus-wide sustainability goals
- Creates a healthier workout environment and promotes athlete performance

FIGURE 4.3 The Greening of College Sports

From National Resources Defense Council (2013), page 10.

 FEEDBACK FROM THE FIELD

Best Practices: High School Sustainability

Andra Yeghoian is the director of sustainability at Bishop O'Dowd High School in Oakland, California. In her unique role at the school, Yeghoian implements a variety of programs to create not only an awareness regarding sustainability but also programs that promote students to increase their sustainability efforts. Yeghoian's work stems from Stephen Sterling, who uses Danielle Meadows's definition that a sustainable society "is one that can persist over generations, one that is far-seeing enough, flexible enough, and wise enough not to undermine either its physical or social systems of support." In addition, Yeghoian uses the framework from the United Nation's World Commission on Environment and Development report, "Our Common Future" (Report of the World Commission, n.d.) (also known as the Brundtland Report), to motivate current and future generations to meet the needs of all changes in society. Yeghoian uses the report to define sustainable development as the "development [that] meets the needs of the present without compromising the ability of future generations to meet their own needs."

In her work, Yeghoian focuses on the three pillars of sustainability: economic development, social equity, and environmental protection. In essence, sustainability can be defined as current generations meeting their needs while ensuring future generations can meet their needs as well. She also stresses

(continues)

FEEDBACK FROM THE FIELD   *(continued)*

to her students in this definition of sustainability that all changes made within our society and our systems should be in harmony and enhance both current and future potentials to meet human needs and aspirations. The reason she uses a combination of meanings within sustainability is to help students understand that it goes beyond just meeting basic needs but also ensuring a full quality of life and meeting all aspirations. In addition, Yeghoian uses the triple bottom line framework, which indicates that within sustainability everything is nested within the environment. The first bottom line is the planet. She explains that if our planet is healthy and doing well, then one is able to focus on people, on society, and on the economy. On the other hand, if the environment is not doing well, it will affect people negatively. The second bottom line is focused on people or society and is focused on culture, health and well-being, community, social justice, and diversity issues. If those things are well taken care of, then there will be a thriving economy. If those things are in turmoil, it is hard for people to prosper. The third bottom line is the economy. The economy is nested within people and the environment. The economy focuses on people's prosperity, reaching their purpose and their livelihood. When she frames this in student discussions, she asks students which one they hear about the most. Their response is the economy. She stresses that even though people focus on the economy, she wants students to realize that the economy is nested within the society and the environment. Yeghoian clarifies that someone who takes a sustainability approach will make sure we balance all three of these elements and understand the relationship between all three.

Yeghoian's role is to bring a cultural change to the school. She has set up a framework for how the institution will approach this change as depicted by three pillars: the campus, the curriculum, and the community, all of which are supported by the base, which is the institutional culture.

Under the campus pillar, Yeghoian's role is to assist in making sure the facility and operations are green. Greening constitutes the energy and water systems, the transportation, waste streams, purchasing, the grounds themselves, and the landscaping. She implements programming to ensure everything is environmentally friendly and healthy for humans. Yeghoian works closely with the facility management team and the administrators who oversee any aspect of the facilities.

The second pillar represents the curriculum. Here Yeghoian works with teachers and departments to help them bring sustainability topics and social, environmental, and economic issues to their classrooms and transform their subject areas so they are solution oriented. She further explains that the goal is to have students examine some of the world's problems through the lens of their English, social studies, or science classes and try to actively solve these problems.

As part of this process, teachers are making space in their curricula for sustainability, making students solve complex global issues. At the community engagement level, one student's project measured food waste at the cafeteria. The student decided to capture the amount of food left or wasted everyday and to figure out how to donate that. Yeghoian indicated her students are getting better at analyzing where the problems are in both local and global contexts and figuring out how they can be change makers.

The third pillar is the community, which focuses on engaging both internal and external communities. Internally, Yeghoian works with both student and staff groups. One example of her efforts was with the admissions department, which is the first point of entry to the private school. The department would give prospective students an inexpensive gift for visiting the campus but one that was not especially useful and would ultimately be discarded. Through Yeghoian's efforts, the admissions department shifted and offered gifts that were useful or organic and still meaningful—and reflected an effort that aligned better with the school's philosophy.

Yeghoian's most recent partnership is with the athletic department, demonstrating the underlying base of institutional culture. Her students decided to host a zero-waste football game with a sustainability emphasis, making sure that what is sold is recyclable or compostable. To accomplish this goal, students stand at waste stations to help people sort trash correctly.

Yeghoian also focuses on sustainable student leadership on campus. She has been working with student leaders on campus, club officers, and sport team captains to have them attend a leadership retreat together to start building a similar skill set. Ultimately, her aim is to get campus student leaders to work in unison to build communities on campus.

Within the athletic department, Yeghoian has focused on transportation. She admits that in the first few years it was difficult or felt unachievable to make a dent in transportation from the standpoint of sustainability. But, by the fourth year, Yeghoian and others on campus were getting into more details, such as asking where the school's largest carbon footprint rests, examining the campus's transportation fleet, and finding ways to transport students more efficiently. Yeghoian is also considering transporting people to and from athletic contests in vans rather than buses and even using alternative fuel vehicles. When asked to provide advice to future athletic administrators, Yeghoian encourages them to think about the attitudes their departments or institutions have toward sustainability and what they can do to reinforce sustainable culture on their campus and in their community events.

Another partnership with the athletic department is community service. Bishop O'Dowd has a four-acre garden on campus and athletic teams do three hours of service, which lends to building community together as a campus outside of athletics. Yeghoian stresses that athletic administrators can reinforce environmental sustainability or social justice issues through community programs. In addition, future athletic administrators should examine everyday operational practices. Yeghoian shared examples of providing athletes with reusable water bottles instead of plastic bottles at games. In terms of health and wellness, she looks at what kinds of sport drinks are offered to their athletes in the cafeteria. The Bishop O'Dowd cafeteria promotes drinks with electrolytes rather than high-sugar drinks. In addition, the campus head chef advertises meals in the cafeteria that are athlete-specific (as an example, extra protein on game days) in an attempt to connect athletics with sustainability.

Clearly, Yeghoian and Bishop O'Dowd are trailblazers in sustainability within the high school setting. Only a few full-time sustainability directors in the country are at the K–12 level. Her school hosts a symposium every year with 25–30 schools in attendance, each sharing ideas to implement greening initiatives at their schools. As stressed by Yeghoian, because athletes are visible role models on campus, the environmental sustainability club works with athletes to participate in educational videos because the athletes are influential with their peers. From a campus perspective, it is important for athletes to showcase their efforts with sustainability because they are culture changers at the school.

another method of going green and minimizes paper use by the organization from signup forms to envelopes, and it even saves on postage (SI Play, n.d.). The YMCA uses clean graffiti (water on dirty sidewalks) for outdoor advertising (thesavageway, 2015).

© Douglas Sacha/Moment/Getty Images.

▶ Maintenance of Athletic Facilities

With the administration of any facility, overall maintenance needs must be included in operational plans. High school athletic administrators must weigh the benefits of rental arrangements with nonschool groups, especially when it comes to the wear and tear of the venue. Questions policy makers ponder include, Who will pay for any repairs or upkeep of the facilities when renting to external groups? If an arrangement could be agreed on in terms of shared maintenance between the school and nonschool community groups, then school administrators may be open to these relationships (Kanters et al., 2014). There are many concerns when balancing facility

© B Brown/Shutterstock.

to a specific school but is hired for district-wide needs (Whithead, 2014). Athletic administrators, along with maintenance personnel, are charged with ensuring all current facilities meet the needs of teams and programs on campus (Hall, 2010).

Event Management

A significant branch of facility management is administration of an entire event from a spectator's perspective. Event management provides a value-added component for spectators. Event managers create activities before, during, and after events to infuse a "feel-good atmosphere" whereby fans look forward to the game-day environment. Simple programs such as coffee with the coach, free hot cocoa for night events in late fall, concession sales, and tented seating areas for parents and fans all are seen as thoughtful gestures on the part of the athletic administrator that lead to satisfied spectators. For larger events, tents, overlook lounges, or larger rooms will be set up to ensure that fans congregate near the playing fields to enjoy the competition. Depending on the scope of the event, the event manager may cater meals or simply provide VIP seating to targeted audiences.

management needs within the overall scope of athletic administration. First, many athletic administrators do not have the training to know the details of turf or field maintenance. Second, many athletic administrators do not have a budget to cover the aspects needed to fully care for the facilities. Third, a designated field maintenance person may not be dedicated

💬 FEATURED INTERVIEW: BEST PRACTICES IN ATHLETIC ADMINISTRATION

Dr. Susan Langlois is the current dean for the Division of Arts and Sciences at Rivier University, in Nashua, New Hampshire. Her expertise in the field of athletics and facility management spans more than 35 years managing sport facilities and contributing as an administrator and consultant to the master planning, design, construction, and maintenance of facilities that support physical education, intercollegiate athletics, and fitness and recreation. She is also a contributing author to *Camp Business, Parks & Recreation Business*, and has written numerous chapters in sport facility planning textbooks. As a professor at Springfield College, the University of Connecticut, and Endicott College, she has taught courses in sport management and facility development.

Although construction and renovation projects may seem like a daunting task for one administrator, Langlois advocates placing as many of the athletic staff on the building committee as possible, allowing all constituencies to "be in the loop" and contribute to the overall direction of the plan and project. A critical piece of building committee meetings are the meeting minutes, which are shared and vetted at the athletic department meetings for those personnel not serving on the building committee, further developing a dialogue on the project and gathering perspectives from others in the athletic department.

Planning for facility management, as Langlois stresses, requires that the athletic administrator identify and connect with key partners. Open and continuous communication with these partners, according to Langlois, allows the athletic administrator to ask core questions and find solutions throughout the facility management process. Key partners include the college president, building committee members, master planner, architect, contractor, estimator, clerk of the works, and project manager. Langlois considers them key partners, "expert partners" who provide advice and expertise, especially when they have been through the facility management process with other projects.

As expected with any type of construction, budgetary concerns weigh heavily on the athletic administrator. Langlois stresses that athletic administrators must be able to anticipate need and avoid asking for change orders; these can be three times as expensive as the work in the original design. If anyone on the design team or the general contractor's team demands a change order, Langlois feels they should determine who is responsible for the needed change and negotiate who should pay for it. A change order comes into play when dealing with any revisions to the contracted plans. One small change can have ripple effects on changes to other areas and costs. For example, simply moving a bathroom from one corner to another could add costs to the project to accommodate the plumbing change. Any changes small or large to the blueprint of the architectural plan can lead to unplanned costs, hence adding to the importance of researching all needs before signing off on the finalized versions of the construction or renovation.

There is a need for systematic, intensive, and regular training of personnel who will develop positive relationships with the public, enforce safety standards, compile seamless documentation on scheduling, participants, cleaning, and maintenance, and treat the facility as if they were the owner. When architects refer to the "program," they are likely referring to the concept of the facility design. It is important for the architect to know that a facilities manager likely refers to the program as the activities that are supported in the facility. The axiom "form follows function" should always be on the mind of the athletic administrator. The facility has to function for the programs, but it also has to be an appealing and attractive environment in which people will contribute, respect, and enjoy their time.

When asked to consider building for current programs or build for expansion, Langlois conveyed there are many discussions underway with the president and board of trustees to determine the direction for the institution, including any changes to the mission that may or may not yet be communicated outside the executive level. In Langlois' case, the institution was planning to move to a coeducational demographic, which supported the need for athletic facility construction. Planning ahead provides the blueprint for the construction and allows athletic administrators to dream a little bit through the master plan. For example, if a second floor is on the planning table for the second stage of construction, the first floor must be able to hold the weight of another floor while also aesthetically matching the theme of the campus. Langlois admits there is no way to anticipate everything, including the wiring needed for Internet (thankfully, wireless access was available) or security cameras. In Langlois' building, the health center was open to alumni and community members. More space was needed to fully accommodate the needs of the students, but a simple dividing wall (which prevented the front desk attendant from having a clear view of the exercise and weight room) limited the opportunity to include more equipment. Because the total need for space was not anticipated, she decided to retrofit the area as a tradeoff, but it was not the best option.

For Langlois, one highlight of the construction project was visiting other schools and facilities that were recently completed or finished 20 years ago to see the renovations added as updates. Langlois fully enjoyed the visits, meeting other athletic administrators, and sharing ideas and challenges. In her words, "The more you listen, you can build a strong foundation to have a building you can really be proud of." Athletic programs evolve, and facilities need to be fitted to accommodate need. For example, Langlois did not plan for a natatorium because there was not a swim team on campus. When a swim

(continues)

team was added, the building was retrofitted to add a pool with an office, and this became the back part of the athletic training room. Her staff raised $22,000 to offset the expansion costs.

Langlois asserts "the smartest things you can do so you can anticipate changes, is not to build the building around the personalities of the staff" but to see the bigger picture of the full needs of the department and ultimately anticipate the institution's growth. By including the athletic staff on the building committee, diverse perspectives are heard, although the athletic director needs to be sure individuals are not pushing their own agendas but are instead focused on what is best for all programs on the campus. Langlois also instituted open meetings; whenever there was a major change or announcement, she invited neighbors to meet architects, believing that transparency is an important piece of the larger puzzle. For example, if meetings were not open, the institutions would not have been exposed to the expertise of one neighbor who presented details on cost-saving, energy-efficient lighting. These open meetings gave people a chance to be included in idea generation and creativity regarding the construction, which in turn created positive relations with community members.

Oftentimes, athletic construction is frowned on because of the spending and the perceived focus away from academics. In the facility planning of Langlois, many classrooms were allocated to academic programs and used for summer camps. Originally, the facility plans did not call for a second floor, but the switch in focus to incorporate academic space, although an additional cost, helped grow the academic program and kept the facility open during evening and night hours.

Unfortunately, many school administrators are dealing with the horrific incidents of shootings on campuses. Langlois reviewed some of the mechanisms that can be implemented to deal with creating safety on campus. Creating a central access point to the facility and alarming all doors provides an initial preventive measure. Adding translucent glass gives the building more privacy, and most people would not want bars on windows. A plan to evacuate the building in case of emergency and designating safe harbors should be part of the crisis-management protocol. In addition, all possible evacuation scenarios should be thought through, including wheelchair access if the elevator is not in use and where people should gather once evacuated to stay out of the line of fire.

Dr. Langlois shared a chronological framework to advance facility projects within athletics, detailing the steps in the process from the realization of needs to the opening of the facility. Under Langlois' tenure, many new teams were developed, which in turn created the need for increased athletic space. Not many athletic administrators have the opportunity or ability to build an entire athletic department from the ground up, starting with no teams to a menu of broad-based offerings. The following chronology showcases the need for an athletic administrator to envision change on a growing campus focused on athletic expansion and facility construction.

- **Year 1.** Intercollegiate athletics on campus (women-only institution) began with the first basketball team. The athletic department added intramural volleyball and new physical education courses in tennis, swimming, equestrian, racquetball, aerobic dance, cycling, and field hockey. The faculty voted to add physical education to the core curriculum.
- **Year 2.** The school added the second intercollegiate team, field hockey. The department also added intramural racquetball, hiking Mt. Holyoke, running club, and faculty fitness club; new physical education courses in advanced lifesaving were offered, and the first athletic field for field hockey was constructed.
- **Year 3.** The school added the third intercollegiate team: equestrian. The department also added intramural soccer, floor hockey, and softball. The institution joined an intercollegiate athletic conference and started to raise funds for intercollegiate athletics.

- **Year 4.** The institution joined the Eastern Collegiate Athletic Conference and added a fourth intercollegiate team: soccer. The soccer team trained and competed at a local parks and recreation field and traveled out of state to compete in tournaments; the college field hockey team traveled to Denmark.
- **Year 5.** The sixth intercollegiate team (lacrosse) was added to the campus offerings. At the same time, the soccer field extension was constructed. Later that year, the seventh intercollegiate team was launched: softball. Because of a lack of facilities, the softball team trained and competed at the local parks and recreation field. The college joined the NCAA while the basketball team traveled to play John Abbott College in Montreal, Canada, and the field hockey team qualified for a first-ever postseason tournament.
- **Year 6.** At the college, a coaching minor curriculum was established. The athletic department organized its first invitational community golf tournament to benefit college athletics.
- **Year 7.** An on-campus softball field was constructed.
- **Year 8.** The college strategic plan established a goal to build a fitness and athletics center.
- **Year 9.** A feasibility study was started, and the department members visited other facilities and asked for tours.
- **Year 10.** The master plan was created, and the school started building a relationship with the Kresge Foundation.
- **Year 11.** Langlois formed a building committee with at least one member of the board of trustees, the director of the physical plant, the vice president of Academic Affairs, and the chair of the faculty senate. Also included on the committee were the athletic director, instructors, and coaches. Langlois sent requests for proposals to four design firms. She cautioned that before a firm would be hired, the committee members should visit facilities that the firm had designed.
- **Year 12.** The athletic department restarted the process by creating a larger "footprint" after realizing the first level was not spacious enough for the programming.
- **Year 13.** New construction began, and the campus lost a parking lot in the process.
- **Year 14.** The Center for Fitness and Athletics opened, and the sixth intercollegiate team, swimming, was added. To support the expansion, the athletic department decided a revenue stream must be created and sustained. The decision was to launch a health club for paying alumni and local residents, along with summer sports camps.
- **Year 15.** The building began to be used, and the venue was dedicated with a ceremony.

Questions for Discussion

1. When dealing with architects, what are some core aspects that athletic administrators should be prepared to understand?
2. What should come first—the decision to build a facility or the decision to add teams? What are the implications for the facility design and future renovations if new teams are added after the completion of a major construction project?
3. Which should athletic administrators accommodate first—the needs of the coaches or the mission of the athletic department? What are the pitfalls of each decision?
4. What impressed you the most regarding the impact Langlois made as an athletic administrator during the facility management process?
5. As a future athletic administrator, how would you include neighbors in the area to participate and contribute to the planning aspect of the facility? Or would you avoid any interaction with the neighbors? Please defend your perspective, using some of the ideas presented in the Langlois interview.

MANAGERIAL APPLICATIONS

Youth Sport: Facility Planning

For one city, there are numerous competing programs trying to secure the limited outdoor and indoor space for their teams. As the municipal director, you are in charge of deciding which youth programs get to use the fields across the fall, winter, and spring seasons. Because you are new at the position, your first task would be to look at other municipal programs to review scheduling and coordination of space utilization among the variety of sport programs. Your goal is to satisfy the needs of all sport programs and present your findings to the youth program directors at your townwide meeting next month.

Questions to Consider

1. What type of priority system will you create so you can rank the order of need for the sports of soccer (played fall and spring), girls' and boys' basketball (late fall, winter), softball (winter indoor and spring outdoor), baseball (winter indoor and spring outdoor), and girls' and boys' lacrosse (winter indoor and spring outdoor)? The facilities under your supervision are the West Elementary School gymnasium and grass field used for lacrosse and soccer, North Elementary School gymnasium and baseball field, the town hall's fields for baseball and softball, and the state's turf field used for lacrosse and soccer. The hours available for use are Monday through Thursday 5:30 PM to 8:30 PM and Saturdays 9 AM to 2 PM. Use a spreadsheet to assign sport teams to time and venue.
2. If you were the president of a youth sport association in this city, what would your proposal be to persuade the municipal director that your program should have priority?
3. Maintenance and overall upkeep of the facilities is costly, so what is your philosophy as municipal director on requesting funding from the youth programs using the space?

 MANAGERIAL APPLICATIONS

High School Athletics: Facility Scheduling

The construction at your high school is finally complete with a new gymnasium, new baseball field with lights and dugouts, new softball field, and new multipurpose turf field for football, boys' and girls' soccer, and girls' and boys' lacrosse (lights). The high school coaches were looking forward to reviewing the schedule for the high school turf field during the summer meeting so they could plan practices and games. It came to the attention of the soccer coaches that the field was to be used by football first and any remaining space would be designated to the soccer teams. In addition, for the ribbon-cutting ceremony for the turf field, only the football team captains were part of the celebration. As the athletic administrator, you have inherited an issue regarding sharing the newly constructed space.

Questions to Consider

1. Do you think that many athletic administrators make the mistake of referring to fields as the "football stadium" and those references define the usage of the space instead of just calling the turf the "athletic stadium"? What are your thoughts on the use of terminology when trying to create a cohesive coaching unit especially when all the staff are excited for the new venues?

2. The softball field does not have lights or dugouts, and the coach refuses to move from the current location of the field off campus. The design of the softball field without the lights and dugouts was an oversight by the planning committee, but now you have an issue on your hands as the athletic administrator. What resolution can you share with the softball coach and players to remedy their concerns?

3. School classes end at 2 PM each day, and teams can practice as late as 9 PM. What would a typical schedule look like for fall sports (soccer, football) knowing that the soccer teams have two games per week (Wednesday and Saturday) and football has one game per week (Friday). Plan for two weeks of scheduling on the turf field when all teams have home contests. List some of the challenges and include some of the value-added features you will incorporate into your planning to create a positive environment for spectators.

4. How can you create an inclusive environment within your staff to ensure all coaches feel their program needs are accounted for specifically under the facility management umbrella?

 DECISION-MAKING CHALLENGE

Case Study: Club Sport Facility Planning

Facility planning requires a vision that couples the current needs of athletic programs with a vision anticipating growth areas and future spatial demands. The checklist of facility planning from an athletic administrator's perspective includes conducting a feasibility study, developing a construction budget, organizing planning committees, researching comparable facilities, and working with experts in the field to determine the best fit of facilities tied to the needs of the program. A new profit-oriented lacrosse club will operate both boys' and girls' teams, and you have been tasked with finding a location suitable for the construction of both an indoor facility with two turf fields and one regulation-sized outdoor field. What are the resources you would use to determine construction costs? What type of financing would be available to your club? Would you be interested in investment partners? Why or why not? Construct a "facility checklist" for planning purposes, list potential members of an organizing planning committee, research comparable facilities, and determine who you would want to work with as the experts in the field to determine the best fit for your facility.

 DECISION-MAKING CHALLENGE

Case Study: Youth Sports

The Americans with Disabilities Act of 1990 (ADA) "is the nation's first comprehensive civil rights law addressing the needs of people with disabilities, prohibiting discrimination in employment, public services, public accommodations, and telecommunications" (Americans with Disabilities Act of 1990, n.d.). You have a parent of your youth team who needs accommodations to watch her child compete in volleyball. What areas do you need to assess outside and inside the venue to fully comply with ADA regulations? Would your handling of ADA be different if you were the athletic administrator at a high school or club volleyball organization?

Wrap-Up

End-of-Chapter Activities
College Athletics

1. Your institution currently lacks a policy for reserving field space for teams out of season. As the athletic administrator, you are finding it difficult to balance the needs of the teams in season versus out-of-season teams. Review facility scheduling policies at two institutions and then craft your own version for your institution.

2. Your campus is the recipient of a donation that is open for usage across the academic and athletic programs at your institution. As the athletic administrator at the institution, you will need to create a persuasive presentation to secure $1 million in funding to renovate your athletic center. What are some of the highlighted points you would use to make the case that your athletic department should be the recipient of funding over competing programs on campus such as academics and student life?

High School Athletics

1. You have been asked by the high school principal to present to the community a proposal for the conversion of your grass stadium to turf. What five points would you make about the benefits of turf over grass?

2. As the athletic administrator, you have been asked by the director of sustainability to create a green initiative for your campus. There has been resistance from many in the physical plant and dining services to adopt more sustainability. Create a memo detailing the benefits of sustainability on a high school campus, citing model programs in your correspondence.

End-of-Chapter Questions

1. You have been charged with setting up a committee for your local high school to determine whether to renovate existing athletic facilities (indoor and outdoor) or build new facilities and field space. Who are some of the key players you would add to this committee and why? What are some of the outlining questions you would pose at the opening meeting for the committee to determine how to assess whether to renovate or to build?

2. Visit two facilities in any of the settings discussed in this chapter (youth, club, high school, college). On your visit, assess the athletic facilities using the following outline:
   a. Describe the facility (location, age, decor, accessibility) and its purpose for use (note whether it is multi-purpose or single purpose).
   b. Visual appearance: How does it look from the eyes of the consumer or user?
   c. What aspects of the facility need major change or improvement and why?
   d. Are there any amenities that enhance the user experience?
   e. Does the size and scope of the venue meet the needs of the organization?

3. *Sustainability* is a buzzword in athletic administration. As a future athletic administrator, describe some of the programs you would implement to create a green movement on your campus or within your entity. Craft a

comprehensive response that details the setting for the activities.

4. Visit the Green Sports Alliance website (www.greensportsalliance.org). Describe five of the activities implemented by college athletic departments that have impressed you the most. How would you incorporate some of the initiatives into the youth sport setting and the club sport setting when a campus may not be available to organize some of these sustainability programs?

5. According to the report of the World Commission on Environment and Development (1987), *sustainability* is "development that meets the needs of the present without compromising the ability of future generations to meet their own needs." First, how would you explain this definition to your staff and to your athletes? Second, what are some implementation ideas you would add to your former high school or current college?

6. Find two articles focused on the topic of ADA and new sport facility construction. Describe the content of each article and share your thoughts on planning for renovations or new construction following the mandates and guidelines provided by ADA legislation.

7. Have you ever visited a site where the access into and out of the bathroom or handicap space was not convenient for visitors? As the athletic administrator, how would you ensure that ADA requirements are fully met at your facility?

8. We are in a construction boom on college campuses. The debate continues to reveal passionate thoughts on where funding should be allocated to support spending. Find two articles online (or within your library database) that review the pros and cons of spending on athletic facilities rather than academic facilities.

9. New construction and renovations on college campuses add to the overall aesthetic beauty of the landscape. Select one college online to explore. What are some of the changes you would make to the athletic facility to remain competitive in recruitment of new students and new staff?

10. Review and critique three articles relating to facility design in two settings (select from college, high school, youth, or club sport). Provide a summary of the articles and include the managerial aspects associated with planning for a new or renovated site.

11. Visit a private sport center (indoor soccer facility, indoor baseball or softball facility) and interview the general manager or athletic administrator charged with renting the venue. Explore the types of teams that use the space across the seasons, the rate changes according to the seasons and demand for space, and the challenges associated with renting to outside groups to generate revenue streams.

12. Craft a list of 10 questions you would ask during your opening meeting with the staff so you can collect a list of needs to be considered for the facility construction.

13. Visit the website for one youth sport organization, one club organization, one high school athletic department, and one college athletic department. Can you determine which designated staff person handles the field scheduling and overall operations within these organizations? Share the job titles for each facility staff person and indicate if their roles are full-time within facility management or whether the responsibility for facility management is rolled into another position. Indicate the pros and cons for each facility management position researched.

References

Americans with Disabilities Act of 1990. (n.d.). Retrieved November 2, 2016, from https://www.eeoc.gov/eeoc/history/35th/1990s/ada.html.

BHS Intramurals. (n.d.). Retrieved November 02, 2016, from http://bhs.brookline.k12.ma.us/intramurals.html.

Boston College (2016, October 16). $200M athletics facilities plan announced. BC News. Retrieved from http://www.bc.edu/bc-web/bcnews/athletics-recreation/department-news/athletics-facilities-plans-announced.html.

Blumenthal, K. J. (2009). Collegiate recreational sports: Pivotal players in student success. *Planning for Higher Education*, 37(2), 52–62.

Byl, J. (2004). Organizing effective elementary and high school intramural programs. *Physical & Health Education Journal*, 70(3), 22.

Case, R., & Branch, D. J. (2003). A study to examine the job competencies of sport facility managers. *International Sports Journal*, 7(2), 25–39.

Dana Hills High School. (n.d.). Intramurals. Retrieved November 02, 2016, from http://www.dhhs.net/intramurals.

Elkins, D. J., Forrester, S. A., & Noël-Elkins, A. V. (2011). The contribution of campus recreational sports participation to perceived sense of campus. *Recreational Sports Journal*, 35, 24–34.

Evans, P. (2016, February 19). Soccer club kicks around $8M tournament complex. GRBJ.com. Retrieved November 01, 2016, from http://www.grbj.com/articles/84561-soccer-club-kicks-around-8m-tournament-complex.

Hall, S. (2010). Impact of facility maintenance on campus recreational sports departments at public universities in the United States. *Recreational Sports Journal*, 34, 103–111.

Henchy, A. (2011). The influence of campus recreation beyond the gym. *Recreational Sports Journal*, 35, 174–181.

Howard, K., Bocarro, J. N., & Kanters, M. A. (2013). Strategies for creating successful joint use agreements: A case study. *Journal of Park and Recreation Administration*, 31(1), 98–107.

Hurd, A. R. (2005). Competency development for entry level public parks and recreation professionals. *Journal of Park and Recreation Administration*, 23, 45–62.

Kampf, S. (2010). Impact of college recreation centers on enrollment. *Recreational Sports Journal*, 34(2), 122–118.

Kampf, S., & Teske, E. J. (2013). Collegiate recreation participation and retention. *Recreational Sports Journal*, 37(2), 85–96.

Kanters, M. A., Bocarro, J. N., Filardo, M., Edwards, M. B., McKenzie, T. L., & Floyd, M. F. (2014). Shared use of school facilities with community organizations and afterschool physical activity program participation: A cost-benefit assessment. Journal of School Health, 84(5): 302–309.

Lower, L. M., Turner, B. A., & Petersen, J. C. (2013). A comparative analysis of perceived benefits of participation between recreational sport programs. *Recreational Sports Journal*, 37, 66–83.

Mather, J. (2016). Lonestar acquires 22 acres to build cutting-edge soccer facility. #OurTurf [online]. Retrieved from https://www.lonestar-sc.com/news/post/ourturf.

Mt. Lebanon School District. (n.d.). Intramural sports at the high school. Retrieved November 2, 2016, from http://www.mtlsd.org/page.cfm?p=1005.

National Recreation and Parks Association (n.d.). CAPRA Agency Accreditation. Retrieved October 23, 2018, from https://www.nrpa.org/certification/accreditation/CAPRA/.

National Resources Defense Council (2013, August). Collegiate game changers: How campus sport is going green. Retrieved from www.nrdc.org/resources/collegiate-game-changers-how-campus-sport-going-green.

NCAA (2013). A greener gameday. Retrieved November 2, 2016, from http://www.ncaa.org/about/resources/media-center/news/greener-gameday.

PAC-12 Conference (2015, June 29). PAC-12 joins its members as official partner of the Green Sports Alliance. Retrieved from http://pac-12.com/article/2015/06/29/pac-12-joins-its-members-official-partner-green-sports-alliance.

Report of the World Commission on Environment and Development: Our Common Future (n.d.). Retrieved November 2, 2016, from http://www.un-documents.net/our-common-future.pdf

SI Play. (2012, April 12). Go green with online sports registration software Retrieved from https://www.siplay.com/blog/go-green-with-online-sports-registration-software

Steinbach, P. (2008, June). For-profit facilities meet demand for community fields. *Athletic Business*. Retrieved from http://www.athleticbusiness.com/Outdoor/for-profit-facilities-meet-demand-for-community-fields.html.

Sullivan, K. (2016, February 10). Stanford athletics is showing its "greener" side. *Stanford News*. Retrieved from http://news.stanford.edu/2016/02/10/green-athletics-muir-021016/.

Sustainability. (n.d.). Michigan Athletics. Retrieved November 2, 2016, from http://www.mgoblue.com/sustainability/.

Tarantino, M., & Andresen. (2015, January 1). So you want to be a facilities manager? Sports Turf. Retrieved from http://sturf.lib.msu.edu/article/2015jan.pdf.

thesavageway. (2015). YMCA takes on sustainable advertising. Retrieved November 2, 2016, from http://thesavageway.com/ymca-takes-on-sustainable-advertising/.

The National Recreation and Parks Association. (n.d.). Retrieved October 23, 2018, from https://www.nrpa.org/certification/accreditation/CAPRA/.

Toperzer, L., Anderson, D. M., & Barcelona, R. J. (2011). Best practices in student development for campus recreation professionals. *Recreational Sports Journal*, 35, 145–156.

Tyahla, D. (2016, February 1). From the power of the permit. National Recreation and Park Association. Retrieved November 2, 2016, from https://www.nrpa.org/parks-recreation-magazine/2016/february/the-power-of-the-permit/.

Webb, E., & Forrester, S. (2015). Affective outcomes of intramural sport participation. *Recreational Sports Journal*, 39, 69–81.

Whithead, B. (2014, September). Maintaining school athletic fields on limited budgets. *SportsTurf*, 26–27. Retrieved from http://sturf.lib.msu.edu/article/2014sep26b.pdf.

Yale University. (n.d.). Case study. Retrieved November 2, 2016, from https://www.nrdc.org/sites/default/files/collegiate-game-changers-Yale-case-study.pdf.

Zhang, J. (2015, October 20). Students promote environmental sustainability in athletics. *The Amherst Student*. Retrieved from http://amherststudent.amherst.edu/?q=article/2015/10/20/students-promote-environmental-sustainability-athletics.

CHAPTER 5

Marketing and Branding

▶ Sport Marketing

Visibility of athletic programs and activities has never been more important for athletic administrators. There is internal and external competition to craft programs to entice sport-savvy consumers while also showcasing optimal elements of each sport program. Marketing is the administrative arm that promotes activities and engages participants to create memorable experiences for fans and athletes. Numerous tools and ideas have surfaced, with the field of athletic administration generating promotional ideas that make the games more of an experience. Although athletic administrators emphasize team performance and individual athletic achievements, the new thrust in marketing includes mascot contests, team rivalries, and pregame promotions, all aimed to entertain spectators beyond the core aspects of the game and into an arena filled with entertainment and interactivity.

Marketing encompasses advertising, promoting, creating awareness about the sport product, and ultimately persuading target groups to initiate some action such as purchasing merchandise, registering for a team, or attending an event. The variety of sport settings—youth, community, club, high school, and collegiate athletics—challenges athletic

© Brand X Pictures/Stockbyte/Getty Images.

TABLE 5.1 Target Markets	
Athletic Setting	**Target Market Focus (Refined or Specific Group of Focus)**
Youth	Parents, children, school
Club	Parents, children
Community	Parents, children, school
High school	Parents, students, student-athletes, community members
College	Students, student-athletes, high school students, parents, alumni

administrators to use a large range of methods to market to target groups. Because of the differentiation of each sport setting and the competition to satisfy participants, athletic administrators continually identify effective modes to connect with target groups (**TABLE 5.1**).

The task of identifying the core group for participation in designated sport programs or delineating which groups should be targeted for fan-related events takes diligence, time, and focus. Target markets are considered the core group of people who will consume or use the sport product. Identifying the needs, wants, and desires of this core group is the first step of marketing for athletic administrators because the majority of promotional programming and advertising will be developed to meet this group's needs. Once target markets are identified, interactions between athletic departments and these consumers is direct and deliberate. Marketing efforts are tailored to the group's unique interests, with the end goal of the target group engaging in some way.

Definition of Sports Marketing

Sports marketing is the practice of using teams, venues, athletes, sports events, and sports media to separate a brand from its competitors. For decades, sports marketing had been perceived as brand-centric, with many marketers aiming to build brands solely through impressions. Recently, sports marketing has migrated to a consumer-centric model with the inclusion of integrated initiatives and programs that interact with the consumer beyond brand awareness. Sports marketers understand how to use the assets of sports entities—individually or in combination—to drive consumers to purchase products and services of one particular brand over another.

Reproduced with permission from Mullin, B.J., Hardy, S., & Sutton, W.A. (2007). Sport marketing (3rd ed.). Champaign, IL: Human Kinetics.

Exchange Relationship

To satisfy the needs of target groups, an exchange relationship develops between the athletic administrator and the consumer (fan or participant). Athletic administrators showcase the worth of the athletic program; in exchange, the target group will join, purchase, and sign up for offerings. From the athletic administration perspective, the programs need to be considered "of value" or "valuable" (enriching, educational, skill enhancement) to the market; in return, the target group will "give up" something of value (e.g., money, participation). In simple terms, the marketing aim for athletic programs across all settings is to persuade participants to affiliate with the program. This is an example of transactional marketing, whereby "transactional exchanges depend on extrinsic factors such as money or other rewards (price discounts, coupons, giveaways) in exchange for a good or service" (Bee & Kahle, 2006).

Marketing is an extension of the culture of the athletic department or program through the communication of events, games, and program highlights. Athletic administrators use many forms of marketing methods, depending on the sport setting, department philosophy, and budget. In terms of personnel assigned to marketing, in the high school setting the athletic director may handle the operational aspects of marketing and then place other staff in charge of implementing the ideas. In the collegiate setting, depending on the size and scope of the department, one person may be in charge of marketing while there could be an entire dedicated marketing staff within the athletic department at another school. For club sports and municipal recreational programs, once again depending on the reach of the programs, there may be a staff member dedicated to marketing and promotions. Within town-based sports managed by volunteers, there may be one person charged with carrying out the program functions, with committee members supporting each initiative.

Sports information directors (SIDs) assume responsibility for connecting with target groups by creating websites, social media accounts, media guides, marketing activities, and public relations within the high school and collegiate levels. The titles or designations attached to the marketing staff managing marketing and promotional efforts have evolved. Today, titles such as sports information director, media relations director, and social media manager are interchangeable when describing personnel overseeing the operations of marketing to constituent groups. In collegiate or high school athletics, positions might include an associate athletic director for marketing; a candidate should possess strong communication and computer skills along with the ability to formulate outreach to students, faculty, community, and media.

▶ Marketing Mix

Marketing encompasses four distinct elements often referenced as the *marketing mix* or the four P's: product, place, promotion, and price. For athletic programs, the *product* is the actual service the sport entity is providing to athletes, fans, and spectators. In the mind of the consumer, the quality of the product attaches value to the given sport program. *Price* refers to the actual cost to participate, including fees to play or memberships. Where the physical events occur (practices and games) constitutes the third component: *place*. Notably, place can be the physical location or the platform used to sell the product or service (online, site store). *Promotion* refers to the varied methods the athletic entity will employ to advertise the features of their sport programming.

Within youth recreation programs, the marketing mix, when executed, can increase attendance and build community awareness (Marquis, 2017). As Marquis further explained, if the cost for a recreational program is too high, potential athletes might not sign up; if the costs are too low, the department risks not covering its expenses. In terms of promotion, the strategy needs to be aimed at parents because the participants are minors (Marquis, 2017). "Successful marketing and promotions will build awareness of the programs your staff has worked so hard to develop and convince your audience that they need to sign-up and participate" ("Promoting Youth Sports Programs," 2017).

Undoubtedly, the 4 P's of the marketing mix have evolved over time. Today, the marketing philosophy has shifted into relationship marketing. Gummesson (2017) mapped marketing changes from the pre-1970s as the traditional marketing mix variables where "services and relationships were absent" to the 1970s to the 2000s timeframe; "relationship marketing," "customer relationship management," and "customer satisfaction" were highlighted aspects of business marketing (p. 17). The 2000s to the present has seen a variety of networks available to reach consumers, with a focus on "cocreation of value in complex service systems is in the making: do with others" (p. 17). Goi (2009) asserts that sentiment is that the current form of the marketing mix may not be an effective management tool, prompting marketers to use new or diverse methods to reach consumers (p. 3).

Much more attention has been placed on satisfying the consumer, and with that shift a new classification for defining the marketing mix has emerged. Lauterborn (1990) depicts the four C's of marketing—*consumer, cost, convenience*, and *communication*—all directed at meeting the needs of the target market. According to Smith (2003), the shift towards the 4 C's does not render the 4 P's obsolete; instead, both components can be fully embraced by athletic administrators to reach target audiences. As Lauterborn asserts, "You can't sell whatever you can make anymore. You can only sell what someone specifically wants to buy." Athletic administrators can look at formulating marketing plans with the 4 P's

Kar, A. (2011). 4Cs of Marketing – The Marketing Mix. Retrieved from: http://business-fundas.com/2011/4-cs-of-marketing-the-marketing-mix/ [Accessed 3 September 2018]

while also integrating strategies that focus on the needs of the athletic participant or fan and building strong relationships and ties with those stakeholders.

Marketing Plan

All the traditional elements of the marketing mix (product, price, place, and promotion) need to be defined before the athletic administrator embarks on crafting any or all of the marketing plan to reach organizational aims. There are several ways to create marketing plans, and the final outcome does not need to be formally written or communicated, but the blueprint does need to include basic elements for successful implementation. A marketing plan includes objectives, strategies, and a budget. Objectives are defined as pathways that lead to accomplishing organizational goals. Although goals are considered the ultimate direction for a company, the athletic administrator who is developing a marketing plan needs to determine how the marketing efforts will contribute to the realization of those goals. Objectives, for ease of understanding, are the tasks and jobs the staff will chip away at each day at work. Meeting marketing objectives will, in turn, lead to the successful achievement of goals. An example of an objective for a club lacrosse team would be to recruit and sign 30 more club players for the fall season. Meeting that objective may help the club team achieve its goal of increasing membership. The marketing plan is a map that prepares the staff to stay on track with marketing efforts. The purpose of a marketing plan is to communicate the goals of the department within the realm of marketing along with the objectives that will help reach those goals. **FIGURE 5.1** showcases a goal within the collegiate setting.

Marketing Strategies

Athletic administrators must craft specific pathways to attain desired marketing results. Marketing strategies lead to achieving stated

It is the goal of the Marketing and Promotions Department at Washington State University to provide the students, alumni, student-athletes, staff, and community with exceptional promotional support for all 17 varsity sports teams. Consistent with the mission and values of Washington State University, our department provides current and fun interactive promotions to enhance the Cougar brand. We are dedicated to building a brand that is larger and richer than wins and losses, and to make the loyal Cougar fan into a supporter of: I am a WSU Cougar. (Washington State University Athletics, 2017)

FIGURE 5.1 Marketing Goals

objectives. For the youth lacrosse club to increase enrollment by 30 players, athletic administrators must adjust their marketing efforts within the marketing mix (product, price, place, promotion). To be effective, the athletic administrator takes one more step in the process by determining which target markets need to be reached and then designing specific and directed programming to appeal to that group (players and their families, in this example). To accomplish the marketing

Target Market

objective, the sport entity needs to devote time and funding to these aims. In some cases, marketing can be a low- or no-cost endeavor. However, best practices in athletic administration suggest the use of realistic budgets to implement marketing strategies. Lastly, in any process, athletic administrators monitor the strategies to ensure the objectives are met and determine if more action is necessary to make the marketing plan a success.

A clear marketing advantage enjoyed by athletic administrators is the existing passion of participants and the fan base toward their sport affiliation. Athletic administrators can leverage loyalty and allegiance because they already have a captive audience in their fan and participant base who are consistently demonstrating their willingness to support the program aims by attending games and even purchasing team gear. Furthermore, "sports consumers [who] exhibit sports-loyal behaviors, such as repeat purchasing and continued attendance, are the key to a sports organization's success" (Bee & Kahle, 2006). The stakeholders in athletic administration all have core needs that can be addressed through marketing strategies. Athletes want to participate and excel in the sporting arena, fans enjoy watching and purchasing

merchandise to show their support and affiliation with sport teams, and spectators (who are often parents) have an emotional stake in the achievements of the athletes along with the success of the program. Savvy athletic marketers leverage the already passionate and emotional stakeholders (participants, fans, parents) to create promotional programs that accentuate those feelings. Engaging sport marketing activities piggyback on the emotional attachment people have with the teams, athletes, and programs. "Given the natural visibility of athletics, the enhancement and further development of brand management strategies may be greatly improved through athletics. For many higher education institutions, athletics may be the most visible form of exposure. Branding and image enhancement are crucial aspects of sport marketing and organizational development initiatives" (Gregg, Pierce, Lee, Himstead, & Felver, p. 157).

Situational Analysis

Before embarking on a marketing plan, athletic administrators conduct a *situational analysis*. This requires researching the current marketplace, offerings, and consumer base. In essence, the situational analysis helps athletic administrators feel the "pulse" of the current sport landscape and where their program is comparably positioned. A situational analysis has two parts: (1) internal (what the entity can control and manipulate) and (2) external (what the entity cannot control but needs to anticipate and monitor). For a lacrosse club, the internal factors might be the colors of the uniforms, the number of staff coaches, the software applications used, the number of tournaments the teams enter, and membership fees. The athletic administrator can easily control or manipulate the internal environment. On the other hand, external factors include aspects that are not controlled by athletic administrators, which presents a bigger challenge.

FIGURE 5.2 Marketing Strategy for Town Softball Program

For a lacrosse club, external elements include the following.

Trends in lacrosse: Do young people in a particular region favor lacrosse over other sports?

Economics: Do consumers have more discretionary income or is unemployment high and thus families are less able to afford club sport?

Regulations: Does the lacrosse governing body have new rules in place that affect the sport such as the size of the lacrosse stick head being changed or a requirement that female players wear protective gear?

Technology: Are there new methods or materials used to produce lacrosse equipment and sticks?

What the competition is doing: Do competitors have a new facility, are they offering discounts, what tournaments are they entered in, and what will differentiate your entity from the competition?

The external factors may not be easily changed or manipulated by the athletic administrator, but they certainly need to be anticipated to stay current in a fast-changing marketplace. After conducting the situational analysis, the athletic administrator assesses opportunities to propel the entity forward.

SWOT Analysis

One step of a situational analysis is to conduct a SWOT analysis—that is, identify strengths, weaknesses, opportunities, and threats—for the sport entity (see **FIGURE 5.3**). Strengths of an athletic department constitute all of the positive elements of the program and what the entity is known for (e.g., competition, player development, sportsmanship). Weaknesses are elements that the athletic administrator must attack to change and improve. Any activities that provide the athletic department with chances to expand its offerings, partner with new groups, or even save money fall

Strengths	Weaknesses
New club with college-level coaching and lower price point than competitors	New club with low name or brand recognition; rents fields and does not own a complex, making practice and game schedules more difficult and costly

Opportunities	Threats
Recruitment of new talent; new option for female lacrosse players; partnership with facility to enhance programming	Securing new players and new coaches for an untested new program in a saturated market space

FIGURE 5.3 SWOT Analysis: Girls' lacrosse Team

under opportunities. Athletic administrators who adopt an entrepreneurial spirit reap the benefits of acquiring new ventures to elevate their programming. Any competition, policies, or legislation that impede the progress of the athletic entity would fall under the threat category. Athletic administrators must be vigilant and steadfast in the anticipation of any threats that may affect future offerings. All of the variables of the SWOT analysis add to the athletic administrator's toolbox and aid in the marketing efforts.

Branding

Branding is the creation of an image or reputation that immediately comes to the consumer's mind when hearing the organization's name. According to the American Marketing Association (1960), "a brand is a name, term, design, symbol, or any other feature that identifies one seller's good or service as distinct from those of other sellers." Branding drives marketing and merchandising and "sticks" in the minds of the consumer, prompting affirmative consumption and purchase-related decisions. *Branding* is a term receiving much attention among athletic administrators partly because of the evolution of marketing, specifically with social media platforms and outlets. Evidence of marketing's critical importance is the process of *rebranding*. Schools are initiating campaigns to increase interest in and the popularity of their programs through initiatives such as rebranding mascots to enhance athletic department and school images. In simple terms, a brand is an entity's essence and determines how others depict the entity. Ultimately, a brand is the athletic department's identity and what is conveyed to the general public. A brand comprises not only the teams but also the coaches, facilities, uniforms, mascots, and even the style of play.

Athletic administrators can tap current literature within the sport management industry to develop a process for launching marketing plans. Welde (2017) published the following general framework that athletic administrators could adopt to enhance the brand of the department:

- Streamline a universal logo for consistency across all teams and programs.
- Define the organization in a consistent and clear message.
- Represent the brand at all times to showcase the commitment to the vision of the entity.
- Network in the community to increase word-of-mouth marketing and position the brand.
- Maximize the benefits of getting involved in community service or goodwill events for community members.
- Have a social media marketing plan.
- Use the alumni database (or a database of past members) (Weide, 2017).

Branding is a significant marketing tool for athletic administrations. Philip Kotler developed a six-step model for companies to

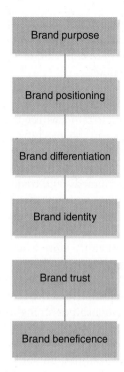

FIGURE 5.4 Philip Kotler's Six-Step Branding Conceptual Model

Kotler (2016)

follow when building a brand. The purpose is to help companies (or sport entities) understand that just establishing a brand by creating a name and logo is not enough. There are other facets of branding necessary to successfully reach the consumer (see **FIGURE 5.4**).

Communication of a sport brand helps consumers identify with the team or program. The mission of the athletic entity is conveyed through the *brand purpose* in terms of what the lacrosse club, as an example, can offer to participants. *Brand positioning* starts "with establishing a frame of reference, which signals to consumers the goal they can expect to achieve by using a brand" (Keller, Sternthal, & Tybout, 2002). Notably, "positioning refers to acquiring a space in the mind of the customer, whereas differentiation is a marketing strategy companies use to make their product unique to stand out from competitors" (Keller et al., 2002). Simply stated, *brand differentiation* is what makes the lacrosse club unique in comparison to the competition.

Brand identity should be a consistent message received by its audience (Lake, 2018). Athletic administrators within the marketing realm intend to shape how participants and consumers perceive their programming through various means of communication, including social media and traditional advertising. Chaudhuri and Holbrook (2001) assert there is a strong relationship between trust and loyalty. Sport participants and consumers trust the sport entity more when the athletic entity is reputable and delivers on its declarations. When trust forms between the participant or consumer and the sport entity, the exchange relationship is strengthened. There have been many social action initiatives by sport entities. Actions such as the green movement in facilities, donations of gear to underprivileged areas, and sportsmanship efforts all lead to serving the community and society as a whole, and is best described as *brand beneficence.*

Several branding initiatives have been introduced by collegiate athletic administrators that focus on centralizing branding campaigns and images associated with the athletic department. Columbia University's branding initiative includes a newly designed website, new signage in the athletic facilities, refreshed athletics wordmark or logotype, and the launch of a new social media hashtag—#OnlyHere—to embody the four pillars of Columbia athletics (Columbia University, n.d.).

The University of Massachusetts Lowell (UMass Lowell) has instituted brand identity guidelines for all staff and vendors working with the school:

> UMass Lowell must capture the affinity of fans, boosters, faculty, students, parents, student-athletes, coaches, staff and the general public in order

to be successful. While logos, colors, and typefaces are not the only elements of an institution's brand, they are its visual representation and commonly what individuals identify with first. To avoid brand confusion and integrity erosion, it is paramount an institution's marks and symbols are consistent. (University of Massachusetts Lowell, n.d.)

The use of athletics as a tool to build a brand is not an uncommon strategy in many higher education institutions. For many campuses, athletics has been used to create awareness not only about athletic programs but also about academic opportunities (Clark, Apostolopoulou, Branvold, & Synowka, 2009). A powerful aspect of athletic administration is the notion that

> A college or university logo is often the most recognizable symbol of the institution. The logo is used on the website, letterhead, campus signage, T-shirts, hats, mugs, pens, and all other miscellaneous swag. This omnipresent symbol represents who you are, what you stand for and what you have to offer. Needless to say, the logo is a big deal. (Vision Point Marketing, 2015)

Email signatures are another branding piece that relays consistency when communicating internally and externally. The matching email signature across the athletic entity demonstrates professionalism in transmitting a uniform and consistent brand to the receiver.

An example of the impact of an athletic logo is showcased by Oregon State University's athletics partnership with shoe and apparel manufacturer Nike, which aims to create new brand identity standards by incorporating "a refined contemporary Beaver mark to be used consistently by all intercollegiate athletic teams, a custom typeface and numeral set, and primary and secondary color palettes" (https://news.nike.com/news/oregon-state-athletics-unveils-new-brand-identity). Within all settings from college, high school, youth, and club sport, the visual representation—whether a logo, mascot, or colors—creates brand recognition for the consumer and leads to an attachment to the sport entity and a feeling or sentiment about the sport organization. Coupled with the image of the sport entity, brand recognition can enhance the reputation of the program, which builds further awareness and attention toward programming—one of the aims of sport marketing.

 FEEDBACK FROM THE FIELD

Best Practices: Marketing and Branding

The primary role of Seacoast United's Director of Media and Communications, Kelly Kelly, involves maintaining websites for the various clubs, e-marketing campaigns, managing mobile applications, and social media management (newly added for Seacoast United is a dedicated person working on the social media accounts). She also operates all aspects of uniforms and apparel for all clubs, management of the online shop, and other projects such as tournament scheduling and staff scheduling. Seacoast United has four designated staff members to handle the club's marketing efforts. In addition, the chief executive officer plays a significant role in advertising and sponsorships.

Seacoast United's footprint has expanded over the years, and the enterprise now operates out of 10 facilities across Massachusetts, New Hampshire, and Maine. Seacoast United originally started as a soccer club, but the organization has made a real effort to expand its reach and the variety of sports it offers. Seacoast United's baseball program was recognized as the largest baseball club in New England in 2017. Seacoast United's field hockey club is the largest in both New Hampshire and Maine. Kelly explains that because of the growth of the organization, Seacoast United currently has dedicated staff members working on various aspects of marketing to ensure that the programs are promoted effectively. She notes that it is "important that families have a good experience with the program(s) they are involved in, as word of mouth goes such a long way." She adds, "Seacoast United is celebrating its 25th anniversary in 2017, and we want to be known as *the* place for sports, to have families associating youth sports with Seacoast United and vice versa. This will continue to build upon the 'New England's Home for Sports' campaign that was started in mid-2016."

Seacoast United has been a trailblazer with the many applications that parents, coaches, and players use for team-management purposes and tournaments. Kelly also connects sponsor companies within those platforms for advertising purposes. She explains that the process originated with the tournament app, an idea that came to her a few years ago while she was coaching one of her teams. As a coach, she always scrambled for all the logistical information for tournaments because information on schedules, events, and field locations were never centrally located on one website. She yearned to pull as much of the essential information together in one place for teams and families attending tournaments hosted by Seacoast United to create a "better experience and include a tool that not all events have available to their guests." As Kelly pointed out, the feedback on the tournament app has been extremely positive and widely used since its introduction in 2013. The Seacoast United Soccer Club (SUSC) mobile app followed with a facility- and organization-based purpose. This app is different than what most clubs use because it goes beyond just displaying rosters and contacts for each team. Kelly wanted an app to keep the

(continues)

client base informed, with special offers available within the club's community and to recognize local businesses.

For Kelly, the app is an opportunity to get more people involved, especially smaller businesses that have been interested in working with Seacoast United but did not have a large advertising budget. The apps, and what Seacoast United now refers to as a "web package," allow those businesses to advertise at a lower cost. Seacoast United will work with these businesses to create special deals for their membership, such as coupons and discounts. As Kelly referenced, these businesses reap the benefits of the app through their exposure to families who use the app and redeem the business coupons and discounts and create more foot traffic at these establishments.

Kelly has created many branding-related activities via social media. Seacoast United incorporated a couple of marketing campaigns that are related specifically to social media and are tied into the web package. Each week, Seacoast United promotes a local business to its followers as the "Business of the Week" (BOTW) and includes any special offers they may have running at the time. The use of hashtags #SeacoastBOTW and #SupportLocal creates a buzz about the business and the collaboration. Kelly points out that the demographics vary on the social media accounts, with Facebook seeing more parental interaction, while Instagram and Snapchat activities appeal to the younger crowd. The players love seeing the posts on Instagram and tag each other frequently. Seacoast United has success in posting action photos and "fun" photos and videos of their players. Kelly feels strongly that "there are so many things that can be posted on the social media accounts to engage the families within our club, and beyond." It is not surprising that the accounts need to be monitored closely when anyone can comment (good and bad) on the posts. Along with that, criticism needs to be addressed, and inappropriate content must be blocked and deleted.

Seacoast United has a systematic outreach process for its numerous corporate sponsors and partners. For Seacoast United, Kelly explained, outreach is broken down into cold calling (75 percent) and referrals (25 percent). In terms of cold calling, Seacoast United identifies businesses that are physically close to their indoor and outdoor facilities. The aim is to have a face-to-face meeting with a decision maker, either at his or her place of work or at the facility. Kelly believes the meeting at the facility prompts the company to be more inclined toward action. For Seacoast United, cross marketing comes into play when working with companies that have a significant presence at the regional or national levels. With so many programs and satellite clubs, sports, and facilities that require attention from a marketing perspective, the biggest challenge is making sure all programs are accounted for and marketed appropriately. As Kelly points out, the marketing team ensures it allows plenty of time to promote programs prior to their start date. If the marketing is left too late or the marketing team is not given enough notice, it is difficult to put an effective campaign together. Their campaigns are multifaceted, involving social media, email, radio, and several other outlets. Another challenge is ensuring these programs do not conflict with one another. For example, during the summer, SUSC offers several residential camps across the club. The club makes a concerted effort to ensure there are no other competing camps taking place that week that might affect player enrollment.

Seacoast United secures many sponsors. With each one, Seacoast tries to create a "partnership" to ensure positive benefits are experienced by both partners in the relationship. This mindset pays off in terms of sponsor renewal rates. Dependent on the partner and the sponsorship package agreed on, there is some cross promotion involved between the businesses.

When offering advice to students planning to enter athletic administration and when it comes to social media, marketing, sponsorship, and branding, Kelly's perspective is for students to "stay up to date on the latest trends as far as marking and educate yourself on how the various outlets appeal to different demographics. Give the client what they want to see (relevant to the organization you're representing) to make them feel that they are a part of your organization, both from a business side as well as participating families."

▶ Market Research

Athletic administrators use research to ascertain which methods of marketing and types of promotions are most effective and resonate the most with their core groups. Athletic administrators may choose to segment the market by various characteristics such as gender, age, participation rates, purchase habits, and economic status to better understand the needs, wants, and desires of core groups and modify marketing efforts to appeal to specific populations. When groups of people share similar characteristics, they can be categorized as a *segment* or segment of the targeted population. Segmenting the market breaks down all the possible consumer groups into a core sector. Once the core market is defined and segmented, the athletic administrator can tailor specific promotional, marketing, and advertising campaigns and activities to this group.

Demographics

Demographics is the first step in identifying a concentrated target market. It is the defining characteristic of a group of people such as age, gender, marital status, income, education, or any traits that assist marketers in knowing as much as possible about these consumers and participants. The information collected and analyzed through demographics lends to a more targeted and focused marketing campaign. For the youth lacrosse club we have been referencing, the target market demographic would include the age, gender, and region of the core target market. The core target market constitutes the primary

group the club aims to target. Perhaps the lacrosse club wants to expand the club to younger players; the club would target girls ages six to nine as the core market, so the materials used to create awareness about the club are geared toward females of this age category and their parents. Conceivably, there may be many novice players in this age category, so the wording needs to reflect the aims of the program as "developmental" and "fun."

The pictures used in any promotions or marketing would also need to depict coaches involved with teaching the game while providing clear instruction to participants, all aimed to appeal to a specific target group: the parents of young females. Athletic administrators seek to learn as much as they can about core groups, collecting information and data to determine what they desire and how to meet their needs. The youth lacrosse club, as an example, may employ an existing database or share a database from similar groups to promote any new programming. Even starting with the database of current members, announcing a new program can be one way for the lacrosse club to solicit interest. Furthermore, the lacrosse club benefits from linking with schools in the area to generate interest through the district-wide email distribution list, and by connecting via social media to announce new programs for specific age groups. The ultimate goal for the lacrosse club is to increase registrants for the program. Driving interest and traffic to the website so parents can learn more about the offerings will increase registrations for the program. The initial perception of the program (i.e., branding) is generated through and by the website's visual and written content. The website serves as the communication hub to visitors, explaining the core aspects of the program and all offerings. The ease of navigation to locate details coupled with the simplicity of the registration process is critical to the success of the marketing efforts. If parents or guardians have difficulty registering children, then they may abandon the attempt and find another sport program.

Mascots and Logos

Athletic programs rely on images and symbols to convey messages about their programs. Both mascots and logos are visual depictions of the strengths of the athletic entity chosen to represent the pillars and vision of the sport organization. In essence, mascots and logos are part of the athletic brand. Mascots have evolved into an effective marketing tool that helps athletic administrators connect with target groups.

It is customary in the athletic setting to rename and redesign outdated mascots to give the athletic entity an updated look and feel or brand. Athletic administrators may still use an original mascot as a way to build connections with target groups. For example, a promotional activity such as naming the mascot is a method to enhance awareness about a program and grow interest from the target groups. Logos and mascots are often consumers' first impression of the entity. Given the power of the visual representation of the sport organization, it is time well spent to invest hours upon hours in weighing the pros and cons of various color patterns and mascot designs.

Uniform Design

Along with logos and mascots, uniform selection and design is a branding opportunity for athletic administrators. Colleges, high schools, and club sports spend a great deal of money selecting uniforms from top brands to elicit an image of quality and athleticism to fans and perhaps even recruit potential student-athletes. When uniforms are appealing, the fan base becomes attracted to the brand and coloring and will, in turn, purchase merchandise to display affiliation with a specific team or program. From athletes to coaches to fans, the consistency in apparel design creates a powerful message of unity and thus embodies the image of the entity.

Public Relations

Public relations is a potent communication method to deliver a clear, concise message through various outlets to inform target groups about programs to prompt a desired action by groups to buy or sign up for programming. Public relations can be "defined as making, developing, protecting mutually sound, correct and reliable relations with individuals or organizations with whom they are in contact, creating positive images in the eye of public opinion and being integrated with the community" (Goksel & Serarslan, 2015, p. 276). Many athletic organizations engage in goodwill events such as free clinics for community groups that, in turn, aid in program promotion. Prompts such as "bring a friend to practice," "early bird registration," and "sibling discounts" generate interest from potential participants. All public relations messaging is controlled by the athletic administrator, allowing for complete design and targeted meaning toward the consumer group(s).

One aspect of marketing is the fact that the perception consumers often maintain about a sport program (accurate or not) in essence becomes the reality and belief about that program. What consumers communicate (written, by word of mouth, or through social media outlets) plays a main role in the messaging shaped around a particular program. The marketing methods used by athletic administrators vary from online communications such as social media and websites to face-to-face interactions, word of mouth, and even traditional forms of publicity such as printed flyers and newspaper advertisements. Athletic administrators can engage current participants to become ambassadors for the program, aiding in positive messaging and recruitment of new participants. Assigning tasks to parents, players, and coaches to solicit new interest for athletic programs serves to broaden the network for the athletic entity while also expanding the brand to new markets.

Marketing does not always need to happen within the walls of the athletic department. There are various opportunities for sport entities to collaborate and link with other groups to promote programming. Cross promotion materializes when athletic administrators join with external partners, serving to increase registration through activities such as passing out fliers at high school events for youth sports, sharing databases between two different sports in the same area to use contact information, or asking schools to send out emails to students regarding sport programming.

Fan Engagement

Spectators have emotional attachments to the teams and athletes they support. Athletic administrators formulate strategies to keep fans interested in the game and connected to the program throughout the season and beyond. Passionate and strong links bind fans to sports and need to be nurtured and supported through pinpointed marketing efforts that appeal to fans who consume a variety of aspects about their favorite sport program, including statistics, game-day reports, season analyses, rankings, and photos. They crave the inner details about their team and athletes, and the athletic administrator controls the platform by which the information is disseminated. Furthermore, these fan-focused strategies serve not only to satisfy fans' needs but also to thoroughly connect fans to the team.

At the collegiate level, athletic marketing directors engage and inform fans by employing strategies consisting of half-time promotions, game-day brochures, local business sponsors, radio advertisements, game-day giveaways, newspaper advertisements, and Internet advertising (Martin, Miller, Elsisi, Bowers, & Hall, 2011). Within town recreational programs, awareness coupled with explanations of the benefits of sport and exercise are the ingredients needed to effectively market programs and offerings. With a variety of competing programs within one town or municipality, "the public park and recreation department might take a lead role in identifying and communicating all the public and private opportunities for physical activity that exist in the community" (Henderson et al., 2001, p. 39).

Promotional activities serve several purposes, including informing targeted groups about programs and building interest in the sport entity. Collegiate and high school programs mirror the promotional efforts commonly used at professional minor and major league sporting events. Attractions such as half-time promotions have dual significance through attraction and retention. The giveaways and entertainment may appeal to fans, in turn prompting them to attend the game (attraction); on a secondary level, the promotion may, in fact, keep fans in their seats for the entire game (retention). Some athletic administrators create teasers that require fans to get a ticket for a giveaway and for the fan to remain at the game in its entirety to ensure a full crowd is supporting the home team. Using "teasers" allows athletic administrators to control the flow of attendance while also providing entertainment value to the fans and spectators. The end result of any promotion is to have a venue full of spectators and support for the teams. When teams at the high school or collegiate levels have low attendance, a simple promotional campaign may be all that is needed to create an influx of interest for the game. Athletic administrators use creative means to get students and spectators to attend the game and to stay for the entire game.

Athletic administrators also create unique promotional campaigns within the game to entice fans to purchase tickets. The University of Maryland offers group packages for 14 or more fans, allowing participants to be part of an autograph session and group announcement during the game. Typically, group sales ticket prices are discounted. Some promotions at University of Maryland games include free winter hats to the first 1,000 fans, high school team night with no charge for attendance, and youth lacrosse night offering admission to players wearing their jerseys (University of Maryland, 2017). At Kennesaw State University in Georgia, some of the promotions tied to ticketing for women's basketball games include free pedometers for the first 250 fans,

$1 hotdogs, postgame autographs, a pajama party, and a postgame movie (Kennesaw State University, n.d.).

Bowen (2016) provides a seven-step plan to increase attendance at sporting events: (1) advertise within the school and to the community, (2) announce game details through social media and within the halls of the institution, (3) engage student leaders to uncover reasons for lack of attendance and present ideas to improve attendance, (4) use social media to strategically connect with fans and the community, (5) be focused on customer service so game times, parking, and hours for workers are convenient, (6) donate empty seats to a youth organization or charitable group, and (7) host a party to create an event within an event to motivate students to attend the games and celebrate together watching the game.

 FEEDBACK FROM THE FIELD

Best Practices: Athletic Director James Coffey, Falmouth High School, Maine

Coffey has a wealth of experience in creating buzz around sporting events at the high school level. Before securing his position at Falmouth High School, Coffey served as athletic director at Winthrop High School and Beverly High School in Massachusetts. Each setting presented emerging opportunities to foster school spirit through marketing and promotional activities. From the start, Coffey believed that student-driven events work best. As he points out, the students enjoy coming up with themes as they show support for their teams. For example, color days such as "Whiteout Days" where all students wear white to the game or Christmas Day in September where students show support dressed in holiday-themed clothes. Any theme that gets the student body excited, Coffey explains, works to build an event within the event.

Coffey shared his experiences with a promotional 50–50 raffle in which the winner gets a chance to win the other half of the raffle funds by shooting and making a half-court shot. Many people came to the game for that chance to shoot the half-court shot, Coffey said, which is another example of how creativity with promotions can serve to increase attendance and energy at these games. Coffey encourages students to write proposals for marketing or promotional activities to be reviewed and vetted by the athletic department. As Coffey indicates, it is important that students have a voice in athletics, and many of their ideas are good, thus fostering engagement and school spirit by the student body and parents.

Coffey is considered by many inside and outside his athletic conference as a trailblazer within the social media domain. When Coffey started to use Twitter and Facebook at Beverly High School, those platforms were not as well regarded as they are today in both educational and athletic settings. Coffey believed that because students were using these platforms, engagement on their level would prove to be an effective communication tool. In addition, Coffey found a social media presence filled a void for parents who could not leave work to attend a 4 p.m. game, allowing them to get real-time updates on the scores and individual player performances.

As Coffey admits, his "following took a while to get going, but I just kept tweeting! It soon grew and people in the community jumped all over it." A secondary outcome to his social media presence, as Coffey further indicated, was that other athletic directors and principals starting noticing. The coverage of athletic teams in print media skyrocketed because the writers and publishers had access to scores or found interesting stories from his tweets. Social media for Coffey grew into a positive following, creating professional opportunities for him to share his ideas through presentations throughout New England on social media's positive influence in education. His work in social media granted him an opportunity to write for the Scholastic company's *Coach & Athletic Director* magazine.

Coffey moved into the athletic director's position at Falmouth High School, where he has taken his social media interests a bit further, adding Instagram and Snapchat. Coffey also started making podcasts consisting of interviews with student-athletes, coaches, and administrators. The end goal for Coffey is to "continue building relationships to bring the entire town together working with students, parents, and being a part of a community is about relationships."

When asked what high school level athletic administrators focus on when it comes to marketing all of their sport teams, Coffey inserts "whether you send out e-mail blasts, use social media, write handwritten notes, newsletters, etc., whatever you do, you need to be equal to all programs and keep everything positive." Coffey truly enjoys tweeting outside of athletics, indicating "my Twitter account is not the 'athletic department,' it's me. It's my picture. I tweet mostly about sports and the school, but I put pictures of my family on there and tweet other fun [and] positive things." Within the school, Coffey enjoys tweeting about the band, cheerleaders, and classroom accolades. He stresses it is "all about showing the positive things done in the school. By doing this, the community realizes you are fair and equitable. They see the success and they trust you. Once they trust you (to always do what's best for kids) then it makes your job a lot easier."

Coffey explored how he manages student body attendance across all games versus the sports that tend to have a core following such as football and basketball. Most athletic administrators are challenged to find creative and tangible ways to fill the seats for all teams to enhance school spirit and overall morale for the teams. Coffey points out that the popularity of the teams depends on the history within the community. At Coffey's first position, the most popular sports were football and basketball; at the next school, the attendance spanned across several sport teams; and in his current position, the highest attended games are soccer, basketball, and ice hockey.

Coffey emphasizes the need to engage students. He has initiated an athlete leadership council working to create support for programs that do not always get the largest fan base. Part of the movement is to make connections between teams in order to build a culture whereby "players from one team (boys' soccer as an example) attend a field hockey game and vice versa." Coffey attributes the success in gaining more attendance to social media. He describes his tennis team's success with a 6–0 record and how, because of social media, students and parents of other sport teams are attending tennis matches because they want to see this team compete. In summary, Coffey believes "it all circles back to how much of a community sense you build and how well you publicize your programs." In the end, Coffey has executed successful marketing and promotional campaigns aimed at managing relationships with the students, athletes, and fans through diverse and innovative ideas.

▶ Social Media Reward Programs

Athletic administrators who use social media may adopt an award program for fans, capitalizing on their interest in the program. To increase attendance at games, students earn prizes and can be awarded for supporting the teams. It is not surprising that many schools (college and high school) will use similar reward structures for other school events, including plays, concerts, and dances, which are all driven to increase attendance. Twitter showcases many tweets by schools to entice student bodies to get involved and show their support for their home teams.

Hashtags

The challenge for athletic administrators is to reach and engage fans on social platforms using creative ideas. For many social media users, the insertion of a hashtag is common to create a buzz before, during, and after games. Social media users on a variety of sites use the hashtag to share or link their message topic or intent with others. The hashtag symbol (#) before any word places the phrase and words into a category, which makes it easier for others to track or search for that topic. For example, during a game, fans may use #GoGullsSoccer when adding pictures or messages to connect their posts with others affiliated with the teams or following that social media site. Athletic administrators' use of the hashtag on a variety of social media platforms serves to link fans to specific sports, teams, events, and players.

Twitter is a digital platform in which users can interact with one another through the use of 280 characters. Twitter users can place hashtags before words or terms to categorize their tweets. Such categorization allows users to easily find tweets regarding a specific theme, topic, sport, or event. Notably, "as Twitter continues to evolve, many business organizations are adopting Twitter accounts within their marketing strategies to interact with their fans" (Witkemper, Lim, & Waldburger, 2012, p. 171). Moreover, Sukjoon, Petrick, and Backman (2017) determined athletics "should be able to effectively build stable, long-term, and profitable relationships between their fans and teams in stages through Twitter" (p. 171).

Dittmore, McCarthy, McEvoy, and Clavio (2013) researched the responses of intercollegiate athletic administrators—including athletic directors, sports information directors, and marketing directors—to determine the use of Twitter in marketing and communicating athletic programs. Dittmore et al. (2013) reported the major thrust of Twitter use was to target alumni, students, and existing ticket holders. The purpose of Twitter use falls generally into three categories: (1) intrapersonal (facilitating two-way interactions between fan and athletics department or coach), (2) informational (providing news, details on upcoming events), and (3) promotional (details on contests and upcoming giveaways) (Dittmore et al., 2013).

A blog from Home Team Marketing (2015) summarizes how high school athletic administrators can fully tap the power of social media. Social media posts can penetrate the clutter of technology by re-creating these ideas: promote ticket sales for events, including images and how to purchase tickets; announce details for upcoming games with clear game-day information plus consistent branding for the season; provide followers with live scoring and updates during events; spotlight high school sponsors by sharing the logo and showcasing the partnership; and highlight student-athlete achievements.

(a)

(b)

FIGURE 5.5 Rewards Program. (a) Hound Nation App is the official rewards program for Assumption College students who attend Athletic Events. (b) Zag Rewards is the Official Student Rewards Program of Gonzaga University Athletics.

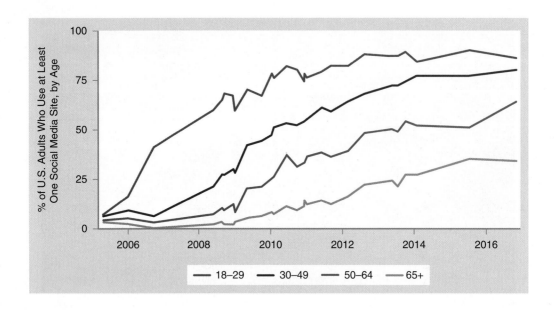

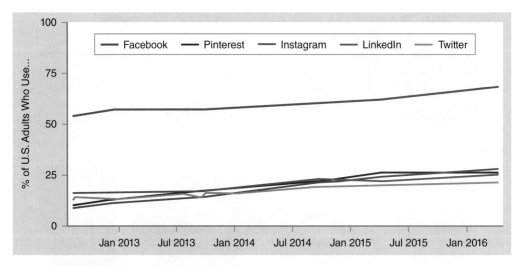

Retrieved from: http://www.pewinternet.org/fact-sheet/social-media/

Athletic administrators use several forms of social media. A common platform is Facebook, assisting in providing information, posting pictures and videos, and promoting upcoming events and games. YouTube is used to share videos with fans about the team or athletes. Abeza et al. (2015) underscore the power of social media to "include social networking sites such as Facebook, Twitter, Google+, and Tumblr; content-sharing sites such as YouTube, Flickr, Pinterest, and Instagram; and blogs" (p. 2).

⚽ FEEDBACK FROM THE FIELD

Best Practices: Marketing and Branding in Recreational Youth Sport

Recreation Director Karen Campbell has been a staple within the recreation department in Wilmington, Massachusetts since 2003. She was promoted to director in 2015. Campbell took the lead in moving the department from a paper registration model to an electronic process. The recreation department publishes a quarterly newsletter, "Recreation Matters," that includes all offerings such as community events, children and adult programs, sports leagues, ticket sales, and day and extended trips. The newsletter is available at their office and the front entrance of the town hall. In addition, the recreation department sends the newsletters to the senior center and the library for additional distribution channels. The Wilmington Chamber of Commerce also distributes the recreation newsletters to new residents and businesses in town.

To stay connected to the community and update residents on the department's offerings, potential customers can subscribe to email alerts through the department's website. Campbell will send out an email blast to alert subscribers to market and promote new programs that are published in a newsletter and when the department has other significant information to share.

The new online registration platform, explains Campbell, allows the department to send out "marketing emails" to targeted groups of people who have accounts in the system. Through the online system, Campbell can target people who have registered for specific programs in the past, or various age groups, or everyone who agreed to receive the marketing emails and has registered for a program in the recent past. Another platform to share information with residents is Facebook, which is also highlighted on the website. In addition to social media, the department still uses traditional print media such as local news publications and local newspapers. Campbell stressed that word-of-mouth advocates are invaluable to her department. She also admits, "it is clearly nothing we can control, and can potentially be negative, but overall we reach many new customers this way." To be present and visible within the community, Campbell and others in the department speak at local charitable organizations or at the "Welcome to Wilmington" events at the library to share their mission and offerings with potential new customers.

There are many competing sport and recreational programs within the town. One challenge for any recreation or sport administrator is deciding which programs to add, retain, or discontinue based on community preference. When asked how decisions are made about the programs, Campbell says she tries to continue any programs that have been "received well." Over her 13 years in the department, the growth of the programs is evident through the growth of the department's newsletter from 4 to 12 pages. The recreation department's website prompts residents to indicate what they may like to see in terms of programs. In addition, Campbell may periodically ask residents if they have any talents or interests and would be willing to lead a program.

The recreation staffers are members of the Massachusetts Recreation and Parks Association (MRPA) and attend regional meetings with representatives from other towns. This membership allows the staff to learn from and identify programs that have been successful in other communities. MRPA holds an annual conference attended each year by two of the three staff members in the department to learn about new trends, ideas, and potential offerings.

To gather information about member satisfaction, post-program feedback is informal. Campbell indicates that "our customers always let us know if a program is disappointing or not up to their standards. With three of us trying to run as many programs and trips as we do, we just don't have time to formalize a process of surveys or other back-end mechanisms. We have, on occasion, called random participants to check on a program if we haven't heard anything at all, and we're considering whether or not to repeat the offering".

(continues)

FEEDBACK FROM THE FIELD   *(continued)*

Since there are so many town programs and private club sport offerings, breaking through all the clutter that exists in the sport/recreational marketplace is a battle for many in recreation management. Campbell continually monitors "other town programs, YMCA and commercial enterprises to compare what they have and what we can do." She will compete "head-to-head" if the department can offer a better value for residents. However, the recreation department will not compete with local school programs, or the large nonprofit sports groups in town. As expected with the growth of certain sports like youth soccer and basketball offered within the town, some programs sponsored at the recreation level may need to change their offerings to support participants seeking other opportunities. As an example, explained Campbell, Wilmington youth soccer now offers its program for four-year-olds that have deflated the recreation Kinder Soccer program, and travel basketball now fields teams for 4th graders, and at least two levels at each grade, so the numbers for recreation basketball have been in a severe decline. Admittedly, Campbell concludes that "when this happens, we can only retreat, and try to find new areas of interest for residents."

Customer service is integral to recreation management while also posing some challenges. There are times when the recreation department deals with various unrealistic perceptions of people as to how things should run and what they should receive for their money. There are always divergent opinions on the level of competition. Campbell shared that she "just had two parents cancel the same class after the first two weeks, one said it was too challenging for their child and the other said it was not challenging enough." For recreation athletic administration the challenge to satisfy all residents is difficult and unrealistic. Weather tests the ability of the recreation department to run events, and they must implement back-up plans for inclement weather.

Even with online registration and continuous communication of program offerings, customers increasingly still want to sign up for programs at the last minute. They do not typically realize the work that goes on behind the scenes regarding planning for minimum and maximum numbers of participants for each program. In Wilmington, the recreation department does not have any of its own indoor facilities, making programs reliant on schools and other town buildings. Unfortunately, the recreation programs can be "bumped" by other users, and sometimes communication falls through the cracks and the department does not have access to a building even after receiving previous permission to hold a program there. As the community grows and develops, the recreation department is relied on for more oversight and contributions.

Another challenge for recreation management are drop-in volunteers over the last decade. As Campbell points out, "more people are working later in life, and there are more two working parent families. We have always relied heavily on volunteers, and this area of recreation management is becoming more difficult to handle." In addition, for the recreational setting, it is often difficult to adhere to a high standard of programming with a high reliance on volunteers. However, with all of the challenges in this setting, Campbell boasts that department employees are all incredibly fortunate to work in recreation. Campbell believes the annual report summarizes their impact the best:

> We aim to provide solutions to new challenges faced by residents in evolving life situations. New residents can meet others, parents can find an array of reasonably priced programs for their children to sample, "empty nesters" might take a class or enjoy theatre or sporting event tickets and residents of all ages continue to reap the benefits of group travel and assorted fitness programs. Every day, we work with and for the residents and for the most part, they are incredibly appreciative and consider us their friends—not just their recreation department staff. We all believe in the power of recreation and its benefits.

Questions for Discussion

1. If you were a staff member within your hometown recreation department, what type of marketing activities would you adopt to effectively promote your programs? Consider the competition of private club sports and other regional recreational offerings.

2. Programs have ebbs and flows in terms of interest. What are some methods you would implement as the recreation director to collect feedback and suggestions to get the "pulse" of what area residents and potential customers would prefer to see in terms of new or enhanced programs?

3. Research the Massachusetts Recreation and Parks Association online. List and describe the various professional development opportunities for MRPA members.

4. There is an increase in "upper-level" sport opportunities for youth athletes, which influences many children to no longer engage in "recreation-level" activities. As the recreation director in your hometown, how will you manage your program offering in light of the shift in participation in recreation versus competitive play?

 MANAGERIAL APPLICATIONS

College Sports

You have just been hired as the National Collegiate Athletic Association (NCAA) compliance coordinator overseeing social media for a Division I athletic department. There are many regulations associated with social media use in athletics. Visit the NCAA website and review at least three social media regulations. What are some of the restrictions you will need to train your coaches and staff to be aware of when dealing with social media posts and high school recruits? Once student-athletes enroll at your institution, what kinds of mechanisms will you have in place to ensure the NCAA regulations and recommendation for social media are followed? Will staff within your department monitor the sites and posts of student-athletes and coaches? What kinds of policies will you develop around the appropriate use of social media within your department?

 MANAGERIAL APPLICATIONS

High School Sports

Often, the athletic director on a high school campus is tasked with handling a variety of duties, including the promotion and marketing of games to fans. It is safe to indicate that most parents and caregivers will be in attendance for home games to support their favorite player. One goal of a high school athletic department would be to increase fan attendance within the student body and from community members. As the athletic administrator in charge of marketing, what are some ways you will balance attendance at both boys' and girls' events and balance attendance between popular and less popular sports on your campus? What are some promotional ideas you can incorporate into your program to get more student-athletes to support other teams on campus? What are some marketing ideas and incentives you will use to engage younger athletes within the community to support your athletic programs?

Wrap-Up

End-of-Chapter Activities

College Athletics

1. You have been hired as the sports information director at a Division III institution. Recruitment of student-athletes has dropped over the last few years, and some athletic department employees blame the lack of exposure on the website and social media platforms.

   a. Come up with a year-long plan to address the identified issue of a lack of presence on the website and social media.

   b. List the social media platforms you plan to use and provide a rationale so that the staff understands your proposed ideas.

   c. Recruitment of student-athletes has been hampered. Locate a promotional brochure you could replicate for your college athletic department that may serve to boost interest in the school and athletic teams.

   d. Identify the plan you will embed into the SID office to fully market home games to fans and promote student-athlete achievement throughout the season.

   e. Many college athletic departments are using their own domain names rather than remain housed within the institutional site. For example, Adelphi University uses Adelphi.edu as its main site and aupanthers.com for its athletic program website. What are the benefits of housing athletics under a separate website?

   f. Review two Division III athletic department staff listings. How many people are employed to work within sports information and sport marketing?

   g. Visit two Division I athletic department websites. How many personnel are assigned to manage sports information and sports marketing? Are you surprised at any similarities or differences between Division I and Division III athletic departments and marketing?

Youth Club Sport

You are executive director for the local recreation department. In this position you must establish a new process for a website and online registration for participants.

Let's get started:

1. Determine how to purchase a domain name for your recreation department. Indicate what sport Club Elite encompasses (example: Club Elite Soccer or Club Elite Softball).

2. Research the costs associated with website development. Is there a recreation website that captured your attention? What elements of that site would you incorporate into your webpage?

3. Processing online registrations needs to be handled by a third-party vendor. Research online-payment options and determine which one may be the best fit for your recreation department.

End-of-Chapter Questions

1. Review three athletic websites (youth, high school, collegiate) and identify the personnel responsible for the marketing for each entity. Is the person full-time? Is the role of marketing assumed by multiple people in

the organization? Describe some of the marketing aims on the websites. Did anything surprise you about the marketing efforts? Would you consider making any changes?

2. Spend time online reviewing websites for athletic organizations. Find one website that exemplifies marketing and showcases the connection between the product and target groups. Explain how the marketing arm is effectively meeting the definition of marketing.

3. Mascots play a role in promoting events for athletic entities. Many programs will change mascots to better engage their target groups. Find two examples of how athletic departments (high school or college) have made mascot adaptations to effectively connect with fans.

4. Creativity is important when trying to sort through the clutter within the sport marketplace. Research three promotional activities for community sport (youth sport, recreational sport) that effectively increased the awareness of the athletic entity within the local or regional community.

5. Club sports have increased in popularity over the last decade. Review two club sport programs from different sports and share two promotional activities used by these programs to recruit new players.

6. Social media has transformed the management of athletics. List all of the social media tools an athletic administrator could use to create marketing strategies to reach the goals of the entity.

7. Branding allows sport entities to present a clear and consistent image and message to audiences to build recognition for its program. Using your institution's library database, review two articles showcasing the power of branding within two athletic settings.

8. What are the advantages of market research? Identify three websites you would use to find statistics or data points regarding sport participation rates in youth, club, or high school sport programs.

9. How would you start to build athletic brand identity? Is there one brand from a college program that stands out that you would try to replicate as a future athletic administrator? Identify the brand and the power of its reach in the sport marketplace.

10. Why do apparel companies compete to outfit college sport teams? Look up deals. What does the school get, and what does the company get from the relationship?

11. Minor league sport franchises are extremely creative in their marketing aims. Visit a minor league website and list some marketing ideas you can transfer to the high school sport setting.

12. Professional sport teams develop a variety of promotional campaigns to engage fans. Visit one professional sport website and review promotional ideas that can be converted for use for college athletics.

13. An aspect of sport marketing is securing participants through online registration platforms. Select a local recreational program website and calculate how many clicks it takes for the visitor to register for a program. Based on your analysis, was the site user-friendly? What are the positive features of the site? What recommendations for change would you make to the website?

14. Social media in college athletics has forced many in the administration to change and revise policies around what constitutes appropriate and inappropriate posts. Review the rules initiated by the NCAA regarding recruitment and social media. What are your thoughts on the regulations governing social media and high school recruitment?

References

Abeza, G., O'Reilly, N., Séguin, B., & Nzindukiyimana, O. (2015). Social Media Scholarship in Sport Management Research: A Critical Review. *Journal Of Sport Management, 29*(6), 601-618.

American Marketing Association (1960). *Marketing definitions: A glossary of marketing terms.* Chicago: American Marketing Association.

Bee, C. C., & Kahle, L. R. (2006). Relationship marketing in sports: A functional approach. *Sport Marketing Quarterly*, 15(2).

Boston College (2017). Sports marketing. Retrieved September 19, 2017, from https://www.bc.edu/schools /csom/departments/marketing/career/sportsmarketing .html

Bowen, T. (2016, November). Increase attendance at your prep athletics events with these 7 tips. State Champs. Retrieved from https://statechamps.com/increase -attendance-at-your-prep-athletics-events-with-these -7-tips/.

Chaudhuri, A., and Holbrook, M. B. (2001). The chain of effects from brand trust and brand affect to brand performance: The role of brand loyalty. *Journal of Marketing*, 65(2), 81–93.

Clark, J. S., Apostolopoulou, A., Branvold, S. & Synowka, D. (2009). Who knows Bobby Mo? Using intercollegiate athletics to build a university brand. *Sports Marketing Quarterly*, 18(1), 57–63.

Columbia University (n.d.). Built to win foundation in facilities, personnel #OnlyHere [online]. Retrieved from https://gocolumbialions.com/sports/2018/6/5 /211462716.aspx.

Dittmore, S. W., McCarthy, S. T., McEvoy, C., & Clavio, G. (2013). Perceived utility of official university athletic Twitter accounts: The opinions of college athletic administrators. *Journal of Issues in Intercollegiate Athletics*, 6, 286–305.

Funk, D. C., & Pastore, D. L. (2000). Equating attitudes to allegiance: The usefulness of selected attitudinal information in segmenting loyalty to professional sports teams. *Sport Marketing Quarterly*, 9(4), 175–184.

Goi, L. C. (2009). A review of marketing mix: 4Ps or more? *International Journal of Marketing Studies*, 1(1), 2–15.

Goksel, A. G., & Serarslan, M. Z. (2015). Public relations in sports clubs: New media as a strategic corporate communication instrument. *International Journal of Physical Education, Sports and Health*, 2(2), 275–283.

Gregg, E. A., Pierce, D. A., Lee, J. W., Himstead, L., & Felver, N. (2013). Giving UE a new face. *Journal of Issues in Intercollegiate Athletics*, 6, 155–173.

Gummesson, E. (2017). From relationship marketing to total relationship marketing and beyond. *Journal of Services Marketing*, 31(1), 16–19.

Henderson, K. A., Neff, L. J., Sharpe, P. A., Greaney, M. L., Royce, S. W., & Ainsworth, B. E. (2001). "It takes a village" to promote physical activity: The potential for public park and recreation departments. *Journal of Park & Recreation Administration*, 19(1), 23–41.

Home Team Marketing (2015, November 23). Five ways your high school athletic department should be using Twitter. HTM School Solutions. Retrieved September 19, 2017, from https://schools.hometeammarketing .com/2015/11/23/5-ways-your-high-school-athletic -department-should-be-using-twitter/.

Kar, A. (2011). Four C's of marketing: The marketing mix [online]. Retrieved September 3, 2018, from http:// business-fundas.com/2011/4-cs-of-marketing-the -marketing-mix/.

Keller, K. L., Sternthal, B., & Tybout, A. (2002). Three questions you need to ask about your brand. *Harvard Business Review*, 80(9), 80–81. Retrieved from http:// www.differencebetween.com/difference-between -positioning-and-vs-differentiation/.

Kennesaw State University (n.d.). Kennesaw State athletics calendar [online]. Retrieved from http://www.ksuowls .com/sports/2012/8/21/FAN_0821120150.aspx.

Knight Commission (2014). *College sports 101: A primer on money, athletics, and higher education in the 21st Century*. Retrieved from http://www.knightcommission.org /collegesports101/chapter-3.

Kotler, P. (2016, March 22). Branding: From purpose to beneficence. *The Marketing Journal* [online]. Retrieved September 19, 2017, from http://www .marketingjournal.org/brand-purpose-to-beneficence -philip-kotler/.

Lake, L. (2018, October 16). How brand identity is defined. The Balance: Small Business [online].

Lauterborn, B. (1990). New marketing litany: Four P's passé. *Advertising Age*, 61(4), 26.

Marquis, A. (2017, November 21). Youth recreation marketing plan using comprehensive marketing mix. *Houston Chronicle*. Retrieved September 3, 2018, from https://smallbusiness.chron.com/youth-recreation -marketing-plan-using-comprehensive-marketing -mix-34311.html.

Martin, C. L. L., Miller, L. L., Elsisi, R., Bowers, A., & Hall, S. (2011). An analysis of collegiate athletic marketing strategies and evaluation processes. *Journal of Issues in Intercollegiate Athletics*, 4, 42–54.

Oregon State University (2013, March 4.). Oregon State athletics unveils new brand identity. Retrieved September 19, 2017, from https://news.nike.com/news /oregon-state-athletics-unveils-new-brand-identity.

Promoting youth sports programs for maximum participation (2017). National Alliance for Youth Sports [online]. Retrieved September 16, 2017, from http://www.nays.org/blog/promoting-youth-sports -programs-for-maximum-participation.

Sanderson, J., Snyder, E., Hull, D., & Gramlich, K. (2015). Social media policies within NCAA member institutions:

Evolving technology and its impact on policy. *Journal of Issues in Intercollegiate Athletics*, (8), 50–73.

Smith, K. T. (2003, April 30). The marketing mix of IMC: A move from the 4 P's to the 4 C's. Retrieved September 3, 2018, from http://chouprojects.com/wp-content/uploads/2015/01/eMarketing.pdf.

Sukjoon, Y., Petrick, J. F., & Backman, S. J. (2017). Twitter power and sport-fan loyalty: The moderating effects of Twitter. *International Journal of Sport Communication*, 10(2), 153–177.

University of Maryland. (2017). Men's lacrosse promotional schedule (2017) [online]. Retrieved September 16, 2017, from https://umterps.com/news/2017/2/14/211475690.aspx.

University of Massachusetts Amherst (n.d.) Auxiliary enterprises [online]. http://umassauxiliaryservices.com/wp-content/uploads/licensing/UMass-Lowell-Athletics.pdf.

Vision Point Marketing (2015, April 27). The higher ed love triangle: A university, its brand and athletics [online blog]. Retrieved from https://www.visionpointmarketing.com/blog/entry/higher-ed-love-triangle-university-its-brand-and-athletics.

Washington State University Athletics (2017). Marketing and promotions. Retrieved September 19, 2017, from http://www.wsucougars.com/sports/2013/4/18/208266771.aspx.

Welde, C. (2017, March 30). Seven steps to build your athletic department's brand. Coach & A. D. [online]. Retrieved September 19, 2017, from https://coachad.com/articles/building-your-athletic-departments-brand/.

Witkemper, C., Lim, C. H., & Waldburger, A. (2012). Social media and sports marketing: Examining the motivations and constraints of Twitter users. *Sport Marketing Quarterly*, 21, 170–183.

CHAPTER 6

Fundraising

LEARNING OBJECTIVES

After reading this chapter, students will be able to:

1. Communicate the importance of fundraising in generating additional revenue to support current and supplemental programming in college, high school, youth, and club sport.
2. Classify the variety of fundraising options available to athletic administrators in college, high school, youth, and club sport.
3. Identify the tasks required to implement a fundraising plan within college, high school, youth, and club athletics.
4. Develop fundraising plans for a college, high school, youth, and club sport athletic entity.
5. Describe the necessity and evolution of various means of fundraising in athletic administration.

▶ Fundraising Defined

Athletic administrators are often asked to enhance program offerings even as their departmental budgets fail to increase. As Stinson and Howard (2010) indicated, "in an era of tightening budgets and decreasing levels of state support for public colleges and universities, private giving has taken on increased importance at many campuses" (p. 312). To sufficiently provide the best opportunities to athletes and even staff members, athletic administrators use budgets to manage the fiscal needs of each team within the department. "Rising costs and a decline of adequate funding requires athletic administrators to seek additional resources through multiple fundraising efforts" (Balog & Connaughton, 2002, p. 38).

Fundraising can be considered an art because individual creativity and ingenuity is involved in mapping out various strategies and deciding on tactics (based on basic fundraising principles, guidelines and knowledge). On the other hand, fundraising may also be viewed as a science because there are general principles and concepts that are applicable for all types of fundraising activities and efforts. (Stier & Schneider, 1999, p. 94)

Because of budget constraints or small allocations of budgets, fiscal management of today's athletics becomes less science and more art. Athletic administrators must be creative in attempting to inject innovation into their broad-based programming. When budgets cannot support program needs, athletic administrators often supplement stagnant budgets through fundraising. As a tool, fundraising is relied on by athletic administrators to not only support current programming but also assist in providing supplemental resources to existing and planned programming. "Many interscholastic and recreational programs are prevented from offering a variety of sports and activities due to rising costs and financial cutbacks" (Balog & Connaughton, 2002, p. 37).

 FEEDBACK FROM THE FIELD

Youth Sports

Stephanie McArdle is the executive director for the nonprofit organization Beyond Soccer. McArdle is a University of Michigan graduate who created a sports-based youth development organization in Lawrence, Massachusetts, a low-income city north of Boston. As an athlete, McArdle wanted to add sport into the lives of young people in this low-income area. To engage these young people, McArdle formed a girls' soccer team from members of a local youth development organization. She organized a complete schedule along with various tournament opportunities. Although the team may have lost games, the experience of playing in tournaments and building self-confidence was the momentum needed to build demand for sport in the lives of children in Lawrence. As McArdle reflected, "I knew very quickly that just that experience of being in the van together as a team, getting to wear a uniform, they had never had that. Even after a lopsided loss, it just rolled off their shoulders and they kept coming back."

McArdle's family was instrumental in the start of Beyond Soccer; her sister became the health and wellness director, her attorney father currently serves on the board of directors, and her boyfriend has served as the finance and operations manager. Beyond Soccer now has more than 2,000 young people in the program. Beyond Soccer also incorporates 35 hours of weekly programming in local schools, including activities such as team building and nutrition education. McArdle requires participants to share their grades so children can be matched with the appropriate academic support. Beyond Soccer also offers various programs for older participants, including coaching courses, guidance on college admission, and help with obtaining financial aid. McArdle admits:

> It's been a labor of love, for sure, with lots of family help and committed friends. I recognized a void in the community [Lawrence] many years ago and wanted to do something about it because that void [soccer] had such a positive impact on my life. I used family and friend connections/relationships I had formed as a high school and college student to bring resources, ideas, collaboration, and attention to the program and the program's important mission.

The majority of Beyond Soccer's funding is generated from private foundations. Beyond Soccer has received some state grants, such as Maura Healey's Summer Youth Jobs Grant. McArdle acknowledges Beyond Soccer has been effective at landing private foundation funding, but her aim is to diversify the base, especially through corporate and individual giving so that it is more sustainable. In fact, increasing individual and corporate support is the top priority of Beyond Soccer's recently adopted strategic plan. The Beyond Soccer board is in the process of mapping out a fundraising work plan to be more tactical with their approach. McArdle feels that having committed board members who champion the mission can be the difference maker on the fundraising front.

McArdle was introduced to the process of grant writing and research by a prior board member and friend, who, when she first started the nonprofit, helped McArdle tell the Beyond Soccer story, including the mission, constituents, community needs, programs, how these programs address needs, and short- and long-term objectives. All of these important pieces were added to written proposals,

(continues)

FEEDBACK FROM THE FIELD   *(continued)*

targeting foundations that Beyond Soccer had connections to first through family and friend networks. Next, these proposals were aimed at foundations whose missions aligned with that of Beyond Soccer (i.e. foundations supporting youth organizations in Lawrence).

McArdle stresses that grant writing is a laborious process in part because no two grants are the same. "Some grants provide space for answers with 450 characters and others, four pages. That can make the process frustrating and tedious, because you cannot just cut and paste." Furthermore, McArdle explains that many attachments are required to support the grant application, so it is important to double- and triple-check the work. Moreover, if a simple list of board member names is omitted, the chances of securing the grant are lowered significantly because grants are so hard to attain. Building relationships with trustees or foundation representatives aids in grant procurement. McArdle notes that like cold calls, "if foundations have not heard about you, it is a tough sell" to acquire a grant.

Beyond Soccer uses a process to identify grants. Because its programs serve Lawrence youth only, it looks to the many well-established foundations that have grants committed to Lawrence. She sought funding from those foundations first, and then as the organization and budget grew, she expanded and started applying to foundations that did not just fund entities in Lawrence, including Boston foundations and national grants (such as the U.S. Soccer Foundation and Women's Sports Foundation). Those have taken more time, but because Beyond Soccer was persistent and has a reputation of running good programs, the process has paid off. McArdle made clear that often once a nonprofit gets "one big funder to take notice, others will follow." Good grant proposals are important and make a difference. For most grants, the decision makers will check the social media pages and website, so the nonprofits must have things current to show they are doing what they say in their mission.

Another time-consuming part of grant writing is reporting. Grants that are successfully funded may require midyear reports as well as year-end reports, signifying that sport administrators must have an excellent calendar system so as not to jeopardize future grants because of missed reporting dates. Because Beyond Soccer's budget is relatively small compared to peer groups in Lawrence, McArdle does not shy away from grants of any size ($1,000 to $50,000), and she has found that similar amounts of work need to be put in regardless of the grant size.

McArdle has many relationships within the city of Lawrence, including city councilors and state and local representatives to champion her efforts. She offers many opportunities for politicians to attend programs, leagues, camps, and events. As McArdle explains, "they need to know you and know about your work. They also want to be seen. You can use that to your advantage."

Finding available fields and field spaces is a major challenge in cities like Lawrence, where 80,000 residents are squeezed into seven square miles. Most other towns in the vicinity are doing a better job with their fields, and many also support turf-playing spaces. McArdle believes Beyond Soccer is falling behind in this area because it does not have a single youth-dedicated field. A recent Parkland Acquisitions and Renovations for Communities Grant for $400,000, plus a $200,000 city match (a two-year process) resulted in a grass field in July 2016. However, now a year and a half later with a host of problems, McArdle laments the field needs to be reconstructed because it does not drain. Currently, a pending city council vote on $150,000 is being debated in Lawrence, and stakeholders are questioning the process as well as the intended use: Is it just for youth soccer or is high school included, and can the field withstand high foot traffic and activity? McArdle recognizes this as an example of how important a good working relationship is with the city, and it also serves as a reminder that more advocates are needed for your cause so that problems get resolved more quickly.

Ideally, McArdle further notes, she would like to push for a more creative private–public partnership arrangement for turf to maximize usage. She is currently negotiating and pushing for a larger turf field capital campaign effort with a local high school. Again, she continually looks for groups to partner with and entities she can trust who have aligning missions. City relationships and collaborations, large and small, require constant work and communication. Another challenge comes from changing leadership in municipalities, which leads to shifts in priorities. As McArdle explains, "You can have a mayor [who] is all about sports and recreation and then four years later have a mayor [who] is not. You just need to make sure you [and] your mission [are] always getting attention and that your families advocate for your programs."

Many students in athletic administration or sport management may not understand the business formation of a nonprofit versus a for-profit organization. McArdle describes a nonprofit as a business just like other large and small for-profits. The same goal exists in that nonprofits do not want to be "in the red" at the end of the year. Just like for-profits, Beyond Soccer sets a budget at the beginning of the fiscal year (FY) (July 1–June 30) voted on by the board, and it is based on the budget from the previous year (meaning what was raised and what was spent). McArdle's fiscal methodology is that Beyond Soccer spends money and makes decisions about programs it relies on as a guide for expenditures. Beyond Soccer also has a budget line item for salaries. There are grants supporting operating costs (personnel and administrative expenses), which are essential for nonprofits to run. Foundations, McArdle emphasizes, like to see that most of their money goes to direct programming, which Beyond Soccer can show, "but at the same time it is frustrating because fundraising and development (for example) are an essential part of any successful and growing nonprofit."

In terms of reporting for the organization's year-end tax return, she breaks down her salary into different areas: 50% program management, 25% spent on fundraising/development, and 25% administration. That allocation gets applied to total program expenses. In closing, McArdle says, "Most days take unexpected turns. It's not easy, but when that kid who started with you, speaking little English, with not much confidence, is now attending college and playing intramural sports, it's worth it. When you get a Mother's Day card from a participant, it's worth it!"

▶ Purpose of Fundraising in Athletic Administration

Effective athletic administrators manage their budgets with precision and care. Unfortunately, in many cases and across all athletic settings, the designated funds for athletic teams cannot fully support the needs of the program. For example, coaches may want specialized practice gear for their teams that is outside the scope of the budget. In other cases, perhaps the entire transportation cost for a high school program needs to be generated by revenue sources outside traditional budget allocation. In theory, it would be ideal for each team to have all its needs met by the budget. However, in reality, perhaps the only way to provide the practice gear, for example, would be to generate revenue from external sources—that is, by fundraising.

Fundraising is a skill set that needs to be a steadfast tool constantly used and galvanized by the athletic administrator to attain fiscal aims. The reach of a sound fundraising plan is limitless. However, athletic administrators require support and assistance from staff members to deliver on raising funds to supplement the budget. Part of fundraising is to direct and motivate staff to sustain a positive effort with fundraising planning. Some coaches may not accept that fundraising is, in fact, an extension of their role as a coach. Athletic administrators need to prepare for this pushback by setting the stage early in the hiring process. Sharing expectations for fundraising limits resistance when athletic administrators ask for assistance and collaboration from staff members.

Adding fundraising to the job position description (for paid and volunteer staff) stresses the priority of this responsibility within the program. Creating a culture within the athletic department whereby fundraising is prioritized helps drive the staff to move initiatives for a full fundraising campaign into action. With the intention of effectively generating funds for requests for practice gear, travel budgets, and team dinners, the athletic administrators along with athletic personnel compile action items necessary to implement these plans.

▶ Budgeting

Athletic fundraising has emerged because of shortfalls within athletic budgets. In some cases, athletic administrators are asked to do more with athletic programs even with budgets that remain the same. On the other hand, many budgets remain the same even though operating costs are on the rise. A variety of costs are associated with the athletic administration of sport across college, high school, youth, and club sport settings. Budget management is a universal responsibility for athletic administrators; however, the methods used to organize budgets take many forms. The first step in budget management is to ascertain the items that need to be accounted for as expenditures. Depending on the setting, expenses include and are not limited to costs for registration (online platforms), uniform and practice-related gear and equipment, travel, officials, awards, meals, rental fees, league fees, general office supplies, technology, and staff salaries.

Budgets are formulated before the start of the fiscal year. For athletic programs housed within education, the fiscal year starts July 1 and runs to the following June 30. For recreational programs and private sport-specific clubs, the fiscal year runs from January 1 to December 31. Note the difference in fiscal years because funding for program needs, collection of information, and deadlines to plan for programs will differ based on the fiscal calendar. Budgets are an estimate of expenses and revenue for a given year. Depending on the scope of the sport entity, the personnel assuming the duty of budget management and financial forecasting (planning for future budgets) can rest with the athletic director for high school or college level, executive director of the sport club, committee member for a town sport league, or recreational director for town programs. Some who study athletic administration may be wary of financial management, but as administrators it is important to understand the overall process of fiscal responsibility, even if other staff members with fiscal expertise take the lead role to facilitate the process.

Budget-Development Process

Typically, athletic administrators will ask coaches and personnel to submit a wish list of items for the following year. The wish list should contain all of the resources needed to operate the program for all games and practices. It is then up to the athletic administrator to prioritize the spending choices by determining when to add wish list items to the budget and which ones to leave off. The gap between the requested items and the actual budget for the department is where fundraising will come into play. The items that the staff and coaches feel they must have to operate a successful budget but are not funded by the department may and can be purchased through fundraising efforts.

Types of Budgets

Over time, athletic administrators deal with the pressure of having to do much more with their operating budget than in past years. When athletic administrators become successful at operating within budget restrictions, they may set themselves up to receive the same budget amount over time rather than receive more funding to enhance programming or add programming. Operating budgets are the accounts or line items used on a daily basis within the athletic departments. Operating budgets are similar to a checking account that individuals use. Capital budgets include high-cost items that may last over a longer period of time like bleachers or a field hockey goal.

These are items with a larger price tag coupled with longer durability. Oversight and management of capital budgets is more strenuous than purchases funneled through operating budgets because of the sheer dollar amount associated with capital expenditures.

Approval for the purchase of capital requests requires an extra layer of review and vetting because of the significant effects those costs can have on the total budget for the sport organization.

Major projects and capital improvements are submitted through the FY Capital Budget Request process, which is initiated by the university chancellor's office annually. Projects prepared by Kansas Athletics are directed and approved by the director of athletics. Capital Budget Requests are prepared by the associate athletic director—Operations/Capital Projects, assistant athletic director—Facilities, the senior associate athletic director, and the chief financial officer and approved by the director of athletics.

Capital Budget Request College Setting

Kansas University Athletics, n.d.

The Park & Recreation Commission is pleased to provide the below information on current Capital Projects and Improvements. We are very proud of the hard work to improve our facilities and parks throughout Arlington. Capital Projects and Park Improvements can be funded by the Town, CDBG funds, and/or Grants. Community [fundraisers] are also accepted. Please note some details of the projects may not take place due to limited funds and the bidding process.

Example from Recreation Department

City of Arlington, Massachusetts (n.d.).

▶ Booster Clubs

Athletic administrators and coaches continually seek the support of parent-driven groups to assist with fundraising efforts. Within many athletic entities there are parent groups, typically called *booster clubs*, that are long-standing committees tied to strong traditions of organizing events and programs with the sole aim of raising funds for athletic teams. Direct oversight over these groups is paramount because monies are being collected and must be accounted for to limit any unethical practices.

One challenging aspect in the administration of booster clubs is the probability that one booster group may be more effective than another, leading to inequities within the department. As an example, the girls' soccer team booster club may have more parents with corporate ties or parents who manage to raise large amounts of funds compared to the boys' soccer team booster club. Within the athletic entity, clear policies and regulations need to be written to ensure discrepancies between teams are limited in order to meet the needs of all programs. One way to offset fundraising discrepancies is adding a percentage amount of total funds raised to be allocated to the general athletic fund. For example, if a booster club raised $10,000,

Fundraising: The principal must approve all fundraising activities (including Booster Clubs) in advance. All student fundraising must be approved by the Cherokee County School Board of Education prior to the activity and accounted separately on the school's accounting record. Students will not be required to participate in fundraising in order to participate in extracurricular activities.

Policy for Booster Club Fundraising

Cherokee County School District (n.d.), p. 20.

a percentage of that total would go to the general budget to be used for program-wide purchases or funneled into the budgets of the other

teams. Pushback may occur from the booster clubs that successfully raise higher amounts; however, policy can govern those disputes.

1. Determine the need.

2. Research fundraising events and opportunities.

3. Solicit volunteers and staff members to help select a fundraising event.

4. Create a realistic timeline to raise enough funds to support program needs.

5. Determine the promotional and marketing efforts to be used to generate interest in the event (publicity).

6. List the expenses associated with the event.

7. Estimate the total amount of monies collected through the fundraising efforts.

8. Execute the fundraising activity.

9. Review the fundraising efforts and identify any areas of weakness to be changed for future events.

Checklist for Fundraising

FEATURED INTERVIEW: HIGH SCHOOL FUNDRAISING

A. J. Armbruster is the tournament coordinator for Volleygrass (http://www.Volleygrass.com), a fundraising event operated by the Port Huron Northern Booster Club in Michigan. Armbruster has been involved with this event for more than six years, serving several of those years as coordinator. The event is a fundraiser at the local high school operated by the booster club. The founder of the event recruited Armbruster to coordinate corporate sponsors, tournament registration, and bracket formation and to manage the entire event from start to finish. He is a president of a local nonprofit, which has given him experience with donors and fundraising. Volunteers and the coaches play an instrumental role in handling a variety of tasks to conduct the event. One way to centralize the process of task delegation is by using Google Docs. Coaches and volunteers can sign up online, which allows task assignment to be more streamlined. One task of the booster club is to match volunteer and coach hours worked to a dollar amount, and the total money raised by the individual is allocated to the sport-specific account. As an example, one hour of work at the event equates to $75, so if the parent of a girls' basketball team member volunteers five hours, a total of $375 is transferred to the girls' basketball account. To use the funds, all purchase requests must be based on need and approved by the booster club. In summary, the more hours the individuals representing a program work at the event, the more funds are raised for program needs.

Typically, there are 80 volunteers for the Volleygrass event. The volunteer coordinator for the fundraiser manages the Google form and disseminating information to the coaches. Once people sign up for a volunteer task, the coordinator places them into positions that best match their personalities with the roles needed for the event. Although volleyball experience is not required, volunteers may be asked to keep score to maintain records for wins and losses at the tournament. For the more intense divisions, where the competition may be advanced and the passion of participants may be elevated, volunteers may need to be stern and direct to better manage the enthusiastic competitiveness. As an example, Armbruster places the varsity football coach on the court, which may be more competitive and hostile than the other division, just because he is well respected, may have attended that high school, and knows most of the community members.

In terms of marketing for the event, Armbruster was asked about the methods used to solicit sponsors, participants, and fans. As he explained, the event has been held for more than two decades. Much of the marketing rests with the repeat registration of returning players, word-of-mouth promotions, and current mailing list along with a running email list. Armbruster explains that the process of outreach starts two months before the tournament when registration forms are mailed to past participants. The mailing includes an impressive list of 3,000 addresses. On the registration form, the collected demographic information includes participant contact details and physical mailing address and email address. Typically, six to eight weeks out, Armbruster sends a mass email to past participants. In addition, social media sites such as Facebook contain an event-hosting page to drum up interest and solicit sign-ups. As Armbruster noted, the process of promoting the event is now a well-oiled machine with a rich history, connection to the school system, and presence in a positive volleyball community.

The physical space for the event includes using as much grass space at the high school, including athletic fields, and lining each area to accommodate 40 courts at the same time, which equated to 211 teams in 2017. Armbruster estimated another 44 courts could be set up on well-maintained grass if the event attracts more participants. Armbruster organizes the teams into divisions, and all pools are in the same area on the high school campus. The grass on the fields is well maintained, and the layouts of the courts are close to each other for a positive tourney field. Armbruster manages to place half of all Volleygrass courts on the high school soccer fields, 15 on the football field, and 6 in the outfield of the softball field. Centrally located among those fields is a concession stand for participants; sales are added to the revenue generated by the event.

The evaluation of an event of this magnitude aids the athletic administrator when planning the next event. Armbruster has only had a few requests or ideas for change in his tenure as volunteer coordinator. However, because the event has been in operation for nearly three decades, it runs "efficiently," according to Armbruster. He stresses that the high school athletic department and teams work collaboratively to make this event such a success. One challenge for the event management is the selection of the date. There are other popular events in the area (e.g., Fourth of July activities), which may affect registration. Planning around other major events helps retain strong participation numbers.

Leading up to the actual event, many tasks and responsibilities must be delegated. The volunteer coordinator—who is a volunteer herself and has had two daughters involved in the high school athletic program—assigns people to specific areas. Armbruster meets with volunteers a few weeks before the event and then on event day to review the expectations. When asked to provide advice to future athletic administrators, Armbruster stresses "try to do everything in person, try to leave things open-ended," he uses an information sheet on the tournament to assess "how things went and how much money was able to be made, if they had to get new signage, and to 'just follow up with people.'" He further explained, "you don't have to be overbearing," just personable while messaging people for your events.

▶ Profit Versus Nonprofit Sport Entities

At times there may be confusion about the organizational structure of profit versus nonprofit sport entities. Athletic entities such as sport clubs and camps operate as for-profit entities, meaning that any revenue generated after expenses is allocated to the ownership or designees. Nonprofit athletic organizations are similar to recreation departments or town or city athletic associations and will recycle any additional revenue back into the budget or program. Salaries and benefits for staff members employed in for-profit and nonprofit athletic entities may be similar. People often believe volunteers solely manage nonprofits, which is not always the case.

Volunteer Management

To have the greatest reach possible with fundraising efforts, athletic administrators will seek the assistance of volunteers. An easy group of people to ask for help with identifying and securing funds from outside sources would be the participants or their families. Many people do not enjoy asking others for money, so the athletic administrator must strategize how to fully use the volunteers to get the most use of their talents. Volunteers have a variety of expertise and talents. A great way to ascertain how they can best assist the sport entity would be to create a simple questionnaire requesting areas of interest from volunteers. This questionnaire serves several functions, including determining the level of interest of the potential volunteer and what skill set can be assigned to the fundraising task.

Volunteer management is one aspect of athletic administration that requires attention because an unpaid but highly motivated workforce is being added to the department. For many athletic administrators, volunteers are a welcome addition to the staff. However, volunteer output needs to match the effort of training and support of those volunteers who simply want to give back to the sport entity. The reasons volunteers want to spend their free time with athletic programs varies from giving back to simply providing a service to the sport program. Placing volunteers in the correct position for the department takes time just—like an informational interview would. The athletic administrator needs to take time to figure out the qualifications needed for the volunteer position. In addition, athletic administrators may want to craft policy in terms of handling money, which may exclude volunteers from holding those positions. As with any position within the athletic department, the volunteer would report to one staff person for directions and supervision.

Volunteers are a unique grouping and often supply a boost to the staff when needed for game day and fundraising activities, two areas that require more effort especially when paid staff cannot perform all of the duties. For fundraising, an athletic administrator creates roles and even job descriptions for volunteers. It is not uncommon for coaches to have job descriptions so they understand the scope of their position, including the expectations and evaluation procedures. Notably, volunteers have an enormous reach within their social, personal, and business contacts, serving to secure leads for donations and gifts for the athletic entity. Committees for specialized fundraising groups are typically formed. Many sport entities adopt a "Friends of XYZ" as a way to link with groups so the donor feels a deeper connection to the sport entity.

Volunteers are also being asked to devote their time and effort across many programs. Sport entities must be flexible not only with the capacity they serve but also with their time commitment. Volunteers prosper when they are provided a schedule; they treat the position just like a paid job with all of the expectations and parameters. It is also challenging to secure volunteers. The need for volunteers is often greater than the supply of people who are willing to give up hours of their time without compensation. Athletic administrators can draw up a rewards program for volunteers. The reward or recognition program can track volunteer hours logged and at specific levels, for example, volunteers could earn merchandise, gift cards, or free tickets to events. Although volunteers may not be motivated by extrinsic rewards, the gesture by athletic administrators goes a long way in retaining highly coveted volunteers. When volunteers return season after season or year after year, they lessen the burden on the athletic administrators who must train new people. The familiarity of having the same volunteers for the athletic department frees the athletic administrator from the continual training and deeper supervision required with new volunteers.

Sponsorships

Athletic administrators must be proactive in attempting to stimulate more growth in the form of revenue streams for their program needs or requests. Another avenue for fundraising is the sport sponsorship. In a corporate sponsorship, a company provides an athletic sporting event or team with money or gifts in kind in exchange for exposure. Sponsoring sporting events is desirable for companies because sport is connected to and rooted in communities, sport is considered a wholesome endeavor, and sport has a far-reaching appeal to participants and spectators. Athletic administrators solicit corporate sponsors at various levels of funding. Corporations analyze which sporting events best mesh with the target population they hope to capture through the sponsorship relationship. Decisions at the corporate level depend on the persuasive nature of the sponsorship deal. For example, companies that have products targeted to ice hockey players

ages 10–15 may not be interested in sponsoring a field hockey event for girls 10–15. Similarly, a company selling products to males ages 60–70, would not invest funds to support an event geared toward Little League players ages 6–10. The sponsorship relationship needs to make sense for the corporation in terms of the connection or overlap with its target market or a target market it hopes to attract in terms of market share. Fundraising is transactional in nature, meaning the entity will receive money or donations to be used for an activity or program, and the corporation will receive market visibility in return (Campbell & Company, n.d.).

Athletic administrators devote large quantities of time and effort into developing outreach initiatives to appeal to local, regional, and national businesses. These initiatives allow athletic administrators to cultivate relationships that can ultimately lead to a gift or monetary donation. The key for athletic administrators is to highlight how the corporations or businesses that provide funding to athletic programs will gain exposure for the relationship. Measuring the effectiveness of sponsorship relationships is not always an exact science; however, the athletic administrator still must stress how the connection would somehow lead to future sales.

Corporations desire to benefit from exposure within their core target base. Sport sponsorship is a viable option to appeal to target groups as a means to reach organizational goals. On many levels, people tend to perceive a corporation's involvement with sport as a form of goodwill. Through sport sponsorships and the relationships cultivated with sport programs, companies tap new or existing markets to assist in growing their reach and sales. In summary, sport sponsorships are rooted in an exchange relationship whereby one side gives up something of value (money or a gift) with the desire to gain something of value (exposure or new market visibility).

Soccer Fundraising - Golf Outing

August 28

Please join us for our 10th Annual Golf Outing. All proceeds this year will go to support the February 2021 Greece Soccer Tour.

Monday August 28
12 pm Registration
1 pm Shot Gun Start
Gentile Country Club

Highlighted Events:

The golf outing includes dinner and awards for closest to hole and longest drive. Attendees can enter our featured event the 'progressive putting contest' the winner who sinks all shots wins $5K. We will also have a raffle event with great prizes!

Select your participation level:

_____$700 Foursome   _____$100 Hole Sponsor

_____$175 Individual Golfer   _____$500 All Golf Carts Sponsor

_____$50 Dinner without Golf   _____ Donation $_____

Group Contact person and cell phone: _____

Identifying Sponsor Opportunities

For athletic administrators to reap the full benefits of sponsorships, the rationale for financial support needs to clearly be identified. Instead of a blanket approach to solicit all businesses in an area, athletic administrators need to focus on specific companies that are good matches for sponsor relations. Athletic administrators must describe how the demographics for their programs or teams match or overlap with the target market for the potential sponsor. Ultimately, business decision makers need to understand and be persuaded that the target markets are linked and that their product or service can benefit from the sponsorship relationship.

Milano (n.d.) provides a list of multiple ways to secure sponsorships for youth sports leagues. First, athletic administrators need to have a business mindset by tapping parents who own businesses to form committees or working groups. To persuade corporate sponsors, athletic administrators communicate all program benefits to showcase to potential companies the value that the sponsor relationship will add. Milano urges youth sport administrators to think locally versus nationally to connect the target market of the company with the sport entity (for example, the athletic administrator solicits restaurants and grocery stores that local families would frequent). Next, identify the amount needed to ensure collection of specific funds to cover program needs. Athletic administrators use the mission or the "warm and fuzzy" aspects of the entity to sell the program to corporate sponsors. Finally, athletic administrators create comprehensive sponsorship proposals to adequately market and sell the sponsorship opportunity (Milano, n.d.).

Types of Sponsor Opportunities

The impact of sport sponsorships cannot be underestimated when it comes down to how much these dollars add to decreasing or stagnant athletic budgets. When athletic administrators secure funding from external sources, the teams and athletes are able to fully benefit from the sponsorship relationship. Crafting sponsor opportunities takes a deliberate and mindful approach by athletic administrators to show how the sponsorship will meet the needs of the corporation. Potential sponsors and donors may require convincing when spending budget money on community outreach. Athletic administrators, in turn, compellingly identify how the financial commitment or contribution will be used along with the frequency of the exposure and marketing for the company before, during, and even after the event or season. Proving that target markets within the event's participant or spectator base overlaps with the company growth areas or core market strengthens the potential for attaining a corporate sponsorship.

In the end, sponsors are seeking a return on their investment in the form of exposure and increased sales. Competition to secure sponsorships is a real challenge for athletic administrators. Many competing groups (other schools, other programs, other youth establishments) seek to attract the same local or regional businesses. The clutter in the sponsor marketplace drives athletic administrators to be persuasive when connecting the funding relationship to the sport entity. Many sport entities exist in the same location, with all of them trying to make and secure connections with the same businesses for sponsor relationships. Breaking through the sport marketplace clutter takes both a

measured approach outlining the benefits for the business and a creative approach to make the sponsorship stand out over the others. A small plaque given to each sponsor by athletic programs is a low-cost yet effective gesture to show appreciation for a company's financial support.

Sponsorship Levels

Fundraising Partnerships

Many companies allow athletes to conduct storefront fundraising. Storefront fundraising may entail "canning" (athletes have a tin can and ask patrons for direct monetary donations), soliciting donations in exchange for a sport entity decal or small gift, or a bake sale or selling discount coupon books or cards to local business establishments. Storefront fundraising is much more prevalent because door-to-door fundraising is perceived as unsafe. Storefront fundraising has its benefits because patrons may feel a community-based connection with the young people initiating the fundraiser.

Home run	Triple	Double	Single
• $1000 • Logo on all publications. • Announcements at start of each inning. • Announcement after each home run. • Banner (at four field locations).	• $600 • Logo on game day program. • Announcements at end of each inning. • Banner in outfield.	• $400 • Banner in outfield. • Announcement at start and end of game.	• $200 • Banner in outfield.

Modified from Wilson Little League (n.d.). Sponsorship levels. Retrieved from http://www.wilsonlittleleague.com/Default.aspx?tabid=1017292.

Summer Sports Camps

One way to promote the athletic programs and raise additional funds is to operate a summer sport camp. Summer sports camps using the open weeks on a college or high school campus serve a dual purpose. The first is to generate revenue for the athletic department; the second is to create a connection between campus coaches and staff and the community. The community connection can serve the program well, especially when the school or entity is trying to get more fans to support the teams. From the club perspective, summer sport camps present an opportunity for program administrators to showcase the program to new prospects. Recreational program directors also organize a variety of summer sport camps to meet budgetary requirements as a non-profit. Many residents take advantage of the diverse offerings of sports that may give novices a chance to experience different athletic opportunities.

Alumni-Based Fundraising

Another fundraising option is to use the existing pool of contacts from past club or recreational enrollments or alumni of the institution. Athletic administrators can tap into the experiences of those alumni and, in turn, ask for donations or gifts to support a program with which they are already strongly connected.

Communication is critical within alumni-based fundraising. Alumni are interested in staying connected to their alma mater. Online access to scores and team stories appeal to alumni who want updates on their athletic teams. By crafting vibrant materials including websites and brochures that list upcoming events. Athletic administrators potentially attract alumni to attend events or give donations. Highlighting accolades of past teams is a guaranteed method to capture the attention of alumni who enjoy reliving their college athletic experiences. To attract a younger population of alumni, athletic administrators produce featured stories with catchy questions or phrases such as "Where are they now?" or "Alumni Stories." Alumni are intrigued to learn what former classmates and teammates have accomplished since graduation. Similarly, at the high school or club sport setting, this spotlight can be for an alumnus who is making an impact on a collegiate program or an alumna who just signed a letter of intent to attend a college on an athletic scholarship.

▶ Athletics and Development Office Relationship

Within the collegiate setting, athletic administrators work closely with the development office. The development office maintains databases with a host of contacts from different programs in academics, athletics, and student groups. The development office typically works with department heads to create marketing outreach programs with the intent to raise money from alumni. Ideas presented by department heads coupled with the broader vision of the development office allow for a pinpointed approach to reaching an already captivated audience (the alumni).

Grant Writing

Another option to supplement the athletic budget is in the form of grants. Grants are cash or gifts in kind from a government agency or any public/private entity (grantor). The grant recipient must complete a grant application to showcase how the program mission/purpose aligns with the criteria for the grant (https://www.grantwatch.com/cat/34/sports-and-recreation-grants.html).

Grant writers can be anyone in the athletic department or associated with the sport entity who complete the grant application or grant proposal process to secure grants.

Field Improvement Grants Available: Multiple States

The Pirates Charities Fields for Kids program provides financial support to improve youth baseball and/or softball facilities via matching grants. The program is open to any independent nonprofit tax-exempt organization, school, or local government unit that operates youth baseball and/or softball programs within the Pittsburgh Pirates market area, which primarily encompasses Western Pennsylvania, Eastern Ohio, and West Virginia.

Pirates.com (n.d.).

Capital Project Grant Funds for Outdoor Recreation and Conservation

Dane County Parks accepts applications year-round for the Conservation Fund Grant Program. This program offers grants to non-profit organizations and local governmental units for the purchase of land or land interests identified in the Dane County Parks & Open Space Plan or for lands in buffer areas immediately adjacent to park lands. *There is no application deadline.*

Grant Gopher (n.d.)

Examples of Grants

Reproduced with permission from GrantGopher.com http://grantgopher.com/Youth-Sports; http://grantgopher.com/Grants-for-Nonprofits/Capital-Project-Grant-Funds-for-Outdoor-Recreation-and-Conservation; Pirates.com (n.d.).

▶ Endowments

Fundraising Ideas

Traditional forms of fundraising include athlete-initiated efforts (asking for money) and corporate sponsorships. Many sport clubs, high school programs, and intercollegiate teams host tournaments during preseason or holiday weekends. These tournaments generate revenue through the fees charged to the participating team, and corporate sponsorships (logos on T-shirts, signage around the venue, logos on website) and through concession

sales during an event. At some tournaments, athletic administrators sell commemorative shirts, sweatshirts, or hats, generating another line of revenue for the program.

Many programs within the club and youth sport setting may host parent-only functions with monies raised earmarked for special events (trip to play in a tournament) or purchases (new uniforms or equipment). Entertainment-based events like music bingo, DJ-themed nights, wine tasting, auctions, and golf outings can generate funds as well as establish a bond among parents within the program. Hall of Fame dinners are specialized events commanding a high price tag covering the meal, entertainment, and venue rental. All athletic settings can take advantage of events to solicit donors and generate funding through attendees purchasing raffle tickets to win prizes. At fundraising events, raffle ticket sales for prizes (wine baskets, tickets to a professional sporting event, gift cards), or 50–50 tickets (half the collected money goes to the winner and half to the athletic program) can potentially generate a few thousand dollars for little effort on the part of the athletic administrator.

💬 FEATURED INTERVIEW: COLLEGE ATHLETICS

China Jude serves as assistant vice president and athletics director at Queens College. Jude has been awarded several accolades, including the 2015 National Association of Collegiate Women Athletics Administrators Division II Administrator of the Year. Jude was honored by the Metropolitan Swimming Official Association in 2012 and named the 2011–12 Alumnae of the Year by the United States Sports Academy. She also serves on the Minority Opportunities Athletics Association board of directors. Queens College sponsors 19 varsity sports and is the fourth largest Division II school in the country and the only Division II college within the City University of New York system and State University of New York system. In 2016, Queens finished 99th in the Learfield Directors' Cup standings, the highest finish in department history.

When Jude arrived at Queens College in 2011, there was already a process in place for fundraising in terms of complying with New York City regulations, adhering to standards set by the Department of Education and the Department of Health. Her responsibility was to update all of the processes, switching everything over to an electronic system. She evaluated the department's revenue flow and how it identified its core demographic group. In addition, she made sure she had the appropriate staff and people. Furthermore, she analyzed whether staff members were getting the appropriate training to make sure they were providing positive customer service while putting out a good product.

At Queens College, fundraising is done in several ways. Jude wrote an NCAA grant to hire an assistant athletic director of development whose main responsibility is to cultivate alumni to make sure the athletic department is staying in touch with recent graduates and alumni who have been out of school for awhile. On arrival at Queens College, she found that there was no development arm for the athletic department. At the time, Queens College had the Department of Institutional Advancement overseeing all of the fundraising and naming rights for the entire institution; however, no specific link was attached to the athletic department. In 2011, Jude started outreach initiatives. She started with alumni who worked in the world of sports such as Donna Orender (former president of the Women's National Basketball Association). Although Jude did not know Orender personally, she called to introduce herself and discovered they knew some of the same people in the industry. That conversation then led Jude to contact another alumnus, and this networking occurred many times with individuals referring teammates, colleagues, and classmates to Jude. From a few conversations, Jude was able to build a base.

From one conversation with one alumnus who spoke eloquently about his time at Queens College, Jude realized she needed to do more to get the alumni base together and formed an Athletics Hall of Fame Dinner. She immediately involved this particular alumnus to be part of the Hall of Fame planning; from that event, other alumni ideas started to spin off, including commemorate gifts, naming rights, and a fundraising campaign for the basketball court. All of these meetings and conversations raised $6 million for the basketball program and honored legendary coach Lucille Kyvallos (Queens College, 2017).

Jude then secured the naming rights for the baseball stadium, cultivating a relationship with Charles H. Hennekens, MD, who was not only a student-athlete but also contributed to medicine in his professional life by discovering that aspirin prevents a first heart attack and can prevent death when given during or just after a heart attack. Dr. Hennekens was part of the Queens College alumni initiative, and as Jude and Hennekens talked, his love of sport was so strong that it led to securing the naming rights for the baseball stadium (CUNY Newswire, n.d.). From these conversations, other rights started to be secured for the baseball timing system and renovation of the aquatics facility, all from phone calls and Jude asking alumni for help in navigating alumni history in athletics.

Before being hired as the assistant vice president of athletics and working in a variety of positions at the collegiate level, Jude also worked for several nonprofit organizations that required grant writing and fundraising. It is interesting that her dissertation focused on athletic alumni and motivating factors for financial giving. In her literature review, she analyzed the tug of war between athletics and institutional advancement. Jude explains that with a small institution or a small pool of prospective donors, there will be questions at the institutional level about which program benefits from those financial gifts.

Because athletic alumni were not being cultivated on a consistent basis at Queens College, Jude had free reign to reach out to alumni for athletic-specific donations. She always included her counterpart from Institutional Advancement to be sure there were no conflicts with the alumni with whom she was developing donor relations. For Jude, it is an unspoken rule that if an alumnus could be at a high giving level, she would loop in Institutional Advancement. Jude points out that any donors giving less than $25,000 were not on the radar for the Institutional Advancement office.

Jude also describes the procurement of a commemorative gift in which the donor wanted to exceed the traditional three- to four-year naming right time frame (contract) to instead develop a lifetime donor relationship for naming rights to the baseball field. A commemorative gift exists for naming a bench, a locker room, a dug out, and anything on a smaller scale ($25,000). The gift naming or plaque stays with the gift for typically three to four years. When the donor wanted to change the parameters of the naming rights contract, Jude contacted the Institutional Advancement office to legally offer this type of arrangement with the donor over a much longer period of time. Jude expresses that she is extremely fortunate to have such a positive and respectful working relationship with the Department of Institutional Advancement. As an example, the Hall of Fame event has been running for many years now, and the director of alumni relations serves on the selection committee so that there is always a link back to the Department of Institutional Advancement.

When asked how she prioritizes and targets different opportunities for donations, Jude said there are three levels: lower, middle, and high ranges. Lower-level giving is when a donor gives $10,000 or less. The athletic department makes efforts to have these donors commit every year. Gifts can be deducted from credit cards or pledges can be in the form of a check. At this level, Jude wants to keep the donors involved and engaged and even tap their time or talents. As an example, the alumnus who inspired the Hall of Fame dinner has been asked to be the master of ceremony for the event. Jude said she is not going after financial gifts from him because he is doing so much work to plan the event; instead she will use his talents to assist with the event. At the lower giving level, the donations

(continues)

are smaller but more frequent, which helps offset the cost of meal money or uniforms for student-athletes. For the middle-level donations, the gifts range from $10,000 to $50,000. The middle-range donations are allocated for facility upgrades such as lockers for the locker room or academic room renovation. At this middle-range level, the gift is substantial, and Jude reaches out to specific donors based on their giving level. On the Hall of Fame application, individuals will report their income level, giving Jude leads on potential gifts so she can cultivate alumni in a more targeted fashion.

The highest ranges of giving start at $50,000. At this level, donors are gifting naming rights, endowments, and scholarships. As Jude explains, at the $50,000 plus level these are not overnight solicitations but take multiple years of conversations, connecting with them at various events, and speaking with them at different functions so she can continue to engage and educate them on the athletic program.

Jude has raised an impressive $6 million for a Division II institution, which compares to the bottom 15 percent of Division I institutions. From the $6 million raised, the department also collects $600,000 from student fees; the institution then allocates $1.1 million to the department. Of the $1.1 million, Jude says $200,000 covers operating expenses, including the cost for buses, officials, and uniforms. The remaining $900,0000 covers five salaried staff members. However, Jude is quick to note she has a staff of 50, so that means that the $4.5 million raised covers salaries, scholarships, and operating expenses because $200,000 does not fully fund 19 athletic teams.

When asked how much time Jude spends on fundraising, she says the percentage varies based several factors. Previously, Jude did not have the associate athletic director for finance position filled. Jude and the business manager handled the finances. Luckily, before the associate athletic director for finance position was vacated, she was already forecasting everything over the next three to four years. Jude had a strategy in terms of creating surpluses and addressing cost-of-living changes that would affect the budget. For that year, Jude spent 45 percent of her time monitoring the budget but not fundraising. Now she spends more time on securing gifts, naming rights, and fundraising campaigns so the percentages have changed. Jude estimates she spends 20 percent of her time monitoring the budget and 50 percent of her time focusing on securing major gifts. Jude notes that the time devoted to fundraising "depends on the dynamics of my staff and the time of year."

The priority of fundraising may vary from institution to institution. Jude knows many athletic administrators from private and public institutions who do not have fundraising as a mandate. Jude adds, "but after experiencing what I experienced at Queens, I am going in every day knowing I have to be on my 'A Game.' Everyday, I cannot make one financial error because it may create a deficit." Jude asserts that "fundraising is not for everyone because some people are not wired that way, but it is a skill set that can strengthen not only an athletic department but [also] help to contribute to the institution as a whole."

Discussion Questions

1. In today's world of athletic administrations, an administrator going into the field should be aware that fundraising is a large part of the position. What are some courses that can help future athletic administrators be competent in fundraising?

2. There are many institutions and communities that feel athletics is not a viable part of the institution and usually spends more money than it makes. Based on this featured interview, what would your response to this statement entail?

3. What is the relationship between the athletics department and the development office at the school you attend or have attended?

4. Soliciting and securing donations is a skill set for athletic administrators. What is your comfort level for asking people for financial support? What are some training exercises or activities you can practice to elevate your skills in this area? Youth Sport: Fundraising

MANAGERIAL APPLICATIONS

As the President of the town wrestling program, your aim for the following fiscal year is to secure at least $15,000 in corporate sponsorships. The challenge is that there are numerous youth sport associations within the town soliciting the same exact local companies and businesses. Since you have many connections in town you feel comfortable with the relationships you have cultivated over time. However, wrestling is not a popular sport, with low participation rates within the community.

Questions to Consider

1. What type of benefits would you list in your sponsorship proposal to persuade local business owners to invest in a sponsorship with your program versus the more popular sports of soccer and basketball within your community? Research local businesses in your community and create a spreadsheet of companies to be contacted for sponsorship opportunities. One column should be titled "Target Market" to map how the core market for your wrestling program (participants and spectators) overlaps with the core market of the prospective corporate sponsor.
2. What type of exposure would be granted to businesses willing to contribute funding to support your program? Please illustrate the exact type of corporate sponsorship exposure and amount of exposure across the year that could be added to the wrestling program.
3. Because there is great competition to secure sponsorships in your community but the efforts are extremely time consuming, craft a proposal for all local teams to share in the sponsorship drives as a collective effort versus a sport-by-sport pursuit. What are the pros and cons of this type of approach?

 MANAGERIAL APPLICATIONS

College Athletics Naming Rights

Finally, the construction on your campus of two major athletic buildings, a baseball complex, and a men's and women's basketball facility is complete. You have been tasked to secure naming rights for both facilities, the locker room space in the basketball facility, and both dugouts for the baseball venue. These are the only facilities on the strategic plan identified for naming rights, but you are considering looking into all possible spaces for revenue generation through naming rights.

Questions to Consider

1. What are some outreach initiatives you will consider to secure alumni donations for the facility naming rights? What events will you craft to engage the alumni to consider giving to athletics in the form of naming rights? What are some of the motives that drive alums to give to their alma mater?
2. The Office of Institutional Advancement has strict regulations on contacting potential donors. What are some ways you can share outreach initiatives with this office? What are some of the overlaps you could communicate to the Office of Institutional Advancement so it understands the mindset of athletic giving over institutional giving?
3. Men's and women's basketball share the same facility and therefore will share the naming rights for the court. List any anticipated issues stemming from naming rights from female versus male alumni. How will you guide both programs to embrace the donation despite where it came from?

DECISION-MAKING CHALLENGE

Case Study: High School Athletics

You are new to the high school and inherited a booster club system with many issues. First, the girls' basketball team has the largest booster club in your program, raising more than $100,000 a year. The budget to operate the girls' basketball team is less than $50,000, including part-time coaching salaries. The district already supports the budget, and the initial goal of the booster club was to just give teams a chance to purchase practice gear and team travel items (jacket and bag). The girls' basketball booster club is demanding that the team get to use the additional funding to travel to a tournament across the country. As athletic director, your dilemma is that you must consider all programs. Allowing one team to spend $50,000 while other teams cannot even raise $5,000 may raise some red flags. What would your response be to the girls' basketball booster club? If you agree to let the team use all of the funds, what rationale would you communicate to the rest of the department and coaches? If you reject the proposal to use the funds, what rationale would you communicate to the booster club members? What policies can you implement to avoid such a difference in fundraising across all of your programs?

 DECISION-MAKING CHALLENGE

Case Study: Youth Sports

Grants can assist sport administrators in supplementing depleting budgets. Many grants are available, but the application process is time consuming. Many athletic administrators spend countless hours collecting information for applications and then many more writing grant requests. As the executive director of a sport nonprofit serving children in a low-income area, what types of grants are available to fund a variety of sport teams (select three)? Find a mission statement of a nonprofit sport entity online. Using the mission statement as your guide, what grants from a mission perspective align with your selected sport entity? What persuasive words or data can you add to your application to showcase the necessity to secure the grants?

Wrap-Up

End-of-Chapter Activities

College Athletics

1. Your institution currently lacks a policy on fundraising for each team. As the athletic administrator, you find it taxing to monitor all of the fundraising after the activities take place. Review policies centered on approving of fundraising activities at two institutions and then craft a version that best matches your philosophy of administration.

2. One way to generate more funds for your athletic department budget is by advertising in sports venues. Advertising space is available on the outfield fences on the softball and baseball fields, the walls of the gymnasium used for men's and women's basketball, and the press box overlooking the multipurpose stadium (used by football and men's and women's soccer). Create a memo seeking approval from the college development office for permission to solicit corporate sponsors to purchase advertising space.

High School Athletics

1. The high school principal has asked you to present a proposal regarding fundraising plans for the next academic year. The request requires that you share ideas for hosting a preseason tournament for at least four teams to generate additional revenue to pay for officials ($150,000) for the upcoming year. Your school sponsors the following sports: field hockey, girls' soccer, boys' soccer, girls' basketball, boys' basketball, girls' volleyball, baseball, softball, girls' lacrosse, and boys' lacrosse. Which sports would you select, how many teams would you invite to the tournament, what additional revenue options would you consider for these tournaments, and what are the challenges for the athletic department to raise so much money to support the programs?

2. As the athletic director, you have been asked to speak to the superintendent and school committee on the evolution of fundraising in high school athletics. Put together a research-based outline of talking points to explain the purpose of fundraising, the evolution of fundraising in this setting, and the challenges and time constraints athletic administrators face when trying to supplement budgets.

End-of-Chapter Questions

1. Fundraising is a core tool that needs to be cultivated by athletic administrators across all settings. In your opinion, which setting—college, high school, youth, or club sport—may be the easiest to generate momentum and the most money raised? Explain the rationale for your response.

2. Asking people for donations is not as easy as we may think. Craft a list of talking points you will use to solicit donations from the following groups; please note that each group has a different investment in the program, so craft individualized talking points for parents of participants, program alumni, and community members. Please adapt the list for the college, high school, youth, and club sport settings.

3. Within some college and high school athletic departments, booster clubs raise a great deal of funding for specific teams. One challenge is to oversee the amount raised compared to other teams that may not have large alumni rosters or have less-effective fundraisers. Craft a policy to address fundraising at either a high school or college to provide oversight to coaches and athletic boosters. Be comprehensive and specific in the regulations crafted. Decide if you want to maintain equity across all programs or allow individual programs to collect 100 percent of the dollars raised. Please also provide a rationale for your decision for this policy decision.

4. You are charged with raising $50,000 for your club field hockey program. The program aims to organize an international trip for 25 players. Craft a one-year fundraising plan to collect the full $50,000 through fundraising. Illustrate a timeline of activities coupled with the dollars raised. Include an Excel spreadsheet that shows the revenue collected and expenditures for the fundraising activities. Use online sources to determine the cost of the fundraising campaign. Along with the budget items associated with the fundraising initiative, list tasks that need to be addressed throughout the year-long initiative.

5. Volunteers constitute an important aspect for fundraising events. What are some incentives you would provide to high school and club parents who

volunteer for events? List appropriate fundraising events to generate revenue to purchase team equipment. Write an email to solicit volunteer involvement from the parents of your program to assist with fundraising.

6. Craft an email to your staff explaining the importance of fundraising within the athletic department. In the email, include the expectations for each coach to raise funds to support his or her team. Inform the coaching staff they need to raise $4,000 each for their programs over the next year.

7. Conduct an online search and locate a grant that you may apply for if you worked in the collegiate, high school, youth, or club setting. Provide the full details of the grant along with some of the past recipients, indicating how they used the funds for their programs.

8. Research the costs associated with attending athletic events (high school or college) in your area. In your estimation, what should the revenue from ticket sales be used for? If one team sells more tickets than another sport, should that team share in the revenue or should it be spread out department-wide? Provide a rationale for your response in managing fundraising at either a high school or college athletic department.

9. Paying for athletic participation at the scholastic level has been common for a few decades. The practice of requiring payment for athletic participation has become the standard of operation in scholastic athletic departments, which supplement budgets by collecting additional funds from families. What is your stand on "pay for play"? How can the athletic department raise external funds to eliminate pay for play, or is this unrealistic given the current economic state?

10. There are two watchdog groups in intercollegiate athletics: the Delta Cost Project (http://www.deltacostproject.org/) and the Knight Commission on Intercollegiate Athletics (https://www.knightcommission.org/). Visit both sites to read some of the work relating to spending within colleges and universities. Share four major aspects of the work of these groups and how it has affected the management of college athletics.

11. Create a fundraising event for a program within collegiate, high school, club, or youth sport.
    a. Describe the purpose of the event.
    b. State the event's goal (e.g., total funds raised after expenses).
    c. Include a complete 12-month planning time line for the event.
    d. Identify the staff involved.
    e. Craft a letter for potential sponsors that specifies benefits a company will receive in exchange for sponsoring the event; incorporate three levels of sponsorship categories.

12. Find two articles focused on fundraising in athletics. Describe the content of each article and share your thoughts on implementing fundraising within your sport entity.

13. Have you ever attended a fundraiser in support of a team or athletic programs? What events or activities have impressed you enough that you would consider adopting them for your fundraising efforts within your own sport entity?

14. Visit the website for one youth sport organization, one club organization, one high school athletic department, and one college athletic department. Can you determine which staff person handles the fundraising arm for the athletic programs? Indicate whether his or her role is full-time within athletics or is in another department on campus (for high school and college sport settings only).

References

Balog, S. E., & Connaughton, D. P. (2002). Fundraising for interscholastic athletic and recreation programs. *Strategies, 16*(2),37–38.

Campbell & Company (n.d.) "Fundraising" vs. "development": A useful distinction? Retrieved from http://www.campbellcompany.com/news/bid/105288/Fundraising-vs-Development-A-Useful-Distinction.

Cherokee County School District. (n.d.). *2016–17 Athletic handbook.* Retrieved from http://cherokeek12.net/freedomms/wp-content/uploads/sites/14/2016/09/SY2016-17-Athletic-Handbook.pdf.

City of Arlington, Massachusetts (n.d.). Capital projects. Retrieved from http://www.arlingtonma.gov/departments/recreation/capital-projects.

CUNY Newswire (n.d.). Queens College athletics program names baseball stadium after world-renowned scientist Dr. Charles Hennekens. Retrieved from http://www1.cuny.edu/mu/forum/2015/10/19/queens-college-athletics-program-names-baseball-stadium-after-world-renowned-scientist-dr-charles-hennekens/.

Delta Cost Project (n.d.). Retrieved from http://www.deltacostproject.org/.

Grant Gopher (n.d.). Capital project grant funds for outdoor recreation and conservation. Retrieved from http://grantgopher.com/Grants-for-Nonprofits/Capital-Project-Grant-Funds-for-Outdoor-Recreation-and-Conservation.

Grant Gopher (n.d.). Youth sports grants, athletic, baseball, football, soccer, physical fitness programs. (n.d.). Retrieved from http://grantgopher.com/Youth-Sports.

Kansas University Athletics (n.d.) Policies and procedures—704B Facilities: Maintenance. Retrieved from http://www.kuathletics.com/sports/2013/6/25/GEN_0625134418.aspx?id=92es.

Knight Commission on Intercollegiate Athletics. (n.d.). Retrieved from https://www.knightcommission.org/.

Marist College (n.d.). Athletic fund raising & support. Retrieved from https://www.marist.edu/athletics/fundraising.html.

Milano, S. (n.d.). Youthletic. Retrieved from http://www.youthletic.com/authors/942/.

Pirates.com (n.d.). Fields for kids. Retrieved from https://www.mlb.com/pirates/community/fields-for-kids.

Powell, F. (2018, October 16). Ten universities with the biggest endowments. *U.S. News & World Report* [online]. Retrieved from www.usnews.com/education/best-colleges/the-short-list-college/articles/10-universities-with-the-biggest-endowments.

Queens College (2017). Queens College to honor legendary women's basketball coach Lucille Kyvallos with Court Dedication. Retrieved from http://www.queensknights.com/general/2017-18/releases/20170922kugnap.

Stier, W. F. Jr., & Schneider, R. (1999). Fundraising: An essential competency for the sport manager in the 21st century. *Mid-Atlantic Journal of Business, 35*(2), 93–103.

Stinson, J. L., & Howard, D. R. (2010). Intercollegiate athletics as an institutional fundraising tool: An exploratory donor-based view. *Journal of Nonprofit & Public Sector Marketing, 22*(4), 312–335. doi:10.1080/10495140802662572.

Volleygrass (n.d.). Retrieved from http://www.Volleygrass.com/.

Wheaton College (n.d.). Athletics—Wheaton College fundraising policy for intercollegiate athletics. Retrieved from http://athletics.wheaton.edu/sports/2012/5/9/GEN_fundraising.aspx.

Wilson Little League (n.d.). Sponsorship levels. Retrieved from http://www.wilsonlittleleague.com/Default.aspx?tabid=1017292.

CHAPTER 7

Risk Management

LEARNING OBJECTIVES

After reading this chapter, students will be able to:

1. Explain the role of athletic administrators in implementing risk management plans for sporting activities and events.
2. Develop sound and applicable risk management plans and training programs for athletic programs at the college, high school, youth, and club sport levels.
3. Identify the challenges associated with managing risk in common areas of athletics, including fan and crowd control, transportation, and selection and training of staff and volunteers.
4. Apply the principles of risk management in college, high school, youth, and club sport settings.
5. Identify the inherent risks associated with athletics in the college, high school, youth, and club sport settings.

The organization and administration of athletic programs requires keen oversight to ensure the safety of participants and spectators. Since the turn of the 21st century, risk management has evolved from the simple management of field space, indoor facility maintenance, and fan monitoring to a much larger charge because of increased litigation, enhanced physicality of athletes, and securing venues from violence within and around the areas of operation. Risk management is the administrative duty to ensure that athletic events function seamlessly and mitigate risk. Fuller and Drawer (2004) define risk management as "the overall process of assessing and controlling risks within an organizational setting and includes

the subprocesses of risk assessment and risk mitigation" (p. 349).

Athletic administrators within college, high school, youth, and club sport create risk mitigation plans in a variety of ways, with safety being the end goal in each setting. Risk management requires the due diligence of all staff members, not just the head administrator, to minimize risk, injury, and harm in the sporting realm. Forecasting impending risks along with staff education to identify and then offset potential risks are ongoing aspects of athletic programming. Risk management assumes many forms, including the management of practices and games under the supervision of coaches and designated contest managers.

▶ Staff Education and Training

Within the college, high school, youth, and club sport settings, monitoring and implementing risk management planning does not rest solely with one athletic administrator. The responsibility of risk management or assessment is vested within all types of athletic administrators and support staff positions. At all times, each staff person must uphold the highest standards of care to offset any chance of harm to participants and spectators. There are levels of care that staff should naturally assume as professionals before, during, and after athletic contests. Staff members are expected to act diligently to ensure playing surfaces are safe for games and practices, bleachers and seating are safe for fans, and the areas around the playing surfaces are also risk free. Risk mitigation is part of the process of assessing whether a playing area should be used or not. The decision to play on a surface after rain or sleet is often determined by the athletic administrator or on-site supervisor. There are occasions when practices and games are underway and foul weather commences. The decision to continue to play or to cancel a game or practice rests with staff members on site whether they are volunteer coaches or paid recreation directors. Often, for sporting events, there are contest managers (college and high school level) who oversee the safety of the venue during inclement weather or other potential vulnerabilities. At the youth sport level, board members may monitor playing venues to decide whether to cancel or postpone events during inclement weather, electrical outages, or public safety concerns. For club-level sports there are typically designated officials acting as "contest managers" or "site supervisors" for highly attended events to monitor and assess risks and decide whether to cancel any session because of dangerous exposure.

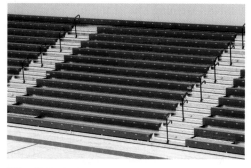

© B Brown/Shutterstock.

Risk management planning and procedures that identify steps to resolve potential issues need to be in place so staff can easily decide and then communicate the assessment to the appropriate participants and staff members. Athletic administrators secure athletic settings by designating staff to manage the facilities from a safety and risk management perspective. Proactive athletic administrators act diligently in protecting the welfare of their participants and spectators by hiring qualified staff, incorporating athletic training and sport medicine teams into the program, maintaining fields, and appropriately supervising athletes during the sport settings to offset hazards and protect the integrity of the sport setting.

Role of Athletic Trainers

Coaches are typically the first responders to athletic injuries. However, coaches have

© De Space Studio/Shutterstock.

limited training in handling traumatic injuries. At the collegiate and high school levels, the employment of athletic trainers (ATs), either full- or part-time, is more prevalent than at the youth or club athletic settings. At high-impact sporting events such as ice hockey and football games, many athletic organizations will employ a physician and even have an ambulance on standby to handle serious injuries. At the youth and club levels, when there are tournaments or highly attended events, athletic organizations tend to hire athletic trainers to oversee the management of injuries. Best practice dictates that athletic administrators take precautions to protect the well-being of participants and spending extra funds on sport medicine is a reasonable investment.

Athletic trainers are the medical personnel associated with supporting sporting events across the college, high school, youth, and club sport settings. Typically, athletic trainers make up a sports medicine team at the collegiate and high school levels. The sport medicine team starts with the coach, who may be the first person to see the cause of injury, and then the athletic trainer, who is under the supervision of a physician. The athletic trainer is a professional who may be certified through the National Athletic Trainers' Association (NATA) or a state-level association, and who completed accredited college-level courses coupled with passing a certifying exam. Once certified, the athletic trainer must complete continuing education courses within the athletic training domain, as well as have up-to-date credentials in cardiopulmonary resuscitation (CPR), use of an automated external defibrillator (AED), and first aid and safety credentials. To practice athletic training, each professional must work under the supervision of a physician. At the college and university setting, there may be multiple athletic trainers on staff to manage

the health of student-athletes. The same may hold true at high schools with larger athletic scopes and staff budgets. Frequently, the high school athletic trainer is contracted to the schools by another medical facility such as sports medicine, physical therapy, or physical rehabilitation. The athletic trainer may be employed full- or part-time by these agencies for daytime staffing and then contracted to support the high school athletic programs starting in the afternoon and continuing through the evening. "As injuries and deaths continue to occur in the secondary school setting, organizations such as the American Medical Association and NATA continue to endorse and support the hiring of [athletic trainers] to prevent unnecessary injuries and deaths related to sport participation and physical activity" (Pike, Pryor, Vandermark, Mazerolle, & Casa, 2017, p. 5).

Close to 8 million high school students competed in athletics during the 2016–17 academic year, according to the annual High School Athletics Participation Survey conducted by the National Federation of State High School Associations (NFHS, 2017). Pike et al. (2017) report that 58% of private secondary schools and 70% of public secondary schools employ athletic trainers full-time, part-time, or through clinical assignment. However, "although different levels of medical care were supplied, a similar percentage of student-athletes had access to AT

© Nestor Rizhniak/Shutterstock.

services in both the public and private sectors" (Pike et al., 2017, p. 8). The NATA delineates the variety of roles for a certified athletic trainer pertaining to the settings of college, high school, youth, and club sport as follows:

Athletic Trainer
Healthcare Program
1. The athletic trainer will be able to demonstrate an ability to perform the following functions regarding athletic injuries: prevention, assessment, treatment (including first aid), and reconditioning as set forth by the board of certification (BOC).
2. The athletic trainer will demonstrate proper taping, strapping, bracing, and fitting of athletic equipment.
3. The athletic trainer will carry out all prescribed treatments and recommendations by the team, program, or event physician.
4. The athletic trainer will maintain BOC and CPR certification in accordance with those respective institutions.
5. The athletic trainer will cover assigned preseason physicals, sports games or matches, and related events under the supervision of the program manager.
6. The athletic trainer must demonstrate knowledge of the principals of growth and development over the life span and possess the ability to assess data reflective of the athlete's status and interpret the appropriate information.

Athletic Trainer: College Level
1. Develop an overall sports medicine program for the university, including injury-prevention programs, injury evaluations, injury management, injury treatment and rehabilitation, educational programs, and counseling for athletes.
2. Provide athletic training services for the university's athletic department, including attendance at scheduled team practices and home and away competitions as necessary.
3. Coordinate and schedule physical examinations and medical referrals for student-athletes to determine their ability to practice and compete.
4. Responsible for the formation of the university's athletic training staff, including hiring, training, and supervision of assistant and associate athletic trainers, graduate assistant athletic trainers, and student athletic trainers.
5. Work in conjunction with the strength and conditioning staff to ensure safety in the design and implementation of fitness, nutrition, and conditioning programs customized to meet individual student-athlete needs.
6. Schedule and coordinate athletic training staff and students for coverage of all team practices and athletic competitions.
7. Assist the athletic director and business manager in the development of the sports medical program budget.
8. Evaluate and recommend new techniques and equipment that would enhance the benefit of the sports medical program.
9. Keep records and documentation.

College Assistant Athletic Trainer
Primary Responsibilities
1. Prevent athletic injuries and illnesses.
2. Evaluate athletic injuries.
3. Treat athletic injuries.
4. Provide counseling and education to student-athletes.
5. Perform athletic training administrative duties.
6. Assist with coordination and scheduling of medical coverage for home and away competitions.
7. Supervise, educate, and recruit student and graduate assistant athletic trainers.
8. Keep records and documentation.
9. Work with doctors and other allied health professionals to deliver care to student-athletes.

Reproduced with permission from National Athletic Trainers' Association https://www.nata.org/career-education/career-center/post-a-job/sample-job-descriptions.

High School Athletic Trainer*
1. Maintain appropriate general treatment orders to be reviewed annually and approved by the team physician.
2. Provide athletic training services for all home athletic contests and away varsity football games. If a conflict arises between an away varsity football game and a home contest, the varsity football event will supersede.
3. Act as liaison between family physicians and specialists, the school district, athletes, and their parents.
4. Maintain accurate records of injuries and treatments and provide insurance claim forms for sports injuries treated by a physician.
5. Develop and maintain a budget for the athletic training program.
6. Schedule and be present for pre-participation sports physicals.
7. Provide the coaches and athletic director with a list of athletes medically eligible to compete under district and state rules and regulations.
8. Assist the athletic director as requested.

*Athletic Training Services: The management and provision of care of injuries to a physically active person as defined in the state practice act with the direction of a licensed physician. The term includes the rendering of emergency care, development of injury prevention programs, and providing appropriate preventative [services] and devices for the physically active person. The term also includes the assessment, management, treatment, rehabilitation, and recondition of the physically active person whose conditions are within the professional preparation and education of a certified athletic trainer. The term also includes the use of modalities such as mechanical stimulation, heat, cold, light, air, water, electricity, sound, massage, and the use of therapeutic exercises, reconditioning exercise, and fitness programs.

Reproduced with permission from National Athletic Trainers' Association https://www.nata.org/career-education/career-center/post-a-job/sample-job-descriptions.

▶ Club Sports

As an entity, club sports has started to use more programs for injury prevention. *Sport performance* is a term that highlights the importance not only of training for a specific sport but also of conditioning the body to handle the stress of an intense sport program. Athletic trainers may be supplemental staff or hired contractors to serve the needs of clubs. Especially for indoor spaces or during off-season training, clubs may add a strength and conditioning program to supplement sport-specific training.

Stretching and rehabilitation are also components of athletic training and sport medicine teams. The trend for many sport clubs is to link with a sports medicine team that offers concussion awareness, baseline testing for concussions, body measurements, and fitness evaluations. The connection to a sports medicine team can be considered value added for members or families who are paying tuition fees for participation in the club. As an example, the Indian Fire Juniors Soccer Club employs a full-time athletic trainer as part of the menu of offerings for its members.

Athletic Trainer in Club Setting

Our Athletic Training services (AT) are available to all NCFC players as part of all Club fees. AT includes, but is not limited to, injury evaluation, taping, stretching, icing, and soccer-specific rehabilitation for any injury. Our Head Athletic Trainer, Jason Bailey, is certified in Athletic Training, Strength and Conditioning, Performance Enhancement, and Corrective Exercise, and he is supported by another certified AT and interns. The training room is conveniently located at WRAL Soccer Park, and is generally open during training sessions on the weekdays and mornings/afternoons on game weekends.

North Carolina FC Youth (n.d.)

 FEEDBACK FROM THE FIELD

Best Practices: Youth Sport Athletics

Luz Quirk is the owner of Reinforce the Game, LLC, in Swampscott, Massachusetts. She earned her bachelor's of science degree in athletic training and applied exercise science from Springfield College and her master's of education in organizational management from Endicott College. Quirk has worked with U.S. Figure Skating, the Cape Cod Baseball League, and numerous youth, high school, and collegiate athletes. Currently, she is an independent contractor for Spaulding Rehabilitation Hospital, Elite Lacrosse, and many other private camps that provide athletic training services. Quirk currently works as a product developer improving protective sporting goods equipment.

From Quirk's experience, risk management and health care are constantly evolving. Specifically, she has witnessed major growth in technology, records management, medical research, and treatment. As she points out, "some great advances available to athletic trainers today are the immediate access to automated external defibrillators (AEDs), applications that can detect the proximity of lightning, and tools that make communication between physicians, parents, coaches, and administrators expeditious and attainable." According to Quirk

"the core areas athletic administrators need to assess as a top priority are implementing risk management procedures, maintaining accurate records, following policy, and ensuring athlete safety. Providing proper supervision by trained professionals, maintaining equipment and facilities, and being diligent and consistent on every facet of the system is critical in managing risk."

Because the topic of concussions is prevalent in athletic administration, Quirk was asked to share how to incorporate the best treatment of care. Concussion prevention depends on many variables, but Quirk says "it works best when coaches, athletes, and the sports medicine team is educated, conscientious, and deliberate," adding that "training and technique, recognition, evaluation, and treatment are essential in prevention and treatment of concussions."

In Quirk's current professional setting, the staff is educated through concussion-safety seminars and online courses through the Commonwealth of Massachusetts. Along with coaches and athletic trainers, Quirk explains, parents and athletes are given resources that summarize the injury and highlight red flags and symptoms. She engages the parents by being thorough during the exam and treatment, being clear with instruction, and available any time to answer questions. Following up after the injury is also critical in the process.

When asked how Quirk would explain the importance of coaches understanding risk management, she would reinforce "athlete safety as the number one priority, the standard policies and procedures of care, and the concerns of negligence and liability." Regarding coaches and their methods of instruction, she provides resources and materials that would be relevant to their sports risks. Quirk communicated the importance of following safety for the best interest of the athlete and "keeping [him or her] in the game and not on the

(continues)

FEEDBACK FROM THE FIELD   *(continued)*

sidelines with an injury." In terms of training and educating the staff on risk management, Quirk reinforces all areas to ensure high standards with "constant review of policies and procedures, injury prevention through strength and conditioning, and proper technique and diligence with records management." Quirk further explained that staff can play a role in effective risk management by noting that "continuing education, collaboration of new methods, and motivation to meet goals will also help the mission." In Quirk's estimation, if risk management procedures are clearly implemented and communicated, there should not be a "blind spot" in the process. "The entire team," Quirk stresses, "must be open and on point with the plans and policies implemented and constant training, evaluation, and education will prevent any deficiencies."

Unfortunately, athletic trainers experience challenges when dealing with risk management protocols, especially "in the moment of a big game or season, perspectives can be blurred by the competitive nature of sport." Quirk details that most athletic trainers have worked with parents, athletes, or coaches who can be dismissive of the severity of an injury and the risks of further injury. In one scenario, Quirk encountered a parent who insisted [his] child was okay to participate in sport with a diagnosis of mononucleosis. The consequences of participating in sport with this condition are severe: Patients with mononucleosis have an enlarged spleen that is fragile and could rupture if hit or strained, which can be a life-threatening injury. Subsequently, Quirk and staff followed the procedure of not allowing the athlete to participate until fully cleared by a doctor and with documentation of clearance to play.

Quirk affirms that future athletic administrators should always be "accountable for [their] decisions and align them with the goals and principles of an effective leader and administrator." She continues to reinforce that athletic administrators "should also put the athlete's safety and well-being as their highest priority. The essential role athletic trainers play in the administration of sport is as the healthcare provider for the 'team,' adding that athletic trainers act as a link between health and successful sport." From Quirk's experience across multiple sport settings and organizations, collaboration and compliance between athletic trainers and athletic administrators "will allow all to work at their best." Quirk notes that "athletic trainers offering exceptional treatment, training, and medical educational resources to the department and always being available to coaches, athletes, parents, and medical doctors will decrease risk of injury."

Another youth club, North Carolina FC Youth, incorporates the athletic trainer at practices and games, providing a variety of services for its membership.

▶ Role of Public Health Officials

Departments of public health across the nation provide oversight for the health and safety of children participating in sport and recreational programming within municipalities. Recreational programs, town youth sport programs, and clubs will often operate programs that require oversight by the public health official in that area. To complement the traditional menu of activities, sports camps are popular offerings by athletic administrators at the youth and club levels. To operate summer sports camps, regulations need to be followed and permits issued by local public health officials. Notably, athletic camps are no longer operated solely in the summer months; there has been an explosion of camps over school vacation periods. Sport camp directors or athletic administrators must comply with many regulations to operate camps under public health codes. Camp rules and regulations may differ from state to state, making compliance for larger athletic entities with multiple offerings in a variety of states more time consuming. The bottom line, however, is that sports camps cannot operate without public health permits. From an athletic administration perspective, the oversight provides another level of accountability, ensuring the camp provides the safest environment for participants and staff.

⚽ FEEDBACK FROM THE FIELD

Best Practices: Youth Sport Athletics

Teresa Kirsch is the public health nurse for the City of Beverly, Massachusetts. She oversees the regulation of athletic camps and clinics, because those programs fall under the authority of the local board of health. As Kirsch explains, public nurses administer the health and safety protocols for recreational and camp programming in their designated areas. Her role is diverse, including many aspects of public health such as the inspection and licensing of recreational camps for children operating within the city. These camps must meet the regulatory standards set forth by the Massachusetts Department of Public Health (MDPH) under state regulation 105 CMR 430.000, Minimum Sanitation and Safety Standards for Recreational Camps for Children.

Within athletic settings are many protocols revolving around concussion education and management. When Kirsch was asked about concussions and prevalence, she indicated that as the public health nurse, her duty is to inspect sports camps for children; however, there is no language in the current camp regulations at the state level that speaks to concussions. She is quick to note proposed draft regulations would require that all camp counselors, junior counselors, volunteers, and staff members complete an online head-injury safety program such as the "Heads Up" training offered by the Centers for Disease Control and Prevention (CDC) (2017) (see the following information) or an equivalent training program approved by MPDH.

Because of the prevalence of sports camps in the City of Beverly, in March 2017 Kirsch invited camp directors, health inspectors, and public health nurses to attend a training course to explain current camp regulations. Two representatives from MDPH's community sanitation program provided a PowerPoint presentation and answered questions from the audience. The purpose of the workshop was to put all parties involved in the business of recreational camps for children on the same page. As an inspector, Kirsch is mandated to ensure that all applicable requirements are met by each camp. As a nurse, she wanted to provide education that allows camp directors and staff to understand why these measures are in place and how they protect campers and staff.

Heads Up

The CDC offers a free course online for coaches and parents. The course contents helps users understand basic information about a concussion and the potential consequences of this injury, recognize concussion signs and symptoms and how to respond, learn about steps for returning to activity (play and school) after a concussion, and focus on prevention and preparedness to help keep athletes safe from season to season (Centers for Disease Control and Prevention, 2017). After completing this course, individuals earn a certificate. Most youth sport entities have started to require documentation of such course completion before an adult can work in a coaching position.

Medical Provisions

Typically, athletic programs across college, high school, youth, and club sports require each athlete to submit an updated medical record, including physical examination (typically within one year of sport activity) and proof of immunization before he or she can participate. Often, the only supervision at practices is from the coaches. In some settings, coaches have limited training in handling medical emergencies but tend to act as first responders when injuries or trauma occurs in the athletic setting. The duty of care extends from the athletic administrator to coaches when it comes to implementing risk management plans. Although accountability for the safety of participants stems from the desk of the athletic administrator, the administrator cannot be present at all sessions and the reliance to carry out risk management plans rests with the staff. Implementing risk management plans, including assessment, focuses on staff preparation and training. Along with acknowledging the specific procedures required by the athletic entity, staff members are normally mandated to complete certifications (CPR, AED, and first aid and safety) before they can engage in any coaching or supervision of athletic programming.

Camper Name: _____ Birth Date: M ____ /D ____ /Y_____ Age: ____

Address: _____

Home Phone: (____) _____ Alternate Phone: (____) _____

Email address: _____

Parental/Guardian Permission And Medical Release

I give permission for my child, _____, to fully participate in the Precision Soccer Camp (the "Camp"). As a condition to my child's participation in the Camp, I hereby agree as follows:

1. I am the parent or legal guardian of the child named above. I recognize that participation in the Camp will involve physical activities and exertion, which, by its nature, may be strenuous and may result in physical injury, and I do hereby acknowledge that I am fully aware that there are inherent risks and hazards involved in such physical activity, and having such knowledge I voluntarily elect for my child to participate. I give permission to the Camp Director and/or employees, during the Camp, to make decisions and provisions for the care of my child.

2. I understand that it is my responsibility to consult with a physician prior to and regarding my child's participation in the Camp. I certify that my child is in good health and that she has no special medical or physical conditions that would impede or prevent her participation in the Camp. I further agree that the decision as to my child's physical fitness to participate in the Camp is my responsibility alone, that I have had ample opportunity to consult with physicians to ascertain my child's physical fitness and Precision Soccer LLC shall bear no responsibility for my decision to allow my child to participate.

3. I warrant that the health history information for my child provided to the Camp is up-to-date and accurate. I understand that in the event of injury or illness to my child, the Camp will attempt to contact me at the emergency contact numbers noted below. In the event the Camp cannot reach me), I hereby authorize the medical personnel selected by the Camp Director to order x-rays, routine tests, and treatment, and to permit the physician selected by the Camp Director to hospitalize, secure proper treatment for, and to authorize injection, anesthesia and/or surgery for my child, at my cost and expense. I also give permission to the Camp to provide routine medical care for my child (including the administering by the Camp's medical personnel of any prescribed medication which my child brings to the camp or which is prescribed while at the camp).

4. In consideration of my child being permitted to participate in the Camp, I accept and assume responsibility for any risks, injuries or damages, foreseeable or unforeseeable, which my child might incur or suffer as a result of participating in the Camp. To the fullest extent under the law, I hereby knowingly, voluntarily and expressly waive and release Precision Soccer LLC, its instructors and staff, from and against any and all liability for injury, illness or damage, to person or property, resulting in any way from my child's participation in the Camp.

I have read the above release and waiver of liability and fully understand its contents. I voluntarily agree to the terms and conditions stated above.

Parent/Guardian Signature: _____   Date: _____

PLEASE COMPLETE THE BACK SIDE

Back side:

CONTACT INFORMATION:

Emergency Contact: _____ Phone: _____

Alternate Emergency Contact: _____ Phone: _____

Physician Contact: _____ Phone: _____

Medical/Hospital Insurance Carrier: _____

Policy Number: _____

Adult name on policy: _____

Please check-off any of the following injuries or illnesses your child has had:

❏ Chicken Pox ❏ Head Injury ❏ Ankle Injury ❏ Asthma

❏ Convulsions ❏ Heart Condition ❏ Diabetes ❏ Frequent Ear Infections

❏ Back Injury ❏ Knee Injury ❏ Fainting Spells ❏ Other

Please record any food, medication or other allergies camper has:

What medication will this camper take while at Camp?

Medicine _____ Dosage _____ Specific times taken each day _____

Reason:

Please record any medical or surgical history this camper has, and whether she has been hospitalized or has visited a doctor for an illness during the past year:

Is there any other health-related information or suggestions that may help ensure this camper's health and safety while at Camp?

IMPORTANT: MANDATORY INFORMATION

ALL CAMPERS MUST PROVIDE THE FOLLOWING PRIOR TO THE START OF CAMP:

✔ **CURRENT PHYSICAL EXAMINATION (must be within 12 months of camp dates)**

✔ **IMMUNIZATION VERIFICATION**

All forms must be signed by a licensed health care provider. **These forms must be on file with the Camp Director three weeks prior to the start of camp.** All forms are required by the Department of Public Health.

Thank you for your cooperation

Concussion Education

Since the late 2000s, concussion prevention and management has dominated discussions across all levels of athletic settings, including college, high school, youth, and club sport. States across the country offer concussion-management regulations along with return-to-play policies after a concussion. Education of coaches, parents, and athletes plays a significant role in the treatment process after a suspected head trauma. The research of Bramley, Patrick, Lehman, and Silvis (2012) revealed an important finding that "high school soccer players who have received concussion education from any source are more likely to notify their coach or trainer of a suspected concussion as compared with athletes with no education, potentially reducing the risk of additional brain injury" (p. 334). An athletic administrator's best approach is to provide resources to participants in their specific sport setting so they have the power to learn as much as they can about concussions.

Spectator Safety

The University of Southern Mississippi launched the National Center for Spectator Sports Safety and Security (NCS4) after the 9/11 attacks, with a centralized focus on the study and practice of spectator sports safety and security. NCS4 works with the NFHS and the National Interscholastic Athletic Administrators Association (NIAAA) to develop a national risk management training and assessment program for interscholastic athletics through coursework and resources (Crumpton, 2015). The topics include vulnerability and risk assessment, planning and preparedness, hazard mitigation, crisis communication, sustaining efficient safety and security programs, and organizational teamwork.

Campuses and sport facilities are soft targets for terrorism. In relation to risk assessment within facility management across the collegiate, high school, club, and youth sport setting,

administrators must be prepared and trained to deal with terrorist threats and incidents. To aid athletic administrators, the Federal Emergency Management Agency (FEMA) offers free online training (http://training.fema.gov/) that athletic administrators can use for their own preparedness. FEMA also provides many resources on its website to assist citizens in learning from others who have managed conflicts (Federal Emergency Management Agency, 2015).

Another component of risk management is the development of an emergency action plan (EAP). The EAP contains the policies and guidelines governing the handling of risk-associated situations and scenarios. Simply stated, "the emergency plan" is considered to be "a blueprint for handling emergencies" (Andersen, Courson, Kleiner, & McLoda, 2002, p. 99). Typically, the EAP contains guidelines on injury reporting, weather protocol (cold and heat), and first aid and safety regulations, along with the evaluation of the athletic facilities. A listing of all potential emergencies and required actions should be written within the EAP procedures. A helpful addition to the EAP is the inclusion of all staff contact information. The NATA provides EAP best practices recommendations for athletic administrators.

As Dick, Agel, and Marshall (2007) report, the NCAA's Injury Surveillance System (ISS) is the largest collegiate athletic injury database in continuous operation in the world. The ISS's primary goal is to collect injury and exposure data across institutions and variety of sports and then share those findings with NCAA sport- and policy-related committees (Dick et al., 2007). A secondary ISS goal is to "provide individual institutions with injury information that can be the foundation for their risk management decision making" (Dick et al., 2007).

Along with incorporating an EAP into the operations for an athletic entity, a facility inspection can assist in offsetting any potential liability. Under the facility management umbrella for risk assessment, a sound plan includes identification of risks, evaluation of the severity of those risks, and selection of

Evidence-Based Best Practice Recommendations	Meets Best Practice Recommendation
1. *Every school should develop an EAP for managing serious and or potentially life-threatening injuries.*	
2. *The EAP should be developed and coordinated with local EMS, venue public safety officials, on site medical personnel or organization administrators.*	
3. *Every school should have a written EAP document distributed to all staff members.*	
4. *The EAP should be specific to each venue and include maps and/or specific directions to that venue.*	
5. *On-site emergency equipment that may be needed in an emergency situation should be listed.*	
6. *The EAP should identify personnel and their responsibilities to carry out the plan of action with a designated chain of command.*	
7. *Appropriate contact information for EMS.*	
8. *Facility address, location, contact information etc. should be identified in the EAP.*	
9. *Plan should specify documentation actions that need to be taken post emergency.*	
10. *EAP should be reviewed and rehearsed annually by all parties involved.*	
11. *Healthcare professionals who will provide medical coverage during games, practices, or other events should be included.*	

EAP Best Practices

methods of treatment for the risks (Wolohan, 2006). Wolohan (2006) directs athletic administrators to take precautionary steps in risk management by "simply walking around the facility periodically and conducting an extensive risk evaluation." U.S. Lacrosse provides an outline for athletic administrators to use as part of the EAP, including the following:

1. Designate someone to be in charge of managing an emergency.
2. Ideally, an adult with a minimum of basic first aid training should be on site.
3. Ideally, at a minimum, a basic first aid kit with materials to clean, cover, and immobilize an injured body part should be on site.
4. Make sure cell-phone access is available for 911 calls. If not, have a backup plan for contacting emergency services. Have needed emergency numbers on site.
5. Ideally, at the youth level, more than one adult should be present to deal with the emergency and other team members.
   a. Number of emergency service if not 911 _____
   b. Number of first person to begin emergency chain _____
   c. Number of backup person to call if needed _____

6. Ideally, at the youth level, a phone chain should be established to notify parents of appropriate situation.

7. Know where the closest emergency care is located and how to give directions to emergency personnel, if necessary.

U.S. Lacrosse (2012)

8. Make sure gates are open and access to fields and athletes are not blocked.

9. Person in charge must control the scene and initiate the preceding plan of action.

 FEEDBACK FROM THE FIELD

Best Practices: College Athletics

Nicholas Gallotto is the associate athletic trainer at Boston College (BC) (Boston, Massachusetts). Gallotto graduated from Endicott College in 2007 with a bachelor's in science in athletic training. He subsequently earned a graduate assistantship (GA) position at Washington State University (WSU) in Pullman working with the men's basketball, men's golf, and women's golf programs. After his GA position, he was hired full-time as an assistant athletic trainer at WSU covering the same sports. Gallotto earned a master's of health administration at the University of Cincinnati and in June 2016 was hired as an associate athletic trainer at Boston College, again working with the men's basketball, men's golf, and women's golf teams. His role at BC includes hiring per diem athletic trainers for coverage of practices, games, and camps and implementing CPR and AED certification of coaches.

In Gallotto's experience, the domain of risk management in athletics and athletic training has evolved. One core area is the push for universal sickle cell testing in NCAA Division I athletics. NCAA institutions are also examining implementation of heart evaluations (electrocardiograms, echocardiograms, stress tests). To that end, according to Gallotto, increasing numbers of athletic departments are looking for data and information on their student-athletes coming to campus in hopes of preventing catastrophic injury. Athletic departments are also engaging other healthcare professionals to improve their student-athletes' welfare while also preventing injuries. Gallotto indicates that more athletic departments are hiring registered dietitians for meal planning and identifying red flags for eating disorders as well as injury through food diaries and blood work while also educating student-athletes about how and when to eat to prevent injuries and improve performance. Sport psychologists, Gallotto points out, "are also being used for performance but also identifying student-athletes who may be struggling with everyday issues and getting them the help they need to prevent further harm."

Within the discussion of concussion education and prevention, at the start of every school year each athletic trainer educates coaching staff members and student-athletes under their care and answers questions they may have and gives information pamphlets as resources, following guidelines from the most up-to-date sport concussion assessment tool (SCAT) form. The SCAT is a standardized method to evaluate athletes after a sustained concussion. BC student-athletes take a baseline impact test along with a baseline balance test for concussion testing that Gallotto repeats with the athletes every two years. Regarding treatment, Gallotto says, "We do not have the student-athlete perform any activity until they are asymptomatic; but under the guidance of our physicians, monitored activity can be done (Buffalo protocol) to potentially help with decrease of symptoms." He adds, "We follow the five day progress of no symptoms before a student-athlete is cleared medically to return to pre-concussion activity."

As Gallotto stresses, risk management plans are "important to have and you do not realize you need one until something horrific happens." He further explains that the staff he works with have yearly in-services to go over spine boarding and weekly meetings with their physicians to review any mental health cases that might be coming up the pipeline. Sometimes, coaches may want to rush athletes back into competition. Regarding this concern, Gallotto uses the practice schedule, noting what student-athletes can and cannot perform during those sessions. An added measure is Gallotto's notation of when student-athletes were injured (and what they were doing) to keep a closer eye when they return to practice and engage in that same drill or activity. Gallotto maintains a spreadsheet of injuries and looks for patterns. At the end of the season, "I look at all the injuries and look to determine if any of the injuries could have been prevented."

Regarding risk management, "Concussion and sickle cell trait education are at the top of the list because each student-athlete goes through an educational program on what these injuries [and] illnesses are and the change of care in the event they have one or both of these." Currently at Boston College is a new educational component focused on sudden cardiac arrest. BC athletic trainers are testing the most at-risk student-athletes (basketball, football, soccer, hockey) and will be moving to test more student-athletes in the near future. As Gallotto reveals,

> "even though we get a family and medical history and a physical from each student-athlete, we have pushed to make sure there have not been any injuries or illnesses that have fallen through the cracks. We educate the coaching staff (who are also CPR/AED certified per NCAA regulations) on why it is important to check their student-athletes and why a student-athlete may get held out [of play] if anything is found."

From Gallotto's perspective, mental health and catastrophic events are two areas designated for more attention in intercollegiate athletics. He remarks,

> "although we utilize physicians and psychologists, mental health needs to be "normalized" through education of the administration, coaching staff and student-athletes alike. . . . At times, student-athletes can be seen as "soft" or "lazy" if they do not want to work hard [o]r are struggling on and off the practice field. While a student-athlete can be "lazy" or have a lower pain threshold, it should not be the go-to reason as to why a student-athlete is struggling."

The safety and well-being of student-athletes is paramount. Catastrophic events can happen at any time, prompting Gallotto to offer that it is important for an athletic department to be ready to respond at any given time in the event a catastrophic event occurs. "The medical staff needs to be ready to act smartly and efficiently, the administration needs to be kept in the loop and ready to help when needed, and the student-athletes need to be helped in the event some are struggling with what occurred."

Athletic trainers deal with many associated challenges when dealing with risk management. Gallotto shares,

> "Mental health can be a tricky situation because it can involve confidentiality if the student-athlete does not want to share with the coaching staff [or] medical staff, yet there can be issues that both groups would find helpful to know in order to improve the healthcare and well-being of the student-athlete."

Gallotto further notes that he does his "best to educate the student-athlete and have them share as much as they are comfortable sharing with myself as well as with the coaching staff so that we can help." Gallotto revealed he has worked with a student-athlete who had suicidal thoughts because of a difficult upbringing. Although the coaching staff was aware of the student-athlete's suicidal ideations, Gallotto did not share the reasons behind the student's thoughts in order to maintain confidentiality.

Gallotto was asked to offer advice to future athletic administrators so they understand the importance of developing a relationship of trust with athletic trainers. "My recommendation is

(continues)

FEEDBACK FROM THE FIELD *(continued)*

to show their faces in the athletic training room and be visible to the staff as well as the student-athlete. Invest in and understand what the staff does and what the student-athlete has to do to get back onto their competitive field." Gallotto notes that in the past he has worked with athletic administrators who are not present, and their visit to the athletic training room would be abnormal for the staff and student-athletes. He suggests athletic administrators "have a good rapport with the athletic trainer and the student-athletes" because it "should be a relationship they should try to strengthen." Another method of connecting with the athletic training staff is organizing a 5- to10-minute meeting once a week "just to touch base and talk about the challenges going on in the athletic training room." Gallotto concludes, "The goal may not be to fix an issue, but to listen to the athletic trainer and understand what the current climate is of the team they are covering and their own mindset."

▶ Role of the Coach in Risk Management

Although sport medicine personnel are educated and trained to handle the prevention and management of injuries, coaches typically spend the majority of time with athletes on the playing fields. Côté and Gilbert (2009) provide an integrative definition of coaching effectiveness as "the consistent application of integrated professional, interpersonal, and intrapersonal knowledge to improve athletes' competence, confidence, connection, and character in specific coaching contexts" (p. 316). Naturally, athletic administrators aim to involve the most qualified staff to provide the most enhanced experience to athletes. Depending on the sport setting, coaches need to understand the physical and emotional needs of athletes. Athletic administrators may be working with novice volunteer coaches in a town program or a college-level coach who has been in the field for decades. Oversight and management of these coaches will vary according to the level of expertise in dealing with practice organization and game-day operations.

Along with understanding the management of practice organization and the effective use of playing space associated with operating sport-

ing events and programs, prospective coaches also need to be well versed in the medical provisions associated with their specific sport setting. Communicating an emergency plan to relay the handling of injuries should be part of in-service staff training. Most athletic departments mandate staff to acknowledge receipt and review of these plans. Simply acknowledging document review is not a surefire way to ensure compliance with risk management procedures, but it is a first step in communicating risk management regulations. Proactive athletic administrators continually review these processes with staff to maintain safe and secure delivery of athletic programming.

Management of the playing space promotes a safe environment for athletes. Coaches who complete sport-specific training learn about proper spacing of drills or activities not only to promote player development but also to lessen the risk of injury. There are times at practices and games when athletes may not be in control of their bodies, which creates an unsafe environment for themselves, their teammates, and their opponents. Knowing and enforcing the rules of play need to be strictly adhered to, not only in games but also in practice sessions. Game-day personnel, including contest managers, facility managers, and game officials, should be supported by the coaching staff at all times. One duty of a coach is to immediately report any issues with the playing surfaces to the athletic administrator so they can be resolved. In addition, if an athlete or spectator is injured, the athletic administrator should be notified in order to handle any subsequent contact from the parties involved and to follow-up with the affected individuals.

Inclusion of a professional code of conduct (dealing with athletes, spectators, and sporting officials and allowing administrators to comprehend and adhere to the rules of the game), injury prevention certifications (CPR, first aid and safety), and sport-specific certification and education should be included within the job description of a coach,

regardless of whether the position is paid or voluntary. From a planning perspective, athletic administrators typically assign coaches based on their level of expertise, preparation, and competence in managing sport programming. In essence, the coach must be able to effectively communicate the rules, techniques, and tactics of the sport to enhance the athletic experience and improve the level of play of the athletes under his or her charge. It is disappointing that coach education in the United States is a splintered movement with some clear and unclear pathways for coaches to navigate professional development and training. The most popular participant sports such as soccer, ice hockey, lacrosse, and Pop Warner football have much clearer coach education pathways than other sports.

US Lacrosse provides both online and face-to-face courses/clinics to members:

Level 1 Certification

Level 2 Certification

Level 3 Certification

Junior Certification

International Certification

According to research, a successful coach…

- is motivational and inspires athletes to improve and work hard,
- is knowledgeable about the skills and tactics of the sport,
- is relational and excellent at communicating with players and parents,
- possesses good character and is a positive role model.

US Lacrosse will help you achieve these goals, whether you played the game, have coached for many years, or are just volunteering for your child's program.

US Lacrosse is proud to partner with the Positive Coaching Alliance to increase your ability to not only help your players with games, but to teach them important life lessons through the sport of lacrosse.

US Lacrosse

U.S. Lacrosse (n.d.)

Even with an emphasis on player-development models and coach education, there still lacks a centralized effort in the United States to ensure the proper credentialing of the staff. However, the National Council

for the Accreditation of Coaching Education (NCACE) is the only accrediting body for coaching education in the United States. Unfortunately, as reported by NCACE, only 12 institutions have achieved accreditation,

USA Basketball Licensing & Accreditation Programs

Coach License Program

- Education & Safety Training
- Youth Development Guidebook
- Coaching Liability Insurance
- Listing in Licensed Coach Database
- Affiliation with National Governing Body
- Online Tools and Resources

Organization Accreditation Program

- USA Basketball Seal of Approval
- Affiliation with National Governing Body
- Listing in Accredited Organization Database
- Online Administrator Resources
- Administrator Management Tools
- Appreciation Offers

USA Basketball

USA Basketball (n.d.)

further accentuating concern for the need for coach education across the athletic setting (National Committee for Accreditation of Coaching Education, n.d.). Athletic administrators can also incorporate the fundamentals of coaching work of the National Association for Sport and Physical Education (NASPE). NASPE publishes the National Standards for Sport Coaches (NSSC). The NSSC categorizes eight general domains of knowledge attributed to quality-level coaching: (1) philosophy and ethics, (2) safety and injury prevention, (3) physical conditioning, (4) growth and development, (5) teaching and communication, (6) sport skills and tactics, (7) organization and administration, and (8) evaluation (Society of Health and Physical Educators, n.d.).

Several youth sport organizations that use the courses offered by NCACE are presented in **TABLE 7.1**.

TABLE 7.1 Programs Offered Through Various Sport Organizations

Organization	Location	Delivery	Available Courses by Subject Area			Price[c]
			Foundations	**Safety**	**Sport / Age Specific**	
American Coaching Academy	Carson City, NV	V	7	1	0	$97[d]
National Youth Sport Coaches Association	West Palm Beach, FL	V, P	2	3	12	$20–$40[d]

Organization	Location	Delivery	Available Courses by Subject Area			Price[c]
			Foundations	Safety	Sport / Age Specific	
Positive Coaches Alliance	Mountain View, CA	V, P	3	0[a]	0	$30[e]
US Lacrosse	Baltimore, MD	V, P	3	2	3	$70[e]
US Soccer	Chicago, IL	V, P	0[a]	1[a]	4	$100–$125
USA Hockey	Colorado Springs, CO	V, P	0[a]	0[a]	7	$50[d]
USA Rugby	Boulder, CO	V, P	0[a]	2[b]	4[b]	$0–$250[d]
USA Swimming	Colorado Springs, CO	V, P	2	1	0[a]	$40[d]
USA Volleyball	Colorado Springs, CO	V, P	2	0[a]	2	$50–$425[d]
USTA	Boca Raton, FL	P	0	0	2	$250[e]
Youth Enrichment in Sports	N/A	V, P	1	0	0	$0–$25[e]

Note. V = Virtual; P = In Person; a = Content included in other courses; b = Courses offered in collaboration with other organizations (e.g. NFHS);
c = Prices reflect an estimate of cost for minimum education level courses offered by the respective organization;
d = Cost for certification; e = Cost per course
Course values represent estimated number of available courses by topic area based on organization website.
Specific breadth and depth of content varies within courses by organization.
Table is not an exhaustive list of available coaching education programs

⚽ FEEDBACK FROM THE FIELD

Best practices in Athletic Administration

Doug Kilgore is the assistant principal and activities director at Central Arkansas Christian School (North Little Rock, Arkansas) and the national voice for the National Interscholastic Athletic Administrators Association. Kilgore had a wealth of experience in administration before his current position as athletic director for two years at Central Arkansas Christian. In his current role, he is charged with the administration of all fine arts groups and activities. He has supervised nearly every extracurricular club group, administered all athletic programs (grades three to 12), and overseen 12 sports plus cheerleading, which includes 55 teams, 18 full-time staff coaches, one full-time athletic trainer, and 16 registered volunteer coaches (10 in grades three through six basketball). Kilgore boasts that approximately 58% of the school's students participate in athletics.

Since 2006, Kilgore has been extremely active in the NIAAA. Through the organization's certification program, he obtained a certified athletic administrator designation in 2004 and certified master athletic administrator designation in 2006. He has been the course chair and revision author of administration of sports medicine programs since 2007. Kilgore is also in the NIAAA's state leadership and has been certification coordinator for Arkansas since 2004, having served the Arkansas High School Athletic Administrators Association as secretary, vice president, president, and past president and is currently on the association's executive committee. He has held the post of secretary of the NIAAA board of directors since 2010. Professional development is a priority for Kilgore, and he has completed 35 courses in the leadership training academy and has taught leadership training courses at the National Conference for Athletic Directors for 10 years and at the state or region level for 12 years. Kilgore instructed 20 different courses in various locations and presented workshops at the national conference articles in the NIAAA's magazine. He has also conducted workshops at state conferences in Arkansas, Colorado, Idaho, New Mexico, North Carolina, Tennessee, and Texas.

Kilgore feels risk management has become a much more critical area in the past decade. It is "not because the needs of the student-athlete have increased—it should have always been high—but because of the increase in the dissemination of knowledge, constituents' increased expectation of accountability and the litigious nature of the 'rage to sue' by various parties." As a result of these and other areas, Kilgore emphasizes that "athletic personnel (and all educators), must be keenly aware of risks and the mitigation of the same. If not, they should be keenly aware of seeking employment in another field." When asked about the core areas of risk management, he deferred to the "Fourteen Legal Duties of Athletics Personnel" (see **TABLE 7.2**) with an emphasis on the duty to supervise (students), duty to assess readiness to participate, duty to instruct (technique particularly), duty to warn, and duty to provide emergency care and duty to select, train, and supervise coaches. These areas, according to Kilgore, "concentrate on the athletic administrators' responsibility and the accountability to providing well trained, professional staff to provide for the oversight and safety of all involved with our athletic programs with primary attention given to the student-athletes in our care."

Kilgore was asked how he explained risk management to his staff. His response highlights the importance of emphasizing and prioritizing safety. Kilgore emphasizes that "with a prime goal of protecting and safeguarding the health and well-being of student-athletes, we must do all within our power to provide a risk-free environment. Risk cannot be totally eliminated but it can be greatly reduced." He further asserts that lives and careers have been damaged, even ended, avoidably by failure to secure environments and activities involving students. He believes we should not rely on the goodness and understanding of our constituents; given the opportunity and need, all will default to protective mindsets that include shifting or transferring blame. The obligation to minimize risk and liability exposure at all

TABLE 7.2 Fourteen Legal Duties of Athletics Personnel
Duty to Plan
Duty to Supervise
Duty to Assess an Athlete's Readiness for Practice and Competition
Duty to Maintain Safe Playing Conditions
Duty to Provide Proper Equipment
Duty to Instruct Properly
Duty to Match Athletes During Practice
Duty to Condition
Duty to Warn
Duty to Ensure Athletes are Covered by Injury Insurance
Duty to Provide Emergency Care
Duty to Develop/Follow an Emergency Response Plan
Duty to Provide Proper Transportation
Duty to Select, Train and Supervise Coaches

Modified from Doleschal, J. K. (2006). Managing risk in interscholastic athletic programs: 14 legal duties of care. Marquette Sports Law Review, 17(11), 295–339.

costs is up to the athletic administrator. Kilgore explains, a twofold duty is to minimize the risk for damage and injury to students as well as minimize the risk to the institution and its employees.

The body of duties to protect student-athletes must be explained early and thoroughly understood by all constituents: staff, student-athletes themselves, and their parents. The importance of each duty should be related so that sufficient attention is given to all areas. Next, an assessment and analysis of the environment and activities should be conducted to identify as many potential risks and causative factors as possible with an eye toward eliminating what can be eliminated and modifying those that cannot be. Sufficient instruction must be given to all parties regarding those areas of potential injury that cannot be eliminated (for example, in any sport, athletes can be injured because of the nature of the competition; these elements cannot be fully eliminated). Finally, in the

(continues)

event of an accident or avoidable event, response actions must be addressed from a basic first aid response to the implementation of an established emergency action plan. This entire process should be relayed soon and often during the course of each school year.

When explaining staff training and education on risk management, Kilgore starts with presenting the Fourteen Legal Duties of Coaches. His emphasis is on preventive measures, primarily the education of all constituents. Coaches should be prepared to fulfill their assigned duties with an eye toward minimizing risks. Coaches should also conduct (with his involvement) parent and student-athlete meetings to address risk areas and relate their critical involvement in the minimization process. Kilgore provides continuing education options for coaches to pursue meeting both ethical and professional requirements, ensuring that most opportunities are "beyond X's and O's." He believes it is his responsibility to provide instruction and options for professional growth first. Staff members may pursue options of "X's and O's" once fundamental risk management and efficiency opportunities are met. He expects no less than a one-to-one ratio of elective professional development involvement between process and product opportunities. From Kilgore's perspective, staff members may also pursue as much professional development learning as they wish on their own time and at their own expense. Finally, he would spend time on his department's coaches handbook to reemphasize areas already covered as well as address the philosophical and practical aspects of working within the athletic department with an emphasis on "Why we do what we do" to encourage buy-in and communicate significance.

One area of improvement relating to this topic is involving student-athletes and parents in the risk management process. In Kilgore's estimation, all parties will be better served by shared knowledge and instruction and acceptance of a shared responsibility to ensure the success and safety of those in our programs. Although the practice of singular student-athlete and parent meetings is widely accepted, he believes repetition of programs and communication with these parties would greatly increase department-wide efficiency and effectiveness while creating an environment of shared responsibility and mutual respect for the rights of all. Kilgore adds, "We work in a team atmosphere yet demonstrate a reluctance to involve all constituents in a team atmosphere approach to our risk management 'game.'"

Questions for Discussion

1. After reading the feedback from Kilgore, what area of risk management do you think is the most challenging to implement within a high school athletic department and why?
2. What are some basic certifications you would require your coaches to obtain within your athletic entity? Be sure to create a list indicating the specific certifications for all settings including college, high school, youth, and club athletic programs.
3. Monitoring field conditions during inclement weather is one of the duties of the coach in the risk management plan. What are some best practices you can share with your coaches when dealing with inclement weather, especially when they are preparing their team for a game and dealing with officials and the opposing team?
4. In-service education offered by the athletic department is one method to ensure the coaches are receiving relevant information about risk management. However, what protocol would you have in place to be sure coaches are fully implementing the plan?
5. In terms of legal duties, the preceding 14 categories constitute an effective risk management program. In the athletic environment of high school athletics, which area do you anticipate spending the most time supervising from an athletic administration perspective and why?

MANAGERIAL APPLICATIONS

Youth Sport: Risk Management

As the president of the town's Pop Warner football program, you have required your coaches to complete the mandatory Heads Up Football certification (USA Football, n.d.). The challenge for the Pop Warner board is to ensure all coaches are implementing these regulations as they coach. During the opening week of the season, the weather is extremely hot (90 degrees) with intense sun.

Questions to Consider

1. With heat preparedness and hydration as part of the Heads Up football program, what types of reminders would you send out to coaches? Write an email message you would distribute to coaches based on the heat preparedness and hydration guidelines for any youth organization.
2. What types of injuries can occur when athletes are competing in adverse weather conditions? If an athletic trainer is not present at the site, what are the responsibilities or duties of the coaches who are operating these practices?
3. Because some coaches have the mindset to focus just on getting the players ready for the first game versus the hot weather conditions, what protocols will you have in place to protect the athletes, and what penalties would you place on coaches who are not adhering to the safety protocol?

 MANAGERIAL APPLICATIONS

College Athletics: Risk Management

Storming the court or field is becoming a ritual on college campuses. Students and fans will leave their seats to rush the court or field to celebrate with their team. The mass of fans on the court or field presents various safety concerns for you as the athletic administrator.

Questions to Consider

1. Fans may not even realize there is an issue or that their actions may lead to unsafe conditions for their classmates (the athletes). Sometimes, when a high-profile coach addresses the crowd and fans directly, it may lead to changes in action. What are your thoughts on getting the coaches involved in the process to address storming issues on college campuses?
2. As athletic administrators, we must take into account all types of risk-related scenarios when it comes to games. We may have a surprising victory or we may have an opponent that just plays an unbelievable game. In all scenarios, the end result is that the athletic administrator along with the staff must be prepared to handle any crowd issues and protect all participants—athletes, coaches, and officials. What resources and training will you implement for your staff to manage game days?
3. Do you think technology and social media play a role in the explosion of storming issues on college campuses? Today's students all have mobile devices and love to capture every moment digitally. Because people can post their storming activities on social media, do you think it might encourage copycats?

DECISION-MAKING CHALLENGE

Case Study: Youth Sport

As the boys' basketball coordinator for your recreational program you receive an email from a parent detailing an injury occurring before the start of fourth-grade basketball practice. One boy slipped on the court and fell into the bleachers, hitting his head on the corner, resulting in a large gash. There was a great deal of blood from the injury. The parent just dropped off her son and realized the coach and the athlete's parent were not in the gym. She proceeded to care for the injured athlete. Once the coach arrived at the practice, he walked over to the injured athlete who needed to be transported to the emergency room. The first problem was that the coach did not have contact information for the athlete's parent. What liability would this present to the town program, and how would you remedy this in the future? Second, there was only one coach at the practice, which left the rest of the players unsupervised when the athlete needed assistance. What should the coach do in this instance if he or she is alone when an injury occurs? Third, the parent was concerned that so many athletes were on the court for so long before the coach arrived. What are the risks associated with leaving a gym unsupervised, and what protocol would you have in place to avoid this occurrence in the future? Finally, what would your outreach response be to the concerned parent and the family of the injured basketball player?

DECISION-MAKING CHALLENGE

Case Study: High School Athletics

The girls' soccer team is having one of its best seasons on record. The team has to win its final game to earn a spot in the conference championship. The leading scorer on the team suffered a head injury at practice the day before the scheduled game. The athletic trainer did not see the cause of impact, but the head coach did witness the scenario leading up to the head trauma. When the athlete went down to the turf, the coach quickly ran on the field and told her to get back up to play. Another player alerted the athletic trainer that her teammate was injured. The coach and athletic trainer had a discussion regarding letting the athlete return to play. Luckily, the practice was near its end, so play did not continue. The athletic trainer is highly concerned that the coach is not being honest about the injury and texts you immediately after practice. As the athletic administrator, what protocol do you initiate to uncover the facts about the incident? What recommendation do you make to the coach and to the athletic trainer to ensure the health and well-being of the athlete is paramount over winning the game? What does this scenario teach you about the role of the coach and athletic trainer in your program?

Wrap-Up

End-of-Chapter Activities

College Athletics

1. Your institution currently lacks a facility audit plan or checklist for coaches to use as part of the athletic department's risk management plan. Research three facility audit plans at the collegiate level. Then, craft your own version for your current institution or an institution with which you are familiar.

2. Your athletic training department currently lacks a formalized return-to-play policy, causing a great deal of confusion for the staff (athletic trainers and coaches). A variety of injuries are assumed by college-level athletes. Select three major injury types and craft a sound return-to-play policy for each.

Club Athletics

1. Your field hockey club currently lacks an emergency action plan. As athletic administrator, you recognize that coaches do not have enough information within the scope of risk management. Research two EAPs at the club setting and then craft your own plan specific to field hockey. Be sure to include what the coaches should bring to each practice and game for emergency purposes.

2. As the director of coaching for the soccer club, you have been asked by the executive director to formalize a coach education pathway for your staff. Research coach education for soccer and one other sport, detailing the courses and offerings for each. What are the challenges you anticipate in mandating a coach education and certification program for your staff? What surprised you the most in regards to the offerings of coach education for the sport or sports you researched?

End-of-Chapter Questions

1. Risk management is an essential topic to examine as an athletic administrator. In your opinion, what area under the risk management umbrella needs the most attention from athletic administrators? Specifically, indicate the challenges of risk management within the college, high school, youth, or club settings.

2. Select two settings to review (college, high school, youth, or club). Create a list of the areas under each that would constitute areas that athletic administrators must monitor in the domain of risk management. As a future athletic administrator, what are your concerns when it comes to protecting the safety of the fans and participants within your athletic department?

3. Conduct online research on risk management. Review three articles delineating the importance of creating and maintaining a sound risk management plan. Also indicate how risk has evolved over the last 10 years.

4. In terms of training and educating staff on risk management, what core areas would you highlight to ensure your programs meet the highest of standards in coach education, preseason and weight-training programs, weather-related policies, and standards of care for athletes?

5. In your estimation, is there a "blind spot" in athletic administration that we need to be aware of when implementing a comprehensive risk management program?

6. Visit your local high school or your current college; please note you may need to schedule an appointment with the athletic director. Inspect the practice and game sites, list any concerns you may have with the space, the perimeter of the space, the playing surface, seating areas, locker rooms, location of AEDs, and cell phones for emergencies. Document any hazards or risks after your inspection.

7. In college and high school athletics, transporting student-athletes to and from game sites is standard. What risk management protocol should be

established under transportation for both the collegiate and high school settings?

8. Athletic trainers play a critical role in maintaining safety within the athletic settings. Research the prevalence of athletic trainers in college, high school, youth, and club athletics. Are you concerned or satisfied with the number of athletic trainers in each setting? Please be comprehensive in your response, citing current literature or research.

9. Visit the website for one youth sport organization, one club organization, one high school athletic department, and one college athletic department. Can you determine what the medical requirements are to allow participation by athletes in each program? If you could not easily locate the information, be sure to indicate so and craft a medical clearance policy for that particular setting.

10. College campuses typically operate summer camps. Research the requirements necessary to secure a permit by the local board of health (use your hometown) for a coach to operate a sports camp.

11. Lightning strikes or threats of lightning present challenges for athletic administrators in terms of determining when to end a practice session or game. Research lightning protocol for one youth sport organization, one club organization, one high school athletic department, and one college athletic department. What would you recommend in each setting based on your findings?

12. Because of increased liabilities within college, high school, club, and youth sport, more athletic administrators are partnering with external agencies for coach education and risk management training. Research the variety of options to fully educate and train your coaches in risk management across all athletic settings.

13. Rules and policies need to be in place to minimize risk to competing teams and

officials. On-court or on-field celebrations often take a turn for the worse, leading to violence, destruction of property, or bodily harm. Multiple institutions craft policies to prevent incidents of storming or excessive celebrations through sanctions and fines. College athletic departments have resorted to issuing fines or sanction for institutions (fans) with crowd control incidents. Examine two court or field-rushing incidents at the collegiate level and the penalties from athletic conferences issued to those institutions.

References

Andersen J., Courson R. W., Kleiner D. M., & McLoda T. A. (2002). National Athletic Trainers' Association position statement: Emergency planning in athletics. *Journal of Athletic Training, 37*, 99–104.

Bloodhounds (n.d.). Sports medicine. John Jay Athletics. Retrieved January 14, 2018, from http://johnjayathletics.com/sports/2006/8/14/training.aspx?&tab=2.

Bramley, H., Patrick, K., Lehman, E., & Silvis, M. (2012). High school soccer players with concussion education are more likely to notify their coach of a suspected concussion. *Clinical Pediatrics, 51*(4), 332–336. doi:10.1177/0009922811425233.

Centers for Disease Control and Prevention (2017, October 04). HEADS UP to youth sports: Online training. Retrieved January 14, 2018, from https://www.cdc.gov/headsup/youthsports/training/index.html.

Clearance Form for New Athlete (n.d.). Retrieved January 14, 2018, from https://cdn1.sportngin.com/attachments/document/0116/0475/MS-NEWAT HandEMERGENCYCARD_non_shoe_sports_17 -18.pdf

Côté, J., & Gilbert, W. D. (2009). An integrative definition of coaching effectiveness and expertise. *International Journal of Sports Science & Coaching*, 4, 307–323.

Crumpton, A. (2015, January). Interscholastic athletics and after-school activities risk management training course set for March 2015. Athletic Business [online]. Retrieved October 29, 2018, from https://www.athleticbusiness.com/high-school-facilities/interscholastic-athletics -and-after-school-activities-risk-management-training -course-set-for-march-2015.html.

Dick, R., Agel, J., & Marshall, S. W. (2007). National Collegiate Athletic Association Injury Surveillance System commentaries: Introduction and methods. *Journal of Athletic Training, 42*(2), 173–182.

Doleschal, J. K. (2006). Managing risk in interscholastic athletic programs: 14 legal duties of care. *Marquette Sports Law Review, 17*(11), 295–339.

Federal Emergency Management Agency (FEMA) (n.d.). Welcome to national preparedness. Retrieved January 15, 2018, from http://training.fema.gov/.

Federal Emergency Management Agency (FEMA) (2015, September 22). Lessons Learned Information Sharing (LLIS) Program Consolidation in 2015. Retrieved from https://www.fema.gov/media-library/assets /documents/104192.

Fuller, C., & Drawer, S. (2004). The application of risk management in sport. *Sports Medicine, 34*(6), 349–356. doi: 10.2165/00007256-200434060-00001.

History Form. (n.d.). (2017, May). School sports pre-participation examination–Part 1: Student or parent completes. Retrieved January 14, 2018, from https://cdn1 .sportngin.com/attachments/document/0103/4945 /New_Physcial_Form_2017.pdf

Indiana Fire Juniors (n.d.). Athletic training and sports performance. Retrieved January 14, 2018, from http:// www.indianafirejuniors.com/page/show/1243585 -athletic-training-and-sports-performance.

Michigan High School Athletic Association, Inc. (n.d.). Medical history [form]. Retrieved January 14, 2018 from https://www.nmu.edu/healthcenter/sites/Drupal HealthCenter/files/UserFiles/MHSAA_Sports _Physical_Form1272039988.pdf.

Minnesota State High School League (2018). 2018–2019 Sports qualifying physical examination clearance form. Retrieved January 14, 2018, from http://www.bing.com /cr?IG=FD4C3E017628425DA6A740866AF6C54F&CID =0F123BA2E458678E1C3430D5E5F76615&rd=1&h=- p9kwL4jaXLnXEMNgPRfL0c5j8tALiesGZYO6r0MIS s&v=1&r=http%3a%2f%2fwww.mshsl.org%2fmshsl%2 fpublications%2fcode%2fforms%2fPhysicalExam.pdf %3fne%3d5&p=DevEx,5064.1.

National Athletic Trainers' Association (n.d.). Emergency action plans. Retrieved from https://www.nata.org /sites/default/files/white-paper-Emergency-Action -Plan.pdf.

National Athletic Trainers' Association (2017, December 6). NATA quick facts. Retrieved January 14, 2018, from https://www.nata.org/nata-quick-facts.

National Athletic Trainers' Association (2015, September 11). NATA sample job descriptions. Retrieved January 14, 2018, from https://www .nata.org/career-education/career-center/post-a-job /sample-job-descriptions.

National Center for Spectator Sports Safety and Security (n.d.). Retrieved from https://www.ncs4.com/about /overview.

National Collegiate Athletics Association (n.d.). NCAA injury surveillance program FAQs. Retrieved from http://www.ncaa.org/sport-science-institute/ncaa -injury-surveillance-program-faqs.

National Committee for Accreditation of Coaching Education (n.d.). Registry of accredited programs. Retrieved from http://www.qualitycoachingeducation .org/accredited-programs/.

National Federation of State High School Associations (NFHS) (2017, September 6). High school sports participation increases for 28th straight year, nears 8 million mark. Retrieved from https://www.nfhs.org /articles/high-school-sports-participation-increases -for-28th-straight-year-nears-8-million-mark/.

National Interscholastic Athletic Administrators Association—Leadership Training Institute (n.d.). Legal issues in athletics: Risk management. Indianapolis, Indiana.

North Carolina FC Youth (n.d.). Athletic training information. Retrieved January 14, 2018, from http:// www.ncfcyouth.com/Default.aspx?tabid=12850.

Pike, A. R., Pryor, R. R., Vandermark, L. W., Mazerolle, S. M. , & J. Casa, D. J. (2017, January). Athletic trainer services in public and private secondary schools. *Journal of Athletic Training, 52*(1), 5–11.

Pop Warner (n.d.). Pop Warner little scholars. Retrieved from http://www.popwarner.com/.

Society of Health and Physical Educators (n.d.). Domains, standards, and benchmarks. Retrieved January 15, 2018, from https://www.shapeamerica.org/standards /coaching/coachingstandards.aspx.

USA Basketball (n.d.). USA Basketball licensing and elearning program. Retrieved January 15, 2018, from https://community.usab.com/.

USA Football (n.d.). Heads Up Football for youth leagues and clubs. Retrieved January 15, 2018, from https:// www.usafootball.com/programs/heads-up-football /youth/.

USA Hockey (n.d.). Coaching education recommended guidelines. Retrieved January 15, 2018, from http:// secyh.org/2e5ca83d-a7fd-45d1-95f7-8735947a7429 /Text/Documents/1269/13718.pdf.

US Lacrosse (n.d.). Become a coach. Retrieved from https://www.uslacrosse.org/coaches/become-a -coach.

US Lacrosse (2012). Youth & best practices guidebook, 2nd ed. [online]. Retrieved from http://files .leagueathletics.com/Images/Club/13692/USL_Boys _Lacrosse_Guidebook.pdf.

US Soccer (2017, April 18). US soccer coaching license pathway provides high-quality education to coaches of all levels. Retrieved January 15, 2018, from https://www.ussoccer.com/stories/2017/04/18 /22/28/20170418-feat-coach-overview-of-the-us -soccer-coaching-license-pathway.

Wolohan, J. T. (2006). A risk management plan starts with a facility audit. Retrieved January 14, 2018, from https://www.athleticbusiness.com/Athelete-Safety /a-risk-management-plan-starts-with-a-facility -audit.html.

© Audrey Kwok/EyeEm/Getty Images

CHAPTER 8

Staff Management

LEARNING OBJECTIVES

After reading this chapter, students will be able to:

1. Explain the role of staff management and human resource management in athletic administration across the college, high school, youth, and club sport settings.
2. Develop hiring policy, including the stages of the hiring process within college, high school, youth, and club sport levels.
3. Identify methods of staff team building within the college, high school, youth, and club sport settings.
4. Apply best practices to developing job satisfaction to enhance productivity and staff retention within the college, high school, youth, and club sport settings.
5. Communicate the role the athletic administrator plays in leading a staff toward desired organizational goals within the college, high school, youth, and club sport settings.

▶ Staff Management

Athletic administration encompasses many responsibilities and core task areas. Ensuring the effective delivery of sport programming to participants is understandably the central thrust for any athletic administration. Moreover, supplying the energy and effort required to sustain a positive sporting environment cannot rest on the shoulders of just one athletic administrator. The role of the staff becomes increasingly important across all settings of athletic administration as the stakes to remain competitive get higher. The pressures to hire the best and most qualified staff members and then retain each over a long period of time are increasing challenges across the range of college, high school, youth, and club sport levels. The process of building a cohesive and well-trained staff takes devotion and time on the part of the athletic administrator. As we have explored in previous chapters, the field of athletic administration is dynamic and competitive. Educational programs in athletic administration and sport management are graduating high numbers of young professionals who aim to secure positions at the college, high school, youth, and club sport levels. Nevertheless, the selection of staff members, even with a pool of eager candidates, demands mindful actions by the administrator to hire the most qualified staff for the athletic entity.

Hoye, Smith, Nicholson, and Stewart (2015) note that "human resource management, in business or sport organizations, is essentially about first, finding the right person for the job at the right time, and second, ensuring an appropriately trained and satisfied workforce" (p. 141). According to the National Collegiate Athletic Association (NCAA) (n.d.), the significance of effective staff management significantly impacts athletic administration, as illustrated in the quote, extracted from the webpage "So You Want to be an AD," "your career as an athletics director depends on how well you manage personnel."

The hiring process can be a daunting challenge for athletic administrators who are balancing the current offering of programs with the process of recruiting and securing new staff for open positions. Similar to other core managerial responsibilities, there should be a process for personnel selection for each open position, with specific steps followed consistently. Equally important is that the hiring process is transparent both internally (within the athletic entity) and externally (to potential candidates and stakeholders). The following core activities should be executed by the athletic administrator before embarking on the hiring process.

Step 1: Position Description

The first aspect of the hiring process is to determine what position is open and what the position requires. The athletic administrator must write a clear job description that details the specific duties of the position and adequately reflects the responsibilities within the athletic entity. According to the NCAA, "a good job description should include: organizational structure, required skills, abilities and core competencies, performance expectations and outcomes, education and experience requirements (including experience working with, coaching, and teaching diverse groups and diverse students)" (2017, p. 5). As indicated by Whisenant, Miller, and Pedersen (2005), within a job description "the qualifications often include minimal levels of education, professional certification, special knowledge and skills, and experience" (p. 914). Typically, the hiring manager (athletic director,

recreation director, or club executive director) starts the human resource management process by analyzing the organization's needs and then developing the position description. Once the formal job description is crafted, the human resource department or supervisor reviews and approves the materials to ensure all legal requirements have been met.

Step 2: Search Committee

The process of reviewing candidates for open positions requires reviewing multiple credentials [résumés or curriculum vitae (CVs), which is similar to a résumé but longer and includes teaching experience, publications, research, awards, and achievements], more so for more attractive roles within the athletic entity. Sorting through and reviewing applications and résumés requires a time commitment along with expertise in understanding the qualifications required for the position. There should be a search committee comprising multiple staff members who not only review the applications but also provide feedback to the chair of the search committee for the next steps in the hiring process.

The search committee chair is the point person or contact person for the entire process. Traditionally, the search committee chair communicates with applicants regarding the specifics of the position, interview schedule, follow-up questions, and eventually an offer if the candidate is the top choice for the position. However, depending on the size of the organization and the role of the human resource department, the search committee chair may not be the person who officially offers the position to the candidate. A member of the human resource department may make the official offer on behalf of the organization and review benefits and salary. The sport marketplace is extremely competitive, requiring a search committee to weigh through the applications in a streamlined fashion. In many cases, the search committee will also review the job description to ensure its accuracy and to clarify the information.

Step 3: Promote the Position

To get the most visibility for the open position, athletic administrators must determine the best platforms to advertise on and promote the position to professionals in the field. There are many web-based job search sites (e.g., Indeed.com, Monster.com) used by athletic entities to reach candidates within the sports domain. In addition to those generic Internet sites, athletic administrators link with professional associations and governing bodies (NCAA and athletic conferences) to distribute information regarding open positions. Athletic administrators generate interest for staff position openings through their own networks. This level of networking, if successful, presents a favorable outlook for the entity and assists in recruitment of highly qualified individuals.

Step 4: Review of Applications

Each open position at the athletic entity may bring a large number of applications, depending on the desirability of the position. Typically, applications are submitted either electronically or, in some cases, via mail, according to the directions of the athletic entity. Proper evaluation of applications incorporates a checklist of minimal requirements. After ascertaining that minimal requirements have been met, the search committee will dig deeper into the credentials of each applicant. The review process takes time and diligence to vet the candidacy of each applicant. Discussion regarding educational preparation, past experiences, and professional accomplishments paints a picture of the potential fit of each candidate. Along with the credentials review, the search committee will link the responsibilities and expectations of the role to the competencies of the candidates.

In athletics (and other industries), positions are filled by internal candidates. Internal candidates could be assistant coaches who want to take a head coaching position or assistant directors of coaching aiming to be the director of coaching. Roach and Dixon (2006) found that

> management literature suggests that the benefits of internal hiring are that it reduces expenses, adds predictability, and enhances the probability of employee commitment and effective performance. The drawbacks, however, are that the organization might have diminished access to important, specialized knowledge from within and might become isolated from sources of new and innovative ideas outside the organization. (p. 140)

The decision rests with the search committee whether to grant interview opportunities to internal candidates. In research by Schneider, Stier, Kampf, Haines, and Wilding (2006) into campus recreation directors, the results showed that job communication skills and experience typically prevailed over grade point average.

Interviews should be consistent and uniform for all applicants.

Conduct an initial phone interview to narrow the pool of candidates to agreed-on number by search committee.

Develop a list of 10 to 15 interview questions to address the skill set and position responsibilities.

Search Committee Checklist

© Photographee.eu/Shutterstock.

Step 5: Interview

Blindly hiring an individual for a position should never happen. The interview process in and of itself is a tiered approach. Depending on the position, top candidates may be subjected to an initial phone interview. Once more, the number of candidates who reach this level of the process depends on their perceived qualifications by the search committee. The intent of the preliminary contact is to review the expectations of the position with the candidate. In addition, the chair can gauge the candidate's interest in the position while collecting responses to a few broad-based questions to get to know the candidate. Once the foundational phone interview takes place, the chair will decide to sit for an interview with the entire search committee.

The interview traditionally entails a face-to-face meeting or video chat to allow the search committee to meet each candidate, see how they respond to questions, and determine how they relate to the committee. To present a productive and informative meeting with the candidate, the same set of questions is used for each interviewee. Ideally, the interview will start with committee members introducing themselves and explaining their roles at the athletic entity to connect and share information with the candidate. The intent of the interview is twofold. First, the committee aims to learn as much as it can about the expertise and candidate suitability for the position. Second, the candidate has an opportunity to learn about the athletic entity and the position through the lens of committee members. Interviews are commonly structured so that similar questions are asked of each candidate. To recruit and showcase the athletic entity to the candidate, committee members will allow time for the candidate to ask follow-up questions. Expectedly, candidates are offered opportunities to ask questions of the group to learn more about the position and the athletic entity as a whole.

Along with the list of prepared questions to ask candidates, athletic administrators must avoid specific questions during the interview process. As the U.S. Equal Employment Opportunity Commission (EEOC) indicates:

> The laws enforced by EEOC prohibit an employer or other covered entity from using neutral employment policies and practices that have a disproportionately negative effect on applicants or employees of a particular race, color, religion, sex (including gender identity, sexual orientation, and pregnancy), or national origin, or on an individual with a disability or class of individuals with disabilities, if the polices or practices at issue are not job-related and necessary to the operation of the business. (U.S. Equal Opportunity Commission)

From a legal perspective, athletic administrators must communicate the appropriate practices throughout the hiring process to anyone who may be involved with the candidate search. Furthermore, athletic administrators and search chairs have legal obligations to monitor the actions of the committee members to avoid illegal actions during the hiring process.

Schneider et al. (2006) reinforce that "the interview continues to be the most widely accepted form of evaluating prospective employees. Positive impressions can occur through positive verbal and nonverbal communications, interviewee qualifications, and the ability of the prospective job candidate to effectively communicate his or her past accomplishments" (p. 143). As determined by the hiring athletic administrator and search committee, the candidates may or may not have extended interview options. In some cases, the candidates will tour the facilities, meet participants or student-athletes, and meet with other staff members and executives who may not be part of the official search committee team. These supplemental interactions serve to give the candidate insight into the internal operations while also allowing search committee members to learn more about the candidate and continue to share information about the opportunity.

In the end, these aspects of the interview provide the search committee with rich information that informs members about the potential impact each candidate might have on the athletic entity.

Step 6: Selection of Top Candidates

After the interviews are complete, the search committee typically reconvenes to discuss the candidates' qualifications. From that list, the search committee typically ranks a set number of candidates from highest to lowest. Once the top candidate is identified, the search committee chair will start the process to officially offer the position to that individual.

Step 7: Extending the Offer

An official offer is presented to the top candidate once all the interview and search criteria are completed. The official offer is made by the human resources office, designated athletic administrator, or the chair of the search committee. Salary, length of contract, dates of employment, benefits, and any special provisions connected to the position are shared with the selected candidate. In a best-case scenario, the candidate will accept the offer. However, if more time is needed, there may be an expiration time on the offer that allows both parties to come to an agreement within a reasonable time frame.

▶ Integration into the Workplace

After all of the steps are complete and the individual is hired, the process of staff management does not end; in fact, it is just the beginning of integrating the new hire into the culture of the athletic department. The process simply converts from the hiring process to staff development. Regardless of the expertise and training the new hire brings to the athletic entity, a learning curve exists whenever anyone starts a new position. The new hire undergoes a process of absorbing information from several resources within the athletic entity. A learning curve is "the rate at which the incumbent masters information about role expectations and the organization's culture to perform effectively" (Minnick et al., 2014, p. 27). Through formal and informal interactions with others, the new hire acquires information about the culture of the athletic environment together with expectations for the position. Orienting new staff to the position and the work environment coupled with cultivating mentor relationships creates beneficial outcomes for the new hire.

Effective athletic administrators will carve out time for new hires to become acclimated to the new setting so the transition is seamless and entry into the position offsets any potential anxiety from the individual. Ideally, staff members, along with athletic administration, aspire to reach high levels of success within their professional role. Nurturing that ambitious desire plays a role in enhancing productivity in the workplace. Moving the staff in the same direction to advance the mission of the athletic entity starts with the leadership.

FEEDBACK FROM THE FIELD

John O'Sullivan is the founder and CEO of the Changing the Game Project, which he started in 2012 after his 20-year involvement as a soccer player and coach at the youth, high school, college, and professional levels. O'Sullivan is the author of the number one best-selling books *Changing the Game: The Parents Guide to Raising Happy, High Performing Athletes, Giving Youth Sports Back to our Kids*, and *Is It Wise to Specialize?* His message has been highlighted in HuffPost, CNN.com, *Outside Magazine*, ESPN.com, Soccer America, and numerous other publications. O'Sullivan is a prolific national and international speaker through platforms such as TEDx, the National Soccer Coaches Association of America, U.S. Lacrosse, IMG Academy, and at numerous other events throughout the United States, Canada, Asia, and Europe. The mission of the Changing the Game Project is:

> to ensure that we return youth sports to our children, and put the "play" back in "play ball." We want to provide the most influential adults in our children's lives—their parents and coaches—with the information and resources they need to make sports a healthy, positive, and rewarding experience for their children, and their whole family. Parenting and coaching young athletes is an art, not a science, and the information you find here can help you navigate the maze of youth sports, and put a smile on your young athlete's face, whether he or she is [six] or 16 years old.

O'Sullivan was asked to reflect on staff management within youth sport organizations. First, states O'Sullivan, with any organization, it is important for youth sport administrators to understand "that changing behaviors takes time, and so the quickest way to do it, is to do it every day." He further adds that the mistake that many organizations make "is that they want changes but then they ignore the bad behavior or the behavior they are trying to change." O'Sullivan urges youth sport administrators to lead. Leading change can take many forms, including bringing in speakers and providing resources to staff and volunteers. The messaging from O'Sullivan's perspective is that youth sport administrators need to stay true to the change and "when there is pushback say, 'Remember we are not doing that anymore.'" From this approach, O'Sullivan asserts

> usually, the train gets rolling in the positive direction but once you ignore certain things then you are basically condoning it and then usually the change doesn't happen, so it takes time and consistency and the willingness to say we are going from A to B and it is going to take some time to get there but it is the journey that is worth taking.

What O'Sullivan gathers from youth sport administrators, coaches, and program directors is that the biggest problem stems from the fact that parents only seem to care about winning. O'Sullivan disrupts this emphasis on just winning by asking athletic administrators, "What are you giving (the participants, including athletes and families) to measure success by, other than 'did we win?'" O'Sullivan adds that some coaches and administrators treat the relationship with athletes and families as transactional— that is, if the club or league uses the player fees to pay for the fields and the officials and "doesn't do anything beyond that, then the only way to measure success is through the wins." So, as O'Sullivan laments in this scenario, "it is only a good transaction if the team is 10 and 2; people are naturally going to be upset when the team goes 2 and 10." To resolve this transactional mindset, O'Sullivan asserts that the most effective youth sport organizations are those that clearly say, "This is who we are, and this is what we do, these are our values, and these are the things we teach and we just happen to teach them through soccer or baseball." From O'Sullivan's experience, those youth sport organizations who are consistent about those values and learning outcomes "are giving people something more to be loyal about than 'did we win?'"

(continues)

FEEDBACK FROM THE FIELD   *(continued)*

From a staff management perspective, the youth sport administrator is relaying the message that the experience is not all about winning, even though most of the time the first question asked of a coach or an athlete after a game is, "Did you win?" O'Sullivan conveys that "it takes a certain maturity as a parent not to ask that question and as a coach not to only judge your success on that." To shed even more light on the prevalence of using wins as the only measurement of success, O'Sullivan cites legendary NFL coach John Madden, who said, "Winning is the best deodorant." From a youth sport administrator's perspective it is important to recognize that "when you win nothing really stinks, but when you lose you start to examine everything." One thing about being a master coach, according to O'Sullivan, is "that ability to look at things unemotionally whether you won or you lost; sometimes you win and it is not very good, and sometimes you lose and it is fantastic."

Professional development for coaches in terms of coaching education is a must for all coaches, according to O'Sullivan. Some sports have a better pathway for coaches to obtain coaching credentials. However, O'Sullivan asserts the biggest problem in coaching education is that the courses and seminars are "almost totally focused on X's and O's, on drills and activities, and yet when we ask kids what are the most important qualities of a coach, they say it is clear and consistent communication, being a good listener, respect and encouragement, being a positive role model, and knowing what you are talking about." The top answers, from athletes, have nothing to do with X's and O's and yet, when we teach our coaches, we teach them drills." To simplify, coaches need to recognize, especially for the younger athletes, that it is about the connection, and, as he states, "they don't care how much you know, until they know how much you care." O'Sullivan and the Changing the Game Project offer youth sport administrators and coaches courses online, including lessons for coaches who are just starting out "putting aside the X's and O's" and discussing "how we connect with athletes, how we communicate, and how do we develop character because that is what kids and parents want out of this experience."

One difficult aspect of coach education in this country versus others is that the United States lacks a "central ministry of sport." Ideally, sanctioning bodies can have more responsibility to prompt members who register with the agency to require "a certain level of coach education" along with "a certain level of parent engagement education that is now expected." As an example, USA Hockey requires coaches to meet a level of coach certification and the governing body "celebrates the organizations that do it right." As parents determine which club is the best fit, they do research online to determine which "are model clubs and model organizations giving them the choice" to sign with a club meeting the standards set by USA Hockey or a club that disavows those ideals.

For future youth sport administrators, O'Sullivan notes the significance of the coaching role in the United States. "[J]ust like being a teacher, it is a vocation, not necessarily a profession, it is something you are called to do because it is not about the money, it is about serving others and working with kids and doing things to make a difference in lives and that is what the best coaches do, that is who our best teachers are." O'Sullivan advises someone entering youth sport administration, "when you first jump in, it is a good idea to be patient and to get the lay of the land, understanding you cannot change everything overnight." He further urges athletic administrators "to pick and choose the things that are most dear to you and work hard on changing them." When a youth sport administrator can change "10–20% of the most important aspects" and "when the staff see those changes that will have a positive effect and they will come back and say 'Hey what else do you have?'" He cautions youth sport administrators against trying to change too much in a short period because "you will bump up against the established politics of any youth sport or adult sport organization and you are probably not going to get anything done at all."

© Matej Kastelic/Shutterstock.

▶ Job Satisfaction

Once the hiring process ends and the staff is fully integrated into the workplace, athletic administrators aim to elevate worker satisfaction levels. "The components of job satisfaction include attitudes toward compensation, coworkers, and one's roles and tasks" (Brown et al. 2004, p. 31).

The importance of job satisfaction within the workplace cannot be underestimated. Staff members who are satisfied are more productive and positive within the work environment. Within the volunteer athletic administration sector, Harman and Doherty (2014) found that volunteer coaches desire to offer the athletic club "technical expertise" and "leadership" and subsequently expect from the club "fundamental resources," "financial support," "coach support," and "formal training opportunities." In their study of the recreational sports setting, Kroth and Young (2014) found that staff desired the following work attributes: "social interaction in the work environment, desire for advancement, salary expectations, and work-life balance" (p. 28). Athletic administrators can apply the work of Kroth and Young and their study of millennials (individuals born between 1980 and 2000) to college, high school, youth, and club sports staff management by incorporating these workplace practices: Focus on team projects so staff can work in a collaborative fashion,

foster creative thinking, allow for autonomy in the completion of tasks and assignments, and allow activities for staff to interact with one another (pp. 29–30).

Bartlett and McKinney (2004) researched the relationship between staff members' organizational commitment and job satisfaction within the recreation setting. Employees within this setting reveal that receiving career guidance from supervisors and satisfaction with career mobility significantly affect organizational commitment, which "focuses on the degree of involvement or fit between employees and their organization" (Mahony, Fitzgerald, Crawford, & Hnat, 2015, p. 17). Within the athletic training arena, Mazerolle and Hunter (2017) stress the importance "for supervisors and administrators to recognize the importance of time off to facilitate rejuvenation, acknowledging the efforts and time of their employees (i.e., saying thank you), and the chance to engage in professionally rewarding activities that benefit the AT, but also, in turn, benefit the organization through the delivery of higher-quality care" (pp. 46–47). Brown et al. (2004) surveyed employees of a multibranch YMCA and from their work shared the following results: managerial employees, part-time, and full-time staff will "hold different attitudes toward the organization based upon their position and experiences;" there is a positive correlation between satisfaction and commitment in that "once positive attitudes toward work are obtained, employees are likely to express commitment (i.e., intentions to stay) to the organization and their job." Staff will experience positive levels of satisfaction and commitment "when employee values are aligned with organizational values" (p. 32). Many factors serve to motivate staff to feel valued, ultimately affecting their satisfaction within their role and at the athletic entity. In the end, athletic administrators can deliberately embed activities the staff desires, which eventually leads to satisfaction and productivity in the workplace.

▶ Retention of Staff

The hiring process and integration of new staff into the work environment is a time-consuming journey that aims to meet the mission of the athletic entity. Job satisfaction and employee commitment to the delivery of the mission are instrumental to retaining staff over time, which is the goal of staff management from an athletic administration perspective. Retaining staff equates to minimizing turnover while also preserving the contributions employees make over time. Seasoned and long-term staff possess the history of the athletic entity and have opportunities to provide direction based on past experiences and knowing the "story" of the organization. Staff longevity presumably promotes a productive work environment while also cutting the costs of filling open positions or having others on the staff fill two roles while empty positions are being filled. As Goodman et al. (2010) note in their study of female athletic trainers at the Division I level, "although a certain amount of turnover is expected and necessary, high turnover can negatively affect organizations" (p. 297). The negative aspects correlate to loss of organizational history, loss of seasoned staff, and expenditures associated with the commencement of the hiring process. Clearly, a core role of staff management is to fully understand what motivates and satisfies employees in order to maintain longevity of staff within their designated positions.

Burnout

Most of the text has focused on how athletic administrators manage and operate within the settings of college, high school, youth, and club sports. Yet even the administrators holding the highest positions within each setting must also report to a supervisor or board of directors. As the field of athletics continues to change and become increasingly competitive, many stressors arise that can lead to burnout among head or top athletic administrators. As Sullivan, Lonsdale, and Taylor (2014) assert, within a dynamic and pressure-filled field like high school athletic administration, the position "can be rewarding but also very demanding, potentially leading to burnout" (p. 256). Maslach, Jackson, and Leiter (1996) depict employee burnout as "emotional exhaustion," cynicism, or holding a "negative attitude" toward work, and a sense of dissatisfaction with work-related achievements (p. 192).

Within seasonal positions in recreation management, burnout is a core concern for athletic administrators. Working with staff on a part-time or on a seasonal basis equivalent to summer camp employment, administrators need to recognize the importance of burnout because it may lead to a reduction in employee performance. Wahl-Alexander, Richards, and Washburn (2017) studied burnout through examining responses from 80 summer camp counselors. The findings reveal differences in male and female camp counselors in emotional exhaustion. Males experienced more exhaustion at the start of camp, and females experienced decreases in personal accomplishment compared to males. However, females detailed more competency and success in their role than their male counterparts (Wahl-Alexander et al., 2017). Raedeke (2004) researched burnout in coaching, summarizing that "not surprisingly, some individuals thrive in the coaching profession and are passionate about their involvement. Others have a less positive view of their coaching experiences, which in some cases culminates in burnout [or] the individual leaving the coaching ranks" (p. 333). In terms of application and strategies to reduce burnout, Raedeke suggests athletic administrators prompt coaches to have "life balance" to reduce stress and to take time to reflect on why they entered this field to "put a spark back into coaching" (p. 347). In the end, supervisors have an arduous task in ensuring employees find enjoyment and satisfaction in their role so they can be highly productive in their work environments.

⚽ FEEDBACK FROM THE FIELD

Gary Colello is the recreation director for the town of Bridgton, Maine. The mission of Bridgton recreation is to provide the community with diverse, fun, and innovative activities for all ages. It is important to promote community health and leisure activities to help individuals reach their potential with an active and balanced lifestyle. Colello admittedly operates a smaller-sized recreation department and is a "one-man show for most of the year." In the summer months, he employs a staff of eight to 10 people to operate the summer camp and various swim lessons over an eight-week period. As with most recreation departments, Colello works with volunteer coaches and parents to deliver a fully functional menu of programs. From Colello's perspective, the recreation department is "interesting and dynamic," especially with the incorporation of so many volunteers within staff management.

The interview process for the recreation department may be less rigid than other settings because of the size of the department and the lack of upper administrators to assist Colello. Individuals apply directly to him for employment; Colello will also visit local high schools and communicate with local colleges to recruit seasonal staff. Colello has a program coordinator review applications, but for the most part he handles the formal interviews on his own.

In terms of staff management and professional development of coaches, Colello requires formalized credentials or training. Colello encourages and offers courses for cardiopulmonary resuscitation (CPR) and first aid certification as an option for any coach. Working within a recreational setting also requires the completion of annual training. Staff and coaches must understand and adhere to municipal codes and regulations, including safety regulations and procedures. The training typically encompasses a half-day to fully expose staff members to the important aspects of recreation management. Over his tenure, Colello learned to deal with changes in town policies and passed the practice down to the staff and volunteers.

Colello shared that the main aspect of his position, aside from delivering the programs to the community, is "finding people who believe in the same values we are trying to offer." To be a cohesive staff, Colello organizes meetings to discuss the department goals and pinpoint outcomes for the children involved in the programs. Colello is a certified strength and conditioning specialist (CSCS), which makes him more motivated to teach his staff about safety, appropriate exercise activities, warm-ups, and dealing with hot weather conditions. Instead of reviewing generalized safety procedures, Colello distributes targeted information "towards what the coaches are trying to accomplish."

Because staff members deal directly with organizing sport-related games and activities, Colello will generate practice plans to assist in managing the programs. Within his recreation department, the experience of the coaches ranges from first timers to college-level coaches. Because the "spectrum of coaches" is broad, Colello offers assistance with planning at a coach's request. In addition, he directs the coaches to use all available online resources—including YouTube—so that volunteers can actually see the activities being implemented. For departmental regulations, Colello is currently writing a policy and procedures manual to assist in guiding staff and volunteers.

Staff retention is a critical element in creating a seamless program from season to season. The benefit of having staff members return season after season is their familiarity with the program and the participants. To increase retention, Colello tries to "pay staff higher than most in similar positions" because he believes paying staffers well demonstrates how much they are valued as employees. "If I am paying someone more, they would put more effort into it (the position) and put more caring into it because they feel like they are worth it." Colello indicates many of the children attending his program are at lower income levels and may not live the most structured home life. Using returning staff who understand the challenges of these participants is an advantage for Colello and the entire recreation department. Colello deals with a population of participants with lower income levels, "63% of [whom] are on free or reduced lunch in our district." As Colello explains the importance of retention, "When

(continues)

FEEDBACK FROM THE FIELD   *(continued)*

you get 10 to 12 kids together who do not have structure, it becomes a mad house sometimes. When you have those staff who can manage those groups, you try to keep them around from their junior year in high school all the way through college." To create job satisfaction, Colello does not have too many requirements for staff members; he wants to make sure they are having fun with the kids, and he makes sure they are taking care of their responsibilities. On some days, to recognize the effort of the staff, he will send them home early or allow them to come in late. These gestures, as Colello clarifies, lend to retention from one season to the next.

When providing advice to athletic administration students within staff management, Colello believes they "should look for character and someone who cares about what they are doing." He stresses that if candidates for a position don't truly care about the role, they are "not going to do anything with [their] degree." He adds, "When we are dealing with 50 kids at the beach, I need people who care. I want someone who is enthused to be there. I want someone who wants to be part of a program." During the hiring process, Colello suggests using scenario-based questions versus "tell me about your experience" only questions. One question he typically asks is, "What would you do if you bring a group to a playground and one kid sprints into the woods?" When it comes to response, Colello confesses that "there is no right answer when it comes down to it. It is case by case." The significance of the question rests with the fact that Colello uses scenario-based questioning to examine "how people respond to it and how quickly they respond to it."

From Colello's perspective, the most challenging aspects of recreation management and staff management are securing volunteers and dealing with the public. As Colello articulates, the most difficult part of his position is making a decision that is not necessarily "the popular decision." As Colello describes, the tougher decisions he makes may not make sense on a personal level but make sense administratively. For example, Colello deals with redistricting in his area. The recreation department policy dictates that participants can only be involved in the recreation department where they reside. However, with redistricting he has participants who live 20 to 30 minutes away, and when they arrive back home from school they would miss the program time frame and the offered activities. Even though Colello would like to allow these young people to participate in his recreation department, he has to decline the request based on established policies.

Because Colello is a CSCS, he is required to maintain his certification by earning continuing education credits. Colello strongly believes these professional development opportunities add to the overall athletic and fitness-oriented activities offered through the recreation department. Colello is also a member of the Society of Health and Physical Educators, an organization providing professional development opportunities and support to professionals specializing in health, physical education, recreation, and dance. He holds credentials from the National Academy of Sports Medicine as a youth exercise specialist. In his role as the recreation director, Colello is also active in New England's parks and recreation association. Because of time constraints and a small department, Colello does not get the chance to attend many conferences, so he opts to complete "classes" for professional development. The town of Bridgton supports and funds these professional development activities.

▶ Employee–Employer Expectations

Another aspect of staff orientation to the workplace involves communicating values and beliefs through formal and informal channels. Agreed-on expectations are formulated and accepted through the official employment contract.

Along with employment contracts that set positional expectations, psychological contracts, which are unwritten, convey the same communal outcomes for the position and workplace. Furthermore, psychological contracts are defined as "individual beliefs, shaped by the organization, regarding the terms of an exchange agreement between individuals and their organization" (Rousseau, 1995, p. 9). Simply stated, psychological contracts exude a "shared set of obligations," which in turn "can create social pressures to adhere to those commitments" (Rousseau, p. 11). As an example, Nichols and Ojala (2009) found in their research of athletic event management that "the key elements volunteers brought to the psychological contract were: reliability, enthusiasm, commitment, good relations and empathy with the public, common sense, local knowledge, general experience of working at events, and in some cases, more specific experience at a particular event" (p. 380). Taylor, Darcy, Hoye, and Cuskelly (2006) assert "the psychological contract relies considerably on the exchange of benefits and rewards, the receipt of which acts as the linchpin in the employment relationship" (p. 126).

As Rousseau (1995) further explains, the psychological contract adds significance to the workplace because "people who make and keep their commitments can anticipate and plan because their actions are more readily specific and predictable both to others as well as to themselves" (p. 9). The process of framing a psychological contract actually starts during the search process. Thus, Fornaciari (2015) advises athletic administrators to "develop a list of characteristics you would like to find in your new coach. It is key to find candidates who have high expectations—for themselves, their assistant coaches, and the athletes." The entire search process ideally lends to adding valuable human assets to the workplace. As Janssen (2012) stresses, to build the best athletic entity you must use your network to "hire, empower, and keep a top-notch staff." Within the club sport setting, Taylor et al. (2006) conclude the "use of the psychological contract in recognizing volunteer organization exchanges can aid in the formation of realistic expectations and provide for a greater mutual understanding of the volunteer organization relationship" (p. 145).

 FEEDBACK FROM THE FIELD

Featured Interview: High School Athletics

Tim Alberts signed on as the athletic director at Wilmington High School (Wilmington, Massachusetts), replacing an administrator who was in that role for more than 13 years. When asked about the transition from one high school to another, he noted that he worked directly with the superintendent of schools to create an entry plan as the director of athletics. The entry plan helped him create a path toward learning and finding areas of need to address within the department. One aspect of the plan encompassed meeting with members of the district leadership team, coaches, parents, program directors, and boosters to get a feel for the Wilmington community. He scheduled meetings proactively and also submitted the entry plan to the local newspaper with an invitation to meet with the community. For Alberts, "it was a great experience and an opportunity to forge new relationships and grow the athletic program."

With any management position, administrators typically make changes to enhance the department as a reflection of their own leadership style. Alberts worked with coaches to make community service a part of their program. A few of the high school sport programs already had this in place—for example, the girls' soccer team already ran a Kick Cancer game with a local school. He also requested that all coaches do their own community service initiative and participate in a sporting goods drive sponsored by the Massachusetts Interscholastic Athletic Association (MIAA). Alberts assisted on making sure these teams were recognized for their good work. To highlight the efforts of his coaches and teams, he nominated the girls' soccer and girls' volleyball teams for MIAA educational athletics awards, and both teams were awarded this prestigious honor.

So that coaches understand the mission and vision of the department, Alberts meets with them individually before the season starts to get everyone on the same page. Following those one-on-

(continues)

FEEDBACK FROM THE FIELD *(continued)*

one sessions, he also conducts a preseason meeting with the entire coaching staff plus an additional meeting with the parents and student-athletes. From Alberts's perspective, these forums help set the tone for the season by detailing expectations of behavior, sportsmanship, and commitment. At these meetings, the coaches also go over team expectations with both the student-athletes and their families. Procedures, schedules for tryouts, and coaching philosophies are the main topics covered at the meeting, along with responses to questions and other concerns.

For professional development of staff, within the Wilmington High School athletic department, coaches are required to be CPR certified, complete an annual Criminal Offender Record Information (CORI) and a one-time fingerprint test, complete a civil rights training, National Federation of High School Sports (NFHS) concussion test, MIAA fundamentals of coaching, and NFHS sports first aid and sport-specific courses. Alberts does not run any in-service activities for his staff but does pass along information on pertinent resources, clinics, coaching associations, and articles and periodicals.

The management of practices and games is a daunting task with the number of sports under the direction of Alberts. At some institutions conflicts may arise in terms of field usage and allocated times but Alberts indicated that he "is lucky as I have a great coaching staff and they get along really well." To effectively plan for playing space, Alberts typically sends out a Google calendar or group email so the coaches can work out the schedule together. The Middlesex League, with which Wilmington High School is affiliated, "does a really good job with the scheduling, so there are few conflicts with sports that might have a home game on the same night," according to Alberts.

There have been many welcomed changes at the school since Alberts's arrival to satisfy the needs of teams. It is an MIAA rule to have a certified athletic trainer at all football games and varsity ice hockey games. Alberts stressed how fortunate his program is to have a fully dedicated athletic trainer at all home games. One supplement to the program from Alberts is a mandatory athletic trainer to cover junior varsity (JV) ice hockey games, and he is committed to having coverage at all varsity events. When possible, the athletic trainer attends JV games, and the department sets an order of priority based on the physical contact involved in each sport. Alberts also switched all lacrosse games (varsity and JV) to the Wilmington High School Alumni Stadium field (versus an off-campus site), which helped facilitate better athletic training coverage.

Alberts was asked what he would like his staff to say about him and his management of the department while also enriching the program for players and fans. He said he wants

coaches to coach and [he] will be supportive and allow them to do their jobs. I trust each coach to be the subject matter expert in their sport, so I give them the autonomy to run practices and games the way they see fit. I am a firm believer that the coach is in charge of picking their team and playing students the way they see fit at the varsity level. At the sub-varsity levels, I encourage the coaches to make sure that playing time is spread out in order to develop students for the varsity team down the road.

In terms of advice to future athletic administrators, Alberts is a firm believer that the most qualified person and right fit should get the position. There are times, he says, that athletic administrators will experience pressure from various constituents on the hiring process, "but it is important to recommend the best person, regardless of politics."

Managing the staff of a high school athletic department presents a multitude of challenges. As Alberts points out, the coaching profession takes a toll physically, emotionally, and mentally on individuals, and coaches face long days for low stipends.

It takes a special person to commit the time and energy to students who are not their own children and it can be a grind. I want my coaches to know that I support them and appreciate their work. I always make sure to thank them and let them know that their efforts are recognized and appreciated.

Entry Plan

For athletic directors, similar to Tim Alberts, who are newly hired, a valuable tool to acclimate staff to their philosophy can take the form of an "entry plan." An entry plan can be a letter/email sent to all staff to introduce the athletic director, sharing their philosophy of management, strategies to implement the department mission, and detailed goals with timelines for accomplishment. The entry plan serves a variety of purposes, especially as a new person in an established athletic department. The staff is probably anxious to get to know the new athletic director as he/she is the leader of the department. The staff is looking for direction and to understand the motives and aspirations of the newly hired athletic administrator.

Although the athletic director went through a formal interview process, the staff benefits from reading/reviewing an entry plan as it is a guiding document with timelines and answers questions that may not have been thoroughly explored through the position search process. Beneficial content areas of an entry plan include: Expressing gratitude for being hired in the position, sharing commitment to the established mission of the department, highlighting the importance of meeting with each staff member within the first month in the position, and communicating the desire to work with the staff to highlight the strengths of the department.

The entry plan can also include a timeline of addressing core needs of the athletic department that are dependent on the scenarios presented at the site. The timeline is composed of meetings with administrators at the superintendent or principal levels for high schools and president and vice president levels for college athletic departments. Staff can review the schedule for opening staff meetings and subsequent meetings to discuss and ultimately implement plans.

The overall intent of the entry plan is to communicate to staff. The newly hired athletic director can use this platform to articulate past experiences that will lend themselves to moving the current department forward while also demonstrating care for the past accolades accomplished by the staff. The purposes of the concluding statements are to reinforce the importance of teamwork among the staff to ultimately create a healthy and productive athletic department serving a variety of stakeholders.

Questions for Discussion

1. Staff management encompasses a great deal of devotion, especially for a newly hired athletic director. After reading how Alberts connected with the existing staff and his entry plan for the athletic department, what type of activities would you model from the information as the new leader of the athletic department?
2. How significant are meetings with current staff members to get the pulse of the athletic department? Should a newly hired athletic director meet one-on-one with each staff member (full- and part-time) or would a group department meeting give the same opportunities for open discussions?
3. Write an opening letter to describe your philosophy as the athletic director and the goals you would have for your department and staff. Use your high school as the setting to craft the letter that should describe your expectations, aspirations, outcomes for teams, and goals for the department.

Jentz & Wofford (2012)

MANAGERIAL APPLICATIONS

Youth Sport: Volunteer Management

Within your town recreation department are several sport teams spanning the fall, winter, and spring seasons. Typically, the same parents volunteer to coach these teams. As recreation director, you have recently observed that many of these repeat volunteers seem tired and have lost a bit of their energy progressing from season to season without a break from their coaching and administrative roles (emails to parents, maintaining organization rosters) for the management of their teams.

Questions to Consider

1. Burnout, as you have studied, can seriously affect retention of coaches. What strategies and activities will you incorporate into the recreation department to offset the risk of losing seasoned volunteers?
2. Because you are concerned that the delivery of the sport programs is dropping in quality because your head coaches have lost energy, should you consider a policy regarding the number of head coaching positions held in a given year by one individual? Research other town recreation programs to determine how the selection and maintenance of volunteer coaches is handled.
3. What types of recruiting systems could you incorporate into the recreation department to increase the pool of volunteers interested in coaching? Many parents want to get involved in coaching their children but may feel apprehensive because of a lack of knowledge in practice planning. What are some in-service opportunities you can incorporate into your recreation department to provide assistance to these potential volunteer coaches?

 DECISION-MAKING CHALLENGE

Case Study: College Athletics

As the athletic director, you pride yourself on providing enriching opportunities to your student-athletes and finding ways to celebrate their accomplishments through social media posts, informal encounters on campus, and formal presentations of awards and banquets. Recently, you overheard a few coaches discussing your lack of acknowledgement when they achieve a level of success (wins, community service, fundraising). As the athletic director, you have spent most of your time focused on the student-athletes but have not recognized the importance of acknowledging your staff. Create a list of activities to incorporate into your management toolbox to praise and applaud the efforts of your coaches and demonstrate your support for their work and their dedication to the student-athletes.

 DECISION-MAKING CHALLENGE

Case Study: High School Athletics Internal Hire

The hiring process requires diligence and patience on the part of all involved, especially the athletic administrator. The head coach, who has been with the girls' ice hockey program for 20 years, is stepping down. She has mentored the assistant coach for the last four years in preparation for this moment. The assistant coach was also a graduate of the high school, and she returned as an assistant coach on graduation from college, where she participated in the Division I women's ice hockey team. Serving as both the athletic director and the chair of the search committee for the position, you have to determine if an internal hire is appropriate for the program. Please provide a comprehensive list of pros and cons associated with an internal hire. Meet with a classmate and compare your lists. What items or considerations did you leave off your list or vice versa?

Wrap-Up

End-of-Chapter Activities

College Athletics

As a future athletic administrator, describe your leadership style while creating a plan for staff management. What types of leadership activities would you implement in which the athletic director and staff can participate together in being leaders/advocates for the department?

1. Please navigate to NCAA.org to research job opportunities and position openings in intercollegiate athletic organizations across the country.
2. Create a list of potential personnel to be hired for a mock institution you plan to create; include job title, job description, educational background, and salary range based on your research.
3. Determine how many athletic teams you plan to offer at this NCAA institution, including support staff. Is there a difference in number of staff in NCAA Divisions I, II, and III?
4. Compare the number of staff within an athletic department at a Division I and Division III institution. What job titles are similar or different within these two levels of the NCAA?

Youth Club Sport

1. You are the executive director for a prominent baseball club. In recent years a few new baseball clubs have entered your area of reach for players. Your concern is that the coaches employed by your club lack the same coaching credentials as the competition.
   a. Determine what types of baseball coaching education and training would be available for your coaches. Include the full details with cost and location.
   b. Research how other club programs promote coaching credentials on their social media sites. What ideas will you incorporate in your social media platforms?
   c. After determining the costs for each professional development opportunity, craft a policy to address the reimbursement for the cost, the expectations for coaches to absorb the cost, or both. Be sure to indicate the frequency of the required professional development for your coaching staff.

End-of-Chapter Questions

1. Staff plays an instrumental role in the composition of the department. Construct a list of 10 questions you would ask candidates applying for a position in the following three areas: college athletic trainer, high school varsity

football coach, and club sport sponsorship coordinator.

2. Review three athletic websites (college, high school, and youth sport) and identify the personnel responsible for the delivery of the athletic programs within each setting. Are the staff full-time, part-time, seasonal, or volunteer? While you were on the websites, did you notice any vacancies within the athletic entity and announcements to fill those roles?

3. Search online for three positions you may be interested in securing within the field of athletic administration. Include the wording of the actual position announcement or advertisement. What aspects of the job description and the athletic entity appealed to you and why? Describe the requirements to apply for these positions.

4. The hiring process requires collaboration from current staff to secure the best staff. For an athletic director job opening at the high school level, which people (give them job titles) would you encourage to form the search committee and why?

5. In a one-paragraph script, explain staff management to a group of newly hired athletic administrators.

6. What are some of the activities you would use to offset the potential for burnout within the college, high school, club, and youth sport setting for your administrative staff, coaches, and volunteers?

7. Promotion of open positions can serve to recruit qualified candidates. Research options to promote positions within the follow settings: college, high school, club, and youth sport. Indicate any costs associated with advertising on the platforms you discovered.

8. Job satisfaction within the workplace is an important consideration for athletic administrators. What activities would you create in the workplace to increase staff members' satisfaction with their roles? What activities would you incorporate that take place outside of the regular hours of operation of the workplace to enhance job satisfaction?

9. From your experience on a team or school group, share activities that served to connect all members to formulate a cohesive working unit. Which activities could you incorporate into staff team building within the college, high school, youth, and club sport settings for team-building purposes?

10. Psychological contracts exist between staff and athletic administrators. From your perspective, what are the benefits of understanding psychological contracts?

11. List some characteristics you would like staff members to exhibit through their psychological contract within the college, high school, club, and youth sport settings.

12. The athletic administrator is in charge of filling the assistant athletic director position at the college level, and you are charged with developing a time line for hire. Use the steps covered in this chapter to detail a specific time frame (use actual dates) with the final date being acceptance of offer. Share the time line with two other classmates and discuss any variance in your work.

13. Within athletic director Tim Albert's interview, details of an entry plan for an athletic department were shared. For the club and youth sport settings, what type of communication should occur when a new hire (at the upper administration level) fills the position? Which words resonates with you the most that you could include in your entry plan for your staff and why?

References

Bartlett, K. R., & McKinney, W. R. (2004). A study of the role of professional development, job attitudes, and turnover among public park and recreation employees. *Journal of Park & Recreation Administration*, 22(4), 62–80.

Fornaciari, J. (2015, January 29). From the ground up. *Athletic Management* [online]. Retrieved August 1, 2018, from http://athleticmanagement.com/2010/04/04/from_the_ground_up/index.php.

Goodman, A., Mensch, J. M., Jay, M., French, K. E., Mitchell, M. F., & Fritz, S. L. (2010). Retention and attrition factors for female certified athletic trainers in the National Collegiate Athletic Association Division I football bowl subdivision setting. *Journal of Athletic Training*, 45(3), 287–298. doi:10.4085/1062-6050-45.3.287.

Harman, A., & Doherty, A. (2014). The psychological contract of volunteer youth sport coaches. *Journal of Sport Management*, 28(6), 687–699. doi:10.1123/JSM.2013-0146.

Hoye, R., Smith, A., Nicholson, M., & Stewart, B. (2015). *Sport management: Principles and applications*, 4th ed. Oxford, UK: Routledge.

Indiana Principal Leadership Institution (n.d.). Interview questions. Retrieved January 18, 2018, from http://www.indianapli.org/wp-content/uploads/Interview-Questions-Athletic-Director.pdf.

Janssen, J. (2012, October 9). Building, sustaining an elite athletic program. *Coach & A.D* [online]. Retrieved August 1, 2018, from https://coachad.com/articles/building-sustaining-elite-sports-program/.

Jentz, B. C., & Wofford, J. (2012). *The entry plan approach: How to begin a leadership position successfully*. Newton, MA: Leadership & Learning, Inc.

Kroth, A. M., & Young, S. J. (2014). New professionals, new desires: What millennials want in their work. *Recreational Sports Journal*, 38(1), 23–32.

Kuchler, W. J. (2008). Perceived Leadership Behavior and Subordinates' Job Satisfaction in Midwestern NCAA Division III Athletic Departments. *The Sport Journal*, 11(2). Retrieved from https://thesportjournal.org/article/perceived-leadership-behavior-and-subordinates-job-satisfaction-in-midwestern-ncaa-division-iii-athletic-departments/

Mahony, D. F, Fitzgerald, S., Crawford, F., & Hnat, H. B. (2015). Organizational justice perceptions and their relationship to organizational commitment, job satisfaction, and turnover intentions. *Journal of Higher Education Management*, 30(1), 13–26.

Maslach, C., Jackson, S. E., & Leiter, M. P. (Eds.). (1996). *Maslach Burnout Inventory manual*, 3rd ed. Palo Alto, CA: Consulting Psychologists Press.

Mazerolle, S. M., & Hunter, C. (2017). A qualitative exploration of the professional commitment of athletic trainers employed in the professional sports setting. *International Journal of Athletic Therapy & Training*, 22(2), 40–47. doi:10.1123/ijatt.2016-0078.

Minnick, W., Wilhide, S., Diantoniis, R., Goodheart, T., Logan, S., & Moreau, R. (2014). Onboarding OSH professionals. *Professional Safety*, 59(12), 27–33.

National Collegiate Athletic Association (NCAA) (n.d.). So you want to be an AD. Retrieved January 20, 2018, from http://www.ncaa.org/governance/so-you-want-be-ad.

NCAA (2017). The diverse workforce [online]. Retrieved from https://www.ncaa.org/sites/default/files/2017DIII_INC_HiringResource_Web_NEW_20170123.pdf

Nichols, G., & Ojala, E. (2009). Understanding the management of sports events volunteers through psychological contract theory. *VOLUNTAS: International Journal of Voluntary & Nonprofit Organizations*, 20(4), 369–387. doi:10.1007/s11266-009-9097-9.

Raedeke, T. D. (2004). Coach commitment and burnout: A one-year follow-up. *Journal of Applied Sport Psychology*, 16(4), 333–349. doi:10.1080/10413200490517995.

Roach, K., & Dixon, M. A. (2006). Hiring internal employees: A view from the field. *Journal of Sport Management*, 20(2), 137–158.

Rousseau. D. M. (1995). *Psychological contracts in organizations: Understanding written and unwritten agreements*. Newbury Park, CA: Sage.

Schneider, R. C., Stier, W. F. Jr., Kampf, S., Haines, S. G., & Wilding, G. (2006). Characteristics, attributes, and competencies sought in new hires by campus recreation directors. *Recreational Sports Journal*, 30(2), 142–153.

Sullivan, G. S., Lonsdale, C., & Taylor, I. (2014). Burnout in high school athletic directors: A self-determination perspective. *Journal of Applied Sport Psychology*, 26(3), 256–270. doi:10.1080/10413200.2013.853328.

Taylor, T., Darcy, S., Hoye, R., & Cuskelly, G. (2006). Using psychological contract theory to explore issues in effective volunteer management. *European Sport Management Quarterly*, 6(2), 123–147.

US Equal Opportunity Commission (n.d.) Prohibited employment policies/practices [online]. Retrieved August 1, 2018, from https://www.eeoc.gov/laws/practices/.

Wahl-Alexander, Z., Richards, K. A., & Washburn, N. (2017). Changes in perceived burnout among camp staff across the summer camp season. *Journal of Park & Recreation Administration*, 35(2), 74–85. doi:10.18666/JPRA-2017-V35-I2-7417.

Whisenant, W., Miller, J. & Pedersen, P. (2005). Systemic barriers in athletic administration: An analysis of job descriptions for interscholastic athletic directors. *Sex Roles*, 53, 911–918. 10.1007/s11199-005-8309-z.

CHAPTER 9

Strategic Planning

LEARNING OBJECTIVES

After reading this chapter, students will be able to:

1. Identify and communicate the components of a strategic plan, including vision statement, mission statement, goals, and objectives for athletic entities within college, high school, youth, and club sport.
2. Evaluate internal factors and external factors in the social, economic, political, and technological environments that influence and affect athletic organizations.
3. Formulate complete and comprehensive strategic plans for college, high school, youth, and club sport entities.
4. Describe tools used to implement strategic plans within college, high school, youth, and club sport.
5. Explain the role of the athletic administration when conducting strategic-planning exercises with stakeholders in the college, high school, youth, and club sport settings.

Strategic planning is a widely used tool by administrators not only to capture the essence of the sport entity but also to move staff forward in reaching department-wide goals through the daily operations within the walls of athletics. Strategic planning is defined as "a managerial process designed to provide outcomes that lead to an organization's improved functioning" (Lake, 2011, p. 225). Strategic planning allows athletic administrators to define the direction of the entity and make decisions on allocating physical and human resources to reach target points contained in the process. The creation of a sound and manageable strategic plan aids administrators in facing challenges and issues within a dynamic and competitive industry. Planning for events and rosters happens at a continuous level within athletic administration. Regardless of how large or small program offerings are, athletic administrators methodically create tactics to operate successfully.

Communication—both articulating the concepts of the strategic plan and actively listening to stakeholders—is a key aspect of the strategic-planning process. The strategic plan is a significant tool of the managerial application within the athletic settings. Because of the importance of the strategic plan, it is understandable that athletic administrators place so much effort clarifying the specifics of it to the staff. Ultimately, it is staff members who carry out the tasks on a daily basis, and this factor cannot be underestimated by athletic administrators.

From the athletic administrator's perspective, the strategic plan guides the staff and shapes the direction of the workflow. First, the plan needs to be created with an investment from all key stakeholders within the athletic entity. Formulation of a cohesive staff unit leads to enhanced contributions within the strategic plan. To foster unified strategic plan writing, the athletic administrator, in this case, becomes a facilitator. Acting as such, the administrator collects input from various stakeholders to determine a true vision and pathway for the sport entity. Actively listening to staff members and considering their ideas augments the strategic plan's content. The strategic plan is enriched when athletic administrators compile information from staff who deal with the daily challenges of the setting because of firsthand work with participants. Embracing and then incorporating the ideas of others fosters a level of engagement among staff members that showcases the value of their contributions toward accomplishing the tasks in the strategic plan. Second, staff members need to identify with specific sections of the strategic plan, especially if tasked with executing those pieces of the document related to their position. Third, distributing the strategic plan and continually referencing it in its entirety to staff and stakeholders intensifies the plan's scope and transforms it into a living element within the walls of the athletic entity. Once the strategic plan is shared and highlighted as a priority by the athletic administrator, the words take on a new dimension and serve to initiate action from the staff. Effective management of the strategic plan results in the benchmarking of milestones and methodically motivates staff members toward accomplishing their specific responsibilities. Finally, the strategic plan cannot remain untouched for a long period of time. Through scheduled meetings, staff retreats, and even quick check-ins with staff, the tasks within the strategic plan need to be revisited, reviewed, and benchmarked to promote an organizational focus to fully execute the facets of this significant document.

The strategic plan must evolve and adapt as needed, as expressed by Weese's (2010) study on leadership within the recreational setting; "directors must clearly, repeatedly, and convincingly articulate a vision and values for their program" (p. 96).

The strategic plan embodies the aspirations of the athletic entity while also steering the administration and staff members on their daily efforts within the workplace. Athletic administrators who consistently incorporate and use the tenets of the strategic plan while communicating to staff reinforce its significance to the entire athletic entity. When the aspects of a strategic plan flow directly into the staff's daily routine, it strengthens the plan's vision. Staff members who know their purpose and connect their contributions to the end goals listed in the strategic plan tend to be more motivated and more productive and even have higher morale.

▶ Situational Analysis of the Athletic Entity

Similar to most other business leaders, athletic administrators aspire to foster a working environment that helps staff be productive and collaborative to meet the established components of the strategic plan. To ascertain the current position and health of the athletic entity, a *situational analysis* is one tool athletic administrators can use. Conducting a situational analysis is part of the preliminary process of developing a sound strategic plan. The situational analysis supplies the athletic administration with an eye-opening assessment of what is happening within and around the athletic entity (internal and external factors), along with mapping steps to tackle opportunities and threats.

SWOT Analysis

As explored in Chapter 5, "Marketing and Branding," one tool to be used for strategic

planning under the situational analysis umbrella is SWOT analysis (SWOT stands for strengths, weaknesses, opportunities, threats). Scanning the internal and external environment allows athletic administrators to best position the athletic entity within the ever-changing and dynamic setting of sport. The SWOT analysis consists of identifying the sport entity's strengths, weaknesses, and opportunities as well as threats to the entity.

The analysis can create powerful conduits of information for use in making sound decisions for future actions. Two sections—strengths and weaknesses—paint a picture of the current scenario or the position of the athletic entity within the sport landscape. According to Dumitru and Puni (2007), "Weaknesses and strengths are the internal parameters of the organization, which can be controlled and which influence the targets of the strategic management process" (p. 13). This analysis provides athletic administrators with data points to identify the department's strengths, in essence identifying what the program is known for and its competitive edge.

One revealing aspect of SWOT analysis is the examination of weaknesses. Athletic administrators can usually pinpoint positive attributes of the entity more easily than they can recognize its weaknesses. In this regard, distinguishable weaknesses can fuel staff improvements and ameliorate these vulnerabilities. Weaknesses extracted from the SWOT analysis predictably turn into the tasks that staff aim to resolve, enhance, and amend to improve the athletic entity's health. Athletic administrators can see the future of the entity through the projected opportunities and challenges associated with threats in the athletic domain. Furthermore, uncovering opportunities provides athletic administrators and staff with renewed passion, reinvigorating individuals to perhaps add new programs, recruit new participants, and expand facilities. Identifying opportunities also motivates the staff by propelling individuals to work on new and exciting projects to once again improve the potency of the athletic entity.

Threats are an obvious concern for athletic administrators. "Threats and opportunities are the uncontrollable external elements belonging to the market where the organization conducts its activity; their potential negative effects upon economic outcomes may be mitigated through optimal planning" (Dumitru & Puni, 2007, p. 14). Naturally, athletic administrators aspire to safeguard current offerings so they can retain their current status. External environmental factors are at some levels unpredictable and beyond the control of the athletic administrator; however, anticipating changes in the external realm can steer the athletic entity out of harm's way or into new ventures. External variables include economic downturns, competition, changes in policies, regulations or laws affecting operational costs,

and technological advances. The external variables comprise one part of the situational analysis and constitute another tool for athletic administrators to incorporate into the strategic-planning review. The second aspect of the situational analysis comprises the internal variables, which describe the current strengths and weaknesses of the entity. The internal factors can be considered elements that the athletic administrator could adapt and change quickly and with certainty. Internal factors that are easily manipulated to better serve the athletic entity may include changing the website design, enhancing social media platforms, adding new programs to accommodate the needs of participants, or adding concessions to home events. Any factors that can be easily deployed to satisfy the consumers and athletic entity as a whole fall under the internal environment for the athletic administrator. The assessment of variables within the SWOT analysis combined with staff insight and feedback supplement the ability of athletic administrators to assemble a sound strategic plan.

Vision Statement and Mission Statement

The first aspect of the strategic plan is the vision statement and then the mission statement. The vision statement focuses on communicating the sport entity's future direction by linking the values articulated in the mission statement. According to Mayfield, Mayfield, and Sharbrough (2015), "effective strategic vision expresses shared organizational goals and values and conveys empathy to stakeholders"; "internal stakeholders (employees) will be more motivated, committed, and perform better—all behaviors [that] lead to better intrinsic and extrinsic rewards" (p. 107). Consequently, from the external stakeholders' perspective, "the strategic vision inspires confidence in the organization" (Mayfield et al., 2015, p. 107).

Swot Analysis: New Albany Parks and Recreation, New Jersey

Strengths	Weaknesses
■ Dedicated staff: Although the staff is small, members are hardworking, efficient, and dedicated to the mission of the department.	■ Adult and senior programming: This is an area where more can be done.
■ Well-maintained parks: With limited staff, the maintenance of the parks is [high priority]. The maintenance staff have positive contact with park users.	■ Lack of passive use areas: The parks are heavily oriented toward active recreation largely because of community needs and lack of additional parkland.
■ Volunteers: A strong volunteer base works with the staff to support many of the athletic activities in the parks.	■ Deferred maintenance: Overall, the parks appear to be in good to excellent condition, but there is concern about deferred maintenance. Buildings, paved surfaces, and equipment needs exceed current budgets.
■ Bevelhymer Park: The size and programming opportunities of this park are a strong asset.	■ Branding: The branding of the department needs to be strengthened and should be tied back to the mission statement.
■ Youth programming: Strong youth programming is a plus. Some programming occurs with in-house staff, but most is provided through agreements with many athletic associations.	■ Fees: Not everyone can afford the fees. A scholarship program is available but not well advertised.
■ Customer service: High level of customer service. Also an opportunity.	■ No indoor space: Indoor programming such as basketball relies on access to other facilities such as schools.
■ Administration: The department has been fiscally responsible. Also work with staff to create a flexible work environment. Staff can work from locations outside the office.	
■ Community oriented: promote healthy lifestyles and community. Buzz words include *fun*, *healthy*, and *active*.	

Opportunities	Threats
■ Partnerships: There is an opportunity to work more closely with other organizations. Among those mentioned were Franklin County Metro Parks and Healthy New Albany.	■ Vandalism and law enforcement: Work with multiple police jurisdictions, including Columbus.
■ Customer service: Although this is seen as a strength, it has not been well documented. Implementation of exit surveys and interviews can verify how strong it actually is.	■ Loss of contracts: Crew Juniors and Rugby; will need to pick up programming.
■ Park capacity: Need to continue to look for opportunities to add parkland to the system.	■ Aging out of board members and volunteers: Will need to recruit new citizens to participate.
■ Communication: There is an opportunity to expand communication efforts through social media.	■ Healthy New Albany and Schools: Duplication of programs.
■ Nonathletic programs: There is an opportunity to expand programming beyond athletics.	
■ Special events: This is an area that can grow.	

Adapted from New Albany Parks and Recreation (2016, October) Retrieved from: https://jerseywatch-files.s3.amazonaws.com/production/organizations/273/downloads/Strategic_Planning_Update_FINAL_12-19-16.pdf

The mission statement can be as short as one sentence or as long as a few paragraphs. The purpose is to give the reader insight into the entity's intended direction. The mission statement encapsulates the purpose of the entity along with the primary groups it serves. "Mission statements define the role an organization plays in society. They represent one of the more visible parts of the strategic management process, and they have become ubiquitous in organizational life" (Ward, 2015, p. 18). Typically, the mission statement focuses on communicating what the athletic entity does or what it is, the key values of the entity, and where it is heading in the near future. According to Babnik, Breznik, Dermol, and Nada (2014), the most important characteristic of an effective mission statement is a "match between the values defined in the statement and the employees' values," which form a source of "employees' emotional commitment toward their organization and its mission" (p. 614).

The following examples of vision statements come from a variety of athletic settings.

Ridgefield High School Athletic Department (Ridgefield, New Jersey)

The Ridgefield Public Schools Athletic Department strives to be an all-inclusive program that provides access and opportunity for its student-athletes, engages its community in review of regular program offerings and best practices, coordinates with its community partners, and places greater emphasis on sportsmanship, healthy lifestyle habits, and safe exercise protocols.

Vision Statement High School

Ridgefield Memorial High School (n.d.)

University of Rhode Island Athletic Department

The University of Rhode Island Department of Athletics will be nationally recognized for excellence in the classroom, in competition, and in the community.

Vision Statement: College Athletic Department

University of Rhode Island (n.d.)

About the A5 Volleyball Club (Roswell, Georgia)

The A5 Volleyball Club was formed in 2004 as a 501-C (3) nonprofit corporation by a group of dedicated men and women who saw the opportunity to create a different club experience in Georgia, and in so doing raise the level of the sport throughout the South. These individuals—A5 plank holders—have left their legacy on the sport and past, present, and future A5 athletes are forever in their debt: Bob Westbrook, Phil Bush, Jeff Choe, Erica Miller, Bayne Tippins, and Dale Smith.

The "A" in our name stands for Atlanta, and "5" refers to our five core values, or the "5 C's":

1. Character Driven: We focus on key character traits that help define a person as he or she grows, including: integrity, intensity, teamwork, leadership, discipline, courage, and sportsmanship.
2. Consistent Coaching: We offer a club environment where coaching is consistent from the first time a player enters a gym at the age of 8 through when he or she graduates from high school. This club insists on uniformity throughout the coaching process and mandatory coaching clinics for all head coaches and assistant coaches. Our coaching staff will continue to update themselves on the most current techniques and strategies used by top coaches in the game, and Master Coaches will be responsible for leading many of the practices and mentoring newer coaches and assistant coaches.
3. Community Involvement: All of our teams are encouraged to give back to the community by undertaking a community service project that may or may not have anything to do with volleyball.
4. Communication—Open and Honest: We practice an "Open Book" financial policy where every parent will have the right at any time to see and understand the financials for their athlete's particular team and the club as a whole.
5. Club Unity and Organization: We aspire to run a well-organized club, including tryouts, practices, tournaments, social events, and overall administration.

We know that the minute our organization focuses just on volleyball is the day that we begin a slide toward mediocrity. We take our mission statement—"Teaching Life Lessons Through the Sport of Volleyball"—seriously and will always emphasize hard work, sportsmanship, teamwork, honor, character development and doing the right thing over "W's and L's", for we know that if we focus on imparting those important life skills to our athletes, winning will take care of itself.

Vision Statement: Club Sport

A5 Pure Volleyball (n.d.)

FEEDBACK FROM THE FIELD

Best Practices: Strategic Planning

Christine Dean is community center director for the town of Lexington, Massachusetts. Dean came from the recreation center in Danvers, Massachusetts, which focused on outdoor and nature-based programming with environmental education. In this position, she worked closely with schools, scout groups, and preschool-aged children. At the Lexington Center, Dean gets to work at a facility that serves many age groups, including the senior population, which was a more personal choice for Dean to get into something different and expand her responsibilities to a senior population while still providing leadership to the typical youth groups and programming at a recreational setting.

At the time of this interview, Dean was in a unique situation as a fairly new employee at the community center of Lexington. To get the full scope of the plans and outlook for the community center, Dean learned as much as she could from the center's strategic-planning documents. When the position became available, she conducted her own research to determine what the center offered and what the town was aiming to enhance. The community center administrators conducted focus groups to generate feedback for the facility that opened a few years before Dean was hired. Dean explained that reviewing the strategic plan gave her significant insight and was the document she referenced the most at the start of her tenure.

When moving from one recreational position to another, athletic administrators seek as much information as possible to ensure the move will be a good fit for them professionally and personally. Several activities assisted Dean in learning more about the Lexington facility and its membership. One driving force in her decision was seeing the facility firsthand and reviewing the variety of programs offered to the residents. Dean was inspired to make the move because the community center offered multigenerational programming. The Lexington Community Center revitalized its offerings, moving from a senior-centric to a multigenerational facility. Much of Dean's expertise was working with youth, so the move to a multigenerational center presented a new and exciting setting with a focus on a variety of demographics and target groups rather than just one. The Lexington Community Center's primary focus now is being a place for all residents.

Dean shared that the new drive of the community center was the focus of the strategic plan. Town officials conducted focus groups to ascertain the needs of residents regarding a recreational facility of this capacity. The results revealed that residents desired a space where the entire community could gather. The town of Lexington was fortunate to have the opportunity and ability to purchase a new space that became available within the same time line as the planning process for change. As Dean explained, residents have several avenues to communicate their desires for specific recreational programming. From the published strategic plan, it was clear that the surveys collected from residents, focus group results, solicited feedback from emails sent to town meeting participants, parent–teacher associations, and all youth leagues provided organizers with considerable information to move the changes to the community center forward. Dean also shared that she currently plans and works with several "'partner stakeholders'" such as the library and a private recreational facility in town. All of these entities work with the same residents, creating a cooperative alliance that ultimately benefits the entire town.

Even though the community center became multigenerational, younger recreational programs did not suffer. In fact, as Dean shared, the biggest shift came from the senior population because that group was moving from a dedicated senior center operated by the senior services department to the new community center. The largest transition was experienced by seniors who felt the change would not given them the priority they were accustomed to having. Of course, as Dean disclosed,

(continues)

FEEDBACK FROM THE FIELD

(continued)

"growing pains" are part of the process when making any changes. However, the senior population has embraced the new facility—the new space, the new offerings, and the new programming. As Dean points out, any community center will garner feedback that is positive and feedback that addresses concerns. Both types of feedback provide athletic administrators with helpful information to meet the needs of their consumer groups while also contributing to the achievement of the strategic plan.

Core values derived from the strategic plan fuel other aspects of the community center's operations. For example, the center uses grants to supplement its budget. Part of grant writing requires proving, through elements of the recreational facility's mission, that the entity meets the criteria for approval. When Dean was asked about the words expressing the core values of the recreational entity, she indicated that they "go back to that idea of the multigenerational space, where all of the community can come together to share and to learn from each other as well as the health and wellness piece." She also indicated that some of the grants awarded for the fitness programs were specifically for seniors. For the older demographic, Dean creates programs that focus on "looking at the quality of life and not only keeping the seniors fit, but teaching them ways to self sustain it, to carry these models and practices home." To gauge member satisfaction, which is another tool to assess the execution of the strategic plan, the Lexington Community Center uses program evaluations. The center frequently uses Survey Monkey but will also offer written evaluations for seniors. Feedback is taken into account frequently, even daily, from a write-in suggestion box.

Nine full-time and five part-time staff members work alongside hundreds of seasonal staff members. To communicate and implement the components of the strategic plan, quarterly staff meetings in collaboration with the human services department to address feedback are attended by 30 full-time staffers. One highlighted component of the plan is safety protocols and the safety and emergency guidelines the town has specific to the occupied building. Discussions at these meetings concern customer service models, ease of operations, registration software for any updates, and software training. Unfortunately, Dean says, this larger meeting for full-timers is only quarterly because individuals are on different schedules, which makes it difficult to connect with such a large group more frequently. However, Dean uses her monthly departmental staff meetings to set agendas based on what upper management is passing down as well as to review feedback collected from the evaluations.

Dean shared some of her core challenges, which as she asserts, are similar to any position in such a dynamic environment. She admits, "at any moment, in this setting one can be easily pulled off task to something else that is going on." She explains that administrators need to know how to divide their attention and prioritize tasks. Ranking the areas that need more attention becomes increasingly difficult when athletic administrators are constantly being pulled away to handle smaller items like a broken piece of equipment, for example. Dean explains,

> Anyone can experience distractions in their job, but given that our operating hours are 8 AM–9 PM and we are open and available to the public, you are constantly being pulled in different directions and just figuring out how to stay on task to accomplish what you need to during the day.

When asked for advice to give future athletic administrators, Dean emphasized that "customer service has always been the core" of what she does, inserting that when challenges arise throughout the day, "customer service is always on my mind." Regardless of the daily obstacles, Dean maintains, "it all comes back to how we best serve our customers without jeopardizing quality or our programming and keeping a sense of humor." Dean summarizes her final advice" "[Y ou can let yourself get frustrated, but remember keeping in mind someone else's perspective and what they are looking to accomplish and just knowing we are here to hopefully provide that."

Lady Legacy AAU Basketball (Richmond Hill, GA)

The FIA Basketball Program and the Lady Legacy Basketball Team's mission is first and foremost to develop character and mental discipline in our members in order to empower them to live exceptional lives. Lady Legacy [also] provides female athletes the opportunity to strive for excellence, through development of their Fundamentals, Intellect, and Agility, opening the door to play at the collegiate level.

Vision Statement: Club Sport

FIA Basketball (n.d.)

Many athletic administrators understand the purpose of vision and mission statements. However, to fully execute the components of a strategic plan requires an investment and devotion of time by the athletic administrator. The words within the strategic plan propel staff to move the ideas into actions through the leadership of administrators. David, David, and David (2016) describe the mission statement as "sometimes called a creed statement, a statement of purpose, a statement of philosophy, a statement of beliefs, a statement of business principles, or a statement 'defining our business,' a mission statement reveals what an organization wants to be and whom it wants to serve" (p. 20). Notably, the importance of the vision and mission statements starts

well before an athletic administrator applies for and then accepts a new position. Before applying for an open position in an athletic administration setting, a candidate will often review the organization's vision and mission statements. The core of the athletic entity is depicted through the words of the mission statement, which should convey to internal and external stakeholders the direction and passion the sport entity embodies. Internal stakeholders consist of current staff members, participants, and community members. The external stakeholders may encompass prospective participants and staff, businesses, potential corporate sponsors, potential employees, and competitors who wish to acquire information about the athletic entity. The mission statement provides the reader with a chance to learn about the core values of the organization while also understanding the direction or future goals. The words and statements in these documents reflect the image of the athletic entity and specify pathways for growth.

Some may wonder how to best apply strategic planning in the day-to-day operations of the athletic entity. The mission statement is the umbrella document that encapsulates the spirit of the athletic entity, focusing in on what the entity has accomplished, its current goals, and its future outlook. In essence, the mission statement communicates what the athletic entity strives to become. The following examples of mission statements are instructive for their variation in tone and length.

Duke University is committed to excellence in athletics as part of a larger commitment to excellence and education.

The guiding principle behind Duke's participation in Division I athletics is our belief in its educational value for our students. Intercollegiate athletics promotes character traits of high value to personal development and success in later life. These include the drive to take one's talents to the highest level of performance, embracing the discipline needed to reach high standards, learning to work with others as a team in pursuit of a common goal, and adherence to codes of fairness and respect. Athletics also plays an important role in creating a sense of community in the University.

Duke's mission defines expectations both on the field and off. In the name of excellence, Duke aims for a level of athletic performance that will frequently produce winning seasons and the realistic opportunity to compete for team or individual championships. Our mission also requires that Duke athletes be students first, that they be admitted with careful attention to their academic record and motivation, that they benefit from Duke's educational programs and make satisfactory progress toward a degree, and that their attrition and graduation rates be comparable to those of other students.

Duke is also committed to the physical and emotional well-being of student-athletes and to the social development of the whole person. We recognize that great demands are placed on students who participate in intercollegiate athletics, and we are committed to providing support to help them manage these demands and get the most out of their Duke experience. Athletes are also expected to adhere to a level of conduct that brings credit to themselves and the University and upholds the values of citizenship and service.

Duke's intercollegiate program shall be composed of nationally or regionally recognized sports that meet the needs, interests, and abilities of male and female students; that provide adequate institutional collateral benefits; that reflect due regard for the athletic traditions of Duke University and the Atlantic Coast Conference; and that fall within the financial capabilities of Duke University to fund at adequate levels.

In view of the health and educational value of athletics, in addition to varsity programs, Duke will create rich opportunities for participation in club sports, intramurals, and individual exercise and recreation.

The mission of the athletics program, ultimately, is that of Duke itself: "to engage the mind, to elevate the spirit, and stimulate the best effort of all who are associated with the University."

Duke University Athletic Department Mission Statement

Reproduced with permission from Duke Athletics. Duke University Athletics (n.d.)

Athletics at Winchester High School play an integral part in the school program. Students have the opportunity to participate in a wide variety of activities that will enhance their educational experience. The sports program is committed to the physical, emotional, social, and mental development of all who participate.

Winchester High School Mission Statement (Winchester, Massachusetts)

Winchester High School (n.d.)

Our mission is to enrich the lives of the residents of Greenfield by providing safe, welcoming parks and recreation facilities and affordable, diverse recreation and cultural opportunities for people of all ages to play, learn, and build community. We create community through people, parks, and programs.

Greenfield Recreation Department Mission Statement (Greenfield, Massachusetts)

Greenfield Recreation Department (n.d.)

▶ Strategic Plan: Goal Setting

The vision statement and mission statements set the stage for the remaining aspects of the strategic plan. Core values are reflected in the words and phrases of the mission statement to illustrate past, present, and future pathways. They are the fundamental beliefs of the athletic entity and serve as guides as the athletic entity strives to reach and accomplish goals. Cooper and Weight (2011) studied the responses of Division III athletic administrators to determine which core values were most important in carrying out the mission of the department. The responses of organizational core values ranked as high priority (first to fifth ranking) were:

1. student-athlete experience (to ensure that student-athletes receive a valuable and rewarding experience on and off field during their career),
2. academic excellence (to achieve high levels of student-athlete and team success in the classroom),
3. health and safety (to create procedures and protocols that ensure health and safety for all individuals in the athletic department),
4. contribution to university mission (to create a culture where individuals embrace and contribute to the educational mission and role of the university), and
5. disciplined diversity (to provide fair and equitable opportunities for all individuals regardless of gender, race, or physical challenges).

The next series of core values were ranked as follows:

6. fiscal responsibility (to implement transparent budgeting strategies that encourage sound, equitable financial decisions),
7. athletic excellence (to achieve high levels of student-athlete and team success during athletic competition),
8. growth opportunities (to create an environment that encourages individuals to develop sound professional skill sets),
9. relationship cultivation (to create an environment that encourages and fosters strong relationships among individuals in the department),
10. sense of shared community (to create an atmosphere that allows stakeholders to feel they are an integral part of the department), and
11. broad-based participation opportunities (to provide a wide range of participation opportunities for individuals interested in different sporting events) (Cooper & Weight, 2011, p. 346).

Core values influence model behaviors and practices within the athletic environment. The National Collegiate Athletic Association (NCAA) publishes core values, and its member institutions share a belief in and commitment to them:

> The Association—through its member institutions, conferences, and national office staff—shares a belief in and commitment to:
>
> ▪ the collegiate model of athletics in which students participate as an avocation, balancing their academic, social and athletics experiences;
> ▪ the highest levels of integrity and sportsmanship;
> ▪ the pursuit of excellence in both academics and athletics;
> ▪ the supporting role that intercollegiate athletics plays in the higher education mission and in enhancing the sense of community and strengthening the identity of member institutions;
> ▪ an inclusive culture that fosters equitable participation for student-athletes and career opportunities for coaches and

administrators from diverse backgrounds;

- respect for institutional autonomy and philosophical differences; and
- presidential leadership of inter-collegiate athletics at the campus, conference, and national levels.

National Collegiate Athletic Association (n.d.)

Discipline

In the classroom and on the field.

Accountability

Every action has a consequence and everyone will be responsible for their own actions.

Sacrifice

Student-athletes play for their school, community, their team, and themselves.

Hard Work

In the classroom, at practices and games, and during the off-season.

Core Values: Maynard Athletic Department (Maynard, Massachusetts)

Maynard High School Athletics. (n.d.)

Core Values

From the depiction of the athletic entity formulated in vision and mission statements, athletic administrators extract the core values of the department to create goals or goal statements. Simply stated, a goal can be expressed as the ultimate direction or ultimate desired result for the athletic entity. As goals are the ultimate direction for the department, they must be written so they are specific, measurable, attainable, realistic, and timely (Meyer, 2003) and will aid staff in easily envisioning their role and contribution in the process. Achievement of department-wide goals requires the deliberate collaboration of senior athletic administrators and staff. When goals are set concurrently between athletic administrators and staff, there is a heightened level of engagement that leads to higher rates of goal achievement. Realizing goals often depends on the management and motivational styles of athletic administrators. There may be athletic administrators who want to push their ideas about goals for the department to all staff members. Conversely, other athletic administrators value and welcome the insight and collaboration of the staff in the goal-setting process. Below are examples of goals covering the athletic settings.

Beachwood High School Athletic Department Goals (Beachwood, Ohio)

To use a continuous improvement process in support of systems and programs that promotes high standards of performance and high expectations for learning on and off the playing field.

To develop a culture of accountability that relies on data, research, evaluation, best practices, and assessment as tools to measure the effectiveness and productivity of our programs and the satisfaction of our stakeholders.

To develop, encourage, and support the athletic department staff, their programs (grades K–12), improve instructional standards and professional development to enhance the student-athletes' knowledge, skills, and performance levels in efforts to achieve a high level of success.

To promote and encourage Beachwood Pride, Unity, Victory, and a Strong Social Conscience among our student-athletes, staff, and community members.

To maintain open and effective communication with the public, the athletic department staff and students in order to be aware of attitudes, opinions, and ideas.

To continue to integrate best practices and advanced technique into all phases of the athletic educational process.

To provide the necessary financial resources for the support of our instructional programs through prudent management and fiscal responsibility.

To ensure that students and staff have a safe and appropriate place to learn, work, and play.

Goals: High School Athletic Department

Beachwood City Schools (n.d.)

Short-Term Goals
- Identify and operate facilities within the park system with the resources available.
- Continue developing strategies to expand the city's wellness program.
- Continue offering activities and developing programs at the community centers.
- Continue partnering with other city departments and agencies to offer additional park enhancements and recreational programs to our citizens.

Long-Term Goals
- Acquire and develop park land with CIP funding, Houston Parks Board (HPB), and private partners.
- Extension of trails in the trail system.
- Search and apply for grants to supplement funding for programs offered at the community centers, adaptive recreation center, and Lake Houston Wilderness Park.
- Identify opportunities with local partners to expand resources for operations and programs.
- Continue to follow [National Recreation and Park Association] standards so that the department may stay in compliance with accreditation mandates and benchmark the system to a national standard.

Goals: The Houston Parks and Recreation Department (HPARD) (Houston, TX)

Houston Parks and Recreation Department (n.d.)

Program Goals
1. Provide each player with the opportunity to learn, develop, and improve their baseball skills on a regular basis.
2. Provide each player with an atmosphere that encourages mental, social, and emotional maturity.
3. Field successful teams at all levels.
4. Prepare players for high school and college advancement.

Seattle Select Baseball Goals (Seattle, Washington)

Seattle Select Baseball Club (n.d.)

Strategic Plan: Objectives

The strategic plan can be considered a living and breathing document, especially when staff members embrace the spirit of the document through their daily routines and actions within the athletic department. Revisiting the document contents through departmental meetings, benchmarking, and celebrating accomplishments of goals encourages participants to meet the strategic plan's overall aims. Understandably, the challenges to reach the stated goals and objectives within the plan take on a new meaning as time lines or events get closer. Strategic planning is a comprehensive approach to ensuring that all athletic department units are connected.

© Monkey Business Images/ShutterStock.

Strategic planning is a managerial instrument that continually moves staff toward reaching the goals and objectives that ultimately constitute living the athletic entity's mission statement. Supporting the department's mission statement entails grasping the significance of the stated goals while simultaneously completing tasks during the workday to attain desired results. Staff productivity pushes the athletic entity closer and closer to meeting the stated outcomes or goals detailed in the mission statement. Once the goals are set, the staff need to work toward achieving them. Objectives are the measurable steps the staff take every day to reach those goals. Objectives are considered the targets or detailed tasks that staff complete during daily operations that can be measured in the form of percentage increases, number of memberships sold, or total dollar amounts from corporate sponsors. Completion of the daily "to-do list" transfers into staff members fulfilling their part in accomplishing the stated objectives.

▶ Implementing the Strategic Plan

Various methods and managerial tools must be pulled into the work environment to motivate staff members to be productive. Productivity can be defined as getting the most effort and end results from the staff. Individuals are motivated to accomplish tasks and to give maximum effort in diverse ways. Athletic administration is a people-oriented field. Athletic staff typically desire to feel the support along with the guidance of senior staff. Effective athletic administrators use their authority and power not only to motivate but also to ultimately stimulate productivity. Authority is the ability to influence others based on the position held by the individual. Typically, within an athletic entity an organization chart outlines the hierarchy or chain of command within the department. Upper management to middle management to lower level management coexist and collaborate to meet organizational objectives. However, administrators who have direct support staff may use sources of power based on their level of supervision within the athletic entity. Based on the research of French and Raven (1959) the sources of power include:

- reward power, which is the ability to grant staff material goods like gift cards to restaurants, days off from work, or extra vacation days;
- coercive power through the ability to punish through loss of wages, demotion, or even removal from the company;

- expert power exists when a staff member has a particular skill set like website design;
- referent power means when staff members are well liked because of their past accolades or even their dynamic personalities; and
- legitimate power is authority to act because of the power vested in the official job description for that individual.

Athletic administrators use sources of power to influence staff to move toward some desired behavior with the outcome leading to the achievement of objectives and then the accomplishment of stated goals.

© LightField Studios/Shutterstock.

▶ Strategic Plan: Review

The final step in the managerial process of strategic planning is to review and evaluate the progress of meeting the objectives of the mission statement. The methods by which athletic administrators carry out control and monitoring of progress toward goal completion may vary by individual philosophies and by the setting. Effective athletic administrators underscore the importance of connecting staff with the strategic-planning outcomes by providing opportunities for staff to participate in the review process to articulate the completion of tasks in their specified work areas or provide tangible examples of how their efforts adhere to the vision and mission of the athletic entity. Open discussion meetings prove fruitful when staff can share what is working and which areas need more attention. Collaboration is best when there is a facilitation of thoughts and ideas in an open forum. Bonds are created through these meetings when a respectful tone prevails and influences staff members to truly share their accolades along with their frustrations when it comes to obstacles or challenges within the work environment. The process stimulates cohesion among the staff and a greater desire to meet organizational strategic plans.

In conjunction with staff meetings, athletic administrators conduct one-on-one meetings with individual members to ascertain their level of contribution toward meeting the strategic plan. Timing of these meetings is critical; waiting too long in the year may not effectively allow for changes to be made that meet the strategic-planning outcomes. Waiting too long to conduct strategic planning check-in meetings does not foster opportunities for the staff to initiate change in a timely fashion. The athletic administrator devotes time to certify that staff members have the tools required to meet their tasks and to determine the progress of meeting the strategic plan.

Another proven method to determine staff performance levels is to require end-of-month reports or a time frame for submission of reports. The platform by which the athletic administrator gathers these "'progress reports" varies, depending on the philosophy of the athletic administrator or the particular athletic setting. Monitoring can occur via email with specific points referenced so that the athletic administrator can determine the progress within that specific area or position. Although it may take a staff member time to write a report that reviews the progress in meeting the strategic plan, it is a valuable evaluation piece.

Observations are another way to monitor progress toward meeting strategic plan outcomes. Athletic administrators simply

FEEDBACK FROM THE FIELD

Best Practices: Strategic Planning

Daniel McCabe was appointed director of athletics and campus recreation at Adelphi University in Garden City, New York, in July 2013. He quickly made his mark on campus in the first two years with the Adelphi Panthers winning the school's second consecutive President's Cup in 2013–14 and finishing second in 2014–15. With McCabe at the helm of Adelphi athletics, his teams won seven Northeast-10 Conference championships, 15 teams competed in NCAA tournaments, and women's lacrosse earned two NCAA national championships. In 2015, the softball team reached the Women's College World Series for the first time as a Division II program, winning the NCAA Division II East 2 Regional. The accolades extend to the classroom, with 12 student-athletes recognized as CoSida Capital One Academic All-District I Team honorees and several Academic All-Americans.

Before working at Adelphi University, McCabe served as the executive associate athletic director at Hofstra University in Hempstead, New York. Before joining Hofstra University, he was the associate director of athletics for external relations at Providence College in Rhode Island for five years. He was also the director of ticket sales from 1998 to 2000 at the University of Miami in Florida. McCabe held positions within marketing departments at Fairfield University (Connecticut) and Fordham University (New York City).

Strategic planning is a widely used tool in athletic administration. Commencing the strategic-planning process within the Adelphi University athletic department begins with focusing on both the university's mission and the athletic department's mission. As McCabe notes, the mission statements are the starting points for his department so staff can value staying true to the core values of the strategic plan and stay true to their specific work-related goals. McCabe works at setting long- and short-term goals for the department. Goal setting provides the consistency, he says, "to staying true to the core values." McCabe describes the strategic plan as "a living document that we go back to every year."

Implementation of the strategic plan happens in a variety of ways under McCabe's leadership. Every three to six months he revisits the strategic plan and "go[es] back and check[s] on how the department is doing with regards to goals within the strategic plan." Through these meetings and discussions, McCabe uses the evaluation process to update the strategic-planning document, making necessary changes if goals have already been achieved. Conversely, if the department falls short of any goals, the strategic-planning meetings serve as a reminder that staff members need to focus on those areas of weaknesses to attain the desired results. But, as McCabe injected, checking in on the strategic-planning document every three to six months helps keep the department as a whole on track. For McCabe, documenting ideas to achieve the goals within the strategic plan comes from what the staff does every day. He maintains that goals come from "the core of what we do every day," adding "we make sure we can document that to make sure we are on the right path."

Adelphi University celebrated the 10th year anniversary of its new athletic turf field. All of the newer facilities were built before McCabe arrived on campus. Another advantage of Adelphi University athletics is the offering of scholarships. However, as McCabe explained, "if you look at those things and you have good facilities and good scholarships, that will give you an advantage for a while but eventually your competitors are going to catch up to you because everybody is trying to open up new or improve [older] facilities." Within Adelphi's external environment, competitors (other colleges and universities) are embarking on similar actions to gain an edge in the recruitment of top student-athletes and expansion of athletic facilities. In Adelphi's case, as McCabe explains,

> there is a limited amount of space to build new facilities and as the competitors are catching up to you in that regard, the question of what else are you going to do to remain ahead and have an advantage, and that is where it comes down to culture and your goals and what you are working

on every day and the support you are getting not just financially but the support you are getting from the alumni and from the campus community.

Implementation of the strategic plan comes from, as McCabe asserts, "getting coaches to buy into it." He indicated that coaches fully comprehend and use the advantages Adelphi holds while also noting the advantages of the competition. He said coaches recognize that "you can never rest" in the dynamic athletic environment, and coaches are looking to "gain any advantage that they can" to stay competitive.

From the administrative perspective, McCabe reports directly to the president of Adelphi University. The athletic director and president meet every month to discuss the department's efforts. The president approves the strategic plan for the athletic department, and she also puts together a strategic plan for the university. As athletic director, McCabe is part of the university strategic-planning process. His role at this level significantly affects the pieces of the strategic plan specifically related to the athletic department.

McCabe is part of the president's cabinet, along with other university administrators who all meet together once a month. Through three positions and as part of the leadership of the university, McCabe aligns athletic department goals with campus-wide goals.

McCabe also involves student-athletes within the strategic-planning process. Adelphi University student-athletes give the department feedback at the end of their respective seasons. McCabe conducts end-of-season surveys of student-athletes that are reviewed by athletic department senior staff members. The surveys provide student-athletes an opportunity to voice their opinions on the department performance in relation to programs, facilities, and support staff, including athletic trainers, sports information, and compliance. In addition, graduating seniors provide feedback through exit interviews. McCabe integrates feedback from student response surveys and exit interviews with seniors to target areas that students perceive as weaknesses or areas requiring more resources. Student suggestions are seriously reviewed by senior staffers, who will then add the feedback to the strategic plan if deemed important to the athletic department mission. McCabe reiterates that plans "get updated all the time, sometimes things get accelerated because it has really become an issue and we need to get this thing done quicker." McCabe admits that in some cases feedback from students may be a larger issue than the department previously imagined, prompting a specific concern to be moved up as a priority within the strategic plan. The end result is that the collected feedback fosters initiatives to enhance the overall delivery of the athletic department's mission and ensures that the department's focus aligns with the work being done through the strategic-planning process. In the end, the strategic plan is not set in concrete, and it can be adjusted as needed by the athletic department shifting its priorities, as McCabe acknowledges.

Alumni are also part of the Adelphi University athletic department feedback system. The alumni group is called the Panther Club. Its executive board meets every three months to discuss the athletic department's positioning and offerings. The Panther Club executive board has formally reviewed the strategic plan, providing feedback to McCabe and his staff. Sharing the strategic plan allows stakeholders to examine what the athletic department is doing so they understand the planning process and goals.

walking through practices or games as a deliberate observer serves as a valuable monitoring tool. Observing coaches and staff in their work environment reveals their effectiveness or ineffectiveness in achieving performance standards as outlined within the strategic plan. A by-product of observation is that staff and coaches may be better prepared to deliver their roles knowing the athletic administrator can visit their work settings at any time. In the end, the goal of all these tools is to monitor the progress toward achieving the strategic plan and following the mission of the athletic entity.

💬 FEATURED INTERVIEW: HIGH SCHOOL ATHLETICS

Scott Garvis has held several leadership positions in athletic administration at a variety of high schools across the nation. He is now director of athletics at Newton High School in Newton, Iowa. In addition to the role at the high school, Garvis is the president-elect for the Iowa High School Athletic Directors Association (IHSADA). As a seasoned athletic administrator with substantial experience, Garvis has many published articles and speaking engagements that focus on the effective management of athletic departments and strategic planning.

Most recently, Garvis embarked on developing a strategic plan for IHSADA. He describes the strategic plan as a long-term plan that provides organizational direction to IHSADA, adding that it is a cohesive statement about IHSADA's mission, goals, strengths, and weaknesses.

The plan-development process included collecting feedback from athletic directors from across the state. Linking so many athletic administrators in a strategic-planning process is a daunting task. As Garvis explained, the greatest challenge to the strategic-planning process was the turnover of organizational presidents. Every time a new president was elected, the group asked the same questions and the target focus areas were overlooked or missed. Garvis made deliberate changes to foster the development of a sound strategic plan. He worked directly with the IHSADA's executive board. One of his charges was to increase membership by bringing in athletic directors who were new to the organization. To better gauge the needs of the athletic programs across the state, the group composition—through Garvis's efforts—evolved to include new athletic directors from large and small school settings. Garvis then divided the athletic directors into segmented groups such as programs, operations, and finance. The Iowa High School Athletic Directors Association was able to meet a few times over the summer (downtime for high school athletic administrators) and also held a retreat. All these meetings were specifically on strategic planning, with the core focus on determining what the organization should look like over the next five years.

Garvis underscores that "the strategic plan is not something to be put together and then thrown up on the shelf," adding "it really needs to be a living breathing document." Garvis and the Iowa High School Athletic Directors Association are in the process of reviewing their target areas of the strategic plan with the aim of reaching those goals. During the spring, Garvis will meet back up with the committee chairs to review the strategic plan and evaluate both the achieved targets and those that need to be developed. Garvis explains that in another five years the organization will review the strategic plan again.

Garvis continually highlights the importance of revisiting the strategic plan within his high school as well. As the high school athletic director, some of the groups he collaborates with for strategic planning are coaches, parents, alumni, business leaders in town, alumni association members and administrators, and some school board members. Garvis aimed to get a wide array of people involved with the strategic-planning process to get the most input from stakeholders.

For Garvis, strategic planning starts with establishing the athletic department's vision and mission. This is followed by evaluation within the strategic-planning process of what the athletic department can tap in terms of facilities, staff, professional development, equipment, and leadership. Garvis described core covenants, defined as *guiding principles*, to be implemented by staff members as part of their daily routine. For Garvis, these covenants "reflect how the staff [is] reinforcing and living up to the mission statement." As Garvis stresses, when individuals attend the high school games or watch practices "they need to see the core covenants in action and how the department is staying true to the mission." Reconnecting with alumni, creating new programming thorough financial management, corporate sponsorships, and staffing needs are all priorities within the athletic department. Garvis uses the vision statement, mission statement, and goals of the strategic plan to facilitate prioritizing how to tackle those needs. From Garvis's experience, engaging many stakeholders (community, alumni, current athletes) allows the athletic administrator to understand how the department *is* perceived and how Garvis and the staff *want* the athletic department to be perceived. As Garvis notes, "engaging those people is the hard part"; however, what he has learned is that bringing in these groups creates an "excitement" around "improving the department and getting better" at reaching elements of the strategic plan.

The core challenges associated with strategic planning are time and getting the stakeholders involved in order to foster buy-in for the direction and ultimate implementation of the strategic plan. As is often the case with athletic administrators, numerous tasks and decisions fall onto their desks on a daily basis. One of the most difficult challenges is scheduling time for the staff to assemble. Garvis suggests setting aside funds to either have a meal during the meeting or reserve a comfortable off-site location to lure individuals not only to attend the forums but also to freely share their input. For Garvis, the most difficult aspects of the strategic-planning process were the time involved and getting all of the stakeholders to connect and meet.

In terms of staff management, with the number of coaches employed at Newton High School, the task of ensuring that staff members are committed to the mission of athletics and the mission of the school as a whole requires benchmarking or systematic check-ins. Garvis directs athletic administrators to "make sure that your mission, vision, goals, and objectives are within your evaluation process." He believes the core values need to be stressed by the athletic administration and adhered to by the staff. The core values according to Garvis are "what you want your athletic department to stand by"; this includes coaches and student-athletes. Some methods Garvis incorporates into the evaluation process for strategic planning include observing coaches during practices and games. Garvis provides quick feedback through a software application after observing these sessions. To continually review progress toward achieving the strategic plan, he meets with the student-athlete advisory council and conducts regularly scheduled staff meetings. All of these evaluation tools generate feedback from student-athletes and coaches toward strengthening the direction of the strategic plan. As the director of athletics, Garvis attends alumni and booster club association meetings to make sure those groups are aligning with the athletic department's core values. Coaches' and captains' conferences are tools to reinforce core values and to monitor that the values are being incorporated into the team programming. Garvis states that sometimes coaches just want to focus on the X's and O's of their teams, but having conversations with them around larger overall goals and how to achieve them pushes them to link core values into their coaching. Three times throughout the academic year, the Newton athletic department meets with the coaches and student-athletes to discuss goals and the process of getting closer to achieving them. On occasion, Garvis invites guest speakers to address the athletic department or members of the coaching staff act as facilitators for these forums.

As with any planning process, athletic administrators must prompt staff to stay on course, refocus, and stay true to the mission statement. Garvis shared that at times a few coaches do put winning above the core values or sometimes coaches are not fully meeting expectations. To resolve the disconnection, Garvis believes in creating positive relationships, having a championship culture, making sure that all participants abide with the focus on academic rigor by making sure student-athletes are performing well in the classroom. Winning is part of athletics, but Garvis stresses that coaches need to meet the athletic department's expectations and the evaluation process is a tool to reinforce the strategic plan. Garvis also shared that athletic administrators may be apprehensive when evaluating coaches, but using an electronic application to communicate an assessment or observation is a simple and time-effective way to provide feedback. According to Garvis, "it all does come down to the time factor"; however, as he also stresses, all of the administrative efforts go "along with the strategic plan and what you want to focus on."

In terms of coach evaluation, Garvis has met with the Iowa Department of Education to inquire about developing a formal process for coaches similar to that of classroom teachers. Taking the discussion on evaluation one step further would be incorporating training for athletic directors to

(continues)

FEATURED INTERVIEW: HIGH SCHOOL ATHLETICS   *(continued)*

enhance communication about reviews given back to the coaching staff. Garvis stresses that "winning is important but not the only thing," adding "living up to the core values and doing all the right things leads to winning." To Garvis, the department wants "to use athletic programs to create a platform to fail, learn, grow, and develop as people." Taking a truly educational approach, he believes athletics is a place where young people can fail and the staff is there to support them. Garvis would "rather have them fail now than when they are adults or in college" adding, "I want them to use this as their experimental time to make mistakes."

Athletic administrators use many tools, including SWOT (strengths, weaknesses, opportunities, and threats), market, financial, and human resource analyses. As for market analysis, Garvis connects with many different people to determine avenues to better promote the athletic department. He has created a "Year in Review" media piece that is distributed to the community. In the past six years, the athletic department benefited from the presence of the Maytag Corporation's office in town. The company has since relocated, along with the families, which has affected the success of the athletic programs, specifically the football team. Today, Garvis is trying to rebrand the athletic department so the focus moves away from just football and highlights the success of all programs. This effort was a focus of the strategic plan. Garvis indicated that his town is different than most because of its geographic isolation and relatively small number of residents (16,000).

In terms of the SWOT analysis, Garvis says the comparisons of the strengths, weaknesses, opportunities, and threats are really against themselves and how to re-create their athletic brand. The focus for Garvis is on what "we want the school to epitomize, what we want to look like, and what we want to portray to our community." Because there really is no other school in the area to recruit or compete against, the SWOT takes on a different purpose. As Garvis explains, in his previous role at a private school in Seattle, Washington, there was a concerted effort to attract students to that school. In this case, Garvis would use SWOT analysis to position his athletic department against other schools competing to recruit the same students. The focus from the private school perspective, explained Garvis, "became a little bit more of what are our strengths versus the other schools," so the institution selected four major points it excelled at to market to student populations. For the financial analysis of Newton High School athletics, Garvis focused on revamping the purchase order process for the athletic department. From the financial perspective, Garvis's ultimate aim was to ensure the inventory-control process was being followed to be certain funds were not being needlessly spent.

Garvis shared that future athletic administrators need to return to making sure the stated vision and mission statements are being followed, which ultimately leads to achieving the strategic plan. Garvis reiterates that establishing core values coupled with hiring and working with a "solid group of people" to assist in the planning process "in the end pays dividends." Although many athletic administrators tend to take on the majority of the workload for the department, the involvement of as many stakeholders as possible takes time. According to Garvis, however, group input is invaluable in attaining the strategic plan. "The strategic plan is what I can focus my energy on, my resources, and time on. It helps me guide my decisions on a daily basis." Garvis puts the needs of the student-athletes first because they are the principal focus for the athletic department. For Garvis, "student-athletes are our end products and that is what we want to focus all of our attention," so linking that to the financial decisions is easy when the expenditure will benefit the student-athletes. Garvis admits that it is easy in this position to get sidetracked by parents or supervisors, but he stresses the significance of looking at the performance at the end of the year and asking, "Did we reach our goals, did we take our specific goals and process and procedures to get to where we wanted to go?"

Questions for Discussion

1. Scott Garvis has a great deal of experience in the administration of high school athletics. His ideas and methods are shared across many professional associations. Research the contributions of athletic directors at your current institution. What are some of their outstanding accomplishments that showcase the value of athletics in our communities?
2. Time management is a large aspect of strategic planning. As Garvis points out, gathering all the staff at the same time has its challenges. List activities you will implement to connect with staff across the year to reinforce elements of the strategic plan.
3. Compare the best practices comments by McCabe (college athletics) and Dean (recreation sport) with the perspective of Garvis (high school sport). What are some of the strategic-planning challenges universal to all athletic settings? Which setting appeals more to you regarding implementing a strategic plan as an athletic administrator?
4. Review an article relating to goal setting, situational analysis, or strategic planning in the high school setting. Share findings with your classmates, along with action plans to achieve stated goals and objectives while adhering to the entity's core values.
5. Conduct an online search of SWOT analyses for high school and club sport entities. As an athletic administrator, what key points from the SWOT review most resonate with you?
6. Review the Iowa Girls High School Athletic Union strategic plan (n.d.) (https://www.ighsau .org/about/strategic-plan/). What areas of the document impressed you the most? How visually appealing is the document shared with stakeholders?

 MANAGERIAL APPLICATIONS

College athletics: Strategic planning

The start of the academic and athletic year is a month away. As the newly hired athletic director of QRS College, you are scheduled to host an opening meeting for your entire staff, including coaches, athletic trainers, and sports information and compliance personnel. The college has charged you with creating a strategic plan specific to your athletic department to span a four-year period. Unfortunately, your predecessor never developed a strategic plan.

Questions to Consider

1. With your entire staff attentive at this mandatory opening meeting, what are some of the talking points you will use to develop an agenda to help identify the components of the strategic plan you need to develop?
2. In what ways can you divide the staff in this three-hour meeting to identify core covenants (see "Featured Interview: High School Athletics") covering all of the staff areas of focus present at the meeting? After a review of strategic plans in collegiate athletics, what are two goals you would like the athletic department to embed into the strategic plan?
3. As the leader of the athletic department, what are some of the words you believe should be embedded into the vision and mission statements from your department? Please locate two online college athletic department vision and mission statements you can use and share as part of this response as model documents to spur discussion from the staff to develop your own statements.

MANAGERIAL APPLICATIONS

Case Study: Youth sport
Mission Statement Development

The current board meeting with the town youth soccer association has an agenda item on the formation of an elite-level team. The board composition is 100% parents with one or more children playing within the local youth soccer association. Currently, the association offers a competitive, recreational menu of programs to boys and girls in prekindergarten through high school. The soccer landscape has evolved, and many more towns are aligning with club soccer programs to provide enhanced training to select players. The agenda item the board is discussing is whether or not to spend $40,000 on hiring club-level coaches to train the higher-level players within the soccer association and whether to create four elite teams (two for boys and two for girls).

Questions to Consider

1. The mission statement of the town soccer association reads: "The aim of the town soccer association is to engage boys and girls in recreational soccer games that promote physical and mental well-being, good sportsmanship, and team experiences." The focus of the soccer association is on recreational programs for all skill levels. How would the mission statement influence your decision to approve or deny $40,000 in funding for an elite soccer program for a select number of players? Please craft a comprehensive response with your rationale.

2. From the town soccer mission statement, what are the core covenants of the town soccer association? In your opinion, would the addition of the elite program align with those core covenants even if $40,000 were removed from the budget for the primary target group of participants within the town soccer association?

3. Because there is a great deal of competition to retain youth athletes in recreational programming, do you think the association in this scenario should revise the mission statement—or do you think the association should continue to serve its core group of recreational-level athletes?

 DECISION-MAKING CHALLENGE: HIGH SCHOOL ATHLETICS

The strategic plan is a document that can be referenced throughout the year in staff meetings and even emails to ensure coaches are reminded that winning is not the primary aspect of high school athletics. You are to write and sign an email that contains the vision statement of the athletic department. You recently asked all athletic department members to use the same electronic signature template. The template reads:

Sincerely,
Coach Dina Gentile
Laine High School
Laine, Colorado
123-456-7890
www.lainehs.org
"Laine High School Athletics places the values of respect, sportsmanship, self-discipline, and learning over winning. Winning at the expense of our values is never accepted."

Two of your coaches refuse to change their electronic signature because they do not believe winning should be a secondary value for the athletic department. Both coaches have had a "win at all costs" attitude, resulting in a handful of meetings with you, the principal, and each individual head coach to reinforce the values of the athletic department. What is your response to these coaches? What assessment methods would you incorporate into your evaluation of these coaches to document their disregard of the core values of the athletic department? If the coaches do not align with the vision and values of the athletic department, what type of recourse should you have as the athletic director?

Wrap-Up

End-of-Chapter Activities
Club Athletics

1. The landscape of youth baseball is changing. Many towns' Little League programs fail to roster enough players to operate multiple teams across age classifications. As a former athlete and baseball enthusiast, you decide to start a club baseball program for participants ages nine to 17. To start this process, you need funding. You have a local business willing to sponsor the club. Before the sponsorship is approved, company executives require submission of the mission statement for the newly established club. Craft a mission statement (eight sentences in length) for LCS Baseball Club to secure your funding. Provide a rationale as to why the words you chose best epitomize the value of LCS Baseball Club.

2. The growth of your club field hockey program has been impressive. However, the mission statement was last reviewed and revamped six years ago; it is brief and does not reflect all of the changes associated with your club. The competitiveness of field hockey as a club sport has evolved, and so has the reach of your club. Using the following mission statement, update the wording to best reflect a field hockey club that has tripled its participant levels, added three new facilities in three different locations (all within 60 miles or one-hour driving time), and secured a sponsorship from Nike. Note that four other field hockey clubs are within 30 miles of your club, signifying the heightened significance of creating a mission statement that captures the essence of your club and markets your values to potential participants and their families. As a reminder, club sports are much more competitive than local town programs, which should be reinforced within the newly constructed mission statement.

Elite Field Hockey Club Mission Statement

Our mission is to promote field hockey within the community, offering participants the opportunity to develop an understanding of the game of field hockey, advance their skills and game strategy in a fun manner while learning the aspects of teamwork and sportsmanship.

End-of-Chapter Questions

1. Strategic planning is a widely used tool in athletic administration. Select two athletic entities within college, high school,

youth, or club sport to research. Compare the elements of their vision statements, mission statements, goals, and objectives. What are the similarities and differences between them? Which entity communicates its strategic plan more effectively? Please explain your response.

2. Select two mission statements for athletic entities within one of the following settings: college, high school, youth, or club sport. Please indicate how effectively the athletic entities communicate and address the following areas within the mission statements: the type of business setting, the target group of consumers, the image of the entity, the nature of the services provided, the defining characteristics to distinguish themselves from competitors, and the values that guide the entities.

3. Craft a strategic plan, writing the vision statement, mission statement, goals, and objectives for a fictitious athletic entity of your choice within one of these settings: college, high school, youth, or club sport. Then compare your strategic plan to an actual plan devised by an athletic entity within that setting. Indicate how similar or different the words were that conveyed the strategic plan and the overall tone of how each plan was communicated. From the exercise, note any changes you would have made to your strategic plan after the review of the actual athletic entity.

4. Implementing the strategic plan throughout the entire staff needs to be systematically incorporated into daily work tasks. What are some methods you would use to reinforce the message contained in the mission statement to staff? How would you evaluate whether the staff is actually meeting the set objectives in a timely manner?

5. Strategic planning takes time and commitment from the athletic administration and must trickle down to the staff. How would you build a sense of buy-in so staff members feel the sense of urgency and passion toward reaching the goals set within the strategic plan? Indicate specific motivational techniques to be incorporated within the daily work environment to increase productivity.

6. Locate a poorly written mission statement online for a college, high school, youth, or club sport. Highlight the words and phrases you would add or change within that mission statement to enhance its delivery and intent.

7. In your own words, how would you describe the meaning and definition of strategic planning to your staff during the opening meeting of the year?

8. Compare and contrast the purpose of a vision statement and mission statement for an athletic entity. In your opinion, what significance does the vision statement add to the strategic plan?

9. You are the athletic administrator charged with writing a strategic plan for a town sports program and for a Division III athletic department. List the individuals within each entity you would solicit to involve in the process and state why. Note if there is any interesting overlap between the personnel enlisted to assist in the strategic-planning process for both entities.

10. What administrative tools would you use if your staff fails to adhere to the values of the vision and mission statements or fails to carry out the action plans of the established strategic plan?

References

A5 Pure Volleyball (n.d.). About the A5 Volleyball Club [online]. Retrieved from https://a5volleyball.com /page/1017/about_a5_volleyball.html.

Babnik, K., Breznik, K., Dermol, V., & Nada, T. S. (2014). The mission statement: Organizational culture perspective. *Industrial Management & Data Systems, 114*(4), 612–627.

Beachwood City Schools (n.d.). Bison Athletics Mission and goals. Retrieved from http://www.beachwoodschools .org/AthleticsMission.aspx.

City of Trenton (n.d.). Parks and recreation vision and mission [online]. Retrieved from http://www.trentonmi.org/index-Page.asp?Page_ID=13&SubPage_ID=54.

Cooper, C. G., & Weight, E. (2011). Investigating NCAA administrator values in NCAA Division I athletic departments. *Journal of Issues in Intercollegiate Athletics, 4*, 74–89.

David, F. R., David, F. R., & David, M. E. (2016). Benefits, characteristics, components, and examples of customer-oriented mission statements. *International Journal of Business, Marketing, & Decision Science, 9*(1), 19–32.

Duke University Athletics (n.d.). Mission statement for athletics at Duke. Retrieved from http://www.goduke.com/ViewArticle.dbml?DB_OEM_ID=4200&ATCLID=152723.

Dumitru, I.-M., & Puni, R. A. (2017). Analysis of the internal potential of a sports organization regarding sales forces—SWOT Perspective. *Sport & Society, 17*(1), 13–29. Retrieved from https://chaos.endicott.edu/cgi-bin/genauth/ecidbauth.cgi?url=http://search.ebscohost.com.proxy18.noblenet.org/login.aspx?direct=true&AuthType=ip&db=s3h&AN=125513014&site=ehost-live&scope=site.

FIA Basketball (n.d.) Lady Legacy basketball. Retrieved from https://www.ladylegacyrh.com/.

French and Raven. https://www.researchgate.net/publication/215915730_The_bases_of_social_power

Greenfield Recreation Department (n.d.). Mission statement and vision statement. Retrieved from http://www.greenfieldrecreation.com/mission.html.

Houston Parks and Recreation Department (n.d.). Department description and mission [online]. Retrieved from http://www.houstontx.gov/budget/12budadopt/V_PRK.pdf.

Iowa Girls High School Athletic Union (n.d.). IGHSAU strategic plan 2013-2018. Retrieved from https://www.ighsau.org/about/strategic-plan.

Iowa Girls High School Athletic Union (n.d.). Strategic plan [online]. Retrieved from https://www.ighsau.org/about/strategic-plan.

Irvine Girls Softball (n.d.). Mission statement [online]. Retrieved from http://www.igsateams.org/igsa-mission-statement/.

Jersey Intensity (n.d.). Field hockey [online]. Retrieved from https://www.intensityfieldhockey.com/page/show/2703538-intensity-field-hockey.

Lake, A. S. (2011, March). Strategic planning in nonprofits: An analysis and case study application. *Special Issue on Contemporary Issues in Business and Economics, 2*(5),

222–235. Retrieved from http://ijbssnet.com/journals/Vol._2_No._5_[Special_Issue_-_March_2011]/28.pdf.

Marietta College Athletics (2016). Mission statement [online]. Retrieved from https://pioneers.marietta.edu/sports/2009/7/27/missionstatement.aspx?tab=missionstatement.

Mayfield, J., Mayfield, M., & Sharbrough, W. (2015). Strategic vision and values in top leaders' communications: Motivating language at a higher level. *International Journal of Business Communication, 52*(1), 97–121.

Maynard High School Athletics. (n.d.). Core values, mission, and vision. Retrieved from http://athletics.maynard.k12.ma.us/home/core-values-mission-and-vision.

Meyer, P. J. (2003). "What would you do if you knew you couldn't fail? Creating S.M.A.R.T. goals. *Attitude is everything: If you want to succeed above and beyond*. Meyer Resource Group, Inc.

National Collegiate Athletic Association (n.d.). NCAA core values [online]. Retrieved from https://www.ncaa.org/about/ncaa-core-values.

Ridgefield Memorial High School (n.d.). Ridgefield Memorial High School athletics [online]. https://www.ridgefieldschools.com/Page/2458.

Seattle Select Baseball Club (n.d.). About us [online]. Retrieved from http://www.seattleselectbaseball.com/about-us/about-us/.

University of Rhode Island (n.d.). Mission & vision statements [online]. Retrieved from http://www.gorhody.com/information/mission_statement.

Ward, R. E. Jr. (2015). Buried accomplishments: Institutional isomorphism in college athletics mission statements. *International Journal of Sport Communication, 8*(1), 18–45.

Washington County Family YMCA (n.d.). YMCA mission, core values, and area of focus. Retrieved from http://wcfymca.org/index.php?option=com_content&view=article&id=57&Itemid=37.

Weese, W. J. (2010). The four steps to exceptional leadership of campus recreation in turbulent times. *Recreational Sports Journal, 34*(2), 95–102.

Winchester High School (n.d.). Mission statement for athletics. Retrieved from http://www.winchesterps.org/Winchester%20High%20School/1.Athletic_Department_Handbook.pdf.

Winona State University (n.d.). Athletic department strategic plan 2015–2020. Retrieved from https://www.winona.edu/ipar/Media/WSU%20Athletics%20Strategic%20Plan%202015.pdf.

CHAPTER 10

Title IX and Gender Equity

LEARNING OBJECTIVES

After reading this chapter, students will be able to:

1. Explain methods of Title IX compliance within college, high school, youth, and club sport.
2. Craft policy around Title IX and gender equity within college, high school, youth, and club sport.
3. Explain the history and evolution of Title IX in college, high school, youth, and club sport.
4. Analyze the challenges associated with Title IX and gender equity in college, high school, youth, and club sport.
5. Apply best practices to provide equitable experiences for males and females within college, high school, youth, and club sport programs.
6. Communicate the athletic administrator's role in leading staff to provide equity in college, high school, youth, and club sport.

One undeniable core purpose of athletic administration is to provide meaningful experiences to sport participants. The benefits and overall well-being associated with athletic participation for males and females should not be underestimated. Unfortunately, even today, with so many advances for girls and women in sport within the scope of amateur athletics, many athletic programs still do not provide or offer similar experiences to male and female participants.

Athletic administrators help create educational and sport-specific opportunities for male and female participants. Likewise, athletic administrators charged with supervising and overseeing athletic programming for males and females ideally aim for the same opportunities for all their athletes. However, the facts paint a different picture when it comes to equity in athletics. Title IX has been part of our culture since 1972, yet discrepancies and inequities persist within athletic programs. Note that Title IX does not even mention sport or athletics; still, this legislation has a strong presence and history within this domain. Proactive management within athletic programs needs to be part of the mindset for athletic administrators. Allocating resources and deliberate planning are all part of the mapping to ensure compliance with Title IX, with the end goal of maintaining gender-equitable programs. Athletic administrators enter this dynamic field because of the positive impact athletics play in the lives of young people. The impact should be valued across all programs and for both genders for the intentional delivery of positive programming for all.

Title IX was legislation enacted as a follow-up to the Civil Rights Act of 1964. Title IX language strengthened protections against sex discrimination at education institutions receiving federal financial aid. Because of the inequities females faced within the sport arena for decades, Title IX in 1972 became the federal law to handle discrimination on the basis of sex in any federally funded program or activity, including athletics. However, compliance with this legislation, despite the fact Title IX has been in effect for nearly 50 years, continues to lag behind in implementation. Implementation and enforcement of Title IX in relation to sports rests with the athletic administrations of college, high school, club, and youth sports. Advocates for equality in sport continue to promote resources and educational tools that athletic administrators can incorporate into their athletic departments to achieve compliance.

At some levels, however, gender equity and Title IX have negative associations, even with the enormous popularity of sport for females across the college, high school, club, and youth sport settings. Ideally, athletic administrators are trusted to offer programs of the highest quality and the most equitable levels for both male and female participants. Realistically, because of the pressures athletic directors may directly or indirectly face regarding spending on marque sports such as football or boys' basketball, many female sport programs have suffered in terms of equity. Circling back to fairness, the National Collegiate Athletic Association (NCAA) document on gender-equity planning best practices promotes that "gender equity should be an organizational commitment and a standard that is embraced by both men and women in order to create an environment that promotes understanding and encourages forward-thinking solution-finding." The document intends that males and females acquire similar athletic experiences (National Collegiate Athletics Association, "Gender Equity Planning," n.d., p. 4).

The impact of Title IX is clear. Female participation rates in athletics have steadily

Title IX Defined

Title IX is a federal law enforced in the United States and part of the United States Education Amendments of 1972. The U.S. Department of Education's Office for Civil Rights (OCR) enforces Title IX, among other statutes. Title IX protects people from discrimination based on sex in education programs or activities that receive federal financial assistance.

Title IX was follow-up legislation to the 1964 Civil Rights Act. It reads:

No person in the United States shall, on the basis of sex, be excluded from participation in, be denied the benefits of, or be subject to discrimination under any educational program or activity receiving federal financial assistance. (National Collegiate Athletics Association, "Inclusion's Best Practices," n.d.)

increased since the passage of Title IX. However, even with tremendous increases in the numbers of girls and women participating in sports and a mandate for providing equity, to date, there is no record of any institution losing federal funding for a Title IX violation (Title IX, n.d.). Enforcement actions in the form of lost funding add teeth to the legislation and help ensure full compliance with the legislation. Without strict penalties, Title IX compliance ends up trivialized, symbolizing a trend of noncompliance. Title IX has three components: participation, athletic financial assistance, and treatment in program areas.

The Office for Civil Rights uses a three-part test to determine whether institutions are in compliance and providing nondiscriminatory athletic opportunities to both males and females. Under the participation component, it is important to note that "Title IX is not a quota system" and "every institution has three options to demonstrate fairness in athletic opportunities" (Title IX, n.d.).

FEEDBACK FROM THE FIELD

Jacqueline McWilliams is the third full-time commissioner of the Central Intercollegiate Athletic Association (CIAA), the first African American female ever to hold the position. The CIAA is the nation's oldest black collegiate athletic conference. In her role, McWilliams provides leadership to 12 member institutions and a board of directors and staff, along with management of 14 CIAA championships. Her athletic administrative experience includes nine years at the NCAA managing championships, holding the role of director of the Division I Women's basketball tournament from 2006 to 2009 and the Division I men's basketball tournament (2007–2012). At Virginia Union University she assumed roles of coach, senior woman administrator, and compliance coordinator. Her credentials also include athletic administration leadership, facilities and operations, compliance and governance, human resources, and external operations. McWilliams is also on the board of directors for Women Leaders in College Sports, the Collegiate Women's Sports Awards, the NCAA Board Ad Hoc Committee for Cultural Diversity, and the John B. McLendon Scholarship Foundation Board. Along with being a motivational speaker, she held the position as chair of the NCAA's Division II management council and was appointed to the NCAA's board of governors.

McWilliams attributes her professional advancement and selection of employment opportunities to the mentors who provided guidance throughout various stages of her career. At the onset of McWilliams's career, an instrumental mentor, Judy Sweet, provided guidance, leading her to serve on a variety of committees with other pioneers in women's athletics. The mentor relationships came when she was a young professional navigating the athletic administration arena. Before joining the NCAA, McWilliams served at Morgan State University (Baltimore, Maryland) as the assistant director of athletics for internal operations, having oversight of compliance, governance, strength and conditioning, facilities management, and day-to-day operations for the department. Before Morgan State, she worked at Norfolk State University (Virginia) for a year in compliance.

As McWilliams points out, her experiences in athletic administration were fulfilling, although there were times when she considered leaving the field because of challenges she faced with "sexism, genderism, and racism." McWilliams explained that some of the individuals she worked with made her question who she was, what she could be, and how she was valued in the space of athletic administration. McWilliams had two stints at the CIAA—leaving for Norfolk State University the first time before returning to the CIAA as the commissioner. McWilliams explained that leaving the CIAA the first time was difficult, because she acquired "great opportunities to do compliance and championships for the conference." She further explained that the athletic director at Norfolk State University was "a leader in college athletics," and she was able to rebuild her confidence in athletic administration because of the "guidance and opportunity that reset my thinking for being in the field." Before Norfolk State University and the CIAA, she worked at Virginia Union University alongside an athletic director who was extremely involved with the governance structure for the NCAA before Divisions I, II, and III separated. In McWilliams' words, the athletic director was "very confident and a leader who always wanted to put me in a position of leadership." She adds, "He would always say that his job was to prepare me to be the next athletic director or as the assistant women's basketball coach to become the next head women's basketball coach." McWilliams said that the position for a 23-year-old was valuable as she gained experience because of the leadership of the athletic director; she was "empowered and encouraged to be at the table with him, on the budgeting side, and talking about Title IX." At the time, McWilliams noted, discussions of gender equity stemmed from scholarships not being funded for female student-athletes at the same level as male student-athletes. A strategic plan, according to McWilliams, was put into place to remedy the scholarship discrepancy and to determine whether to add sports to enhance women's experience at Virginia Union.

At the NCAA, McWilliams experienced racism, but those challenges, she asserts, prepared her for her role at the CIAA. McWilliams quickly pointed out that she loved working there, particularly the intensity of the men's and women's basketball championships. Plus, she gained respect and value for sports she was less familiar with such as the individual Olympic sports of fencing, golf, track and field, and rowing, ultimately gaining leadership within those programs. Within a year and a half, McWilliams was promoted to an associate director position at the NCAA. However, internal challenges emerged because several colleagues also applied for the position. McWilliams's strong background and credentials in athletic administration within a conference setting coupled with managing compliance and events across the NCAA divisions set her apart from her colleagues, which ignited unfavorable responses and gender-based comments as to why she was elevated into the new position over others. McWilliams also explained that even as she was promoted to director of women's basketball she faced challenges. At the time, she was a newly married mother, and athletic leadership did not think she would be able to handle additional job responsibilities. McWilliams explained this wasn't true, adding, "I do not think it was intentional; I think as leaders sometimes you feel those things would be a burden if you add more to the plate and they did not discuss that with me to allow me to determine if it was too much, so I had to deal with that as well." McWilliams reflects that it has been "a ride of a career with some challenges." She indicates that she always tells people "the 'isms,' no matter what color you are or gender, they do happen, they exist, it is just a matter of how you deal with them and manage them through your career."

McWilliams says she was able to manage the challenges with support. When she started at the CIAA, there were just two female board members on the 12-member board, which could be daunting. Initially, she felt a lack of support from female leaders. However, a majority of board members demonstrated their support for McWilliams to appoint her as commissioner because they were looking for progression and advancement for the conference. Unfortunately, many women in the workforce do not have the full support of their female colleagues. Women face many obstacles, especially in a male-dominated workplace. As McWilliams emphasized, however, linking with mentors paves a supportive pathway. Recently, McWilliams had a friend with three children who questioned her own ability to assume an athletic director position. McWilliams's advice was that an effective administrator "allows people around you to succeed and do well," and in most cases there is "flexibility in the schedule once in a leadership role."

As a conference commissioner, former athletic director, and former athlete, McWilliams understands what equitable opportunities should look like so that all student-athletes can enjoy a great experience. On the topic of gender equity, for McWilliams, even "after 45 years, the fact that we are still having the discussion is crazy to me. . . . [W]hen you are in a leadership position, you can identify ways and find ways to provide equity."

The CIAA operates one of the largest NCAA conference tournaments in the country, generating more than $50 million annually for the city of Charlotte. The revenue generated from the event is necessary to help the conference provide equitable experiences to all student-athletes for all of its sponsored sports. In terms of hiring practices and equity, McWilliams is highly cognizant about having males and females equitably represented in administrative positions. As an athletic administrator, McWilliams asserts that decisions and choices are selected based on one's "belief in equity, diversity, and Title IX." Working with 12 college presidents, McWilliams acknowledges they have to be mindful about the leadership on their respective campuses, Title IX, and the overall mission. The CIAA has progressed by bringing in consultants to explore equity.

When she was a college athlete, McWilliams says, her coaches had to defend their gym space on rainy days when the football team wanted to practice indoors. She recalls her basketball coach advocating for new uniforms because the sizes were too small. As McWilliams states, "those are simple things," and in her own roles she always wanted her student-athletes "to feel valued." Although there are many men coaching women's sports today, it is important to recognize that women tend to be more aware and connected to the inequities in athletics because "it happens to us all so often." In terms of high-level discussions regarding gender equity, those conversations do take place, but for McWilliams the core issue is how to funnel the message to the student population. At the Division II

(continues)

FEEDBACK FROM THE FIELD   *(continued)*

level, McWilliams spends more time on the general message to try to keep all offerings equal. Sometimes when administrators make changes to create more equity, they encounter pushback from various groups. Still, behind the scenes, administrators do all they can to balance the opportunities for men's and women's sports. Athletes, however, just "want to play the game," McWilliams says, and are less worried about start times and locations than administrators might be. "I believe student-athletes already believe their coaches and administrators are working on their behalf," she says.

McWilliams believes all her experiences with sexism, genderism, and racism have allowed her to deal with the professional challenges associated with providing leadership to athletic programming. When speaking to young people who feel a certain position may not be the best fit, she offers this advice, "it may not feel right now and there will be something else," adding that "if you can take every opportunity, you will learn something about you and others." McWilliams underscored that her experiences and mentor relationship molded her leadership.

Significant Lawsuits and Legislation Affecting Title IX

- *Grove City v. Bell,* 1984: This case grew out of the 1978 requirement that all schools sign statements that they were in compliance with Title IX. Almost all schools did so, even though few actually were. Grove City College refused to do so based on its long-standing rejection of any federal intrusion on its campus. There was no allegation of sex discrimination on campus, but Grove City's refusal to sign the letter triggered a move to withdraw the only federal money connected to the campus: BEOG (now Pell) grants given to students directly who then used the money to pay their tuition at Grove City College. The college sued the federal government to block the withdrawal. Two points of significance were the result of the Grove City decision. First, the U.S. Supreme Court ruled that even indirect funding was sufficient to trigger Title IX jurisdiction. Second, Title IX's jurisdiction extended only to the subunit of the institution that received federal money. The impact of the first ruling maintained Title IX's broad jurisdiction of education programs, but the second effectively removed Title IX's jurisdiction over physical education and athletics programs. Physical education and athletics programs almost never enjoy federal dollars and thus were *not* institutional subunits that would fall within Title IX's reach. Almost instantly after the Grove City decision, many colleges withdrew scholarship aid for their female athletes, and some even terminated women's teams. High school programs were not affected by the Grove City decision because their federal money is mixed into entire operating budgets.
- Civil Rights Restoration Act of 1987: Enacted over a presidential veto in 1988, the act effectively corrected the second part of the Grove City decision. The act stated that Congress had indeed intended Title IX's jurisdiction to be triggered for the *entire* institution whenever one dollar of federal money appeared anywhere on campus. Thus, in 1988 college athletics and physical education programs were again within the sweep of Title IX.
- *Franklin v. Gwinnett Public Schools,* 1992. Before this U.S. Supreme Court case, the best that a complainant to OCR or a plaintiff in a Title IX lawsuit could hope for was the withdrawal of all federal money from the campus of a noncomplying education program. OCR, however, has never withdrawn any federal money for a Title IX violation, and Title IX's teeth were dull before Franklin. The unanimous Franklin decision found that both compensatory and punitive damages were available to the successful plaintiff who proved intentional discrimination under Title IX. The court further indicated that any school with an athletics program that violated Title IX was most likely doing so intentionally because Title IX was then already 20 years old and its provisions well known. The Franklin decision provided sharp teeth for those seeking to enforce Title IX via the courts, and

many schools decided that it was fiscally sound to move to compliance rather than spend money on attorneys defending the indefensible.

- *Jackson v. Birmingham,* 2005: The 5–4 decision in this Supreme Court case was handed down in March 2005. If decided differently, it would have significantly hindered Title IX enforcement. Jackson is coach of a high school girls team. He discussed potential Title IX violations with his superiors and was fired in retaliation, an act prohibited under Title IX, which covers employees as well as students (although for most issues, employees find better help from Title VII or the Equal Pay Act). In this case, the issue was whether Coach Jackson's remedies are limited to filing a complaint with OCR, which has no meaningful value to an employee who was fired or if Coach Jackson (who was later rehired) has access to a "private right of action" (the right to use a lawsuit, not just a complaint) that carries the potential of money damages (both compensatory and punitive). The decision means that when an employee is fired in retaliation for talking about Title IX, the employee has a significant remedy available. If Jackson had lost, coaches and teachers who value their continuing employment would likely have been silenced on Title IX topics.

Carpenter and Acosta (n.d.)

Compliance with Title IX: Three-Part Test

Participation Component

An institution is in compliance with the three-part test if it meets any one of the following parts of the test:

1. The number of male and female athletes is substantially proportionate to their respective enrollments; or
2. The institution has a history and continuing practice of expanding participation opportunities responsive to the developing interests and abilities of the underrepresented sex; or
3. The institution is fully and effectively accommodating the interests and abilities of the underrepresented sex.

Office for Civil Rights, n.d.

Athletic Financial Assistance

The total amount of athletic aid must be substantially proportionate to the ratio of female and male athletes. For example, consider a college with 90 female athletes and 115 male athletes and a scholarship budget of $100,000. An equitable distribution of funds would award $44,000 in scholarship aid to female athletes and $56,000 to males.

Title IX (n.d.)

Institutions found to be "not in compliance" with Title IX are required by the OCR to implement a plan as well as changes to the institution's policies; "in rare cases, OCR will declare a university in violation, and could move to cut off a school's federal funding, such as student loans and Pell grants, though the agency has never done that" (HuffPost, 2014).

Because of the outcry from advocacy groups seeking gender equality in sports, the workings of many athletic departments are becoming increasingly transparent, and some institutions are publishing their strategies for compliance on institutional websites.

▶ Title IX Coordinator

Athletic departments are required by law to enforce all provisions of Title IX. To do so, an athletic administration must fully understand the scope of Title IX and its implementation requirements. In addition to providing leadership in the athletic administration, the Title IX coordinator is responsible for enforcing the law within the system. The position of Title IX coordinator was created to facilitate implementation of Title IX. According to Staurowsky, Zonder, and Riemer (2017),

> in theory, a functioning Title IX enforcement scheme entailed a communication chain that started at the U.S. Department of Education and was connected to schools through principals and presidents, legal counsels, and Title IX coordinators. Failure to appoint a Title IX coordinator or reduce the role to a title only with little authority effectively broke that communication chain resulting in a failure to activate the rest of the enforcement scheme. (p. 32)

Unfortunately, as Staurowsky and colleagues report, college athletes have limited knowledge of Title IX, adding to the lack of implementation by athletic administrators of this legislation. Staurowsky et al. suggest that "in an ideal world, college athletes should be introduced to the history of Title IX through government, American history, and women's studies courses long before they enter college" (p. 40).

Athletic Positions and Title IX

Title IX has increased opportunities for females in sport but not for all women holding coaching or administrative positions. Within the coaching realm, female athletes are less likely to have a female coach than ever before. This statistic can be troubling because there was a larger percentage of women coaching female teams before Title IX. Stark (n.d.) reports that "in 1972, 90% of coaches for female sports were women" whereas today that number is "fewer than half."

The Tucker Center is an interdisciplinary research center that examines how "sport and physical activity affect the lives of girls and women, their families, and communities." The center produces an annual report card on Title IX. Consistent with the work of Stark, the Tucker Center indicates that "in the 40+ years after the passage of Title IX, female sport participation is at an all-time high but the percentage of women coaching women at the collegiate level has declined from 90+% in 1974 to near an all-time low today of 40%" (University of Minnesota, n.d.). Reasons attributed to this shift include the simple fact that male coaches who could not secure coaching positions with male programs now have two avenues to find employment in coaching because resources have poured into female programs. Female coaches had been limited to coaching girls and women in sport, and these positions are now saturated by male coaches.

Similar to collegiate and high school athletics, discrepancies exist in youth sports and female volunteer coaches. Messner and Bozada-Deas (2009) studied sport volunteers over multiple years, finding the presence of a "gender category sorting system" that directs most men

into coaching and most women into being "team moms." (p. 49). LaVoi, Becker, and Leberman (2009) provide strategies for athletic entities to recruit and retain female coaches in youth sport, especially because less than 20% of women serve as coaches (LaVoi, Becker, & Leberman, 2009). The associate director of the Tucker Center for Research on Girls and Women in Sport offers that women in coaching provide diversity within athletic entities, a pathway for young females to enter coaching, and same-sex role models for girls (LaVoi & Leberman, 2015).

Within athletic administration positions in the NCAA, women lag behind their male counterparts in athletic director roles. Vollman (2016) reports the number of women in the NCAA holding the position of athletic director increased from 2006 to 2012; "however, prior to the 1972 passage women served as athletic directors over women's programs in great numbers." According to the NCAA's report ("Sport Sponsorship, Participation, and Demographics Search," n.d.), for the 2016–2017 academic year, women continue to hold a small percentage of leadership positions as athletic directors across all three divisions. In summary, within all levels there are 1,134 athletic directors, 899 of then male and 235 female. At the Division I level, of 354 athletic directors, 314 are male and 40 are female. At the Division II level, of 323 athletic directors, 270 are male and 53 female. At the Division III level, of 457 athletic directors, 315 are male and 142 female.

Similarly, within the high school setting, Whisenant (2003) analyzed the number of women in athletic director positions within the National Interscholastic Athletic Administrators Association and found results parallel to those of the NCAA, with only 13% of women versus 87% of men holding interscholastic athletic administrator positions. Efforts to turn around these statistics have been spearheaded by several advocacy groups such as the Women's Sports Foundation, National Coalition for Women and Girls in Education, the American Association of University Women, and the Alliance of Women Coaches. Regrettably, "while

Title IX has led to greater opportunities for girls and women to play sports, receive scholarships, and obtain other important benefits that flow from sports participation, its goal of equal opportunity in sports has yet to be realized (National Women's Law Center, n.d., p. 1).

Senior woman administrator (SWA) is a designated position at NCAA member institutions and signifies the highest-ranking female within an athletic department (National College Athletic Association, "Senior Woman Administrators," n.d.). Hatfield, Hatfield, and Drummond (2009) studied the role of the senior woman administrator, finding that "overall, SWAs seem to be satisfied with the contributions they are making to their respective athletic departments, yet there still exists today some ambiguity regarding the role and function of SWAs." The SWA position was first called the *primary woman administrator* and was meant to give women a voice in the management of intercollegiate athletics (NCAA, n.d., "Senior Woman Administrators"). Despite these efforts, as Tiell, Dixon, and Lin (2012) indicated, "a discrepancy persists between senior woman administrators and athletic directors regarding the extent to which SWAs are and should be involved in decision making within athletic departments" (p. 247). Without the authority vested in the SWA position, the administrative muscle of females in athletic departments continues to be weaker than that of their male counterparts.

NCAA Gender Equity Task Force Definition of Gender Equity

An athletics program can be considered gender equitable when the participants in both the men's and women's sports programs would accept as fair and equitable the overall program of the other gender. No individual should be discriminated against on the basis of gender, institutionally or nationally, in intercollegiate athletics.

—NCAA Gender Equity Task Force, 1992

Gender Equity

In 1992, the NCAA created an initiative to assist member institutions in establishing gender equity within collegiate athletics. The NCAA Gender Equity Task Force served to provide guidance to member institutions by publishing a free manual (National Collegiate Athletic Association, 2010) that explained Title IX and to provide gender-equitable policies for athletic departments along with strategies to implement these policies. The NCAA Gender Equity Task Force was also instrumental in the creation of the *NCAA Emerging Sports for Women Process Guide* (n.d.) because only 30% of athletic offerings in the early 1990s were available to female athletes. Furthermore, "NCAA bylaws require that emerging sports must gain championship status (minimum of 40 varsity NCAA programs as reflected in the

Gender Equity Definition

Gender Equity is the process of allocating resources, programs and decision-making fairly. It does not mean providing the exact same programs to both girls and boys. Some girls' activities may be the same as those offered to boys, some may be altered, and some may be altogether different. (British Columbia Recreation and Parks Association, n.d.)

The Equity in Athletics Disclosure Act of 1994 made it mandatory for colleges receiving federal funds to make all gender-equality information about their athletic programs publicly available. (Ross, 2015)

NCAA Sports Sponsorship Database) within 10 years or show steady progress toward that goal to remain on the list."

 FEEDBACK FROM THE FIELD

Kathleen Walsh is chief operating officer (COO) for the Metro North Y in Massachusetts. In her role working with the support of the chief executive office, the board of directors, and the senior Y leadership, Walsh aims to execute the strategic plan of the organization, which serves 30,000 people at seven unique locations within an urban and suburban footprint. Walsh has been with the Y for more than 20 years in various leadership positions.

Walsh explains that in her tenure at the Y over two decades, the discussion on Title IX and gender equity has shifted significantly. In the early part of her career, the Y catered to men's programs, men's memberships, elite men's locker rooms, and men's laundry services. Women did not have the same offerings. Since the late 1990s, a female leadership presence has increased. At the executive leadership level, Walsh says 70% of the positions are now held by females. The organization previously known as the Young Men's Christian Association (YMCA) underwent rebranding, changing the name to the "Y." As Walsh explains, dropping "Men's" and the Christian terminology allowed the Y to focus on "being an all-inclusive organization so all that we do now is weighted equally for males and females." In terms of gender equity, the conversations for programming focus on one community at a time and serving community interests as a whole. Today, the discussions on equity are considered special topics because of the progress made over the last 20 years in programming.

One set of issues that has been discussed recently relates to transgender members and how to fully accommodate these individuals within the Y. The transgender subject is, according to Walsh, "real to our community and as a community-serving organization we want to address it with dignity, kindness, and everything else we stand for." Walsh explains the Y, as a national organization, abides "by whichever gender that the person affiliates with and we accommodate accordingly." With any decision, leadership is exposed to dealing with adverse commentary from members holding traditional views of human sexuality. Walsh stresses, however, that "we support whichever gender the individuals identify with, and we have changed some of our policies because of it." Policies regarding locker room tours have also shifted at the Y. In the past, staff would walk prospective members through the locker room space. Under the new policy, Y "staff across the board do not accompany our members into the locker room." According to Walsh, uniformity with policy changes will exist whether dealing with males, females, or transgendered individuals. In the end, the Y intends to be sensitive and consistent in policy making.

Naturally, when dealing with a historic entity such as the Y (with some facilities as old as 140 years), changes to the physical space take planning. For newly constructed facilities, changes and equity in spacing are easier to implement. Today, when the Y engages in construction, the building components are "across the board 50–50." A good example of this mindset and commitment is at the newest Y where the new locker rooms for males and females are exactly the same square footage rather than four times larger than the women's space as previously. The Y organized information sessions about the new building. It is not surprising that the change in the facility space prompted some members to express concern about the reduction of locker room space on the men's side. According to Walsh, the process has been enlightening for the members. It is important to remind those who give some pushback to ultimately be loyal to the Y's cause over their own needs. As Walsh notes, "the transition has been an educational process for [seasoned members] as well to have them understand that the Y is a charity providing scholarships, and it is really about shaping the community as opposed to accommodating just a few members."

When challenged on the changes to the facility center, Walsh emphasizes the value the Y provides to the community and the power it has to transform the city and area. In the end, members with concerns typically retreat from complaining once they acknowledge the effects of the Y in the community, Walsh says. She further notes that the Y evolves as the community landscape evolves. When presented with criticism, Walsh points out the "Y is a fluid organization adapting to changing needs, and our members need to embrace that." Operating seven different Y's, Walsh's team designs programs based on each community's needs.

In terms of equity, youth basketball is one of the biggest Y programs. Now if the Y offers a travel basketball program for boys, it will offer the same activities to girls. Walsh and her staff work at eliminating gender discrepancies by listening to members and understanding the demographics of the community. Swim classes and teams are coeducational, and the activities for sports programs are offered to boys and girls. Even for a predominantly female sport such as gymnastics, the Y offers the same opportunity to males. For children after second grade, the sport programs move from coeducational to single gender; Walsh points out that "we have balance between the girls' and the boys'" menu of sport options. The Y relies on the support of volunteers; in the basketball program, there are more male volunteer coaches but the swim program has more female volunteers.

In terms of staffing and gender balance, Walsh thinks the "Y needs to find a better way to recruit strong female board members." She is in favor of blind hiring of people by "taking name and gender off the résumé and just look at experiences and how they present themselves in interviews" to avoid gender stereotyping for certain positions such as sports director or coach. The Y's executive board assumes the operational aspects of the organization, whereas the senior staff works on programs that are inclusive and balanced for the membership. Walsh stresses that the Y "has been around for 170 years and keeps evolving with what is going on with the world, touching so many people along the way."

Many students entering the fields of athletic administration and sport management may not think the Y is a "viable or flashy career option,"

© Sergey Ryzhov/Shutterstock.

(continues)

FEEDBACK FROM THE FIELD   *(continued)*

but as Walsh underscores, "the Y is a multibillion-dollar organization serving hundreds of thousands of people." As COO, Walsh manages a $24-million business with 700 employees; "the impact that I am doing that with is significant." For students with a desire to make a difference at a nonprofit organization, she says the Y provides individuals with more upward advancement than most sport-related organizations. "There is a huge opportunity for people who love this kind of work, which is everything from athletics to finance to marketing, and to be able to have a passion behind it. People need to look at the Y more for a long-term career." In her final comments, Walsh says she believes young people should follow their heart and the rest will follow, especially if the desire is to make a difference in people's lives.

The following checklist was prepared to assist you in meeting some minimum requirements of the Title IX Regulations. It is not an exhaustive checklist and therefore should not be used as a substitute for careful reading of the regulation itself.

§106.8 Designation of Responsible Employee and Adoption of Grievance Procedures

- At least one Title IX coordinator has been designated to coordinate efforts to comply with Title IX, including investigations of any complaints.
- All students and employees have been notified of the name(s), office address(es), and telephone number(s) of the coordinator(s).
- Grievance procedures for students have been adopted and published.
- Grievance procedures for employees have been adopted and published.

(Authority: Secs. 901, 902, Education Amendments of 1972, 86 Stat. 373, 374; 20 U.S.C. 1681, 1682)

§ 106.9 Dissemination of Policy

The following have been notified of a policy of nondiscrimination on the basis of sex:

- applicants for admission and employment,
- students and parents of students,
- employees,
- sources of referral of applicants, and
- unions, and professional organizations.

Notification of a policy of nondiscrimination on the basis of sex has been placed in the following:

- local newspapers;
- school newspapers and magazines;
- memoranda or other written communications distributed annually to each student and employee;
- announcements, bulletins, catalogs, student and faculty handbooks; and
- application forms.

The above-listed publications are free of text and illustrations suggesting differential treatment on the basis of sex.

- Admission and recruitment representatives (including counselors or student advisors and personnel officers) have been advised of the nondiscriminatory policy and are required to adhere to the policy.

Basic Checklist for Title IX Compliance

Title 34 Education (n.d.).
Authority: Secs. 901, 902, Education Amendments of 1972, 86 Stat. 373, 374; 20 U.S.C. 1681, 1682); [45 FR 30955, May 9, 1980, as amended at 65 FR 68056, Nov. 13, 2000]

FEATURED INTERVIEW: BEST PRACTICES IN ATHLETIC ADMINISTRATION

Dr. Donna Lopiano is president and founder of Sports Management Resources. She is considered one of the most significant forces in scholastic and collegiate athletic administration. Dr. Lopiano is the former chief executive officer of the Women's Sports Foundation (1992–2007), has been named one of the 10 most powerful women in sports by Fox Sports, and repeatedly listed as one of the 100 most influential people in sports by the *Sporting News*. On the national and international stage, her efforts to advocate for gender equity in sports have been recognized by the International Olympic Committee, the National Collegiate Athletic Association, the National Association for Girls and Women in Sports, the National Association of Collegiate Women Athletic Administrators, and the National Association of Collegiate Directors of Athletics. Her recent publications include *Unwinding Madness* with Gerald Gurney and Andrew Zimbalist (Brookings, 2017) and *Athletic Director's Desk Reference* with Constance Zotos (Human Kinetics, 2013).

Dr. Lopiano's experience within athletics is extensive and extremely impressive as she has become an influential change agent in athletic administration. She was the director of women's athletics for 18 years at the University of Texas, is a past president of the Association for Intercollegiate Athletics for Women, and is assistant professor and assistant athletic director at Brooklyn College of the City University of New York. In addition to running her own sports management consulting business, Dr. Lopiano is now an adjunct faculty member within the sports management program at Southern Connecticut State University.

As a national expert on gender equity and Title IX, Dr. Lopiano has testified about Title IX and gender equity before three congressional committees, served as a consultant to the U.S. Office for Civil Rights; the Department of Health, Education; and the Welfare Title IX Task Force; and she has testified in more than 30 Title IX and Title VII lawsuits. Dr. Lopiano has operated as a consultant to school districts, institutions of higher education, and state education agencies on Title IX compliance. As an athlete, Dr. Lopiano participated in 26 national championships in four sports and was a nine-time All-American at four different positions in softball, a sport in which she played on six national championship teams. She is a member of the National Sports Hall of Fame, the National Softball Hall of Fame, and the Connecticut and Texas Women's Halls of Fame, among others.

Dr. Lopiano has championed many issues in athletics, with Title IX being at the forefront of her work. She says there are two "musts" of athletic administration and Title IX that athletic administrators must understand: what Title IX requires and understanding how to complete a Title IX assessment. The reality, according to Dr. Lopiano, is that schools have traditionally not been in compliance with Title IX, and athletic directors are not informed enough about the requirements of the law to make a good assessment or bring an athletic program into compliance. Subsequently, Dr. Lopiano explains, this lack of knowledge from athletic directors places schools in an unfavorable position if there is ever any Title IX litigation. This is particularly important, as Dr. Lopiano shares, because college presidents are asked annually to verify that their institutions are in compliance with Title IX as a condition for receiving substantial higher education funding that equates to millions of dollars for their institutions. Therefore, one important obligation of any athletic director is to adequately inform the college president about the status of Title IX within the athletic department.

For students studying the legislation of Title IX, Dr. Lopiano advises the use of the U.S. Department of Education's Equity in Athletics Data Analysis (EADA) online database (https://ope.ed.gov/athletics/#/) to review participation data on institutions with regard to compliance. The EADA is an "analysis-cutting tool" designed to provide rapid customized reports for public inquiries relating to equity in athletics. The data are drawn from the OPE Equity in Athletics Disclosure Website database. This database consists of athletics data that are submitted annually as required by the Equity in Athletics Disclosure

(continues)

Act via web-based data collection from all coeducational postsecondary institutions that receive Title IV funding (i.e., those that participate in federal student aid programs) and have an intercollegiate athletics program (U.S. Department of Education, n.d.). This database discloses "participation rates" and other indicators of how institutions are or are not likely to be in compliance with Title IX, but such information is insufficient for conducting a full Title IX analysis.

Dr. Lopiano opines that since Title IX's passage in 1972, it is "highly unlikely that any institution can comply with Prong 2 or Prong 3 options of Title IX" that would allow exceptions to the requirement that the percentage of male and female athletics participants be equal to the proportion of males and females in the undergraduate student body. She highlights the three core components of Title IX: participation, lists of benefits and treatments, and financial aid. The EADA database, according to Dr. Lopiano, provides a quick assessment about whether an institution is in compliance with Title IX under the participation and financial aid requirements by providing "a count of male and female athletes and gives the enrollment figures from which the individual can determine what percent of athletic participants are male and female compared to the undergraduate student body male and female." An individual can also see financial aid expenditures, which allows administrators to determine whether athletic scholarships are being distributed proportionally to the same percentages of male and female athletes. Furthermore, she describes that because most schools use Prong 1 for Title IX compliance, "athletic participation rates for men and women need to be equal to the percent of male and female undergraduates." As explained previously in this chapter, Prongs 2 and 3 are compliance options under Title IX; however, Lopiano asserts she has "never found an institution that can legitimately comply with Prong 2 or Prong 3." Lopiano cautions against using EADA data alone when it comes to compliance because "Title IX has a great many subtleties specific to the fact situation at each institution that require more extensive examination." Furthermore, she prompts athletic administrators to "do your homework because the devil is in the details and the reason why people get sued is because they don't understand the details. That is why they lose in court."

Dr. Lopiano's book, *Athletic Director's Desk Reference* (2013), contains more than 300 cloud documents in Excel format, including Title IX assessment worksheets, a guide on how to conduct a Title IX athletics assessment, gender-equity policies, and much more to assist athletic administrators in understanding Title IX. According to Dr. Lopiano, the suggested time frame to complete these assessments is once every four years to remain in compliance with Title IX and to ensure "coaches do not put you out of compliance." Also available for download in Excel and Word forms are sample model policies for general departmental issues and forms to handle operational areas like travel and injury reporting; these can be easily customized for institutional use.

Dr. Lopiano stresses that Title IX compliance is a "continuing obligation" for the athletic director. She shared an example of a football coach who has a donor willing to gift $10,000 for new uniforms. In this scenario, the new uniforms equate to 100 football players now having three sets of uniforms versus the two sets of uniforms for all other sports. As Dr. Lopiano explained, under the Title IX "laundry list," the football coach "can inadvertently put the institution out of compliance if he is allowed to provide that additional uniform benefit to male football players and an equal proportion of women athletes don't get the benefit of a third set of uniforms." The athletic director is the only administrator who can see how all sports are treated, so she or he cannot allow the football coach "to discriminate on the basis of sex albeit unintentionally. This is how institutions go 'off the wheels' in terms of gender equity by allowing coaches to do special things for athletes." This is why Title IX requires "constant oversight on the part of athletic directors on expenditures and especially the use of fundraising accounts that are separate from operating budgets. The use of both funds is countable under Title IX," according to Dr. Lopiano. To remedy such fundraising issues, Dr. Lopiano recommends departments develop a set of policies that deal with these issues. For instance, in the case of uniforms, equipment, and supplies, the athletic director should develop a gender-neutral policy that mandates that every team have a sufficient number of uniforms as required by the rules (i.e., that basketball and football both have home and away uniforms) and the purchase of any other additional set of uniforms requires the approval of the athletic director." In this scenario, the athletic director is not saying a third set of uniforms cannot be purchased, but as the department head you are making sure these purchases are happening for an equal percentage of male and female athletes.

Within certain divisions, many institutions prioritize sports, treating some sports better than others with regard to funding, the number of coaches provided, recruiting budgets, and allocation of full scholarships. Many athletic directors "tier" sports incorrectly. For example, a school might put two men's sports such as football and men's basketball and two women's sports such as basketball and volleyball into the top tier. Title IX requires an equal proportion of male and female participants in each tier (i.e. 20% of all male athletes and 20% of all female athletes) rather than an equal number of teams. If an athletic director wants to put the programs into different financial tiers, they "still need to be in compliance with Title IX." Dr. Lopiano recommends "Constructing a Tiered Sports Program for College Athletics" by Connee Zotos (2006) as the best way to "stay on the right side of gender equity."

Dr. Lopiano said she doesn't know of any athletic department "that financially prioritizes the support of sports in ways that don't affect one or more Title IX laundry list areas." In her experience, "because of historical factors, most athletic programs do not treat sports programs equally." Even at the Division III level where the prevailing philosophy is to treat all sports equally, "financial reality doesn't allow" athletic directors to do so—and thus prioritization of sports persists. Dr. Lopiano provided an example of a

> Division III men's lacrosse team that may be able to travel nationally or is able to go on a spring break trip because of a long history of program success and generous financial support from former players. No other sports' operating budgets can afford such trips. It is not acceptable under Title IX to say to all other sports that you have to raise your own money for spring break or national travel just like lacrosse if your operating budget money won't cover it. Title IX treats money from all revenue sources as institutional money. If institutional money is provided for such extensive men's lacrosse travel, the athletic director needs to identify another funding source to allow an equal proportion of female athletes to benefit from a similar trip. If the money isn't there, the men's lacrosse team should not be allowed to travel in violation of gender equity requirements.

> This is another example, Dr. Lopiano says, of

> decisions that are made by a single sex team that are going to be gender discriminatory if the athletic director does not exercise his or her Title IX referee responsibilities. Athletic directors must continually ask themselves the question, "Is an equal percentage of male and female athletes getting this benefit or being treated this way?" It becomes their daily job to exercise such oversight and make those decisions.

Dr. Lopiano also cautions that athletic directors should pay particular attention to coaches looking "for the edge," because they will make numerous requests for special treatment in the name of being able to better compete in recruiting wars. The athletic director's responses should not put the program "on the wrong side of gender equity."

There are scenarios whereby athletic departments do not promote or publicize games for both genders in an equitable fashion. Dr. Lopiano explains that promotion and publicity cannot be overlooked. Simple concepts such as game-day programs at each event or one general athletic department program at all events "promotes males and females in the same way and you get the same results with publicity." At the University of Texas, Dr. Lopiano was head of the women's athletics program, which was administered separately from the men's athletic programs with its own athletic director. The women's program had

(continues)

FEATURED INTERVIEW: BEST PRACTICES IN ATHLETIC ADMINISTRATION *(continued)*

all of its teams in the "top 10 nationally, was able to hire the best coaches, and sold 8,000 women's basketball season tickets." As Dr. Lopiano explained, "we were able to treat female athletes as well as our male athletes because no one said women's sports had to come second to men's sports." Dr. Lopiano stresses it is common sense when dealing with promotions that if the men's and the women's teams are "treated the same—same quality coaches, same number of scholarships, same recruiting resources, same promotions—the same things happen" in terms of attendance and ticket sales.

Critics of Title IX may blame the legislation for cuts in men's sport programs, but Dr. Lopiano urges individuals to review the data from NCAA participation sponsorship annual reports. These reports show the number of sport teams dropped and added. Dr. Lopiano reveals, "the only division in which net losses for men occur is Division I, the institutions with the richest athletic programs." She further explains that "the money saved by cutting a men's sports isn't going toward Title IX compliance; rather, the money for cutting these men's sports is going to fuel the men's basketball and football arms race." In fact, Dr. Lopiano discloses that when examining "Division II and Division III, these programs are on a net basis adding sports for men." In the end, "to disprove a myth, you have to present factual data."

Dr. Lopiano also discussed the influence of athletic department structure on the achievement of gender equity by making an analogy to a U.S. business model, arguing that higher education institutions "don't have to have administratively separate men's and women's athletic departments to treat women equally." She suggested that "within an athletic department serving both men's and women's sports staff, a separate athletic department staff needs to invest time and effort into the development of new products separate from developed products because the marketing strategies and sales for those products are not the same." According to Dr. Lopiano,

> corporations have it right; they have to put a lot of money in the development pipeline so when the developed product sales start to level off, which is inevitable, or sales level off in athletics due to factors like limited arena seating or bad team performance, if you don't have something coming out of the development pipeline to offset that, then you are in trouble. Diversification of product lines is the hallmark of corporate success in a capitalist society. We don't do that in athletics; we put all of our athletic eggs into one or two baskets, usually basketball and football, rather than developing other sports.

Dr. Lopiano further explains that if these flagship men's programs fail, the impact on the athletics business is exacerbated when

> we fire coaches, pay a million dollars to get out of the multiyear contract we gave the coach who is being fired and then up the ante to get a new coach; it's a bad business to do so if such costs result in pulling back on the development of new sport products.

In the end, Dr. Lopiano advises athletic administrators "do their homework" on Title IX and to "pay attention to liability risks, as we know that most programs are not in compliance with Title IX."

Questions to Consider

1. Navigate to the Equity in Athletics Disclosure Act (EADA) (https://ope.ed.gov/athletics/#/) for three institutions. What surprised you the most about the schools you reviewed? Are there areas of compliance that concerned you, and how will you remedy the inequities?
2. Prepare a policy within the high school or college setting to manage single-sport booster clubs. When each team has its own booster club, it can create challenges for the athletic administration. Be sure to address the creation of equity within your policy.

3. Inevitably, some sports gain more of a fan following than others on high school and college campuses. Develop a marketing plan to promote all your teams equitably for the fall season. Be sure to research ideas from other institutions that have been effective in enhancing the overall athletic environment.

4. What impressed you the most about Dr. Lopiano's impact on the sport landscape for both males and females?

5. As a future athletic administrator, how would you operate your athletic department to ensure males and females had similar experiences under the three compliance areas of Title IX (participation, athletic financial assistance, and treatment)?

Good Ware from flaticon.com

 MANAGERIAL APPLICATIONS

College Athletics

The Title IX coordinator is responsible for ensuring compliance with Title IX—but the entire athletic department must adhere to the legislation. Unfortunately, many coaches and athletic staff members do not fully understand the law. In fact, when you as athletic director of a Division II institution asked each coach to explain Title IX and gender equity, their facts and information were not accurate. Without properly knowing about Title IX and gender equity, your staff is not equipped to assess any discrepancies between the male and female programs. Furthermore, if your staff does not possess accurate information on Title IX and gender equity, the communication of these essential components within athletics are not transferred accurately to student-athletes and their families.

Questions to Consider

1. Do you think athletic administrators assume the staff has full knowledge of Title IX and gender equity? How will you promote the position of Title IX coordinator to help explain the components of Title IX to your staff?

2. Gender equity focuses on fairness and providing similar opportunities to male and female athletes. You sense there are issues regarding the field space allocated to the girl's field hockey team. The venue has not been upgraded along with the other athletic facilities over the last five years. Because there have been no grievances filed regarding this space, do you as the athletic director need to act and make changes to provide similar treatment between male and female programs?

3. How can you create an inclusive environment within your staff to ensure all coaches are able to operate their program in a similar fashion under Title IX using the three components of participation, scholarships, and treatment?

© Jon Osumi/Shutterstock.

DECISION-MAKING CHALLENGE

Case Study: Youth Sport

Within your town's athletic program, the major concern each season is the recruitment of volunteer coaches. Over the years, you have noticed only one or two women have been added as assistant coaches and none have been placed as head coaches. You reside in the town, so you know that many residents are athletic, attended college, participated in sports, and seem especially interested in youth sport programs. You are concerned that women do not make up a larger percentage of coaching roles in your town program.

What type of outreach would you create to recruit new coaches to the youth program? Explain your plan to recruit women to volunteer as coaches within the program. Do you feel there needs to be a specialized communication plan to attract women to coaching their children, and why? What are the key points to be communicated to retain women coaches within your program from season to season?

 DECISION-MAKING CHALLENGE

Case Study: High School Sports

Booster clubs fall under the purview of Title IX. As the newly hired Athletic Director at Quinn High School, you discovered a disparity in the booster clubs for your boys' and girls' teams. From your investigation, you uncovered that the booster clubs were providing benefits and services to the boys' teams resulting in greater benefits and services for the boys' teams than the girls' teams. As Athletic Director, you shared your concerns with the School Principal and Superintendent of Schools, who charged you with immediately developing a new policy and practice to oversee booster club involvement with the interscholastic athletics program. This may be a challenging task, as the boys' programs have been generating revenue over 5 years and the girls' programs have lagged behind. What are some best practices you have discovered to assist in this process?

Wrap-Up

End-of-Chapter Questions

1. Compose a well-worded statement that lays out the reasons why Title IX was enacted.

2. Conduct an online search for Title IX compliance issues at Division I, II, and III institutions. Describe the discrepancies at the institutions uncovered by the Office for Civil Rights and the steps that need to be taken to ensure compliance with Title IX.

3. In your own words, describe gender equity and its effects on athletic programs

at the collegiate, high school, youth, and club sport settings.

4. Title IX has changed the participation rates of females but has decreased the opportunities for women in coaching. What do you think has caused the decline of females in coaching and athletic administrations within both the high school and collegiate settings?

5. Within the youth sports setting many more fathers than mothers volunteer to coach their children. What are some strategies you can list to recruit and

retain more females within the youth sport setting?

6. Trace the evolution of Title IX after reading this chapter and conducting an online search of milestones. What surprises you most about Title IX in the more than 40 years since its inception?

7. Visit the Women's Sports Foundation website (https://www.womenssports foundation.org/advocate/title-ix-issues/). Describe an action plan you can implement at the high school or collegiate level to comply with Title IX and create gender equity within your department.

8. What is the purpose of the Office for Civil Rights regarding Title IX?

9. Title IX has changed the sporting landscape for females, but some critics blame the legislation for decreasing the numbers of opportunities for males. What is your position on that belief? Use data points to support your conclusion.

10. Find two current articles focused on gender equity in the youth sport setting. Describe the content of the articles and share your thoughts on the challenges athletic administrators must overcome to generate equitable opportunities for their male and female participants.

11. Have you experienced a difference in treatment as a student-athlete or youth sport participant? Please describe the scenario and how the discrepancy was resolved. As an athletic administrator, how can you ensure that your participants are treated equitably within your offerings?

12. Dr. Vivian Acosta and Dr. Linda Jean Carpenter have researched Title IX for decades. Visit their website (http://www.acostacarpenter.org/) to review their report, *Women in Intercollegiate Sport: A Longitudinal, National Study Thirty-Seven Year Update*. Select three topical areas to review within this report.

References

British Columbia Recreation and Parks Association (n.d.). Gender equity in sport and recreation [online]. Retrieved from https://www.bcrpa.bc.ca/media/34879/genderequity.pdf.

Carpenter, L. J., & Acosta, R. V. (n.d.). Title IX in a nutshell [online]. Retrieved from http://www.acostacarpenter.org/Title%20IX%20in%20a%20nutshell.pdf.

CUNY Newswire (n.d.). Queens College athletics program names baseball stadium after world-renowned scientist Dr. Charles Hennekens. Retrieved April 3, 2018, from http://www1.cuny.edu/mu/forum/2015/10/19/queens-college-athletics-program-names-baseball-stadium-after-world-renowned-scientist-dr-charles-hennekens/.

East Stroudsburg Warriors (2018). NCAA Division II compliance information for prospective and enrolled student-athletes, parents, boosters and others. Retrieved August 10, 2018, from https://esuwarriors.com/sports/2009/9/14/compliance.aspx.

Hatfield, L. M., Hatfield, L. C., & Drummond, J. L. (2009). The perceived role of senior women administrators in NCAA Division I institutions. *Sport Journal*, 12(4), 8. Retrieved from https://chaos.endicott.edu/cgi-bin/genauth/ecidbauth.cgi?url=http://search.ebscohost.com.proxy18.noblenet.org/login.aspx?direct=true&AuthType=ip&db=ccm&AN=105146143&site=ehost-live&scope=site.HuffPost (2014, May 2). Education department clarifies Title IX "Compliance reviews are not random" [online]. Retrieved from https://www.huffingtonpost.com/2014/05/02/education-department-compliance-reviews-title-ix_n_5254075.html.

Laney College Athletics (n.d.). Title IX statement. Retrieved from https://www.laneyathletics.com/title-ix-compliance/.

LaVoi, N. M. (2015). Why women matter in sport coaching. College of Education, Human Development [online]. Retrieved from https://cehdvision2020.umn.edu/blog/why-women-matter-in-sport-coaching/.

LaVoi, N. M., Becker, E., & Leberman, S. (2009). Mother–coach generated strategies for increasing female coaches in youth sport. http://www.cehd.umn.edu/tuckercenter/library/docs/research/Mother-Coach%20Generated%20Strategies.pdf.

LaVoi, N. M., & Leberman, S. (2015). A rationale for encouraging mothers to coach youth sport. *Canadian Journal for Women In Coaching*, 15(1), 1–4.

Lopiano, D. (n.d.). Q: Is there a methodology for "tiering" or "prioritizing" sports programs? Sports Management Resources [online]. Retrieved from https://www.sportsmanagementresources.com/library/q-there methodology-tiering-or-prioritizing-sports-programs.

Lopiano, D. (2013). *Athletic director's desk reference*. Champaign, IL: Human Kinetics.

Messner, M. A., & Bozada-Deas, S. (2009). Separating the men from the mothers: The making of adult sex segregation in youth sports. *Gender & Society*, 23, 49–71.

National Collegiate Athletics Association (NCAA) (n.d.). Gender equity and Title IX [online]. http://www.ncaa.org/about/resources/inclusion/women-gender-equity-and-title-ix.

National Collegiate Athletics Association (NCAA) (n.d.). Gender equity planning: Best practices. Retrieved from http://www.ncaa.org/sites/default/files/Final%2Bonline%2Bversion.pdf.

National College Athletics Association (NCAA) (n.d.). Inclusion's best practices [online]. Retrieved April 3, 2018, from https://www.ncaa.org/sites/default/files/InclusionsBestPractices.pdf.

National College Athletic Association (n.d.). NCAA emerging sports for women process guide [online]. Retrieved from http://www.ncaa.org/about/resources/inclusion/ncaa-emerging-sports-women-process-guide.

National College Athletic Association (NCAA) (n.d.). Senior woman administrators. Retrieved from http://www.ncaa.org/about/resources/inclusion/senior-woman-administrator.

National Collegiate Athletics Association (NCAA) (n.d.). Sport sponsorship, participation, and demographics search [online]. Retrieved from http://web1.ncaa.org/rgdSearch/exec/instSearch.

National Collegiate Athletic Association (NCAA) (2010). Gender equity in intercollegiate athletics [online]. Retrieved from http://www.ncaapublications.com/DownloadPublication.aspx?download=GEOM11.pdf.

National Women's Law Center (n.d.). The battle for gender equity in athletics in colleges and universities [online]. Retrieved from https://www.nwlc.org/wp-content/uploads/2015/08/2011_8_battle_in_college_athletics_final.pdf.

Office for Civil Rights (n.d.). Intercollegiate athletics policy: Three-part test—Part three [online]. U.S. Department of Education. Retrieved from https://www2.ed.gov/about/offices/list/ocr/docs/title9-qa-20100420.html.

Queens College Knights (2017). Queens College to honor women's basketball coach Lucille Kyvallos with court dedication. Retrieved from http://www.queensknights.com/general/2017-18/releases/20170922kugnap.

Ross, T. F. (2015, March 18). What gender inequality looks like in collegiate sports. The Atlantic [online]. Retrieved from https://www.theatlantic.com/education/archive/2015/03/what-gender-inequality-looks-like-in-collegiate-sports/387985/.

Southwest Minnesota State Athletics (n.d.). SMSU Athletics Department mission statement on gender equity. Retrieved from https://smsumustangs.com/sports/2012/10/16/AA_1016120210.aspx?id=568.

Stark, R. (n.d.). Where are the women? NCAA Champion Magazine. Retrieved April 3, 2018, from http://www.ncaa.org/static/champion/where-are-the-women/.

Staurowsky, E. J., & Weight, E. A. (2011). Title IX literacy: What coaches don't know and need to find out. Journal of Intercollegiate Sport, 4(2), 190–209.

Staurowsky, E. J., Zonder, E. J., & Riemer, B. A. (2017). So, what is Title IX? Assessing college athletes knowledge of the law. Women in Sport & Physical Activity Journal, 25(1), 30–42.

Tiell, B. S., Dixon, M. A., & Lin, Y.-C. (2012). Roles and tasks of the senior woman administrator in role congruity theory perspective: A longitudinal progress report. Journal of Issues in Intercollegiate Athletics, 5, 247–268. Retrieved from https://chaos.endicott.edu/cgi-bin/genauth/ecidbauth.cgi?url=http://search.ebscohost.com.proxy18.noblenet.org/login.aspx?direct=true&AuthType=ip&db=s3h&AN=89496631&site=ehost-live&scope=site.

Title 34 Education (n.d.). Retrieved from https://opi.mt.gov/Portals/182/Page%20Files/Title%20IX/Title%20IX%20Compliance%20Check%20List.pdf?ver=2017-08-25-093416-373.

Title IX. (n.d.). Retrieved April 03, 2018, from https://www.sadker.org/TitleIX.html.

University of Minnesota (n.d.). Women coaches research series and report card. Retrieved from http://www.cehd.umn.edu/tuckercenter/research/womencoaches.html.

U.S. Department of Education (n.d.). Equity in athletics data analysis. Retrieved from https://ope.ed.gov/athletics/#/.

U.S. Department of Education (2015, October 15). Title IX and sex discrimination. Retrieved August 10, 2018, from https://www2.ed.gov/about/offices/list/ocr/docs/tix_dis.html.

USLegal (n.d.). Title IX and other women's issues [online]. Retrieved from https://sportslaw.uslegal.com/title-ix-and-other-womens-issues/.

Vollman, A. (2016, February 15). Female athletic directors: A scarce but positive influence. Insight into Diversity [online]. Retrieved from www.insightintodiversity.com/female-athletic-directors-a-scarce-.

Whisenant, W. A. (2003). How women have fared as interscholastic athletic administrators since the passage of Title IX. Sex Roles, 49(3–4), 179–184.

Women's Sports Foundation (n.d.). Title IX and issues [online]. Retrieved from https://www.womenssportsfoundation.org/advocate/title-ix-issues/.

Women's Sports Foundation (n.d.). Beyond X's and O's. Retrieved from https://www.womenssportsfoundation.org/wp-content/uploads/2016/10/wsf_infographic_final.pdf.

Women's Sports Foundation. (2008). Show me the money: Title IX and booster clubs. Retrieved from http://www.womenssportsfoundation.org/Content/Articles/Issues/Title-IX/B/Booster-Clubs-and-TitleIX.aspx.

Zotos, C. (2006). Constructing a tiered sports program for college athletics [online]. Retrieved from https://www.sportsmanagementresources.com/library/q-there-methodology-tiering-or-prioritizing-sports-programs.

CHAPTER 11

Evaluation Tools

▶ Purpose and Definition of Performance Appraisals

One major component and core responsibility for effective management of athletic programs is the performance review of staff members. Personnel across the athletic settings from collegiate to youth sport are added to the staff to fulfill various positions. The obligations for paid staff may differ from those of volunteer staff, but the requirements to meet the agreed-on expectations are identical. The end result of the contributions of paid and unpaid staff toward the designated athletic settings is measured (on varying scales and levels) to ensure the core mission and goals of the sport entity are achieved.

Performance appraisals serve both the individual and the organization. They have a variety of functions:

at the individual level, performance appraisals (1) reinforce and sustain good performance and/or improve performance, (2) provide insights into career goals, (3) pinpoint areas of strength and weakness, and (4) suggest training needs. From the organization's perspective, performance appraisals also facilitate informed personnel decisions such as linking rewards (e.g., pay, promotions, etc.) to performance and determining training needs. (MacLean & Chelladurai, 1995, p. 195)

The performance-review process begins at the end of the hiring process when the stated job requirements are acknowledged and formally agreed on. It is those stated job standards and requirements that are transformed into measurable tasks or performance assessments. Simply stated, once the hiring process is complete, staff have daily responsibilities to achieve.

There are two components of monitoring performance levels for both paid and volunteer staff. First, athletic administrators conduct informal reviews through daily observation of task completion and follow-through on assigned duties. Because of the dynamic nature of the operations, at most athletic entities the staff typically works in close proximity with one another, allowing for supervisors (athletic administrators) to monitor performance benchmarks of the personnel. Through informal means—such as verbal instructions and feedback or email reminders to a staff member or a remark while walking through the department or on the fields—an athletic administrator can spark change in employee action. Informal methods can become embedded parts of the athletic administrator's routine to oversee staff within their daily operations versus a formal evaluation that may occur in a meeting. Examples of informal evaluation activities may also include simply walking around and being present in the physical space where staff members work to ascertain the pulse of the operations. These informal observations provide a current picture of the workplace environment. Informal observations allow athletic administrators to supervise how the staff operates in work-specific scenarios. Walking around the department, attending practices, or sitting in on small staff meetings provides athletic administrators with enriching and timely data to assess the overall strengths and weaknesses of staff members and the entire athletic department or program. Furthermore, the observable behaviors are data that eventually become talking points during the formal performance-evaluation process. The formal evaluation of staff varies by athletic setting. As an example, a youth soccer club employing part-time coaches may only have meetings once a year with the coaches; in contrast, a collegiate athletic department may require supervisors and staff to have written evaluations and meetings as part of the full evaluation process. All of these tools demonstrate that evaluating the performance levels of staff is a process that requires both time and planning to fully execute.

Athletic administrations use staff evaluation as the managerial function of control. The overall aim of control is to have everything in the organization running smoothly. Determining performance levels and motivating staff to change is one method of accomplishing that aim. Under the evaluation process, athletic administrators collect performance-related documentation about staff in the areas of excellence and areas needing improvement, all in an attempt to reach organizational or departmental goals.

⚽ FEEDBACK FROM THE FIELD

Bob Bigelow, former player in the National Basketball Association, conduct seminars and workshops for youth sport teams across the globe. The central focus and top priority for his work is to help create positive change for young athletes. Bigelow played for the University of Pennsylvania and then the Kansas City Kings, Boston Celtics, and San Diego Clippers. Since 1993, he has shared his work through more than 2,500 talks and clinics. For his efforts, he has been selected as one of the "100 Most Influential Sports Educators" by the Institute for International Sport at the University of Rhode Island.

Through his speaking engagements, Bigelow is focusing on educating adults involved with youth sport. From his perspective, the biggest gap in the youth sport setting is that most adults are not well versed in child development or physical education. As he explains, 98% of American adults do not have any background in these fields. The adults who get involved in youth sport "have played high school sports or watch professional games on television and that is where it has gone off the tracks." Bigelow often asks adults how many played high school basketball, and he goes on to confirm that they learned from their coach. He then goes on to ask how many took English as a subject in high school and all hands go up. The next question he poses is, "How many of you would feel comfortable teaching English?" Naturally, he explains, no hands are raised, proving the point that most youth coaches feel competent and qualified enough to coach because they played high school sports. Bigelow tries to point out the lack of training and experience most youth coaches have in educating young athletes. Instead, through television, most adults mirror their coaching from professional sport coaches who are working with the best athletes in the world. Bigelow argues, "we already start with the awareness of education gap. But so many people think you played high school basketball or college basketball and that makes them automatically qualified to coach youth sports."

The evaluation of youth sport coaches may not be as advanced or formal as we see in the high school or collegiate sport settings. However, as Bigelow points out, the true indicator of a coach's effectiveness is "no matter how good or bad you think your team is" the true measure is "do all the kids who want to play come back next year?" Full team retention of young athletes, according to Bigelow, proves the youth coach has created a positive environment for all his or her players. In Bigelow's estimation, "there are much better youth coaches coaching winless teams, for one major reason—they are playing all the kids," adding "the worst kids are getting more time and are getting better." On the flip side, Bigelow explains "there are coaches with a 10–2 record but the coaches are not playing all of the kids and that is not a good youth coach." Allowing all the athletes to play, according to Bigelow, is "the first thing about being a youth coach" and "to recognize the number one reason kids play sports is to play." Unfortunately, when evaluating the full scope of youth sports, Bigelow suggest the problem with adults organizing these programs is that most adults are involved in sport "to win." According to Bigelow, "we automatically run into that clash, and the problem with organized sports is a certain percentage of adults believe winning is too important." He suggests these coaches "don't know any better" because "they are conditioned that when you win it is a good day, when you lose it is a bad day." Bigelow asserts that children would still enjoy playing, regardless of the win–loss record of their teams. He adds the children "would play every minute on a losing team" rather than have limited playing time on a winning team. As Bigelow stresses, "these players signed up to play" the sport. Bigelow laments that "until you get adults understanding that kids want to play and adults want to win, we are always going to have troubles in this field."

In terms of evaluating coaches in the youth sport setting, the efforts focus on the education of adults. As Bigelow explained, adults are conditioned to win rather than teach the game when they are coaching. Unfortunately, he says, a culture exists within youth sport organizations that, unless changed, will persist in generating the same win versus teaching attitude among youth coaches. Most youth organizations cite several resources on their websites promoting player development and coach education. Nonetheless, Bigelow thinks the challenge is that the messaging on the websites does not always match the actions of the coaches. In essence, Bigelow describes the youth sport setting as having "the fox guarding the hen house." This is the major challenge for youth sport administrators when it comes to evaluating programs, teams, and coaches. The youth sport boards are "living organizations," but the "culture is the way we do things here and if they are not doing things too well, that is the culture you absorb."

(continues)

When youth sport administrators evaluate the coaches and programs, it is important to determine what the young players gain or acquire from their participation. As Bigelow stresses, children need to get far more from their participation in sport than scoreboard results. As Bigelow describes, he has lost many games but played everyone, even though he admits that he would have won many more games if he just played the best players. However, he measured his coaching effectiveness on the full participation of his athletes in games. The outcome, according to Bigelow, of any successful sport season is that all the players want to come back next season. As Bigelow emphasizes "the primary duty as coach is to make sure everyone wants to play next year, not just the kids you favor with playing time. If you don't think that is the mission as a youth coach then go coach with a high school team." Bigelow would rather those individuals in youth sport who focus on just the wins coach instead in a setting where winning is the priority over "player development."

Following up on player-development models, Bigelow contends "some coaches and some sports are better than others at player development." Using soccer as an example, Bigelow asserts that "there is so much action in the game that is not controllable by coaches," adding that "coaches cannot be micromanagers in soccer." But in a sport like "basketball (due to more stoppages in play), it is more controllable, which leads to more micromanagers." At the very minimum in terms of coach performance, youth sport organizations should support coaches in practice development for them to have a "sense of what to do with an hour-long practice." Today, Bigelow asserts it is common for "local youth organizations and clubs to promote training and development for coaches." Bigelow credits "online resources and training"; however, the end result even after all of the coach education, in his opinion, must be that "coaches are interested enough to play all kids and to be able to understand how to talk to a kid so they can improve."

In the youth sport setting, most coaches are volunteers or parents or both. To effectively monitor the performance levels of coaches, some youth associations have designated observers attend games and provide feedback. Bigelow offers that "every youth sport board should have someone who is well respected and has been around a while who goes out and watch[es] the coaches coach." The aim of this process is to evaluate the coach's strengths and weaknesses and give the youth board authority to "pull out the coach in question and say this is what we need to improve upon or you cannot coach anymore." To achieve positive results from coaches and retention of players, athletic administrators must "explain to the volunteers what a good coach is and that is the problem, too many forgo the softer stuff to win a lot of games. I tell people to watch the five kids on the sidelines who are not playing and what is their body language." As Bigelow continually stressed, coaches should be evaluated on how many players want to return to play in the next season, not on the number of wins accumulated.

▶ Collection of Job Performance Information

Formal evaluations contain a variety of documentation, depending on the athletic setting. Typically, at the collegiate and high school levels there are established procedural components for performance appraisals designated by the institution. Notably, the evaluation procedures established by institutions may or may not be specific to athletic staff. The criteria for evaluation, when not specific to athletics but created more for classroom educators, may not give the athletic administrator the tools needed to fully examine the productivity and performance objectives of their staff. The evaluation tools render the data and forthcoming results used for performance evaluations. Most important from an athletic administrator's perspective is to allow staff through the evaluation process to demonstrate their effectiveness in their designated positions or roles. Without an effective measurement tool, the performance-appraisal results will not paint the full or true picture of staff performance levels. In these cases, athletic administrators may incorporate supplemental methods to specifically evaluate the scope of work conducted by staff members. In the evaluation arm of athletic administration, staff members are assessed on their productivity directly related to the tasks they are required to accomplish as outlined in employment contracts or position descriptions. A major thrust of effective staff evaluation is to openly communicate the criteria for evaluation and the time frames for the review of milestone achievement within the workplace.

An essential component of the evaluation process includes feedback. Typically, staff members complete a self-evaluation that includes a rating scale or written summary of their productivity over a designated time frame. In conjunction with the self-evaluation, the athletic administrator would, in turn, complete a performance evaluation. To provide a data-based and collaborative performance assessment, both instruments (from the staff and from the athletic administrator or supervisor) would be compared and then used to provide enriching feedback to the staff member. As DeNisi and Pritchard (2006) indicate, "the ultimate goal of performance appraisal should be to provide information that will best enable managers to improve employee performance" (p. 255). The process is most effective when it is collaborative in nature, giving both the supervisor and the staff member opportunities to freely discuss performance achievement and goals.

The underlying objective of performance appraisals is to evaluate a staff member's strengths and weaknesses while creating open lines of communication in the chain of command, which serves to motivate staff to reach and exceed performance standards. Through self-evaluation tools, the athletic administrator can tap into staff members' reflections regarding their level of productivity. The athletic administrator can also use evaluations to provide a complete assessment coupled with constructive feedback to allow a staff member who may be struggling to make plans and take initiative for improvement.

A variety of performance criteria are offered by the Business of Small College Athletics that can help provide objective evaluation feedback. The athletic administrator or supervisor can be specific in terms of what needs to improve to realize change and to implement a process for change. Many people assume performance appraisals point only to the negative, but it is important for the supervisor to highlight the positive contributions of the staff member. Performance reviews operate to give honest feedback to initiate change. Creating an agreed-on plan of change allows supervisors to help promote improvement. As with any process, it is important for the supervisor and staff to follow up on the evaluation and plans for improvement. Finally, effective athletic administrators will ask staff members to evaluate their leadership and department offerings (Business of Small College Athletics, n.d.).

Measuring the performance of athletic coaches at the collegiate level presents many challenges for athletic administrators. Cunningham and Dixon (2003) propose that intercollegiate coaches be evaluated on "six dimensions of coaching performance," including "team athletic outcomes, team academic outcomes, ethical behavior, fiscal responsibility, recruit quality, and athlete satisfaction" (p. 189). Coaching at the collegiate level requires not only the management and execution of practices and games but also the effective administration of program budgeting, recruitment of new talent, and education of student-athletes. A coach may be well versed at practice and game day operations, but he or she may lack the requisite competency to effectively recruit, hence the rationale for incorporating multiple evaluation criteria.

Clearly, the evaluation process is challenging as Moltz indicates "coaches at Division I programs in the National Collegiate Athletic Association are judged not only by their players' performance on the field but also by the players' performance in the classroom" (Moltz, 2011). According to Turner and Chelladurai (2005), coaches are essential human resources because "they recruit the athletes (i.e., mobilize the human resources), attempt to develop them into excellent athletes (i.e., motivate and train them), and mold them into effective teams (i.e., coordinate their efforts and activities)" (p. 194). At the program-wide level, Bryant (2015) incorporates the following questions into the evaluation process:

1. What is the quality of the experience our student-athletes are receiving? Does it match our mission, vision, and value statements?
2. How are our coaches performing?
3. Is the department running efficiently and effectively?
4. How are our facilities?
5. How are our department finances?

Similarly, at the volunteer level it is essential for athletic administrators to uncover what motivates individuals to give their time to an athletic entity. As Bang and Ross (2009) suggest, "event managers must understand what motivates people to volunteer for special sporting events, and how to help each volunteer achieve a sense of personal satisfaction through the identification of various motivations" (p. 70). Volunteer satisfaction leads to enhanced performance levels. Athletic administrators who can identify motives of volunteers can use those intentions to harness productivity. Moreover, especially with volunteers, retention is crucial in order to hold onto the same individuals each season or year who have a core understanding of the athletic entity or event. Through this review process, athletic administrators can uncover methods to increase the volunteer's connection to the athletic entity or event. In the end, these types of activities can translate into volunteers feeling a "sense of camaraderie" with a possible outcome of increasing staff retention (Pauline, 2011). A by-product of the evaluation process is learning how to satisfy the needs of the staff, whether paid or volunteer, to retain individuals and work with motivated staff.

At the youth sport setting, performance evaluations are incorporated into the operations of the athletic entity even with the heavy reliance on volunteer coaches and volunteer athletic administrators. The Positive Coaching Alliance (PCA) (www. https://www .positivecoach.org/) provides member sport associations with a list of postseason evaluation tools for coaches. The first piece of the PCA evaluation process is to allow coaches to reflect on the season by responding to the following three questions based on the work of Garcia: (1) How did you redefine winner, (2) how did you honor the game this season, and (3) how did you fill the emotional tanks of your athletes? Garcia adds, "[T]hese questions get coaches to think about their performance in terms of positively influencing athletes, and helps them de-focus on the outcome on the scoreboard from their season (Positive Coaching Alliance, 2017). Richards (2012) studied the confidence of youth sport coaches in teaching the sport, highlighting that athletic administrators can "expect

⚽ FEEDBACK FROM THE FIELD

Brad Rose is the activities director at Valley High School in West Des Moines, Iowa. In this role, he manages the athletic and fine arts programs. He has 15 years of experience as a baseball coach (named the Iowa Coach of the Year twice), and for the 2016–17 year he was the Iowa State Athletic Director of the Year and in 2017, Central District Athletic Director of the Year; he has also coached basketball, track, and football. The National Interscholastic Athletic Administrators Association has honored Rose for his leadership in 2011 with the State Award of Merit and in 2014 with the Jim Teff Achievement Award for Excellence.

© ArrowStudio, LLC/Shutterstock.

Rose has a wealth of experience managing athletic department staff; his accolades and achievements in athletic administration have made a lasting impression on many elite associations and his department. His perspective on the topic of staff management and evaluation is revealing, and coupled with his accolades it provides an insightful understanding on the importance of performance reviews in athletic administration. Fundamentally, the core purpose of staff performance evaluations at the high school level, according to Rose, is "to support the coaches as good teachers through the best instructional practices." To be on the same page, athletic administrators must give weight to the importance of communicating to the entire staff the purpose of performance evaluations. To gain the full benefits of growing and learning from performance evaluations, the athletic administrator conveys not only the purpose of the assessments but also the connection to the mission of the department and ultimately, the institution.

Rose incorporates a few levels of evaluation planning to disseminate and collect useful details about overall staff performance levels. First, Rose schedules a preconference meeting with all coaching staff to review the process. Second, individual pre-evaluation meetings are arranged with a coach to discuss goals and areas of improvement. The last step is the actual evaluation and scheduling of multiple walk-through sessions, which all lead to a final meeting with a teacher or coach on areas of strength and goals for improvement.

In Rose's department, the evaluation process is not based on one tool or one meeting but on various performance assessment points and multiple opportunities for the coach or teacher and athletic administrator to interact and determine strengths and weaknesses. For example, Rose incorporates multiple emails or conversations within the process, but "most important is developing trust with the teacher [or] coach so any correction or suggestions are taken as ways to improve instruction and ultimately, the team improves."

Rose applies the values within the mission statement to connect the work of the staff and goals of the athletic entity to the evaluation process. "We just have a school mission statement and academics will always lead our decisions. We do have some athletic guidelines, and they do lead us in some ways. We do not cut, and we want all kids to have a great experience, not just the varsity."

Performance evaluation is a managerial tool activated to move staff in the same direction, motivate individual effort, and collect valuable information to assist staff in achieving program-wide initiatives. However, challenges exist, especially within a systematic process like performance assessment. As Rose indicates, some common challenges for athletic administrators and supervisors regarding staff evaluation center on time commitment, communication to staff, and developing trust from staff. Rose revealed another challenging task: finding ways to help staff understand how to teach and develop relationships with students so they trust coaches along with team building.

(continues)

FEEDBACK FROM THE FIELD   *(continued)*

Rose incorporates several tools to review staff productivity. One is Ewalk, which is a walk-through program and is tied to Applitrack, which his school system uses for evaluations. As Rose points out, both tools enhance the evaluation process because "when you can't seem to set up a meeting, it will go to the staff member by email and it can happen right away." Rose stresses that within the evaluation process, "timely responses and discussions [are] important when providing feedback." He also emphasized "our goal is not to 'catch' someone doing something wrong but to improve instruction." Circling back to the purpose of evaluations, athletic administrators aim to provide feedback to prompt staff to elevate their performance to deliver the best programming possible.

When asked to provide future athletic administrators advice on best practices for conducting staff evaluations, Rose urges them to write their plans down. He also underscores that it is important to "make the coach a part of the evaluation." As an example, coaches should provide input to the process regarding what they want you to watch, how do they want to improve, and areas of emphasis." Rose counsels future athletic administrators to "follow up." The evaluation process needs to come full circle for changes to occur within performance levels and ultimately, with productivity. As Rose indicates, "when you have those difficult evaluations, write down your goals for the meeting, then stick to the plan." When providing feedback to staff, athletic administrators are encouraged to share "improvement ideas and plans" with staff throughout the evaluation process.

that they (coaches) be entirely committed to their role as coach, but it is not appropriate to assume this ensures they are qualified to coach youth." Richards expresses that coach education programs play a vital role in the abilities of coaches to teach requisite skills. One aspect of youth sport administration that is linked to the performance evaluation of volunteer coaches is to measure and promote attendance at educational workshops and to assess credentials obtained through coaching education programs.

Evaluation Tools

A variety of methods can be used to evaluate staff performance. Each setting under the athletic administrator allows a myriad of tools to help determine overall staff effectiveness. Willenbrock (2015) created a rubric by which his coaches might understand the elements to be evaluated.

Four Coaching Essentials: Evaluation Criteria	
Team Cohesion	**Creating a Culture**
Clear direction	Culture of motivation
Rules and policies	
Explicit authority	Culture of respect
Stability	Culture of responsibility
Appropriate traditions	
Communication	Culture of safety
Player Development	**Role Modeling**
Progressive teaching	Sportsmanship
Fulfilling potential	Ethics
Support systems	Cultural competency
Feedback	Authenticity
Rewards	Positive nature
	Working with assistants

Willenbrock (2015)

⚽ FEEDBACK FROM THE FIELD

Dr. William R. Watson is the director of activities and community education for the Urbandale Community School District in Urbandale, Iowa. He has been recognized for his excellence in athletic administration and has been named the Robert D. and Billie Ray Center's Character Champion and the Athletic Director of the Year by the Iowa Girls Coaches Association, and he has been nominated for the National Athletic Director of the Year with the National High School Athletic Coaches Association.

From Watson's perspective, the purpose of staff evaluations at any level is improvement. A central aspect of performance appraisals is to give staff members feedback to allow them to grow from the evaluation process. Watson adds that improvement "includes not only individual improvement but also program improvement." As staff elevate their contributions and performance levels, the entire department or program, in turn, reaps the benefits of that progress.

Watson stresses that all of his communication to the staff about evaluation is focused on improvement. Although performance evaluations may be "on the individual coach, it provides an opportunity to reflect back on how that individual coach impacts the entire program (team) and how improvement can be made in that regard." To deliver a cohesive evaluation process, Watson incorporates a step-by-step plan for implementation. First, he gives a "notice of evaluation provided both in writing and in a presentation to all coaches at the beginning of the school year." Annually, an impressive number of more than 100 staff coaches are evaluated. Next, Watson requires head coaches to set individual goals each year. Once goals are set, the process incorporates the observation of coaches. Watson explains that part of the evaluation process is conducting informal observations at practice and games throughout the year. He attends 95% of all varsity games and "utilizes road games to evaluate more than games at home because there are far less duties on the road." After the observation step, each coach completes a self-evaluation two weeks before the end of the season. This self-evaluation is submitted to Watson ahead of the evaluation meeting. The evaluation form has been integrated into the evaluation process and is approved by the board of directors with the focal area on improvement. After Watson reviews the coach's self-evaluation, he will then add his perspective on the evaluation form. A formal evaluation conference commences once the documentation is completed and submitted by the coach to Watson. At the evaluation conference, both parties review the evaluation instrument and discuss a plan for improvement. As Watson notes, "the conversation and plan that is in place after the meeting is far more important" as these formulated plans serve to "help coaches and programs improve."

When asked what connection the mission statement of the athletic entity has with the staff evaluation process, Watson shares "our mission statement is at the focus of everything we do." Watson further explained that "one area within our evaluation is focused on relationships with athletes, and in this section, we tie directly into the mission of the District. This is perhaps the most important area we address through the evaluation process."

Even with the seamless evaluation process that Watson has created and follows, challenges still present themselves. The time factor is the primary challenge in the evaluation process. As Watson details, the challenge is to find "time to observe practice, time to be in the locker room after a game, time to talk with students, time to talk with coaches, and time to talk with parents."

The athletic department comprises assistant coaches who are evaluated along with head coaches. Watson says he manages "all assistant coaches and all head coaches the same in terms of my expectations for their performance and evaluation." However, he does spend more time and go into greater detail with head coaches annually, but the full coaching staff is observed and evaluated.

The evaluation tools used by Watson to evaluate the staff are developed around the district-wide mission and vision and also specific criteria for athletic department staff. Watson shared that the "Evaluation Instrument" was developed and then approved by the board of directors, the "Self-Evaluation Form" was developed after the evaluation form, and the "Goal Setting Form" for coaches is not a requirement but

(continues)

⚽ FEEDBACK FROM THE FIELD   *(continued)*

certainly something that is available for their use. For observations, there is an "Observation Form," but Watson uses "note cards and then files those with each individual coach in their file."

Watson provided six points for future athletic administrators managing staff evaluations. First, he highlights that the process feeds into "important conversations and almost every employee wants to get better," adding that "those that do not probably should look for another line of work." Second, the evaluation process

> takes time and is something that should be done annually because the nature of team development is that it changes and it changes annually. In the math classroom, while your students might drive some of the direction you go, the basics are going to stay the same. In team sports, the actions and reactions of all involved impact the direction of the program.

Third, by and large the process prompts athletic administrators to "build a system." Watson explains athletic administrators "set deadlines and listen to coaches both in terms of what works and what does not work for observation and evaluation setting." Fourth, athletic administrators must "be visible; it not only demonstrates support but also demonstrates outwardly that coaches are held accountable for their actions." Fifth, Watson encourages athletic administrators to be honest. Watson notes that "too many administrators are friends with their coaches; this clouds the line between the two." As Watson communicates, athletic administrators must "ensure that you maintain those boundaries so that you can be honest and supportive and still demand excellence." Sixth, speak to students and collect their feedback. From Watson's expertise in staff evaluations, he considers students to be "very honest and forthright with good and bad as it relates to coaches." In summary, Watson incorporates several approved forms to streamline the evaluation process so it delivers consistent feedback focused on overall improvement of individual staff and the entire department offerings.

💬 FEATURED INTERVIEW: COLLEGE ATHLETICS

Ali Cantor has been the athletic director at NCAA Division III Simmons College in Boston, Massachusetts, an all-women's institution since 1995. Her tenure at Simmons College reflects a body of work that includes highly competitive teams winning multiple conference championships, participation in NCAA tournaments, regional rankings, and individual student-athlete recognition. Notably, Simmons College received three Commissioner Cups as the top women's athletics program in the Great Northeast Athletic Conference.

Most recently, Simmons College's athletic department opened the Art Daly Athletics Complex, which includes a venue for soccer and lacrosse, tennis courts, a field hockey field, and a softball field. Simmons was the recipient of the Priscilla McKee Award from the Simmons Alumnae/i Association at the college's Service Awards Reception in 2016 for exceptional service to the Simmons College community. Kantor is highly active on and off campus as an instructor for the Simmons College First Year Experience Seminar, former assistant commissioner of the Great Northeast Athletic Conference, chair for the New England NCAA Field Hockey Championships committee from 1997 to 1999, member of the NCAA Field Hockey Championships Committee from 1998 to 2000, chair of the Great Northeast Athletic Conference Swimming and Diving Championships from 2000 to the present, member of the Simmons College Strategic Planning Committee in 2007, and member of the Grants Allocation Committee for Women's Sports Foundation and GoGirlGo in 2008.

Kantor has been able to build a staff of young professionals over the years to assist with developing competitive and successful athletic programs. A major component of effective staff management stems from a leader's ability to motivate individuals, provide feedback to prompt enhanced performance, and deliberate communication. Kantor uses performance evaluations to systematically motivate and drive staff to reach agreed-on goals. To that end, Kantor incorporates annual merit-based performance reviews for her staff. The process of performance evaluation starts the summer before the academic year begins. As Cantor explains, the staff will conduct a self-assessment, and she will use a performance review to assess athletic staff performance levels. She articulated that the performance-evaluation process incorporates extensive meetings totaling three hours per staff member, which includes one hour to review the self-evaluation. A collaborative session follows for one hour in which Cantor and the staff member formulate goals in tandem for the upcoming year. In the third hour, her formal evaluation is reviewed and discussed.

One important component of the process, as Cantor explains, incorporates a reflective review on the process—in essence, a discussion on whether goals were met for the prior year. Simmons College allocates a percentage of funding toward merit awards. Cantor will use performance evaluations to determine if staff members met their goals; from the review and subsequent approval from her supervisor, the athletic staff can be awarded money for their goal achievements. Cantor says, "I really use the merit as a motivator, I take it seriously and I think it is the motivator. I have given zero or I have given as much as I can." There are several performance measures used in the evaluation process for her athletic staff, including: goals; job competence; goal attainment; commitment to the brand, strategies, and goals of the college; organizational skills; communication skills; results, orientation, and problem solving; and, finally, management leadership. The performance measures used within the athletic department are consistent across the entire college for all departments. Cantor only employs two part-time coaches, but merit considerations may apply to those individuals as well at the discretion of the college. The merit pool of funds is generated by a designated percentage of the total salary figures at the college. Each department head will be allocated a certain dollar amount and then Cantor decides the percentage to be distributed to her individual staff members. Cantor explains she can give 0 percent or as much as 5 percent to 6 percent of the total figure, and she finds the process to be highly "effective in setting goals and meeting goals."

Within the athletic department performance review Cantor incorporates three evaluation components. One focuses on recruitment with four general areas: (1) geography, with the aim to "try to recruit from outside of New England"; (2) academic rank of prospective student-athletes as they would be eligible for the "highest merit awards"; (3) African, Latino or Hispanic, Asian, and Native American students and "diversity recruitment"; and (4) "overall prospects you want to deposit" once admitted to the college. Cantor adds that the win–loss records and advancement to postseason play are also part of the evaluation process. Cantor sets goals with the coach with the intent to "strive for all the sports to win the championship or at the very minimum to make the championship tournament." For teams that need more attention and may still be developing, she "formally documents within performance goals the win–loss records, and for those teams it can definitely be about recruiting, and it is about roster size as part of our goals." Simmons College teams will use the NCAA roster size limit for all teams, but Cantor encourages coaches to go over that number "in certain sports that can carry more." For example, swimming has 31 athletes and cross-country and volleyball have more than the limit. Cantor acknowledges "we do not have junior varsity sports or club sports, but I encourage the programs to keep higher rosters and establish a few practice players because it is hard to get your team at practice every night."

The role of the athletic department staff includes coaching and administrative duties. Currently, only one person within the athletic department does not coach because of an administrative role, which includes managing the new athletic complex and transportation.

(continues)

When prompted to discuss how she handles the effective coach and poor administrator combination or vice versa, she pointed out that "I don't have much of a problem since I have been here so long, I hand pick people, we pay them well, we have a lot of longevity." Cantor has been with Simmons College for several decades, and she has made a concerted effort to rearrange administrative duties "based on career goals and what they (the staff) want to be and what they want to do; I try to keep them stimulated and challenged." During the interview process, she discusses the rotation of duties because it certainly serves as a motivator to rotate through the administrative positions.

Part of the performance evaluation is to connect with staff to enhance workplace satisfaction and staff retention. In Cantor's case, all but two coaches have been with her for less than 10 years. She attributes that retention to her leadership styles, describing herself as a collaborator. "I make the final decision but I am big on getting buy in, collaborative thinking and collaborative problem solving." Cantor credits the hiring of "really good people and giving them a lot of latitude" in their positions. However, Cantor also has "high expectations, and I am not afraid to tell them when they don't meet those expectations." Cantor advocates for her staff through merit awards, but she believes staff satisfaction starts with the hiring process, "giving them new challenges," and stems from the support received from the college president.

While Cantor supervises and evaluates her staff, the vice president of enrollment management, in turn, evaluates her. The reporting structure changed in 2015 from reporting to the dean of students to now reporting to the vice president of enrollment management. Cantor proposed this shift because the vice president has a direct line to the college president, and partners athletics with "admission counselors with communication for recruiting being more coordinated."

The performance evaluation is not limited to documentation, and Cantor spends a great deal of time assessing and working collaboratively with staff through department meetings every other week to 30-minute meetings with her direct reports. She spends a great deal of "face time" with the staff and is a proponent of "face-to-face meetings." Cantor expects her staff to attend the department meetings, given these sessions are only twice a month and allow the department to stay informed. Cantor wants the staff to be "advocates for themselves" through these meetings. In some cases, Cantor has to "coach the coach," and in those scenarios Cantor admits that an employee may not have been a good hire if she is constantly instructing him or her on how to perform a role. Ultimately, she mentors and gives "a lot of independence to her staff with the expectation to keep me informed and run it by me."

In addition to meetings and formal evaluations, Cantor incorporates team-building elements into the athletic department. Cantor "praises" staff in front of groups for jobs well done while also giving constructive feedback privately. She acknowledges her staff in campus-wide events and credits individuals for specific accomplishments. She believes that all of these gestures and expressions of appreciation for staff performance make up an effective form of management and department leadership. Every summer, she organizes off-campus outings for the staff to prepare for the upcoming year and to connect as a team. One excursion was to a therapeutic riding center on a farm in western Massachusetts as a retreat. The center incorporates leadership development, work with horses in the corral for group problem solving, and goat yoga. During Christmas, she also takes the staff to lunch or orders a special lunch for the group to enjoy.

Another large aspect of Cantor's position is to solicit staff feedback. Cantor sees her role as a "facilitator and leader of the department" aiding in supporting and advocating for resources. Cantor is focused "on keeping them informed," noting that "I am transparent on keeping them informed, I think that is motivating. They are my team, we set our goals, I hold them accountable,

I recruit good employees, every now and again I don't have a good one and I am not afraid to move them out."

To paint a complete picture of staff performance levels, Cantor uses student evaluations. From Cantor's standpoint, student evaluations are a helpful tool, especially when information needs to be collected on a poorly performing coach to support her performance review. Student-athletes complete the evaluations two weeks before their seasons end. Through this tool, student-athletes evaluate training staff, athletic administrators, head coaches, and assistant coaches. The student evaluations provide insight on the operations of the department and an added layer of documentation and information for the complete performance-review process.

Performance evaluations provide supervisors with an opportunity to share with employees the areas requiring improvement while also highlighting positive achievements. Cantor urges future athletic administrators to "treat others the way you want to be treated," and she doesn't "expect anything from my staff that I do not expect for myself. If I am not working hard I cannot expect them to work hard." Cantor believes her management and leadership styles stem from her coaching philosophy: "I set the bar high, and I work hard and lead by example. And I treat them with respect, and I give them a lot of latitude. It goes a long way. I am not a micromanager, but I have expectations." In the end, Cantor encourages athletic administrators to lead by example.

Questions for Discussion

1. Performance evaluations are a method used by athletic administrators to provide feedback to direct staff. After reading the steps, Cantor incorporates such feedback into her staff evaluations. What impressed you the most about her commitment to the process?
2. In the classroom, students are continually evaluated on their work and progress in the course. Cantor uses her department meetings to get the pulse of the department and monitor the productivity of her staff. Based on your classroom experiences and the work of Cantor, create a list of performance-evaluation milestones you would incorporate into your athletic department, recreation department, or youth sport organization.
3. One objective of performance appraisals is to determine if an individual is a good fit for the department or organization. Cantor has used performance evaluations as one tool to dismiss an individual from his or her role. What are your thoughts on the process of dismissal, and how many pieces of evidence would you require as the athletic administrator?

Good Ware from flaticon.com

MANAGERIAL APPLICATIONS

Youth Sport: Volunteer Evaluation

Relying on volunteer coaches is the standard for youth sport associations. In your local town are many individuals who apply to coach their children's sports teams each season. To streamline coach selection for teams, the board has created an application process. The application asks about previous coaching experience, previous playing experience, and coaching credentials from coaching education programs or attendance at coaching workshops. Once the coaches are selected, your local sport association does not have a formal evaluation process. As a member of the board, you recognize this is a missing aspect to the overall management and delivery of an effective sport experience to participants.

(continues)

MANAGERIAL APPLICATIONS

(continued)

Questions to Consider

1. What type of evaluation process would you present for board approval? What performance standards would you highlight in this process, and how do these standards link to the mission of youth sport?
2. How do you think the current coaches would react to a new process that evaluates their performance levels? What are some mentoring programs you can adopt to facilitate a seamless transition to the evaluation process?
3. Because communication is critical when changes are implemented, what would your messaging (email or social media post) read to explain the new process, and how will it ultimately promote a more educational sporting experience for participants?

MANAGERIAL APPLICATIONS

High School Sport: Coach Evaluation

As the newly hired athletic director at XYZ High School you have researched performance appraisals specific to coaches over the course of the last year. Currently, your school requires that department supervisors use the same evaluation for all staff. You recognize the need for a designated and consistent form across the campus; however, the performance standards in those forms are not consistent with athletic department tasks or coaching tasks.

© Sergey Kuznecov/Shutterstock.

Questions to Consider

1. As the designated figurehead in athletics, you acknowledge coaches are educators, but you disagree that a standardized evaluation form appropriately captures the productivity of your staff. What resources can you present to the school committee to identify the need for a specific evaluation form for athletic department staff? What overlapping criteria can classroom educators and coaches share that can remain in the evaluation process?
2. The current evaluation form does not meet the objectives of fully evaluating the performance of coaches, and you have several part-time coaches to evaluate. Would the evaluation of part-time head coaches differ from that of full-time head coaches who may teach at the high school? What criteria would change or remain the same when evaluating part-time versus full-time staff members at the high school level?
3. Because you have only been employed at the school for one year and the current evaluation process has been used for decades, what are examples of athletic-specific performance appraisals you would share with the school committee to initiate change in this area?

⚾ DECISION-MAKING CHALLENGE

Case Study: High School Sports

As the athletic director at Calhoun High School you employ more than 60 coaches (head and assistant levels) to operate your broad-based sport programs. This season you spent considerable time informally evaluating coaches by walking through practices and listening to the coaching points, observing game-day preparation, and watching games and training sessions. The boys' basketball coach has exhibited behavior that is inconsistent with the school's mission. As the athletic administrator, you have documented these negative behaviors to present to the coach during the formal evaluation process. You also have collected evaluations from the players. The results from the players were overwhelmingly positive for the coach. In addition, this coach has a history of high winning percentages and capturing league titles over the last five years. How do you handle a beloved coach with high winning percentages who does not meet the expectations of your institution? How would you use the results of the evaluation process to prompt changes in the behavior of this coach?

Wrap-Up

End-of-Chapter Activities
College Athletics

1. Your institution currently lacks a policy for formal evaluation of head and assistant coaches. As the athletic administrator, you recognize that once the hiring process commences and contracts are signed, the failure to include performance evaluations cannot be added to agreed-on aspects of the position. Annually, coaches are required to be rehired and thus sign new contracts. Craft a new statement to be entered in the coaching contracts that enables annual performance evaluations.

2. In college athletics, the expectation to win often overshadows all other elements of coaching effectiveness. Craft an evaluation form you would use at the college level, including criteria that mesh with the work of Cunningham and Dixon (2003), who propose that intercollegiate coaches be evaluated on "six dimensions of coaching performance."

Club Sport

Your elite soccer club highlights the credentials of your coaches, who are required to obtain coaching licensures and attend at least two coaching workshops or seminars each year. As the club director, you consistently promote these achievements on social media and the club website. The issue is that your coaching staff is not effectively transferring the knowledge obtained from these professional development opportunities to their practice preparations or game-day tactics. How can you assist in bridging this gap, especially when coaches tend to stick to their routines and to what has worked best in the past? What evaluation methods can you employ to link the professional development to positive changes in the delivery of the knowledge to the players?

End-of-Chapter Questions

1. In your own words, describe the role performance appraisal plays in the management of an effective athletic department.
2. Research performance-evaluation processes and forms for college, high school, youth, and club sport. Explain the similarities and differences in program-evaluation methods for college, high school, youth, and club sport.
3. Review athletic-specific performance evaluations and craft four separate policies, including procedures for managing staff evaluations for college, high school, youth, and club sport.
4. Describe the purpose of staff evaluations and their connection to the mission of the program for college, high school, youth, and club sport. In your response, provide a rationale for the differences or similarities within each setting.
5. Based on the content in this chapter, how would you define informal evaluation methods, and which of these informal methods would you feel most comfortable implementing in your athletic program? Do you envision differences in the ways informal evaluations are conducted for athletic administrators at the college, high school, youth, and club sport settings?
6. Athletic administrators must balance numerous managerial tasks on a daily basis. In a given year, depict the time line for staff evaluations. Indicate all of the tools, forms, meetings, and other methods you would incorporate into the full evaluation process of your staff over a given year.
7. In your estimation, what are the benefits of employing informal evaluation methods into the performance appraisal process?
8. What criteria would you want to see in staff members' self-evaluations of their own performances? How would you use the self-evaluation in your overall analysis of the performance achievements of staff members?
9. What is the importance of using a variety of criteria (versus just winning) when evaluating the performance and effectiveness of coaches in college, high school, youth, and club sport? Be sure to identify any differences within each setting in your response.
10. What role does job satisfaction play in performance achievement? What methods would you use to enhance job satisfaction in each setting (college, high school, youth, and club sport)?
11. Create a list of criteria you would implement as athletic supervisor to evaluate assistant coaches at the high school and collegiate levels.
12. Create a list of criteria you would implement as the athletic supervisor to evaluate volunteer coaches at the youth sport setting.

References

Bang, H., & Ross, S. D. (2009). Volunteer motivation and satisfaction. *Journal of Venue and Event Management*, 1(2), 61–77.

Bryant, K. (2015, January 29). How am I doing? Athletic Management [online]. Retrieved April 21, 2018, from http://athleticmanagement.com/2012/03/31/how_am_i_doing/index.php.

Business of Small College Athletics (n.d.). Evaluating performance. Retrieved April 17, 2018, from https://www.smallcollegeathletics.com/evaluating-performance.

Cunningham, G. B., & Dixon, M. A. (2003). New perspectives concerning performance appraisals of intercollegiate coaches. *Quest*, 55(2), 177–192.

DeNisi, A. S., & Pritchard, R. D. (2006). Performance appraisal, performance management and improving individual performance: A motivational framework. *Management & Organization Review*, 2(2), 253–277. doi:10.1111/j.1740-8784.2006.00042.x.

MacClean, J. C., & Chelladurai, P. (1995). Dimensions of coaching performance: Development of a scale. *Journal of Sport Management*, 9, 194–207.

Mascoutah School District Number 19 (n.d.) Coaching Evaluation. Retrieved April 21, 2018, from https://www.ncacoach.org/uploads/JohnsonAD2.pdf.

Moltz, D. (2011, May 16). Evaluating community college coaches. Inside Higher Ed [online]. Retrieved April 21, 2018, from https://www.insidehighered.com /news/2011/05/16/oklahoma_community_college _evaluates_coaches_based_on_academic_success _of_athletes.

Pauline, G. (2011). Volunteer satisfaction and intent to remain: An analysis of contributing factors among professional golf event volunteers. *College Research Center*, 26. https://surface.syr.edu/researchcenter/26.

Positive Coaching Alliance. (n.d.). New: The grand prize. Retrieved April 21, 2018, from https://www .positivecoach.org/

Positive Coaching Alliance (2017, November 08). How to conduct post-season coach evaluations. Retrieved April 21, 2018, from https://community.sportsengine .com/news_article/show/854159.

Richards, M. (2012). Coaching education and a survey of youth sport coaches' perceptions of their coaching efficacy. *Inquiry Journal*, 8. http://scholars.unh.edu /inquiry_2012/8.

Turner, B. A., & Chelladurai, P. (2005). Organizational and occupational commitment, intention to leave, and perceived performance of intercollegiate coaches. *Journal of Sport Management*, 19(2), 193.

University of Nebraska at Omaha (n.d.). Head coach intercollegiate athletics positions: Performance evaluation for Office/Service, Managerial, Executive/ Administrator Employees. Retrieved April 21, 2018, from https://www.unomaha.edu/.../performance -evaluation-form-athletics-headcoach.docx.

VAHA (n.d.). Coaching evaluation survey [online]. Retrieved April 21, 2018, from http://www .viroquathunder.org/coaches_eval.html.

Willenbrock, P. (2015, January 29). Defining success. Athletic Management [online]. Retrieved April 21, 2018, from http://athleticmanagement.com/2012/08/18/defining _success/index.php.

CHAPTER 12

Technology in Athletic Administration

▶ Technology in Athletics

With the advent of social media, the realm of athletic communication has exploded since 2010. Within the college, high school, youth, and club sport settings, the responsibility for handling communication for the athletic programs may rest with one or several designated athletic administrators or staff. The variety of technology platforms and customized approaches to reach targeted groups makes the arena of athletic communication dynamic, engaging, and vibrant. Full use of technology tools offers athletic entities across all settings the opportunity to strengthen their promotional and marketing arms through creative endeavors.

The channels by which athletic information is communicated spans platforms from websites to social media posts to Twitter to stories to video streaming. The options to promote and market athletic events and share the activities within programs across the college, high school, youth, and club sport settings are limitless and often cost-effective to administer. Although athletic departments typically have good intentions while incorporating social media into their communication plans, as Clavio and Walsh (2013) indicate, administrators may need to learn more about fan engagement within these platforms. Clavio and Walsh suggest that those in athletic communication "vary their social media strategies" (p. 277). Operating a communication plan on multiple social media platforms such as Twitter, Instagram, SnapChat, and Facebook, among others, has a great potential to reach diverse groups of fans tailored to their social media preferences. In essence, there is not a one-size-fits-all approach to marketing with social media; instead, an effective campaign uses several social media channels.

Vaughn (2016) highlights the importance of athletic administrators grasping the changes in expectations from parents and fans when it comes to consuming information about their athlete or team. To meet the heightened demands of the fan base, athletic administrators must embrace new technological offerings to reach targeted groups—in essence, changing their strategic communication process. Addressing the evolution of the athletic administrator role, Vaughn details "expectations have changed. Instantaneous information is at everyone's fingertips through real-time social media, and mobile technology has changed how people communicate" (Vaughn, 2016).

Technology and Recruiting

Advances in technology not only elevate the marketing and promotional aspects of athletic programming but also enhance opportunities to engage potential student-athletes and participants in programming across all sport settings. At the collegiate level, student-athletes interact with athletic coaches through the completion of online questionnaires on the athletic department website. From the collection of demographic information entered by the prospective student-athlete, coaches, admission counselors, and athletic administrators connect with these individuals to market the institution.

In the high school setting, technology can help assess interest in particular programs through online questionnaires and allow participants to register for tryouts and upcoming sporting events.

Within college athletics, virtual reality exemplifies a shift in the operations of athletic recruitment. Virtual reality simulates viewing the landscape from the comforts of mobile devices and computers. Using virtual reality, college-level athletic administrators can now show prospective recruits the visual layout of fields and locker rooms before they visit a campus (Heitner, 2016). Recruits get a glimpse from the comfort of their own devices of the college campus, athletic venues, and resident halls without stepping foot on the campus. Virtual reality is another recruitment tool to reach a demographic of tech-savvy student-athletes.

 FEEDBACK FROM THE FIELD

Susan Byrne is associate director of athletics for marketing and sales at Harvard University's Department of Athletics. Byrne started at Harvard University in 2008 and is responsible for marketing 42 varsity sports. Her responsibilities encompass managing the areas of marketing, promotions, and sales, including ticket, merchandise, concession, and corporate sales. Before joining Harvard University athletics, she was the vice president of advertising and promotions for the Boston Bruins of the National Hockey League (NHL). Her tenure with the NHL team spanned

(continues)

19 years as she held positions from public relations assistant to director of marketing and community relations, as well as serving as chief marketing officer and community relations liaison to the NHL. Byrne launched her career at the New England Sports Network. Byrne also has served on the board of directors for several nonprofit organizations, including the Boston Bruins Charity Foundation, the Bay State Games, and MetroLacrosse. She is a member of the National Association of Collegiate Marketing Administrators, the National Sports Marketing Network, and the Sport Marketing Association.

Byrne's expertise spans the spectrum from professional to collegiate sport. She asserts that the biggest difference within the professional sport setting is that revenue is the top priority. Working for a Division I nonprofit entity such as Harvard University, the emphasis is on integrating academics and athletics: "[I]t is a different mindset; revenue is important but there are also a variety of other priorities that revolve around the student-athletes." When professionals are in a field as dynamic as communication and technology, the tools used are continually evolving. As Byrne relayed, since 2008 there has been quite a change in all types of communication tools in both the professional sport and intercollegiate athletic settings. According to Byrne, "the emphasis on innovation in higher education is significant. An area of growth over the years throughout the sports industry has been the use of analytics." Today, "decision making," as Byrne explains, "is based on data and analytics, where in the past, it wasn't as readily available and not utilized as much as it is now." In fact, as Byrne points out, many sport-related career opportunities exist under the analytics framework. *Analytics* can be defined as collecting information and then interpreting that data to make decisions.

For Byrne, analytics is "important in my day to day job." She and her department staff review websites, social media, and ticket data. When the athletics website was designed (through the collaboration of key stakeholders), the goal was to have a user-friendly site where information could easily be accessed. The website for Byrne "became a great tool for us to provide information, but people needed to know it was there." To drive traffic to the website, a branding strategy was created for gocrimson.com and then tested by reviewing analytics on how many people accessed the website and where they clicked most often. It became essential data for potential sponsors. As technology advanced, Byrne focused on "outbound communication by developing a database so we could sell tickets and disseminate information through email marketing campaigns. In order to better serve our consumers, we made a switch from inbound communication to outbound communication in order to get our messaging out effectively and increase our sales efforts." Byrne admits that "the website is still a valued communication tool, but it is not as valuable as it was 10 years ago." Mobile applications are common tools in communication and marketing now, with Byrne acknowledging that "10 years ago we were not even thinking about an app." Along with the injection of mobile applications, live-streaming events are now common in intercollegiate athletics. The Ivy League created the Ivy League Digital Network, which is a paid subscription to view live-streamed sporting events. With the Ivy network, a multitude of games from the 42 sport offerings can be streamed and consumed by families, alumni, and fans. The Ivy network was an initiative generated from the conference commissioner's office. The Ivy network, in Byrne's perspective, is "one example of how technology has changed our ability to market all of our sports."

The management of the Harvard athletic department's social media is a shared responsibility of the marketing and communication offices. From a marketing standpoint, social media focuses on building engagement, according to Byrne. A few examples of social media engagement are compelling photos that get "shared" and off-the-field storytelling. Because the realm of social media is so vast, Byrne and her staff discuss strategies to "build engagement, realizing that different generations are using different platforms." Byrne examines the data for generational usage for social media platforms, including Twitter, Facebook, Instagram, and Snapchat. She explains that Facebook may have an older age demographic than Instagram or SnapChat, "so we try to take that into consideration as we try to market through the social media platforms." Byrne's department still considers email marketing an effective sales tactic. Instead of emailing the entire database, though, communication can be targeted to smaller lists based on purchasing patterns. Byrne explains: "The future of ticketing revolves around identity, and the more we can learn about who is buying our tickets, the better we can engage, connect, and accommodate our customers."

To avoid a buildup of too many social media postings or outbound emails, the staff communicates often. Along with an assistant director are several interns who handle social media and marketing for the department. To enhance marketing support to all 42 sports and increase communication and collaboration between the marketing department and varsity teams, Byrne created a chief marketing officer (CMO) initiative whereby designated student-athletes take on the promotion of their team events and contests. Byrne explains that the CMOs

> become an extension of our staff because the student-athletes really know their team and their sport the best and they can be a significant help in marketing, especially to their peers. The chief marketing officer may suggest a popular giveaway such as burritos or design a T-shirt for a featured game to help increase student attendance. Some are featured in videos in a fun and authentic style, letting other students know about a giveaway or special event. Based on feedback from the CMOs, most of their peers are active Instagram users. Therefore, in an effort to promote their sports, the videos are posted to Instagram "stories." This is a feature that allows users to post videos or photos that disappear after 24 hours. Back to analytics and segments of the market, according to the data showing our interactions and reach, Instagram stories are helping engagement and reaching our target audience. The chief marketing officer initiative has provided a unique leadership opportunity for our student-athletes and has helped us in our marketing efforts, especially to students.

One challenge for Byrne—even running a nonprofit entity—is prioritizing revenue goals among 42 marketed sports. The revenue targets her department must reach are primarily in "ticket sales, sponsorship sales, merchandise sales, and concession sales." These goals are an important priority, but as Byrne points out, "the nature of sports is dynamic and at any given time something unplanned will surface." As an example, weather can have a significant effect on football ticket revenue. " If it rains for the first two of five home games, we need to make up lost revenue in the last three games to meet our revenue goal."

Staying current on a college campus like Harvard University—where "being innovative and using technology are promoted"—is encouraging for Byrne. In fact, Byrne participates in professional development courses for all staff offered by the university. At the end of the year, staff performance reviews include use of technology and innovation. In essence, the aim is to share implementation of new technology within performance evaluation. As Byrne notes, it can be "challenging to stay current, but it is critical for the success of my department." Byrne describes how over the years new hires have brought "a certain expertise" to marketing. Many people may believe that younger hires are more adept at social media because they have been using it longer, but as Byrne explains that "utilizing technology to communicate with friends or for personal branding isn't necessarily the same as utilizing it to market an athletic department." In her office, the staff present a "combination of being technically savvy and also strategically smart." The focus of Byrne's position is "to be able to use technology in a strategic and effective manner to meet our own priorities and goals, including those of the entire athletic department. We are always tying what we do back to our overall mission of educating through athletics and building community and pride in Harvard."

One major shift in technology is the use and prioritization of video content for both communication and marketing. Byrne showcases the impact of video content, noting that in the past each game had a written recap on the website, whereas today every team has a highlight video after the game on both the website and social media pages. The swing in content focuses on the fact that individuals today with access to mobile devices do not have to be video experts or editors to capture video footage.

(continues)

FEEDBACK FROM THE FIELD *(continued)*

Byrne aims to "be fair and balanced" when marketing the vast sport programs at Harvard University. In the end, Byrne tries "to do whatever we can to make the student-athlete experience the best one possible" for all participants. To offset the challenges of a small staff, embracing the chief marketing officer initiative has helped Byrne's department have a greater marketing presence. To stay current with the latest tools, she allows her staff to explore new applications or platforms that may fit with the menu of marketing techniques for the department. Even when contacted or solicited by new technology companies, Byrne delegates the review of these tools to her staff that may benefit the department. An example of this process is an application called SuperFanU, a student reward app. Students get points for attending games and within the app there is a leaderboard and prize store. Byrne shares that the student rewards application has "been helpful for us to engage with students and increase attendance by utilizing a technology that is familiar to students." She further notes that "when you have more students at an event you typically have a lot of energy and enthusiasm, so we encourage student attendance, and through the student rewards app we have been able to use technology in an effective way." To provide guidance to future athletic administrators, she concludes that "you have to be receptive to testing new ideas and technologies, and, most importantly, you must evaluate what's really helping you achieve your goals."

▶ Social Media and Athletics

The shift from traditional means of communication to social media communication has transformed the delivery of information and, therefore, consumption of information to athletic stakeholders—participants, consumers, and fans. At the collegiate level, the majority of athletic departments host their own websites rather than use the general sites for their institutions. As an example, the Endicott College athletics website is now ecgulls.com ("Gulls" is the college mascot) where a decade ago the department was a link off the institutional website Endicott.edu. The decision to move away from the institutional website is threefold: more content control by the designated athletic administrator, increased capacity to host video streaming and other high-end multimedia content, and branding opportunities for athletics.

Negative Aspects of Social Media

Although social media presents athletic administrators with opportunities to connect with fans, consumers, families, and participants through a wide array of technology platforms, this emergent tool does have a downside. Social media can be inappropriately used by coaches, athletic administrators, fans, athletes, and families. The comfort level in using social media in personal and daily occurrences enables individuals to freely express their thoughts and share images. Unfortunately, sometimes these social media posts have negative outcomes. As DiVeronica (2017) found,

> any student–athlete or not—can cause or get in trouble with one bad tweet, picture, or online conversation. Teens complaining about playing time, cyberbullying someone or taunting an opponent have forced parents, coaches and administrators to be more vigilant about online activity and interactions because you never know who is watching their online activity.

Even though athletic administrators organize presentations to explain the negative effects of social media, incidents continue to repeat themselves, leaving athletic administrators with no choice but to create policies to govern social media use in athletics. Williams (2017), as a seasoned athletic administrator, suggests "our society has enjoyed tremendous benefits from the technological development of the Internet, Facebook, Twitter, Instagram, blogging, and other types of electronic communication. However, as with so many great inventions, problems have developed. Many of these issues have raised concerns at our schools."

 FEEDBACK FROM THE FIELD

College Athletics

Stefanie Howlett has worked for more than five years in sports information, social media, and athletic communication at several institutions from Division I to Division III in the Boston, Massachusetts, area. She is currently employed at an elite preparatory school as the digital marketing manager. In her role as a sports information director (SID) at a Division I school, she handled the promotion of six athletics teams, serving as the primary contact between the media and student-athletes and coaches. Within this position, Howlett traveled with the women's basketball team for the entire season as well as postseason for the other five sports. Howlett organized press conferences, coordinated interviews, and was the game-day point of contact for television, print, and online media. She wrote and edited extensive "game notes" that play-by-play and color commentators used during broadcasts for information on the team. In addition, Howlett was responsible for all website updates and game-day statistics, among many other duties as assigned, which Howlett jokes will be her autobiography title someday: "Other Duties as Assigned." Later in this position her role included the integration of social media. Howlett revealed her department was "one of the earliest adopters at the collegiate athletics level to embrace social media as we saw the benefits of getting scores, statistics, and interesting game notes out immediately."

Howlett earned previous experiences at an Atlantic Coast Conference school, completing a year-long postgraduate internship. After leaving collegiate athletics full-time, she maintained

> a foot in the door by working at athletic events as the game-day statistician at the Division I, II, and III levels, which has given me a unique perspective on the differing challenges that athletic communications professionals face depending on which division, the structure of the college [or] university, and the resources the department has for marketing and public relations purposes.

As Howlett explains, at almost every school in the NCAA, SIDs use a program called "StatCrew" to input statistics. This software generates box scores, season statistics, and career statistics. Howlett compares the programming capabilities of StatCrew to "dial-up computers from the late 80s and early 90s." Although Howlett admits it

> may seem archaic, it gets the job done, you input each play by code and it generates everything from field goal percentage to points in the paint, fast break points, and much more. A side effect of learning a DOS-based system is that I have a good understanding of how computers, servers, and coding works.

Other technology tools that Howlett used in her role are content management systems for websites, Adobe Creative Suite (Photoshop, InDesign), and Final Cut Pro (or other similar video-editing software). Photoshop and InDesign were primarily used to create marketing materials such as posters, roster sheets, and game notes, along with media guides (printed and online). As the industry has evolved, Howlett added, "video editing has also become a function of an SID's job" plus "being able to put together highlights quickly is a new and important piece of the job."

Howlett has been in athletics for more than a decade, and the biggest evolution she experienced in the industry is the "visual component"; in much the same way that the newspaper industry has evolved, athletic communications has evolved with it. There's an appetite for strong visuals and video (especially in the last few years). When Howlett first entered the industry, she was focused on writing long recaps for the website and media; however, "now it is much more focused on writing about the

(continues)

FEEDBACK FROM THE FIELD *(continued)*

highlights of the game, along with photo galleries, highlight reels, and postgame video interviews with student-athletes and coaches." She adds, "I think it's a more sophisticated operation; websites look sleeker and communications are more strategic."

Howlett points to resources such as College Sports Information Directors of America (CoSIDA) and other professional organizations where SIDs can share ideas, especially in a setting within athletic administration that is rapidly changing. She has also found that the SID community is "closely knit . . . especially ones in the same conference, creating a feeling as though they are on the same team." This close-knit community, Howlett notes, "understand the challenges and work ethic it takes and are always willing to help each other out, whether that means bouncing ideas off each other or providing extra game-day assistance if needed."

Using and monitoring social media is a large part of sports information, and Howlett has experienced social media's growth firsthand. Early on, she was using just Facebook and Twitter, but later she added Instagram and Snapchat. "You have to have a presence," she says. "Wherever your resources allow. . . . you have to have a strategy for each platform." SIDs, in the earliest stages of social media, were "just handling the nuts and bolts" in the form of scores, play-by-play, and monitoring records that were broken. However, Howlett quickly saw the need to have a "voice." Although some schools are focused on brand management, there has been a shift with social media when student-athletes are offered a personal presence on this platform.

When prompted to provide recommendations to students completing athletic administration coursework on the impact of technology and working with designated staff who deal with technology for the department (SIDS, game day staff, social media), Howlett said, "being an SID is not just about being a good writer and storyteller, although that is important. Be as well rounded as possible. Take graphic design classes, learn video editing, and take computer science classes." She encourages individuals to have an overall understanding of all of those areas so they can have an advantage over other candidates applying for the same position. Howlett also urges students to "always be willing to accept constructive feedback because it's there to improve you (much like a coach gives feedback to his/her student-athletes.) And, after you've edited a piece . . . edit again." Howlett concludes,

> it's a hard industry; you put in long hours and you often live out of a suitcase for months on end, but it's all worth it if you love the work and love sports. Even after all these years, I still have an idealistic view of what sports can teach us. There were times I felt burnt out, but the joy and adrenaline of seeing your work come to life made it worth it.

The highlighted benefit of social media rests with the opportunities for the athletic entity to enhance promotion of programs along with branding of the department, school, association, or club. Cooper (2010, p. 26) listed the strategies and technologies that NCAA athletic departments can insert into their communication plan about the **TABLE 12.1** on page 271.

Following the work of Cooper, athletic administrators aim to build brand equity value and social network sites, texting, and video-sharing sites to meet that critical communication objective. Undeniably, administrators are increasingly challenged to stay current with communication and promotional tools, but the fiscal support to fund these initiatives is lacking. To promote programming, to communicate information, or to share athletic stories, athletic administrators turn to the Internet simply because the platform is a simple and inexpensive tool to use for communication (Doran, Cooper, & Mihalik, 2015).

Notwithstanding the popularity of social media components in athletics, many aspects of these technology tools require oversight by athletic administrators. As Sanderson (2011) cautions, "because social media can be accessed from any computer or mobile

TABLE 12.1 Survey Items Related to Electronic Branding Strategies

Survey Section	Question
Athletic Department Website	*The following website technologies are critical when attempting to build brand image with consumers on your athletic website:* Audio Broadcasts Blogs Interactive Chat (Coaches/Players) Interactive Fan Polls Message Boards Newsletters Podcasts Video Broadcasts
Independent Media Platforms	*The following independent communication mediums are critical when attempting to build your brand image with consumers:* Blogs Message Boards Podcasts Social Network Sites Text Messaging Twittering Video Sharing Sites
Role of Technology in Future	*Social network sites will become a primary database marketing tool to reach younger fan segments.* *Video sharing sites will become a primary marketing tool for organisations looking to build their brand image with consumers.* *Database text messaging will play a much larger role when promoting events to consumers* *Younger generations will continue to grow more reliant on the Internet and technology in the future.*

Note. Six-Point Likert scale used to rank items (1=strongly disagree; 6=strongly agree).
Cooper (2010, p. 26).

device with an Internet connection, sports organizations have little control in filtering athletes' and sports figures' public commentary" (p. 492). On the positive side, a tool like Instagram allows athletic administrators "to share all aspects of the athletic department, especially in the areas of marketing, media relations, and recruiting" (Bowles, 2016, p. 236). Bowles investigated trends in the use of the photo-sharing media platform Instagram within the NCAA Division I Southeastern Conference. Emerging from the full-year content analysis of Instagram activity within this conference were such themes as action, behind-the-scenes events, fans, landmark events, promotions, and success. Furthermore, Bowles linked each theme with a definition of usage to assist athletic administrators in understanding the value of each category see Table below Bowles.

TABLE 12.2 Trends in Photo-Sharing Platforms	
Theme	**Definition**
Action	Post Shares on-field or in-game images. This includes instances of sideline, practice, and pre-game imagery. Videos that include replays or game action were also added to this theme.
Behind the Scenes	Post includes off-the-field, exclusive images of events not generally seen by the average spectator. i.e., practices, photo shoots, interviews, players traveling, and locker room images.
Fans	Post is focused on fans and spectators. i.e., photos sent by fans, pictures from around the world, fan groups, and athletes or coaches with fans.
Landmark	Post is focused on facilities or campus artifacts. i.e., stadiums, arenas, historical images, recognizable campus locations, and alumni.
Promotional	Post promotes or markets both events and student-athletes. i.e., giveaways, fan contents, and informational event previews.
Success	Post shares success or victories by teams and student-athletes. i.e., award announcements, broken records, victory announcements and images of trophies.

Bowles (2016, p. 231).

Sport-Automation Platforms

Youth sport organizers rely on websites and sport-automation platforms to help announce sport programming and to register participants. In recent years, sport automation for youth, recreation, and club sport has exploded. Many companies offer youth sport athletic administrators a variety of options from website design, website hosting, and registration to fundraising in some packages. Increasing numbers of youth sport administrators are balancing larger enrollment with the need to satisfy stakeholders' current technological use habits. Beginning around 2000, most youth sport organizations used paper-and-pen mail-in registration in which parents or guardians would also mail a check. Today, the process is streamlined, integrated, and completely online, containing point-of-registration demographic information

(age, gender, address, contact details), program-specific information (level of play, experience), a health questionnaire (upload or proof of current physical examinations and immunization records), parent or guardian information (volunteer opportunities to coach, raise funds, act as team liaison), and collection of payments. The competition to solicit the business of youth athletic administrators is high, making decisions to select an appropriate interface extremely daunting. Many sport-automation companies continually market to youth sport organizers to land their business because the pool of potential consumers, given sport-participation rates, is extremely high. Sport-automation encompasses placing all of the management of athletic programs under one simplified and user-friendly interface. Sport-automation companies provide a convenience feature to

sport organizers who are continually search-
ing for online components to simplify not only
the registration process but also scheduling
and tracking player availability across seasons.

The continued growth of sport participation coupled with the desire to manage
and simplify participants' sport experiences
leaves little doubt the sport-automation
setting is blossoming into a big business.
Sport-automation offerings are evolving to
match the technological needs of youth sport
entities with consumer needs to easily access
information through a variety of platforms
and register their athletes for sport programming. Evidence of this growth potential is
revealed through one application, TeamSnap,
which is "used by almost 15 million players,
parents, and coaches and has been adopted
by 1 million teams" (Gillham, 2017, p. 365).
In essence, "mobile and digital technology
have become commonplace in every industry as businesses strive to modernize time-
consuming processes that were previously
done on paper" (Sports Board, 2016).

 FEEDBACK FROM THE FIELD

Kristie Cavanaugh is an account manager at Champion's Choice (Wilmington, Massachusetts), a
leading athletic outfitter for sport entities across the college, high school, youth, and club sport
settings. Since 1999, the company has consistently improved its operations, transitioning from a
small entity to one of the largest athletic distributors in the country through deliberate planning
within its customer service model along with incorporating technology to best serve its customers.
The mission of Champion's Choice reads: "We will support you with the commitment you expect
from every member of your team. Our mission is simple. Customer service takes precedence in every
aspect of our business."

Several workplace attributes set Champion's Choice apart from its competitors. The company fully
executes many functions within its own building, allowing professional teams to handle embroidery,
screening, and uniform numbering. Another major factor in the company's growth is the ability
of athletic administrators to receive the lowest pricing because of the "institutional buying power,"
whereby Champion's Choice can tap all of the "partner institutions' annual purchases," passing along
discounts and distributing "promotional stipends" (the more you spend, the more benefits to the
athletic entities) to their clientele. In terms of technology and information security and protection,
Champion's Choice offers its consumers "brand and identity protection and uniformity across their
athletic program." In addition, Champion's Choice is committed to gender equity. As the company
promises. "You won't find female athletes wearing down-sized men's gear; Adidas products suit the
unique fit and performance requirements of male and female athletes." Over the years, Champion's
Choice has evolved to become the "largest volume team provider in New England for Adidas, Reebok,
and Champion." In 2011, the company opened a new building to include an office, warehouse, and
manufacturing facility. In 2009, the company became an Adidas "3-Stripe Dealer" and two years later,
the largest Adidas team dealer nationally.

As Crampton explains, Champion's Choice has helped athletic administrators in both operations
and team outfitting. The company works with all NCAA levels, including New England preparatory
schools, which have extremely large budgets to support their athletic needs. Crampton homed in
on what Division I schools received from the bigger brands in the past, and her company made
concerted efforts to provide the same opportunities to the Division II and III schools. In Crampton's
opinion, brand identity is extremely important for athletic administrators to consider. She details that
"nowadays, athletes have the ability to order things online and order things from random websites

(continues)

FEEDBACK FROM THE FIELD *(continued)*

© Steven Bade/Alamy Stock Photo.

where the colors may be off; the brand identity as far as your marks is not necessarily what you would want it to be because athletes have access to that technology." Champion's Choice considers itself the central point in the athletic outfitting process where "we are being protective of your brands and your marks and schools have different levels of protectiveness over their marks." From the institutions Champion's Choice works with, "some athletic departments have a one-page document that gives a general sense of their logo, and some have 65-page PDF files to protect their marks." The role of Champion's Choice is "to guide and help the school to develop a style guide if they don't have one, even at the high school setting." Once Crampton and the staff at Champion's Choice learn more about the needs of the department they will "steer you toward a specific brand so when you get off the bus everyone knows you are XYZ." The highlighted services that Champion's Choice provide to athletic entities are "brand identity and protection." As previously stated, gender equality is woven into the operations of Champion's Choice. Unfortunately, as Crampton details, many top brands still do not manufacture female options for athletes. Champion's Choice has advocated for female athletes and has even "driven some products to vendors" when the only option provided was a men's extra small versus a women's cut. According to Crampton, "we are fortunate to have that buying power so we can drive products from customer requests all the way up to the actual process."

Interestingly, Crampton defines Champion's Choice as "acting as a virtual equipment manager" and a "virtual employee of the school." Champion's Choice handles the quality control for uniforms and practice gear, sorting of equipment, distribution (each individual gets the order in their own bag versus all of the pieces in large boxes) and budget planning which, as Crampton points out, aids the fiscal manager when they are dealing with larger expenditures like transportation and facility rentals.

Another tier to the services provided by Champion's Choice is engaging the parents and fans in the process of ordering team gear. Champion's Choice creates password-protected websites streamlined to protect the brand identity of the athletic entity so only the athletes and/or designated individuals have access to purchasing the official team gear. Password-protected websites are offered for fan sites and alumni sites "where it acts as a fundraising portal that acts as a virtual extension of the athletic department." The athletic administrator just sends off the link to the website while Champion's Choice handles "payment collection, sorting, shipping to people's homes" and in turn, "the department gets a credit to their account or a check to their program so it is a nice, easy, tangible fundraiser where they are not taking any risks on goods."

Champion's Choice "evolved so quickly, and we just caught on" to the changes in the athletic space "before similar companies." A change in the process for Champion's Choice is the elimination of individually meeting with coaches and teams. Instead, Champion's Choice deals with "the purchasing department, business department, or the athletic director so it is the actual decision maker" with the information in one meeting versus multiple meetings with each coach.

In the youth sport setting, business is more challenging because the company is dealing with volunteers who are parents. Most of these volunteers do not have years of experience with the program because their children typically age out of these youth associations, which also "may not necessarily have the resources in terms of a legal department or finance department." At the start, Champion's Choice had experiences in which youth sport groups were left with unsold but unpaid for goods. Today, Champion's Choice has "safeguards in place" to assist youth sport associations, typically because multiple people are involved in the ordering process and it is a volunteer role. The volunteers are "dealing with late sign-ups who need a uniform," "collection of checks," "dropping off items at the homes of individuals," and "entering data into Excel spreadsheets." Crampton and Champion's Choice handle all of those areas, and "we make the process easier." "Champion's Choice provides a link, then it is sent out to the group with a specific order date, and then you get a box with everyone's name on it." Champion's Choice makes the entire ordering process user-friendly. In addition, the company has security procedures in place for online payments.

When asked about strategies she would give to the president of a youth club, Crampton indicated she "would make sure you are working with someone who understands your target market. We are the largest Adidas dealer in the country; that doesn't mean that every program can afford an Adidas product." To accommodate her clients, Crampton may suggest a branded Adidas jersey and then a generic sock and generic short. Champion's Choice embeds discount codes for scholarship athletes. In some cases, athletic administrators are dealing with scholarship players, payment plans, and athletes with financial hardships. To extend discounts to these parties, Champion's Choice provides discount codes for use on the ordering website. As Crampton stresses, this is "important because you want to keep sport accessible for kids considering the cost to play these days."

Champion's Choice also works closely with booster clubs, creating websites, providing products, directing them with fundraising trends, and presenting a variety of artwork to the groups. In essence, Crampton describes Champion's Choice as a "department of the school that is off-site handling any questions the parents have on orders directed towards us." In some cases, Crampton details, "coaches may go rogue and order funky colors, but it stops here because we are the filter through the administration in making sure the brand is protected."

When anticipating the future of the space technology and sports outfitting will inhabit, Crampton sees quite a shift in the education and backgrounds of the athletic administrators making the decisions. More than ever, Crampton works with athletic administrators who hold degrees in either sport management or athletic administration. In Crampton's experience, this has affected social media by allowing more athletic administrators to tweet about uniforms and logos more than ever before. Because of social media, parents are also more involved, and fans are monitoring scores and are more aware of logos and uniforms, "which is not something they would know unless they were at the game." Crampton indicates "social media is driving athletics in terms of parents, in terms of student performance and how they are being monitored, apparel trends because athletes will show me an item, and in terms of a recruitment tool."

Champion's Choice is a company typically ahead of the competition in the athletic outfitter space. National conglomerates with national buying power are purchasing many smaller-sized companies, but unlike Champion's Choice they don't have a sound customer service process. Crampton revealed many schools break contracts with the competition because of poor customer service. From Crampton's perspective, the next stage of growth in this part of the athletic administration industry is "within technology, the enhancement of security with online ordering, and the impact of 3-D printing in footwear."

▶ Athletic Scheduling and Facilities

With the expansion of new or renovated facilities paired with increased facility rentals by outside groups, athletic administrators across the college, high school, youth, and club sport settings are finding much-needed assistance in facility-scheduling technology. Within college and high school athletic departments, tracking student use of weight rooms and athletic performance centers supports not only the planning process for hours of operations but also reinforces the need to spend (or not spend, depending on usage) within these areas. Tracking software and applications can serve to collect much-needed data to the athletic administrators. Athletic administrators can use that data to determine high or low usage times and change staff schedules accordingly. The data can also demonstrate a need to add more equipment or even more hours to the venue to meet participants' demands. Scheduling software may also be integrated into other online platforms to serve as a calendar for parents and participants to easily view and download to their mobile devices. Scheduling software solves administrative challenges associated with placing teams and programs in available spaces, collecting rental fees, and preventing double bookings for space. Within athletic entities, coaches and staff members can easily view open times to schedule their own programs with ease.

▶ Athletic Administration Technology Tools

In the domain of sport officiating technology tools, companies such as ArbiterSports (https://www.arbitersports.com/) centralize the process of allocating referees and officials to athletic contests. For athletic conferences, an assignor places officials to work games. The assignor is typically a current or former sport official employed by specific leagues. Assignors use online platforms to match officials with athletic contests based on their availability. Online software such as ArbiterSports plays a critical role in athletic management; in fact, "sports leagues and associations make nearly 15 million assignments to more than 400,000 officials every year using ArbiterSports technology" (n.d.).

 FEEDBACK FROM THE FIELD

College Athletics

Rob Palardy is the assistant athletic director of strategic communications at Endicott College in Beverly, Massachusetts. Before holding his current position at Endicott College, he was the sports information director for five years. In his current role, he supervises athletic communications, oversees intramurals, and coordinates outreach for the athletic department. As SID, Palardy managed to promote 700 student-athletes, handling regional and national media exposure for the athletic department, content creation and management of the department online through its website and a variety of social media platforms, and the administration of game-day tasks, including statistics and pre- and postgame outreach. Palardy has been instrumental in the redesign at least four times at Endicott College and Lesley University (Boston). In addition, he has a wealth of expertise and knowledge using website-management companies, including PrestoSports and SIDEARM, and HTML coding for web editing. Palardy is active in CoSIDA and the Eastern College Athletic Conference Sports Information Directors Association.

As Palardy explains, "the sports information industry over the past decade has dramatically shifted away from the traditional methods of communication into a more modern, digitally driven environment so as to keep with the tendencies and behaviors of today's sports consumer." The evolution of sports information has moved from SIDs writing long-form articles and using "traditional technologies like the telephone, electronic mail, and fax machines." "With the advent of social media," Palardy says,

> and the need for all sport entities—high schools, all levels of collegiate sports, professional organizations and leagues, and the growth of online media coverage—to bring their game day experience directly to their followers via mobile devices, sports information professionals have been asked to evolve their approach to not only communicating but also connecting with their supporters.

© Rido/Shutterstock.

The largest takeaway from the evolution of sports information is the simple fact that "technology is everything; what technology you are using and how you are implementing it across a variety of platforms in an integrated fashion." For Palardy,

> integration enhances efficiency for sports information workers who are asked to not only continue the traditional tasks of being a statistician and journalist for teams or organizations but are now required to be social media experts, graphic designers, video editors, website user experience and maintenance professionals, and spokespersons for the entities they represent.

In essence, since 2008, not only have the tools of communication changed in dynamic fashion but also, so has "the skill set needed to be successful in the sports information field."

Palardy puts to use a variety of technology tools within his role, including the web, social media, and graphic- and video-editing software. As Palardy notes, for the web, "the majority of institutions at the NCAA level use web providers like PrestoSports or Sidearm Sports to give their collegiate athletic brands an online presence." These web providers give athletic administrators platforms that are customizable in terms of design, look, and feel.

Another aspect to the web platform at Endicott College is the use of a coded integrated system that allows the institution's website to communicate instantaneously with a college opponent. The integrated platform allows for sharing of game scores, statistics, recaps, video, and audio links, all communicated throughout the web provider's network. The integrated platform provides instant updates with a live statistics feed, a video webcast, and score updates in real time for a game between two institutions. The importance of this feature is that the information is then shared immediately with all potential followers, spanning current students and their families, prospective

(continues)

students and their families, alumni, faculty and staff, supporters, and external media outlets for both institutions.

Palardy notes that most NCAA Division III institutions have social media presences across the four major platforms: Facebook, Twitter, Instagram, and YouTube. Palardy adds that some institutions have gone a step further by including Snapchat, but he explained the updated "Instagram platform now includes the 'story feature' so it is not entirely necessary to have a presence on Snapchat." Nevertheless, "social media has become the primary outlet for sport promotion and recruitment for college athletic departments." Palardy stresses that social media is a "direct link" to the "institution's constituencies." Furthermore, he offers "the features within each individual platform provide a unique method of communicating with those groups and, in most cases, demand that sports information professionals find creative ways to reach audiences with the same material but in a different manner." One essential piece within the athletic communication setting is the monitoring of social media. Monitoring is a core aspect of administering "the workflow for sports information teams as well with the use of third-party software like Hootsuite or Tweetdeck, which offer free versions, or more expansive software like Sprout Social and Falcon.io, whose paid versions can include more in-depth analytics, posting, and monitoring services."

For graphic design and video editing, the sports information team typically uses software for photo editing, video editing, and creating motion graphics. Palardy's workflow incorporates the use of Adobe Creative Suite, which offers Photoshop (photo editing and graphic design), InDesign (document layout and design), Adobe Premiere (video editing), and After Effects (motion graphics) as a total package among other ancillary products. All of these programs "are integrated and help sports information professionals accomplish their goals of creating engaging content for their followership."

The SID is an extension of the public relations arm for the athletic department and the school. The content areas that are most important for a sports information department are twofold: "athletics-related material and institution-related material with a focus on the student-athlete." Moreover, according to Palardy, "sports information departments that only focus on the athletics portion are missing an opportunity to properly connect the mission of the athletic department to the greater college community."

Staging information encompasses the workflow for the athletic administration's sport communication arm. First, "sports information departments must deliver their athletic-related content that is engaging and creates a sense of excitement and pride in the athletics brand." From Palardy's perspective, this content "must be delivered on a daily basis to avoid being stagnant and stale and must represent all sports at the varsity and club levels to reflect the broad-based sport sponsorship the department has instituted." The content Palardy is referencing includes game-day pieces in the form of live statistics, live webcasts with broadcasting talent, pre- and postgame recaps, and social media coverage. Features written for the web could also be tailored to fit in social media posts. These posts may include weekly awards, preseason and postseason accolades, annual Hall of Fame inductees, and articles on student-athlete, coach, team, and department successes. Similarly, developing a rich, detailed statistical archive of all-time leaders and records is also important for tracking current student-athlete progress and serves to further engage the fan base.

Second and most important, according to Palardy, are the nonathletic-related content pieces. The nonathletic pieces serve an integral purpose for the athletic department because they "help position athletics as a pure reflection of the mission and values of the institution and a part of the overall success of the institution." Some nonathletic content focuses on academic features such as the "dean's list, academic all-conference team academic awards from outside organization, regional and national academic honors for standout student-athletes, and pieces on experiential learning pursuits of student-athletes." For Endicott College, these features include "internship and study abroad experiences that give student-athletes an opportunity to showcase how the institution prepared them for their professional experience, how it reflects their academic learning, and what it means to build a resume for postgraduate success." To showcase the off-the-field presence of teams, "other nonathletic content features may include initiatives that student-athletes or teams are involved with that promote healthy living, community service, the overall college experience, and the relationship between academia and athletics."

When asked to share some of his favorite technological tools for use in athletic administration, Palardy says he favors cloud-sharing services such as Google Drive (file management and transfer) and WeTransfer (larger file transfers such as raw video). Communication tools such as Ryver (team communication) and Podio (project management) have been important in communicating with other departments across campus such as marketing and communications, publications, and web services. Skype (video conference) and GoToMeeting (conference calls) are also useful for connecting with external colleagues. Within the scope of athletic administration, a connection and collaboration exists as "the sports information collaborates with web services (general webmaster) and marketing and communications [public relations] on a regular basis." Notably, one of the key projects for Palardy is coordination with the Endicott College webmaster on web accessibility as they aim to find methods of "communicating our web content in such a way that is readable and accessible to persons with a variety of disabilities." Palardy clarifies that "accessibility laws will soon go into effect within the next two years that will require all websites to meet a standard of accessibility. The features of accessibility include the use of alt tags and text, video closed captioning and audio transcripts, website color contrast, and header usage."

> An outcome of athletic communication at Endicott College is to promote the greater impact of being a member of our college community, it is important to be in regular contact with the marketing, communications, and public relations department for the institution. Policy and strategy oftentimes comes down from these departments and it is our responsibility to implement within our athletic realm.

> The sports information department at Endicott College includes the following positions, all under the supervision of Palardy:

- assistant athletic director,
- strategic communications director,
- sports information director,
- assistant sports information director,
- sports information coordinator, and
- graduate assistant for sports information.

In addition, the athletic department uses a group of approximately 15 to 20 federal work-study students to assist with day-to-day responsibilities ranging from office work to game-day coverage.

Palardy's advice to future athletic administrators working with sports information departments is to use their skill sets to their fullest.

> These professionals have a wide-ranging list of skills ranging from writing for the web and social media, graphic design for print publications and social media, and video-editing capabilities. Their mission should be to promote the athletic, academic, experiential learning, and community accomplishments of student-athletes, coaches, teams, administrators, and the overall department. Come to them with ideas, collaborate and strategize with them on how to implement these ideas across a variety of platforms, and monitor the success of those campaigns to see what worked and what needs improvement. Sports information will also be an ever-evolving field and athletic administrators themselves need to stay up-to-date on what the most effective methods are to communicate with the vast constituencies that exist for one singular institution.

(continues)

FEEDBACK FROM THE FIELD *(continued)*

Questions to Consider

1. Research the definition of innovation. How would you apply the principles of innovation to the department Palardy oversees? Aside from the word *innovation*, what other word describes the evolution of technology in athletics? Please provide a comprehensive list.
2. Palardy operates a department that promotes more than 700 student-athletes at a Division III level. Compare the work of Palardy at ecgulls.com and comment on the content compared to what a visitor might see while reviewing a Division I institution.
3. The athletic department at Endicott College employs several staff members in sport communication. Are you surprised at the human resources applied at a Division III institution or do you think Division III athletics require more attention in the sport information area because they are a major recruitment arm for the school?

 MANAGERIAL APPLICATIONS

College Athletics

The sports information director's role within college athletics has been transformed from transmitting informational content to creating interactive and engaging content. Many social media platforms are available for college athletic administrators to incorporate into communication options for their institutions.

Questions to Consider

1. Because you as the athletic director are hiring staff to oversee the communication of athletics, what process and resources would you use to monitor the social media content being shared across multiple platforms?
2. Social media access is available to your staff and student-athletes. Much of the content that is transmitted through social media channels often goes unnoticed by athletic administrators, yet the overall brand and institutional reputation need to be protected. Research two policies relating to regulations associated with student-athletes' postings on social media and two policies relating to regulations associated with coaches' postings on social media.
3. As a future athletic administrator, how often will you monitor social media to ensure that all teams under your supervision are adequately represented across all integrated communication platforms?

 DECISION-MAKING CHALLENGE

Case Study: High School Sport

As the high school athletic administrator, you incorporate a variety of workshops on topics to help student-athletes improve their decision-making skill sets. Young people often use social media for personal communication and informal commentary without recognizing that what is transmitted may reach unintended targets. When used properly, social media can help high school students promote their achievements through posts of videos or highlights. Conversely, when social media is not used as a positive personal branding tool, high school athletes may lose admission opportunities to colleges or scholarships. You were just informed that your star point guard has tweeted something offensive about the opposing team.

Questions to Consider

1. After conducting an online review, what are the resources you can use to develop a workshop to teach your student-athletes the proper use of social media?
2. What policies should athletic departments have in place to prevent this type of negative post from occurring?
3. What type of punitive action should be taken toward the student-athlete in question, the team, and the coach? What type of apology would you issue to the athletic department and individual targeted in the negative post?

 DECISION-MAKING CHALLENGE

Case Study: Youth Sports

Sport-automation companies provide tools for youth sport organizers to help simplify the administration of programming from database management to scheduling facilities. You are the newly elected president for the flag football association in your hometown. Currently, all of the registration materials are communicated through an archaic website. To register, participants must print out forms and mail them to the athletic entity via mail. There is no online processing of registration, which is causing many parents and guardians to consider looking at other flag football opportunities in neighboring towns because the registration process is so tedious. You are committed to securing a sport-automation company that can provide all of the requisite content and technology tools to families before registration starts in two months. Research five sport-automation companies' packages and costs. Provide a detailed analysis of each company and the technology interface offered. This report is to be shared with members of the board so a decision can be made that will enhance management of the flag football association.

Wrap-Up

End-of-Chapter Activities

1. Create an athletic department website for a mock NCAA institution using pbwiki.com, geocities.com, or weebly.com. Use fall sports as the vehicle for adding content that includes space for schedules and results, highlights, polls, contact information, and other relevant details. Compare your website ideas to three other coursemates'.

2. Trace the effects that social media, technology, and technological tools have made on the college, high school, youth, and club sport settings. Which setting has experienced the most growth in the area of technology, and to what do you attribute this growth?

3. Explore three athletic department websites at the high school level. What are the common areas or sections of content across all sites? What do the websites lack in terms of content and fan engagement? What changes would you make to any of these sites?

4. Investigate the titles for the designated athletic administrator tasked to handle fan engagement through the department website and social media platforms within the college, high school, youth, and club sport settings. Compare and discuss the variation of staff titles and number of staff members employed to handle technology within the college, high school, youth, and club sport settings.

5. Fan engagement takes on many forms. Conduct online research to determine the most effective ways that college, high school, youth, and club sport athletic administrators who handle communication can fully connect and link with the fan base.

6. Select five successful promotional campaigns within the college, high school, youth, and club sport settings that you would consider embedding in your department. Explain the benefits of these promotional campaigns and the details relating to the outreach to connect with fans.

7. List the advantages and disadvantages of social media usage within the college, high school, youth, and club sport settings.

8. The needs of fans and parents are changing when it comes to their consumption of information regarding athletics. Trace the evolution by using a time line of the trend of moving communication away from traditional means toward social media within the college, high school, youth, and club sport settings. Insert the changes in the platforms used and the target groups likely to favor or use those tools.

9. Consumers of sport include fans and participants. The technology tools each group uses may not be the same. List and describe the technology tools parents of high school students use to find information on high school athletics. Compare the technology tools high school parents use to college parents who are looking for information about their child's athletic details. In your estimation, which athletic settings (high school versus college) provide the most user-friendly option to parents in terms of ease of navigation along with sufficient information?

10. Select three high school athletic department websites to review. If you are in a classroom setting, work with two other classmates. Compare the websites using the criteria of ease of use (user friendliness) and content (schedules, graphics, video stream) and then rank them from best to worst website with rationales for your decisions.

11. Residents of cities and towns rely on Y's and recreation departments for many athletic offerings. Review your hometown Y or recreation department website to determine ease of navigation and content areas. Then research its social media presence (if any) and the types of platforms used to communicate program offerings to residents.

12. Select two youth sport organizations to research. Act as a parent who is looking to sign up your child for that sport. Describe the process of first locating the sport entity, finding the correct program, locating the registration information, and then starting the registration process. What changes would you make to simplify the registration process? Also indicate the sport automation interfaced used by that youth sport entity.

13. Live streaming of athletic events is common in college athletics. Locate two

Division I athletic department websites to determine the cost associated for fans to have access to live game streaming. Then compare the options for live streaming at Division II and III athletic departments. What are the similarities and differences within each setting?

14. Athletic conferences comprise schools at the collegiate level that are similar in size and philosophy. To give fans greater access to viewing games, many athletic conferences are offering live-streaming options. First, summarize one article depicting live streaming as a revenue generator for Division I athletic conferences. Second, visit the website of two athletic conferences and list the packages available to fans under live-streaming options. From a fan perspective, are these packages cost-effective? From an athletic administrator's perspective, what is the value of your athletic conference's live streaming of events on behalf of your department?

References

Arbiter Sports (n.d.) About. Retrieved from http://www.arbitersports.com/company/.

Bowles, J. (2016). Instagram: A visual view of the Southeastern Conference. *Journal of Contemporary Athletics*, 10(4), 227–240. Retrieved from https://search.proquest.com/docview/1864521063?accountid=43872.

Clavio, G., & Walsh, P. (2013, March 4). Dimensions of social media utilization among college sport fans. *Communication and Sport*. doi: 10.1177/2167479513480355.

Cooper, C. G. (2010). New media marketing: The innovative use of technology in NCAA athletic department e-branding initiatives. *Journal of Marketing Development and Competitiveness*, 5(1), 23–32.

DiVeronica, J. (2017, September 6). Don't let one bad tweet ruin an athlete's future. Democrat & Chronicle [online]. Retrieved August 10, 2018, from https://www.democratandchronicle.com/story/sports/2017/09/06/cyberbullying-social-media-student-athletes-scholarships/464543001/.

Doran, A., Cooper, C. G., & Mihalik, J. (2015). A content analysis of NCAA Division I track and field team's twitter usage: Defining best practices in social media marketing. Journal of Contemporary Athletics, 9(4), 227–247.

Gillham, E. (2017). TeamSnap app. *International Sport Coaching Journal*, 4(3), 365–366.

Guidelines for Student-Athletes (n.d.). Retrieved from https://hs.collingswood.k12.nj.us/ourpages/auto/2011/7/13/52579351/Social%20Media%20Guidelines%20for%20Student%20Athletes.pdf.

Heitner, D. (2016, November 23). Golden Gophers go with virtual reality to tempt football recruits. Forbes [online]. Retrieved from https://www.forbes.com/sites/darrenheitner/2016/11/23/golden-gophers-go-with-virtual-reality-to-tempt-football-recruits/#29eb7d722e47.

Sanderson, J. (2011). To Tweet or not to Tweet: Exploring Division I athletic departments' social-media policies. *International Journal of Sport Communication*, 4(4), 492–513.

Sports Board (2016, October 24). The technology landscape in youth sports is changing . . . quickly. Retrieved from https://sportsboard.io/the-technology-landscape-in-youth-sports-is-changing-quickly/.

University of Southern Maine (2017, August 15). Athletics social media policy. Retrieved August 10, 2018, from http://www.southernmainehuskies.com/information/SocialMediaPolicy.

Vaughn, R. (2016). The evolution of the athletic director as the world gets smaller. Sport Techie [online]. Retrieved from https://www.sporttechie.com/34242the-evolution-of-the-athletic-director-as-the-world-gets-smaller/.

Williams, J. (2017, November 7). Creating a social media policy for athletes. Coach & A.D. [online]. Retrieved August 10, 2018, from https://coachad.com/articles/creating-social-media-policy-athletes/.

© Audrey Kwok/EyeEm/Getty Images

CHAPTER 13

Career Preparation

▶ Careers in Athletic Administration

The athletic administration domain is dynamic and ever changing. Curricula within academic programs in athletic administration and sport management evolve to meet the industry's transforming needs. Athletic administration can be considered an umbrella with its ribs covering collegiate sport, high school sport, recreation, youth sport, and club sport.

Many positions within athletic administration exist to move the mission of athletic programs forward in an environment of increased attention to sport participation. Positions within the athletic administration domain change and adapt as the sporting domain alters to effectively serve the demands of participants and spectators. Emergent technologies and increased opportunities for athletes add to this transformational nature of the field. Today, young professionals aiming to secure positions in athletic administration must possess a core skill set that aligns with management in an intensely competitive space with high-profile interactions.

In the 1970s, physical educators assumed the roles of athletic administrators across many colleges and universities. Decades later many retired coaches moved from the sidelines into athletic administrative positions. The current trajectory for the athletic administration career pathway requires professionals to obtain specialized education and work experience. With the growth of athletics on college campuses and a shift to a business and

© Yuri Arcurs/ShutterStock.

development model, "There has never been a greater need for professionals who bring both a dynamic and robust set of skills to manage these complex, multifaceted business operations" (Belzer, 2015, p. 1).

The number of colleges and universities offering preparatory programs and degrees in athletic administration and sport management gives individuals a chance to develop their skill sets in more focused ways than ever before. Before institutions began offering specific programs in athletic administration and sport management, aspiring professionals majored in business management or physical education without having strong links or academic ties to the sporting industry. Tying concepts of athletic administration into core academic programs and course syllabi provides aspiring professionals with a tangible way to connect theories to actual workplace scenarios. Without specific academic programs in athletic administration, sport management, or recreation management, students lack the core knowledge to meet the needs of a unique market that is emotionally tied to sport as a product. Hurd (2005) defines competencies as "the essential skills, knowledge, abilities, and personal characteristics needed for effective job performance" (p. 46).

Case (2010) studied athletic directors in the state of Virginia. The intent of the study was to showcase the top competencies valued by athletic administrators so that college preparatory programs in athletic administration

or sport management could benefit from the study. Based on this work, the following top 21 athletic administration competencies were revealed in rank order by respondents (athletic directors):

1. sound judgment;
2. knowledge of VHSL rules, policies, and so on;
3. ability to multitask;
4. ethical decision making;
5. leadership and delegation;
6. budgeting;
7. time management;
8. problem solving;
9. event management;
10. event scheduling;
11. risk management;
12. personnel supervision;
13. planning and organization;
14. legal liability;
15. public relations;
16. oral and written communication;
17. staffing and hiring;
18. crowd control;
19. performance evaluation of staff;
20. transportation scheduling; and
21. facility management.

These competencies provide a snapshot of what students entering the field of athletic administration should master or at least become proficient in to operate within positions in the college, high school, youth, and club sport settings. Because these competencies are so valued, it benefits the individual to include these words and phrases on résumés and in cover letters.

▶ Internship Opportunities

Academic preparation ultimately builds a core knowledge base within the field of athletic administration. Many colleges and universities also offer experiential learning in the form of internships. An internship offers an opportunity to integrate knowledge and theory learned in the classroom with practical application and skills development in a professional setting. In the academic setting, the internship acts as the capstone experience at the end of the degree to assist students not only in applying their knowledge in a practical setting but also in preparing them for future career options (Odio, Sagas, & Kerwin, 2014).

Internships are a catalyst for networking and often create connections that lead to future opportunities or full-time positions in the industry. For the most part, internships are woven into the academic experience whereby students earn college credit for their work in the industry. Several settings are available within athletic administration for students and young professionals to explore. The first step in learning about the athletic administration field is to research the variety of positions that exist under each setting. Each athletic administration setting presents a variety of challenges, rewards, time commitment, and expectations. The listing of positions can be exhaustive, and students must take the time to sort through the areas within athletic administration that best suit their interests and potential for growth. Subsequently, students should examine the size and scope of the athletic entities they wish to pursue for prospective jobs or internships. On exploration, individuals may decide to pursue smaller athletic entities that better suit their personalities and career outlook, whereas others may determine that a larger setting better suits their career aspiration. In addition, location of positions plays a role in deciding on a particular setting. If a student desires to stay closer to home, then that choice may limit their career opportunities. Students who desire to travel or relocate may have many more choices to explore a variety of settings within the athletic administration domain.

The umbrella of athletic administration covers many diverse and interesting career opportunities. Creating a guide to systematically research and ascertain which setting is best

suited for a student can make the process operationally easier. One way to start the process is to list out potential sites within the athletic administration setting to explore for internship opportunities. Once 10 to 20 sport entities are listed, the student can review the variety of positions and job opportunities within that particular setting. From that list, students can eliminate sport entities that are not appealing or do not fit the scope of their full interest. Most people anticipate that internships serve to affirm a student's interest in a particular setting, but the experience may, in fact, present an alternate outcome. An internship that may not fully meet the desires of a student may point the individual toward a different career path within the sporting industry.

In some cases, internships uphold and sustain a student's interest in the field. Conversely, internship experiences also help to eliminate settings that may not be the best fit for the individual. Through research, interviews, and trial and error, students gain enriching experiences and knowledge regarding career pathways. For students, knowing what they do not want to pursue is equally as important as knowing what to pursue. In the end, "a challenging internship, with increased levels of responsibilities, can result in new skills being learned and the testing of theories and concepts taught in the classroom" (Ross & Beggs, 2007, p. 4). The overall internship experience encourages students to develop professional networking skills, enhance professionalism, acquire professional competencies, gain training to secure an entry-level position within the industry, and allows for bridging of theoretical concepts and applied knowledge (Beggs & Hurd, 2010).

▶ Volunteering

Volunteering in a college athletics or recreation department is a convenient way for students to supplement work experience on their résumés. Most academic programs at the undergraduate and graduate levels encourage and may even require students to take advantage of volunteer roles in sport and community services. Many college athletic departments seek the assistance of student volunteers to market and promote events and support the administration in controlling contests and managing competitions on campus.

Bravo, Won, and Shonk (2012) surveyed NCAA athletic administrators who said career-related work experience as the top attribute during the hiring process. This finding supports the need for students within the field of athletic administration to secure internship positions along with volunteer roles so they can be considered viable candidates within the workforce. The researchers stressed "the need for *career-related experience* and [underscored] the importance that sport management educators should place on practicum and internship requirements and the necessity of stressing volunteering and trainee programs to students" (Bravo et al., 2012, p. 11). Findings from another study related to careers in athletic administration corroborate the work of Bravo et al. (2012), emphasizing that "career-related work experience was the most important candidates' attribute" during the hiring process (Won, Bravo, & Lee, 2013, p. 1). Not all internship experiences are glowing or positive. Sheptak and Menaker (2016) found task frustration when volunteers were not used to "their fullest potential," creating a negative experience. Moreover, "the younger college students who volunteer to gain experience and help further their career, spoke of training, or the lack thereof, as the key to their frustration when trying to complete tasks" (Sheptak & Menaker, 2016, p. 840). In the recreational setting, athletic administrators have reported that volunteering has significant benefits to individuals and the National Intramural and Recreational Sports Association (NIRSA) (Tingle, J. K., Hazlett, D., & Flint, A., 2016).

Similar to researching potential jobs or internships, students seeking volunteer experiences need to adequately sort through opportunities to ensure their expectations are clearly defined and roles are specific to their needs. Because internships and volunteer opportunities are common in athletic administrations, most sport entities develop position descriptions that outline specific tasks and duties along with handbooks for volunteers and interns. Athletic sites that have placed effort in developing these documents and policies most likely create positive experiences for students because of their organization and dedication to the learning and educational process. The job description acts as a quasi contract for the student experience, informally binding the athletic entity to the intern or volunteer and vice versa. The job description should not be overlooked because the required assignments and tasks stem from written responsibilities contained within those documents. Typically, academic programs require students to generate learning agreements spelling out the specific learning outcomes and work-related tasks ultimately approved by the sponsored site supervisor, university faculty, and student intern.

To fully explore the industry, students must actively collect information to analyze potential internship, volunteer, and career opportunities. Core aspects to research for internships or volunteer positions include:

- career opportunities,
- mission statements,
- vision statements,
- profit versus nonprofit status,
- changes over the last two to 10 years (short-term and long-term),
- size of the entity (including number of full-time staff, part-time staff, volunteers),
- type of product or service offered to the market,
- organizational objectives,
- industry competitors,
- organizational charts and listing of positions and names of personnel, and
- review of social media feeds to feel the pulse of current conditions and recognize opportunities at the sport entity.

▶ Résumé Building

Few students, let alone industry professionals, can produce a résumé packed with specific and lengthy athletic administration experiences. However, students promote their expertise, skills, and achievements through the words and descriptors they add to their résumés. Any résumé should be treated like a marketing piece or elevator pitch in which the candidate persuades and impresses the reader. The aim of the résumé is to highlight a candidate's managerial, communication, and athletic management skills to prove she or he will add value to the desired position and sport entity. Students should review syllabi and notes from classes to select terminology consistent with industry standards to add to their résumés and cover letters. Extracting industry terms and core competencies from course syllabi and course outcomes starts the process of identifying key terms, phrases, and words to highlight the candidate's capabilities in the eyes of the hiring committee or person.

© Antonio Guillem/Shutterstock.

▶ Interview Process

Once the cover letter and résumé are reviewed, candidates are asked to meet for interviews. Interviews can take many forms, including the traditional face-to-face meeting, phone interview, and videoconferencing. The purpose of the interview is to convey a candidate's strengths and capabilities to the prospective employer or internship supervisor. Preparing for an interview entails researching the company, reviewing job requirements, reviewing current social media posts and releases, and learning about the staff at the organization.

Of note is the importance of understanding the process sport entities use when vetting the qualifications of candidates for athletic administration positions. Bravo et al. (2012) shared the top attributes in the job-screening process as career related. However, during the hiring process work ethic was the top-rated attribute, which is not surprising because "employees in collegiate athletics work long hours and must exhibit a strong work ethic" (Bravo et al., 2012, p. 69). The most common lacking attribute was communication skills. Bravo et al. (2012) further described the results from their study as indicating "the need for *career-related experience*" which "underscores the importance that sport management educators should place on practicum and internship requirements and the necessity of stressing volunteering and trainee programs to students" (p. 73). In the recreational setting, a "diverse and applied work experience portfolio" was more valued for hiring candidates over those who only had degrees in parks and recreation (Fulthorp & D'Eloia, 2015). Recreation and sport practicum students and supervisors rated being punctual and being professional as top criteria within the volunteer and internship experiences (Sibson & Russell, 2011). "Supervisors and students were in general agreement that the placement should enhance a range of employability skills such as communication, teamwork, and problem-solving, as well as providing opportunities to apply knowledge learnt in the classroom" (Sibson & Russell, 2012, p. 9). These studies underscore the importance of learning as much as possible about desirable attributes when entering the athletic marketplace.

Among the preparation activities for an interview are writing down questions prospective employers may ask and preparing sound responses to each. Organizing a mock interview with colleagues or friends can also prepare individuals to make seamless responses to questions. Deciding on the outfit to wear may not seem like an essential piece of the preparation process, but candidates need to feel comfortable and professional when trying to present themselves in the best light for the position. Individuals should bring copies of their résumé in the event the interview committee does not have the material for review. All of these actions provide candidates with a sense of being organized, prepared, and confident as they aim to enter the competitive sport marketplace.

▶ Finding the Right Fit

Students and young professionals learn about positions and discover their talents by completing their academic coursework and having practical experiences. Being open to a variety of positions within athletic administration will broaden students' career landscapes so they can look beyond specific settings that may not have openings or opportunities. In many cases, no two positions within athletic administration are alike, making the industry extremely unique and challenging. For example, although the job title of "athletic director" within collegiate athletics may be the same from place to place, Wong and Matt (2014) stress that differences exist between Division I and III roles, citing "the size of the athletic department staff, the attention by fans and media, and the compensation" (p. 26). They add that the most significant difference is the revenue generation required by Division I athletic directors who manage media deals, sponsorship deals, marketing contracts, and ticket sales (Wong & Matt, 2014). Meshing the personality of the candidates to the athletic administration position can be paramount to the success and

effectiveness within that setting. According to Belzer (2015),

> The modern-day college athletics director brings with them a wide range of experiences and skill across a number of different verticals, but most importantly has the ability to adapt to an ever changing and volatile business environment. The best candidates, and subsequently the most successful administrators, are the ones who conduct their own research and determine whether they are both qualified and fit for a particular institution. (Belzer, 2015, p. 2)

▶ Mentoring

Students can seek mentors if they want to gain an advantage in learning about and connecting with industry professionals within the athletic administration field. Mentoring is "a process in which a more experienced person (i.e. the mentor) serves as a role model, provides guidance and support to a developing novice (i.e. the protégé) and sponsors that individual's career path" (Weaver & Chelladurai, 1999, p. 25). Bower (2008) defined *mentor* as "a wise, experienced, and trusted adviser, teacher, or counselor helping to advance and nurture the protégé both personally and professionally" (p. 39).

Effective mentors guide and counsel young people navigating education and career. Undergraduates often work closely with their academic advisors to determine the best career pathway based on their interest in the industry. Academic advisors have contacts in the field and typically a vast network of professionals with expertise and knowledge about a variety of responsibilities to share with students. Cultivating mentor relationships requires effort on the part of students, who may need to go outside their comfort zones to connect with various professionals on campus. Many professionals in athletic administration have busy work schedules, but they seem increasingly willing to connect with aspiring young people in this field. College coaches often act as counselors, providing undergraduate students with needed guidance through mentor relationships (Bjornsen & Dinkel, 2017). Mentors serve as advisors, counselors, and motivators. Pauline (2011) emphasized the importance of mentorships to advance professional development at both the informal and formal levels for students. Professional and academic advisors share research, career expertise, and professional membership options with students, sparking new interests and perspectives on the athletic administration domain. Mentorship affects both professionals and students. Weaver and Chelladurai (2002) found that male and female athletic administrators who served as mentors to individuals were "more satisfied with work and extrinsic rewards than their nonmentored counterparts" (p. 113). Not surprising in a people-oriented field like athletic administration, mentorship is mutually beneficial for all parties involved.

Introduction: Candidates should mention the job position they are applying for, linking experiences and talents to the specific tasks of that role. The language used in this section needs to be persuasive so the reader will want to review the résumé.

Body: In this section, a candidate must prove she or he would be the right fit for the position by convincing the reader that the candidate's experiences and talents will enhance the athletic entity. The managerial and administrative terms used in this section should match the wording in the résumé.

Closing: This is a candidate's opportunity to prompt the reader to act. The candidate desires to have the reader review the résumé with the intent of securing an interview. "I look forward to meeting you in the next weeks to discuss my qualifications" or "I look forward to further exploring the opportunity within your athletic department" are statements that stimulate the reader to act.

Sample Cover Letter

▶ Professional Credentials: Cover Letter

Before reviewing a professional résumé, the organization will read and review an individual's cover letter. The cover letter introduces a candidate and his or her interest to the sport organization. An effective cover letter will prompt the reader to review the candidate's résumé. In fact, the cover letter is the first point of contact with the potential internship or employment site and thus is important in communicating qualifications and potential contributions to the organization based on prior experiences.

▶ Professional Credentials: Résumé

The task of résumé writing can be daunting for many students. An easy way to start the process is to list all work experiences from volunteering to summer positions to any part-time or full-time employment. Students can include any athletic administration and sport management experiences to their advantage by highlighting how these skills are applicable to the position. The list of experiences should contain dates, positions, and locations. Undergraduates may not have a vast listing of experiences, which can make résumé writing difficult. Often, however, volunteer experiences or school group participation can fill gaps when work-related experiences are lacking. Participation on athletic teams may highlight leadership roles and should be listed in the achievements or accomplishments section. Many activities stem from athletic team participation that parallel the functions required to administer a sport program. Fundraising, as a prime example, is a major requirement for team membership. In some cases, players raise large sums to supplement budgets, and the skills involved and the experiences can be tied into professional experiences. Many students in athletic administration may have held the position of captain or earned all-star status on sport teams, which lends to leadership and communication skill sets.

The goal of the résumé is to underscore an individual's talents and abilities. The task of résumé writers is to fully illustrate their strengths so they are viable candidates for open positions, especially in a marketplace as competitive as athletic administration. For an undergraduate student, the typical length of a résumé is one page. In some cases, when the student has more work-related experiences coupled with references, the résumé may be two pages. The résumé needs to look visually appealing and professional. Font size and style of text all make an impression on the reader, who is ultimately the one who decides whether the applicant gets contacted for an interview or hired for a position.

Name

Education

Work Experience

Skills

Activities

Accomplishments

Achievements

Professional References

Sample Resume

Résumé Writing Tips

Students can devote time to fine-tuning the tools needed to enter the athletic administration realm. Simple actions to formulate the résumé include the following.

1. List all descriptors that accentuate the individual's talent and experience. Use terms and keywords extracted from internship positions, course notes, job positions, and current course syllabi.

2. Provide an accurate timeline of employment and volunteer experiences, including month and year. The résumé should detail the location of work and volunteer experience, including name of company and location. In addition, the résumé should highlight the position occupied at that site.

3. Gaps in résumés resulting from a short employment history or few volunteer experiences can be substituted with participation on athletic teams, including year, captainship, and awards. Adding involvement on sport teams showcases an obligation to a unit, leadership potential, teamwork, and the ability to follow directions from a superior (coach).

4. Leadership and creativity are linked to participation in student groups or committees. Supplementing résumés with any type of service-oriented committees or groups demonstrates an individual's dedication to a cause or purpose.

5. Sport knows no language barriers, and candidates who are bilingual have an advantage over other candidates, especially when athletic entities aim to capture new demographics in a language other than English. In addition, fluency or conversational knowledge of a language showcases one's ability to listen and learn new concepts.

6. Technology has a major role in the transformation of athletics and sports. Candidates must possess basic skills in using Excel, PowerPoint, and Word and have evidence of managing or using social media platforms.

7. Professional and academic references support student credentials. References who are listed on the résumé can be contacts from school-based activities, advisors, and supervisors from work and internship experiences. The professional reference section includes name, place of employment, title, and phone and email address for the contact.

Collectively, the elements on a résumé draw attention to a candidate's strengths and expertise with the intent to secure an interview and, if successful, ultimately earn the position.

▶ Professional Portfolio

A portfolio is a collection of someone's work over time, including achievements or artifacts of completed academic and professional work. Students can electronically preserve the materials completed for academic courses or internships. Examples of portfolio items include sport-marketing plans, fundraising proposals, strategic plans for athletic entities, policies and procedures manual for athletic departments, and sponsorship proposals for athletic events. In some cases, employees may want to review past work to forecast the candidate's abilities and creativity. In the academic setting, portfolios can serve as a reflective exercise. Student reflection prompts individuals to explain what they have learned and illustrates their professional growth and development within a certain topical area or experience.

▶ Professional Associations

Holding a professional membership in an athletic administration helps an individual stay abreast of current changes in the industry, networking opportunities, and how to implement new tools and ideas into the workplace through attendance at conferences or consuming published research and best practices information. Benefits for memberships in these associations range from employment alerts to monthly publications, among others. Membership costs vary for professionals and students in these associations; however, benefits outweigh the fees, especially when individuals take advantage of the vast platforms connecting them to industry trends.

Professional associations in athletic administration include the following:

The National Association of Collegiate Directors of Athletics (NACDA) "serves as the professional association for those in the field of athletics administration, providing educational opportunities and serves as a vehicle for networking and the exchange of information to others in the profession" (NACDA, n.d.). With more than 12,500 individual members and more than 1,600 institutional members, the NACDA is the largest association of collegiate athletics administrators throughout the United States, Canada, and Mexico. NACDA members encompass such positions as athletics directors, associate and assistant athletics directors, conference commissioners, and affiliate individuals and corporations. NACDA is an umbrella professional body administering multiple organizations, workshops, and forums to continually meet the diverse needs of constituents while linking to changes in athletic administration. The following list and descriptions showcase the reach of NACDA:

■ The Division I Athletics Directors Forum is an annual event for Division I athletic administrators.

■ The College Sports Information Directors of America (CoSIDA) boasts more than 3,000 members in sports public relations, media relations, and communications and information professionals working in collegiate athletics in both the United States and Canada. In 2008, CoSIDA became an affiliated partner with NACDA (www.cosida.com).

■ The Collegiate Event and Facility Management Association (CEFMA) offers educational programs, professional development, networking opportunities, and best practices to enhance event and facility management (CEFMA, n.d.).

■ The National Association of Athletic Development Directors (NAADD) is an organization of individuals with a mutual interest in collegiate athletics so that (1) an agreed-on standard of excellence can be established, (2) educational and development successes can be shared, and (3) a united voice of opinion can be heard on key issues facing collegiate athletics in general and collegiate athletics development specifically. NAADD has 1,500 members in collegiate athletics (NACDA, n.d.).

■ The National Association of Collegiate Marketing Administrators (NACMA) offers tools, training, and networking for collegiate sports marketers to successfully generate revenue, manage brands, and develop fans (NACDA, n.d.).

■ The former National Association of Collegiate Women Athletics Administrators (NACWAA), has been rebranded to be Women Leaders in College Sports. Women Leaders in College Sports aims to empower, develop, assist, celebrate, affirm, involve, and honor women working in college sports and beyond (Women Leaders in College Sports, n.d.).

■ Facilities Workshop is an annual session for NACDA members to discuss facility management from innovations in facilities to financing and marketing.

■ *Athletics Administration* is the official journal published by NACDA. The contents include a variety of topics and current issues within the collegiate athletic administration setting.

■ The National Association of Collegiate Marketing Administrators (NACMA) is an organization for those in marketing positions within the college athletic setting.

■ The National Association of Athletic Development Directors (NAADD) serves individuals in the college athletic administration setting working in the fundraising area.

■ The International Collegiate Licensing Association (ICLA) meets the needs of members operating as collegiate licensing administrators.

■ The National Association for Athletics Compliance (NAAC) works with athletic administrators involved with compliance issues in intercollegiate athletics.

■ Members of the College Athletic Business Management Association (CABMA) are those who are college athletics business managers and administrators.

■ The Minority Opportunities Athletic Association (MOAA) is sponsored by NACDA and offers "opportunities to exchange ideas, advocate increased participation and administrative opportunities for minorities in athletics" (https://nacda.com/sports/2018/7/17/moaa-moaa-overview-html.aspx).

- NIRSA, founded in 1950, comprises and supports leaders in collegiate recreation (https://nirsa.net/nirsa/about/).
- The National Interscholastic Athletic Administrators Association (NIAAA) "preserves, enhances and promotes educational-based athletics through the professional development of interscholastic athletic administrators" (http://www.niaaa.org/).
- Since 1920, the National Federation of State High School Associations (NFHS) has "set directions for the future by building awareness and support, improving the participation experience, establishing consistent standards and rules for competition, and helping those who oversee high school sports and activities" (https://www.nfhs.org/).
- The National Recreation and Park Association (NRPA) "is the leading non-profit organization dedicated to the advancement of public parks, recreation and conservation to enhance the quality of life for all people" (http://www.nrpa.org/).

▶ Graduate Degrees

A graduate degree is another option for students and young professionals who want to continue to hone their skills and specialize in athletic administration programs. Numerous academic programs in sport management, athletic administration, and recreation management currently exist. Sorting through the best institution takes a great deal of vetting because programs have unique links to the industry and variety in course selections. In Spenard's work (2013), only 13.1% of athletic directors in the study held a bachelor's degree, and 68.7% possessed a master's degree as their highest educational level.

TABLE 13.1 Percentages for Highest Degree Earned for Athletic Directors as Reported by Division and Sex

		Bachelor (%)	Master (%)	Doctorate (%)
Division I		17.8	62.5	19.7
Division II		16.6	68.8	14.6
Division III		16.6	70.9	12.5
Division I	Male	18.8	61.7	19.5
Division I	Female	7.4	70.4	22.2
Division II	Male	15.4	70.1	14.4
Division II	Female	21.7	63.0	15.2
Division III	Male	19.9	66.8	13.3
Division III	Female	8.5	80.9	10.6

Lumpkin, A., Achen, R. M., & Hyland, S. (2015). Education, experiences, and advancement of athletic directors in NCAA member institutions. Journal of Contemporary Athletics, 9(4), 249-265.

Wrap-Up

End-of-Chapter Activities

1. Write a professional résumé and share it with at least three people to collect feedback and critique.

2. Identify an internship or job position. Write a cover letter to inform the athletic entity of your interest in working at the organization. Be persuasive and direct with your professional expertise. Include a few sentences on why the company would benefit from having you work there. Share the cover letter with at least three people to collect feedback and critique.

3. Determine which contacts (academic or professional) you can list as your references. Be sure to reach out to the contacts to get approval to add each one to your résumé.

4. Create a list of terms typically used in job descriptions for the college, high school, club, and youth sport settings. Highlight the terms that you can include in your résumé and cover letter to depict your skill set.

5. Write a list of prospective questions you may be asked during an interview in the college, high school, club, and youth sport settings. Once you have listed the questions, craft comprehensive responses to each one.

6. Write a list of prospective questions you can ask the interviewer in the college, high school, club, and youth sport settings at the end of the interview.

7. Conduct a mock interview with one person and then again with another person. Reflect on what changed from the first interview to the second. What areas would you aim to improve for the next interview? Are there responses you can improve so the communication of ideas is flawless and speaks to the strengths of your candidacy for the position?

8. Review the list of professional associations. Visit the website of at least one professional association in each setting (college, high school, club, and youth sport), listing the purpose and benefits to members. Based on your collection of materials, which organization best matches your interests within the college, high school, club, and youth sport settings? How much does it cost to join the association?

9. In previous chapters, professionals within the college, high school, youth, and club sport settings have been highlighted. Select one professional in each setting to research. Review any changes in the position the person holds and his or her educational background. What parallels can you draw from the person's experiences to your own academic and professional development?

10. Street and Smith's *SportsBusiness Journal* has listed the top 40 sport managers under age 40. Research the publication and award list for the 40 under 40. Which three professionals resonate most with your career interests and why? What educational and professional background details most impressed you about these individuals?

11. Interview one professional in the college, high school, youth, and club sport settings (total of four interviews). Probe the professional to determine the challenges associated with entering a competitive sport marketplace. Ask the professional to provide assistance regarding preparation for professional interviews along

with cover letter and résumé development. In comparing and contrasting responses from college, high school, youth, and club sport settings, what surprises you the most from this exercise?

12. Once your résumé is written, review the following items as modified from a checklist from Collegial Services (n.d.). Be sure to add and revise to meet the following benchmarks.

Résumé Checklist

- ☐ Use a professional email address.
- ☐ State your objective.
- ☐ Be sure to customize the résumé for the industry and job type you are applying for.
- ☐ Under "Education," include school, degree earned, and date of completion.
- ☐ Under "Coursework," include relevant courses such as communication, public speaking, and business.
- ☐ Under "Skills and Awards," include awards and certificates that are relevant to the profession you are pursuing.
- ☐ Under "Experience," include work history, projects, and internships.
- ☐ Under "Activities," check for industry-related terms that are misunderstood or misused.
- ☐ Use action words.
- ☐ Customize your résumé for every position.
- ☐ Check for spelling and grammatical errors.
- ☐ Be consistent and symmetrical in spacing and layout.
- ☐ Remove any unprofessional photos or posts from your social media profiles.

13. LinkedIn is a social networking site connecting professionals in the field. Use the checklist retrieved from Collegial Services (n.d., "LinkedIn Profile Checklist") to develop an effective profile:

LinkedIn Profile Checklist

- ☐ Profile picture
- ☐ Heading
- ☐ Email address
- ☐ Customize profile URL
- ☐ Profile settings
- ☐ On–off activity broadcasts
- ☐ Activity feed privacy
- ☐ Connections visibility
- ☐ Explore recommendations
- ☐ Communication settings
- ☐ Groups, companies, an applications
- ☐ Account settings
- ☐ Summary
- ☐ Experience
- ☐ Education
- ☐ Skills and endorsements
- ☐ Projects, volunteer work, associations

References

Beggs, B., & Hurd, A. R. (2010). Internships bring the classroom to life. *Parks & Recreation*, 45(2), 31–34.

Belzer, J. (2015, February 19). The dynamic role of the modern day college athletics director. Forbes [online]. Retrieved from https://www.forbes.com/sites/jasonbelzer/2015/02/19/the-dynamic-role-of-the-modern-day-college-athletics-director/#58d292ba6076.

Bjornsen, A. L., & Dinkel, D. M. (2017). Transition experiences of Division-1 college student-athletes: Coach perspectives. *Journal of Sport Behavior*, 40(3), 245–268.

Bower, G. G. (2008). Developing effective mentoring relationships with women in the health and fitness industry: Suggestions from the perspective of the protégé. *Women in Sport & Physical Activity Journal*, 17(1), 38-46. Retrieved from https://search-proquest-com.proxy18.noblenet.org/docview/230658069?accountid=43872.

Bravo, G. A., Won, D., & Shonk, D. J. (2012, March). Entry-level employment in intercollegiate athletic departments: Non-readily observables and readily observable attributes of job candidates. *Journal of Sport Administration & Supervision*, 4(1), 63–78. Retrieved from https://quod.lib.umich.edu/j/jsas/6776111.0004.110/--entry-level-employment-in-intercolliegiate-athletic?rgn=main;view=fulltext.

Case, R. (2010). A study to examine the nature and scope of school athletic administrator positions in the state of Virginia. *Virginia Journal*, 31(1), 4–8.

CEFMA (n.d.). Key info [online]. Retrieved from https://nacda.com/index.aspx?path=cefma.

Collegial Services (n.d.). LinkedIn profile checklist. Retrieved from https://collegialservices.com/wp-content/uploads/2015/03/LinkedIn-Checklist.pdf.

Collegial Services (n.d.). Resume checklist. Retrieved from https://collegialservices.com/wp-content/uploads/2015/03/Resume-Checklist.pdf.

Fulthorp, K., & D'Eloia, M. H. (2015). Managers' perceptions of entry-level job competencies when making hiring decisions for municipal recreation agencies. *Journal of Park & Recreation Administration*, 33(1), 57–71.

Hurd, A. R. (2005). Competency development for entry level public parks and recreation professionals. *Journal of Park & Recreation Administration*, 23(3), 45–62.

Lumpkin, A., Achen, R. M., & Hyland, S. (2015). Education, experiences, and advancement of athletic directors in NCAA member institutions. *Journal of Contemporary Athletics*, 9(4), 249–265.

NACDA (n.d.). Mission statement [online]. Retrieved from https://nacda.com/sports/2018/7/17/nacda-nacda-missionstatement-html.aspx.

NACDA (n.d.). What is NACDA and what does it do? [online]. Retrieved from https://nacda.com/sports/2018/7/17/moaa-moaa-overview-html.aspx

Odio, M., Sagas, M., & Kerwin, S. (2014). The influence of the internship on students' career decision making. *Sport Management Education Journal (Human Kinetics)*, 8(1), 46–57.

Pauline, G. (2011). The role of educators in building the next generation of female leaders in the sport industry. *Journal of Physical Education, Recreation & Dance*, 82(8), 4–5,12.

Ross, C. M., & Beggs, B. A. (2007). Campus recreational sports internships: A comparison of student and employer perspectives. *Recreational Sports Journal*, 31(1), 3–13.

Sheptak, R., & Menaker, B. (2016). The frustration factor: Volunteer perspectives of frustration in a sport setting. *VOLUNTAS: International Journal of Voluntary & Nonprofit Organizations*, 27(2), 831–852. doi:10.1007/s11266-015-9635-6.

Sibson, R., & Russell, D. (2011). Sport, recreation and event management practicum placements: What do stakeholders expect?. Paper presented at 20th Annual Teaching and Learning Forum. Perth, WA. http://ro.ecu.edu.au/ecuworks2011/354.

Spenard, J. C. (2013). An examination of National Collegiate Athletic Association Division I athletic directors. *Kinesiology, Recreation, and Sport Studies Publications and Other Works*. http://trace.tennessee.edu/utk_exerpubs/2.

Weaver, M. A., & Chelladurai, P. (1999). A mentoring model for management in sport and physical education. *Quest (00336297)*, 51(1), 24–38.

Weaver, M. A., & Chelladurai, P. (2002). Mentoring in intercollegiate athletic administration. *Journal of Sport Management*, 16(2), 96.

Women Leaders in College Sports (n.d.). Our purpose [online]. https://www.womenleadersincollegesports.org/WL/about/our-purpose/WL/About/our-purpose.aspx?hkey=44fec3dc-e1fe-4825-8645-286560bb09a9.

Won, D., Bravo, G., & Lee, C. (2013). Careers in collegiate athletic administration: Hiring criteria and skills needed for success. *Managing Leisure*, 18(1), 71–91.

Wong, G., & Matt, M. (2014). An inside look at Division I and Division III college athletic directors. *The NACDA Report*. Retrieved from http://grfx.cstv.com/photos/schools/nacda/sports/nacda/auto_pdf/2014-15/misc_non_event/oct2014.pdf.

Glossary

A

ArbiterSports Centralized online platform used to schedule referees and officials to athletic contests.

Athletic director (AD) A person in an athletic department who provides leadership, supervision, and fiscal accountability for competitive athletic programs.

Athletic facility manager or athletic facility coordinator A person in the college or high school athletic department who is responsible for the coordination or scheduling of venue space.

Athletic trainer Health care professional under the supervision of a physician who treats injuries, manages illness and injury prevention, and helps rehabilitate injuries and medical conditions.

Authority The ability to influence others based on an individual's position.

B

Booster club Group that seeks to raise funds for an athletic team.

Brand The communicated identity of an athletic entity.

Branding The identity of an athletic entity as shown in its image, reputation, and logo.

Budget A plan for the allocation of dollar amounts to effectively support athletic activities.

Burnout Exhaustion from a work position; often results in an individual leaving an entity or organization.

C

Capital budgets Athletic department budget that includes high-cost and long-durability items.

Centers for Disease Control and Prevention (CDC) Federal agency that offers courses for athletic administrators in health management.

Central scheduler A person in high school athletics who secures and manages venue rental agreements and schedules across districts or shared school spaces.

Certificate of liability insurance An insurance policy that licenses athletic entities to conduct business within a specific state or town.

Certified Park and Recreational (CPRP) An agency offering exams for facility management professionals.

Club sports Athletic programs offered to players across towns or regions that attract competitive players and professional coaches.

College head coach A person who manages college-level teams from recruitment to practices and game-day operations.

Communication Part of the 4 C's of marketing.

Compliance coordinator A person in collegiate athletics who is responsible for maintaining compliance and eligibility with designated governance entities and conferences, as well as institutional regulations for the university.

Consumer Part of the 4 C's of marketing.

Consumer fans Individuals with strong bonds who supporting a team or program because of personal connections to the team, a team's talent level, its location, and its reputation.

Contest A game, match, or play day between one or more teams.

Contest management The comprehensive administration of games from setup to breakdown.

Controlling The managerial function to create a checks-and-balances system within the department.

Convenience Part of the 4 C's of marketing.

Corporate culture A shared beliefs and value systems that is accepted and adopted by staff members.

Corporate sponsorship Relationship whereby company provides an athletic sporting event or team with money or gifts in kind in exchange for exposure

Cost Part of the 4 C's of marketing.

Cover letter Component of the hiring process in which a candidate demonstrates interest in the sport organization.

D

Decision making The process of selecting choices in a thoughtful and systematic process to achieve organizational objectives.

Delegating The managerial function of assigning responsibility and tasks to staff members.

Demographics Characteristics of target groups, including by age, gender, marital status, income, and education.

Director of coaching (DOC) A person in club and youth sport who identifies and recruits new coaches, assigns coaches to teams, and creates and coordinates coaching-development sessions.

Director of sport marketing A person in athletics who coordinates ticket sales, increases fan attendance, and creates sponsorship opportunities and external business relationships.

E

Efficiency The production of high-quality work with little waste.

Emergency action plan (EAP) Policies and guidelines governing the handling of risk-associated situations and scenarios.

Equipment manager A person in college or high school athletics who coordinates, washes, and maintain athletic team equipment and student-athlete practice and game-day apparel.

Event management A branch of facility management aimed at creating activities before, during, and after events to engage fans.

Exchange relationship A relationship in which an athletic entity provides value (sport experience) in exchange for something of value from the consumer such as money.

Executive director A person in club and youth sport who manages enrollment, creates marketing plans to recruit players, secure facility contracts, and handle the fiscal responsibilities of the club from membership fees to coaching contracts.

External environment Part of the situational analysis not easily controlled or manipulated by the athletic administrator.

F

Facility management An administrative function that encompasses staff management and venue maintenance and operations to support participants, spectators, and organizers in sporting endeavors.

Facility manager A person who manages athletic staff and provides a safe environment for athletic participation, coordination of internal and external programming, and the generation of rental revenue.

For-profit entities Revenue generated after expenses are allocated to owners or designees.

Fundraising Administrative tool to generate revenue to support current or future programming.

Fundraising and development personnel Persons in athletics who identify and cultivate donor relationships to secure athletic department gifts and funds.

G

Game-day operations coordinator or contest manager A person in athletics who maintains all aspects of athletic game-day management.

Gender equity An environment that promotes fairness in athletic offerings for males and females, usually by organizational commitment.

Goal The ultimate direction or desired result for an athletic entity.

Governing bodies Entities such as leagues and conferences that set standards on participant eligibility, participation outcomes, game-scheduling procedures, season start and end dates, and sportsmanship.

Grant writers Designated individuals in the athletic department or associated with the sport entity who complete the grant application or grant proposal process to secure grants.

Grants Cash or gifts in kind from a government agency or any public or private entity (grantor).

H

Human resource management The process of selecting, training, and satisfying the most effective individual for a position.

I

Identification camps (ID camps) Specialized athletic programming on college campuses to evaluate prospective college players.

Implementing A managerial function to drive plans forward by designated staff members.

Injury surveillance system (ISS) The largest collegiate athletic injury database in continuous operation in the world; run by the National Collegiate Athletic Association.

Intercollegiate sport clubs Programs organized and led by students with supervision and oversight by college administrations.

Internal environment Part of the situational analysis controlled and manipulated by the athletic administrator.

Interview Method for search committee to learn about the credentials and expertise of candidates through face-to-face meeting, video chat, or other means.

Intramurals Extracurricular and recreational sport programming offered at college-level and high school–level programs.

Itinerary A listing of participant expectations and timeline for athletic travel.

J

Job description Summary of the qualifications, education, professional certification, special knowledge and skills, and experience relevant to a position.

Job design A managerial function to establish positions or role descriptions and balancing responsibilities or staff to complete tasks at the highest quality level.

L

Leadership A managerial characteristic that reinforces values embodied through sports, such as teamwork, respect, collaboration, selflessness, and decision making.

Lodging Room accommodations for overnight athletic trips.

Long-term plan A plan created to be accomplished from over four to 10 years.

M

Management style The philosophy to direct and motivate staff to achieve organizational tasks.

Market segmentation Dividing consumers into groups based on shared characteristics.

Marketing The promotion of activities to engage participants at sporting events.

Marketing mix Contains the product, place, promotion, and price.

Marketing plan A map to communicate department goals along with strategies to reach desired objectives.

Marketing strategies Actions leading to the achievement of the stated objectives.

Mission statement A grouping of ideals detailing past accolades and vision of the athletic entity.

Motivation A managerial function to change and sustain valued behaviors of staff.

Municipal official A designated position within town or community sports to manage sport facilities to maximize usage across all town sports.

N

National Association of Sports Officials (NASO) A membership group for officials offering educational resources and research publications.

National Athletic Trainers' Association (NATA) Certification body for athletic trainers.

Nonprofit entities An organization that recycles any additional revenue back into its budget or program.

O

Objective A pathway leading to the accomplishment of organizational goals.

Offer Employment offer tendered to a selected individual on completion of a job-search process; communicates salary, length of contract, dates of employment, benefits, and any special provisions connected to the position.

Operating budgets Accounts or line items used on a daily basis within the athletic department.

Opportunity Activities that can help an athletic entity grow; part of SWOT analysis.

Organizational hierarchy A flowchart depiction of each staff position, unit, or department.

Organizational structure The hierarchy of positions created to implement the plans and activities of the department or athletic organization.

Organization chart The hierarchy or chain of command within a department.

Organizing A management function to ensure staff productivity.

P

Participants Athletes and coaches who compete within their specific sport domain.

Performance appraisal Evaluation tool to measure strengths, weaknesses, accomplishments, and staff productivity.

Permit A scheduling procedure to apply for municipal field usage.

Place The physical location or the platform used to sell a product or service (e.g., online or site store).

Planning A management function to create blueprints for department operations.

Policies and procedures manual A guide to illustrate the pertinent recurring themes, questions, concerns, and steps in the operation of athletic programs.

Policy A clear statement providing guidance to employees.

Portfolio A collection of work over time, including achievements and artifacts of completed academic and professional work.

Positive Coaching Alliance (PCA) A national nonprofit organization that seeks to create enriching sport experiences.

Price The actual cost to participate in athletic programming and game attendance.

Procedure A set of directions or steps communicated to employees.

Product The merchandise or service provided by a sport entity to athletes, fans, and spectators.

Productivity A measure of the effort and end results produced by staff.

Promotion The use of marketing or advertising to highlight sport programming.

Psychological contract Includes a shared set of characteristics, expectations, and obligations for a specific position or role.

Public health officials Provide oversight for the health and safety of children participating in sport and recreational programming within municipalities.

Public relations A communication tool to deliver clear and concise messages through various outlets.

R

Résumé Component of the hiring process in which a candidate highlights work experiences, accomplishments, and skills.

Risk management The process of assessing and controlling risks within the sport setting.

S

Scheduling The creation of practice and game schedules.

Search committee Designated group formed to review and interview candidates for positions.

Search committee chair Point person or contact person for the entire interview process.

Senior woman administrator (SWA) Designated position at NCAA member institutions of the highest-ranking female within the athletic department.

Short-term plan A plan created to be accomplished from one month to three years.

Situational analysis Examination of the current marketplace, offerings, and consumer base from internal and external perspectives.

Sources of power Tools to influence staff to move toward desired behavior and the achievement of objectives and goals.

Specialist sport official assignors The professionals who handle the organization and management of officials.

Sport-automation platform Tool for athletic administrators to perform website design, web hosting, player registration, fundraising, and scheduling.

Sports information director (SID) A person in college and high school athletics who is responsible for developing, administering, and distributing news and statistics through social media channels.

Sports marketing The practice of using teams, venues, athletes, sports events, and sports media to separate a brand from its competitors.

Staff retention Minimizing turnover while preserving the contributions employees make over time within a position.

Strategic planning Administrative process to assist athletic organizers to direct the entity to reaching goals.

Strengths Part of SWOT analysis in which positive elements of an athletic program are identified.

Sustainability Efforts by athletic programs to reduce energy usage, reduce chemical and water usage, reduce waste, and enhance education and awareness on reducing carbon footprints.

SWOT analysis Identifying and analyzing a sports entity's strengths, weaknesses, opportunities, and threats.

T

Target market The core group of people who will consume or use a sport product.

Threat Competition, policies, or legislation that impede the progress of the athletic entity; part of SWOT analysis.

Title IX Federal law from 1972 that forbids discrimination on the basis of sex in any federally funded program or activity, including athletics.

Title IX coordinator Person who facilitates the implementation of Title IX on college campuses.

Transactional leader A leader who motivates by the exchange of valued characteristics.

Transformational leader A leader who motivates by engaging the staff to fully satisfy their needs.

V

Volunteer management Arm of athletic administration that manages the services of unpaid workers.

W

Weaknesses Elements that need change or improvement; part of SWOT analysis.

Wish list Inventory of resources desired for operating a program for all games and practices.

Y

Youth or community sport The channel to offer sport options for participants at Y's, town- and city-based programs, travel-based programs, and recreation departments.

Index

National Association of
    Intercollegiate Athletics
    (NAIA), 11, 93
National Association of Sports
    Officials (NASO), 75
National Athletic Trainers'
    Association (NATA),
    160, 161
National Collegiate Athletic
    Association (NCAA), 2, 7,
    11, 54–55, 60, 93, 131, 213,
    229–231
National Council for the
    Accreditation of Coaching
    Education (NCACE),
    173–175
National Federation of High School
    Sports (NFHS), 196
National Federation of State High
    School Associations
    (NFHSA), 294
National Interscholastic Athletic
    Administrators Association
    (NIAAA), 176, 177, 294
National Junior College Athletic
    Association (NJCAA), 11
National Recreation and Park
    Association (NRPA), 294
National Standards for Sport
    Coaches (NSSC), 174
NCAA Field Hockey Championships
    Committee, 256
NCAA Gender Equity Task Force,
    236
Nonprofit sport entities. See Profit
    sport entities

O

O'Connell, Kristina, 77
Office for Civil Rights, 229
Officiating, 75–76
Off-season event, 71
Organizational culture
    club sport, 26
    Coaching Peace, 26–29
    high school sport, 25
    local corporate cultures, 23
    mission statement, 24
    PCA, 24–25
    shared beliefs and values, 23–24
    standard of care, 25
    student-athlete, 25

Organizational structure
    associate/assistant levels, 12
    athletic director, 11–12
    athletic trainer, 12–13
    College Athletic Department, 11
    compliance coordinator, 12
    contest management, 13
    director of sport marketing, 12
    equipment management, 13
    facility manager, 13
    fundraising and development, 13
    game-day operations, 13
    head coach, 13
    SID, 12
Orlando, Paul, 63–64
O'Sullivan, John, 189–190

P

Palardy, Rob, 276–280
Park & Recreation Commission, 141
Partnerships, 147–148
Performance appraisals
    component and core
        responsibility, 247–250
    information collection
        athletic administrators,
            251–252
        Business of Small College
            Athletics, 251
        designated positions/roles, 251
        employment contracts/
            position descriptions, 251
        evaluation tools, 254–261
        event managers, 252
        feedback, 251
        institutions, 250
        PCA, 252–254
        players' performance, 252
        staff member's strengths and
            weaknesses, 251
        volunteer satisfaction, 252
Plan-development process, 220
Policy making, 42–43
Positive Coaching Alliance (PCA),
    24–25, 252–254
Professional associations, 292–294
Professional portfolio, 292
Profit sport entities
    alumni-based fundraising, 148
    partnerships, 147–148
    sponsor opportunities, 146–147
    sponsorship levels, 147

sponsorships, 145–146
summer sports camps, 148
types, 147
volunteer management, 144–145
Public health, role of
    camp rules and regulations, 164
    concussion education, 168
    medical provisions, 165–167
    spectator safety, 168–170
Public relations, 122–123

Q

Quirk, Luz, 163–164
Quirk, Sean, 74–75

R

Rebranding, 117
Recreational sport programming,
    93–95
Review process, 186, 217–219
Risk management, 158–182
    club sports, 162–164
    college athletics, 170–172, 179
    high school athletics, 180
    public health, role of
        camp rules and regulations,
            164
        concussion education, 168
        medical provisions, 165–167
        spectator safety, 168–170
    role of coach, 172–178
    staff education and training,
        159–162
    youth sport athletics, 163–164,
        179, 180
Rose, Brad, 253

S

Scheduling process
    agreements, 66–67
    alumni/homecoming events, 69
    away game costs, 68–69
    budgetary tool, 67–68
    communication, 76–77
    cost application, 68
    definition, 59
    game-day contract, 67